seventh edition

ADVERTISING MEDIA PLANNING

JACK Z. SISSORS and ROGER B. BARON

New York   Chicago   San Francisco   Lisbon   London   Madrid   Mexico City
Milan   New Delhi   San Juan   Seoul   Singapore   Sydney   Toronto

The McGraw·Hill Companies

2 3 4 5 6 7 8 9 10 11 12 13 14 15   DOC/DOC   1 9 8 7 6 5 4 3 2 1 0

ISBN   978-0-07-170312-3
MHID   0-07-170312-8

Library of Congress Cataloging-in-Publication Data

Sissors, Jack Zanville, 1919–2004.
      Advertising media planning / Jack Z. Sissors and Roger B. Baron. — 7th ed.
          p.   cm.
      ISBN-13: 978-0-07-170312-3
      ISBN-10: 0-07-170312-8
      1. Advertising media planning.   I. Baron, Roger B.   II. Title.

   HF5826.5.S57   2010
   659.1'11—dc22   2010004379

Interior design by THINK Book Works

McGraw-Hill books are available at special quantity discounts to use as premiums and
sales promotions or for use in corporate training programs. To contact a representative,
please e-mail us at bulksales@mcgraw-hill.com.

This book is printed on acid-free paper.

CONTENTS

PREFACE

Throughout history, the form of mass media has been determined and limited by the technology of the age. In 1439, Gutenberg's printing press first delivered words to the masses on paper. Until the 1950s, short personal messages were printed on strips of paper that were pasted to forms and handed to recipients by Western Union delivery boys. The radio first delivered audio through a large piece of furniture in the living room, only to be eventually replaced by Sony's Walkman delivering audio directly into the ear. Sight, sound, and motion used to be delivered primarily at the local movie theater or on a small black-and-white television screen in the living room.

The technology limited each of these forms to a single type of content: printed words, sound, still pictures, and moving pictures, at first in unnatural black and white. Each was limited to one-way communication from the few who produced the content to the masses who received it.

It could be argued that the digital revolution and the Internet changed all that—words, pictures, moving pictures, and interactivity are all just different kinds of digital media that have converged on the three screens of video: the television set, the personal computer, and the nearly ubiquitous mobile cell phone. The nature of the content has changed also. In addition to professionally produced material, user-generated content populates YouTube, social networks, blogs, Wikipedia, Twitter, . . . and new media forms are emerging every day. The Internet gives users the ability to search for and retrieve in seconds information about virtually any subject on earth, creating the opportunity to deliver advertising to people with a demonstrated interest in the product or service.

But the digital world is constantly changing. Media that were new in 2003, such as MySpace, are already beginning to show their age, challenged by newer options like Facebook, LinkedIn, and Twitter. Search engines like Google and Bing, now key drivers of online marketing, are vulnerable to start-ups that offer still further improvements. The list could go on and on. Furthermore, the research tools available to evaluate online media are evolving, with enhancements coming out seemingly every month.

Given this constant state of change, the reader might reasonably ask, "How can the seventh edition of a 30-year-old text remain relevant to today's media professional?" The answer lies in the characteristics of the traditional media that continue to meet the fundamental marketing needs of advertisers. They must deliver a message to a large percent of the population in a single day, give a piece of paper or a product sample to the residents of a community, quickly create awareness of a new product nationally or in one market, reach people in their car on the way to the store, deliver a detailed message to the people most likely to use a product, place the message within a compatible editorial environment, or quickly reach a large percentage of a niche marketing target, to name just a few of the nearly infinite marketing needs.

Digital media cannot replace the ability of traditional media to meet all these needs. They will supplement traditional media's capabilities, and in a few cases may even replace them, but only for those products and services where it makes marketing sense. Quick-serve restaurants, automobiles, and hotels have different marketing needs that the planner must match to the capabilities of the different media, regardless of whether they are traditional or digital.

As planners evaluate alternatives, they will rely on the same fundamental measures that Jack Sissors wrote about 30 years ago: coverage (the percent of the advertiser's target in the medium's audience), composition (the percent of the medium's audience in the advertiser's target), selectivity (composition of the medium compared to the population universe), campaign reach/frequency, effectiveness (however that is defined), and cost-efficiency. Planners must understand these basic characteristics of all media, including the new online venues, to ensure the most effective use of the advertising budget.

Accordingly, this seventh edition will continue to focus on the fundamentals of media planning, with an emphasis on traditional media that continue to receive the great bulk of advertising dollars. It will cover the basics of planning and buying online display advertising (banners and rich media), and it will give an overview of planning and buying search advertising on sites such as Google and Bing. But a detailed discussion of the many new forms, from mobile to Twitter to social media to blogs is simply not possible, both because of the space required and because anything said today in the spring of 2010 is sure to be obsolete over the 10-year life of this book. We will, however, show examples of how the new media can be creatively used to enhance the effectiveness of advertising delivered by traditional media.

So it is in this spirit that I begin the seventh edition of *Advertising Media Planning*. I am indebted to the many people across the industry who have helped me with this project—especially to my wife, Margi, who put up with me disappearing into the den for hours at a time, and to the people in the media department at DRAFTFCB Chicago, who continue to inspire me with their intelligence, creativity, and devotion to the media planning art.

Roger B. Baron

I t is said by many that Erwin Ephron invented media planning. This was back in the 1970s when, as those of us who were in the business remember, media had backroom status in agencies. Erwin said in the foreword to the last edition of this book, "For decades planning media has had a . . . modest persona." This was true for long after the media planning concept was first practiced, but as he says, "That has changed . . . today media is one of the best career paths in advertising." Or, as far as I am concerned, any practice that is marketing related.

But the role that Mr. Ephron described, that of planning and strategy being the reason "an agency can provide continuity in brand advertising management," has been achieved today. Mr. Ephron's many other thoughts on media can be read on his website at www.ephrononmedia.com.

So if you are opening this book to begin a career in media planning, further your professional or academic education, or use it as a tool to teach others, you will find it instructive and hopefully complete. Media options change so rapidly, even exponentially, but the fundamentals you'll find here are timeless.

How Has Media Planning Changed?

The first serious moves for digital advertising as we know it today started in 1995 with Yahoo! (portal), I/PRO (metrics), and InfoSeek (search). But a bubble had to burst and then recover before there was enough consumer critical mass for media planners to take the Internet seriously. Today, options include Web display (HTML banners, rich media, flash, and streaming audio and video), search, social media, emerging media technologies, and many others we cannot begin to foresee, which will eventually become commonplace by the time you read this book.

Digitization

We have gotten to the point where the digitization of TV is a *fait accompli*. The way three-dimensional television will further unfold, whether the medium will have the ability to deliver a custom creative message to individual homes or neighborhoods, whether it will be primarily delivered through cable companies, phone companies, or Internet service providers—these are among the many interesting battles that have yet to be fought during the age of digitization. The fastest growing of all digital media types are digital out-of-home displays in gas stations, shopping malls, retail stores, and so on. Other media, in fact, *all* media will leverage all of their digital capabilities in the upcoming years.

Digital advertising also brings with it new challenges when it comes to metrics and measurement. Historically, media research has emphasized the front-end metrics of audience and audience effectiveness. Back-end metrics have been left to market research (attitude, usage, and awareness research) and the world of direct response for sales purposes. The Web allows for more sophisticated options on the front end, although getting industry agreement on a standard way of measuring these options is still a challenge.

Types of targeting abound. Just a short time ago, targeting was primarily about demographics. It still is, especially in traditional media, but the types of targeting available in the digital space include demographic, product usage, sociographic (lifestyle/psychographic), contextual, behavioral, relevancy, social (birds of a feather), retargeting people who have previously responded, keyword search, and more.

Digitization is inherently about technology; media planners today must be technologically astute. They must know how to deploy ad-serving tags, understand the value of rich media versus banners, and be able to advise creative groups on these issues. They must understand the technical considerations regarding banner specification and be prepared to lead the team, including the creative group, account management, and clients, on their execution.

The media planner must also understand the back-end metrics that define return on investment (ROI), because they represent the success or failure of a campaign in the eyes of the advertiser and the agency. These do not include just sales, but engagement metrics such as Cost-Per-action, CPinquiry, CPdownload, CPregistration, CPvisitation, or CP whatever other metrics are deemed relevant.

Search

Search is today the largest and fastest-growing part of the interactive marketplace, yet it is not necessarily controlled by the media planner or even the chief marketing officer (CMO). For many companies, the website and search are the responsibility of the information technology (IT) department. We expect this to change over time as advertisers recognize their importance to the overall marketing plan.

Emerging media technologies abound. It is problematic to predict which will receive critical mass, but for some the future is clear. There is not much advertiser acceptance yet, but mobile has consumer critical mass and is sure to grow. Applications, also known as apps, widgets, or gadgets, have the potential to become major advertising units. We are also sure to see video everywhere (on smart phones, mobile, and out of home). Nevertheless, television is expected to remain the principal place where video is watched, although the ways in which it is delivered to your living room or family room may change.

Social media has become a fact of life for the advertiser. The biggest aspect of social media turns out not to be as a major advertising medium, however. It is that consumers now feel they have permission to comment on everything from ad campaigns to products and services to corporate policy. The consumer engagement in communications will probably affect creative more than media, although the media planners' tools for measurement should come in handy here.

How Has Media Planning Stayed the Same?

As much as it is popular to talk about how media has changed or evolved, it is important to realize how much has remained the same—the basics and fundamentals of media planning still need to be practiced. It has never been more important to understand who your target audience is and then to properly implement the plan to reach them. Accurately translating the advertiser's marketing objectives into the advertising message and then into the media objectives and strategy remains crucial.

While many new metrics for measuring media effectiveness have been proposed, such as the continued "fuzzy" metric of engagement, tools like reach (how many of your target has the opportunity to see your message) and frequency (how many times are they exposed) remain the best way to compare the impact of alternative plans. Reach and frequency and their building block, the gross rating point (GRP), are expected to survive in the new world of digital metrics, as are important concepts like audience composition and the value of a medium's content. Digital media have learned from their traditional media forbearers the value of having commonly accepted, standard ways of defining and measuring advertising exposure.

At first, the Web planners resisted standards; they wanted to talk about the improved metrics that the Web could provide. Over time, the digital industry has come to realize that standards do not reduce the value of the new media. Instead, they bring comparability and order to the marketplace so that all are talking the same language and are on the same page. Efforts to standardize metrics are expected to continue through important organizations such as the Interactive Advertising Bureau (IAB), American Association of Advertising Agencies (4As), the Media Rating Council (MRC), and many others. A budding media planner could do no better for his or her career than to get involved with these organizations as they work to develop standards. It not only represents a great learning opportunity, but also provides exposure to the leaders in the industry.

What About a Career in Media Planning?

As mentioned earlier, this book is a great resource if you are contemplating a career in media.

Starting a career as a media planner can prepare you for many different marketing and advertising roles, including that of a media strategist, media researcher, or media director on either the agency or client side. Many go on to successful careers in advertising sales. More than a few CMOs had their first job in media.

Some benefits you gain with a career in media planning include the following:

1. An understanding of marketing and media data and analytics. The business world is driven by data today; data is the new creative in the media business.
2. An understanding of marketing strategy.
3. An understanding of the creative process and the knowledge of what works and what doesn't. Even CEOs need this.
4. Some great lessons on dealing with others. Everything is a learning experience, a negotiation experience, or both.
5. How to prepare an effective and persuasive written or oral presentation. After all, you have to sell your work every day.

As a media planner and buyer, you will be responsible for ensuring that the substantial amounts of money you are entrusted with are properly spent and accounted for. Beyond that, you will come to understand the value of honesty and fair dealing as you work with your client, your coworkers, and the media sales representatives.

Enjoy this book—it is a great resource. For those of us who have spent a career in media and love it, the book Jack Sissors started has been and always will be a primary reference because of its solid and in-depth information on everything you want to know about advertising media planning. This new edition is expected to carry on that tradition. Thanks to Roger Baron for making this happen.

David L. Smith
CEO and Founder
Mediasmith, Inc.

CHAPTER ONE

Introduction to Media Planning

The Art of Matching Media to the Advertiser's Marketing Needs

It was the client's annual advertising review at a large Midwestern advertising agency. The creative team was presenting digital animatics of the new campaign from the flat-screen monitor on the wall. The media director was glancing at the BlackBerry in his lap below the table, waiting for a response from ESPN about the base package for this client. The light in the corner was still blinking green as the creative director finished up, but he could see from the smile on the client's face that it was a success. The creative director had sold the campaign. Now it was media's turn.

The client turned to the media director and said, "This creative is great. Now I want to know how you're going to spend the $100 million I'm giving you so my customers will see it. I want to know what my competition is doing, who you are targeting, what media you are going to use and why, where it will run, and when it will run. I want to know how many of the target audience will see the campaign and how often they will see it. But mainly, I want to see how you plan to creatively integrate this campaign across all the different platforms we have today—the conventional TV set, the PC, the online search, and the mobile, social, and other opportunities from emerging media that didn't exist just a few years ago. If you make a good case, I'll authorize the $100 million. So let's see your media plan."

A bit overdrawn perhaps, but it is the job of the media planner to answer these questions and to develop a plan that delivers the creative message to the target as effectively and efficiently as possible. It is a fascinating job that combines marketing, psychology, show business, law, research, technology, and the planner's sensitive, creative insights into the human condition. It has the planner playing the dual roles of both salesperson and client—sometimes alternating between the two from one minute to the next. In the sales role, planners must convince the advertiser and his or her own agency team that they have developed the most effective media plan. Then with a ring of the telephone, a planner becomes the client of the media sales representatives who want their website, cable television network, magazine, or other medium included on the plan—that is, included so they receive an order for some of that $100 million budget. These are the outward manifestations of the core job of the media planner: to make the most effective use of the advertiser's media budget.

Media: A Message Delivery System

Media exist primarily to deliver message content—entertainment, information, and advertisements to a vast audience. Media should be thought of as both carriers and delivery systems. They carry advertisements and deliver them to individuals who buy or choose media first on the basis of the kind and quality of entertainment and information and second on the kinds of advertisements they deliver. Advertisers find media to be convenient and relatively inexpensive delivery systems compared to direct mail or other channels that do not carry entertainment and information.

This definition applies to online media as well as traditional mass media—the banner ads on websites and the sponsored links that accompany paid search keywords serve the same function as the commercials and printed advertising that accompany information and entertainment in traditional media.

It is important to recognize that consumers have specialized needs that media can meet, such as providing information about certain kinds of products and brands. Readers can browse a magazine or newspaper, stopping to look at any advertisement that seems interesting. When there is a clear need for information, 15 minutes spent with Google, Bing, Wikipedia, and the other search engines will give a person top-line knowledge about any topic on earth.

Advertisers who want to reach both a mass and a specialized audience find it is more expensive to buy media that reach the specialized audience. However, no matter which kind of audience advertisers want to reach, it is imperative that someone plans the purchase of media as far ahead of publishing or broadcast dates as possible. Advertisers cannot afford to buy media impulsively or capriciously. Therefore, the planning function is a major operation in advertising and media agencies and at client companies. There is too much money involved to not plan ahead of time, and this book concentrates on the planning function.

Two words are sometimes used as if they mean the same thing: *medium* (the plural is *media*) and *vehicle*. They are not exactly the same. A *medium* refers to a class of carriers such as television, newspapers, magazines, and so on. In other words, it refers to a group of carriers that have similar characteristics. A *vehicle* is an individual carrier within a medium. For example, the website CNN.com is a vehicle within the online medium. "60 Minutes" is a vehicle within television. *Martha Stewart Living* and *People* are vehicles within the magazine medium.

Media Planning

Media planning consists of the series of decisions made to answer the question, "What are the best means of delivering advertisements to prospective purchasers of my brand or service?" This definition is rather general, but it provides a broad picture of what media planning is all about.

A media planner attempts to answer the following specific questions:

- How many prospects (for purchasing a given brand of product) do I need or can I afford to reach?
- In which media should I place ads?
- How many times a month should prospects see each ad?
- During which months should ads appear?
- Where should the ads appear? In which markets and regions?
- How much money should be spent in each medium?

When all the questions have been asked and the decisions made, the recommendations and rationales are organized into a presentation (usually PowerPoint) and a written document called a *media plan.* The plan, when approved by the advertiser, becomes a blueprint for the selection and use of media. Once the advertiser has approved the plan, it also serves as a guide for actually purchasing the media.

It would be a mistake, however, to think of media planning as nothing more than finding answers to a list of questions about media. Such a view is too narrow to provide the necessary perspective. Rather, it is better to assume that each question represents certain kinds of problems that need to be solved. Some problems are relatively simple, such as, "On which day of the week should television commercials be shown?" Other problems are much more difficult, such as, "In which media will ads most affect the prospect's buying behavior, resulting in the most additional sales?"

Media planning should be thought of as a process or a series of decisions that provides the best possible answers to a set of problems. It is the planner's recommended way to balance the many trade-offs within a given budget. A planner might find that a recommended solution to a given marketing problem does not make sense when other factors are considered. Finding the best solutions to a set of marketing problems represents the main task of planners. That is what makes media planning such an intellectually challenging activity. In a sense, media planners are marketing professionals with media expertise.

The Changing Face of Media Planning

Some marketers believe the traditional media forms such as television, newspapers, magazines, and radio are passé. This is a mistake. Although the Internet as a whole is now accessible to 86 percent of the U.S. population,[1] its fragmentation across thousands of sites (the so-called Long Tail) makes it costly to deliver advertising to large numbers of people with enough frequency to communicate the message. Mass media, especially the top-rated television programs and large-circulation magazines such as *People*, continue to define popular culture in the United States and in the world. Mass media are essential to create broad awareness of new products and services and to reinforce awareness of existing brands. But today's consumers want more information than can be communicated with the traditional media. Because they expect to get this information from the Internet, marketing plans must consider how this medium, and especially search tools such as Google and Bing, will be used to build on the awareness that has been created with mass advertising.

At the same time, advertisers want to reinforce awareness with frequent brand mentions in media that are part of the target audience's daily life. Exhibit 1-1 on pages 6–7 presents the example of Coors Light's use of ESPN cable television, *ESPN: The Magazine*, mobile advertising on cell phones, and online exposure to men of legal drinking age during the annual personnel draft of the National Football League (NFL).

Traditionally, media planning has asked questions revolving around how media can reach the right persons. The "right" persons came from broadly aggregated data, such as "women ages 18–49" or "men ages 25–54." But these broad demographic characterizations were developed to accommodate the sale of broadcast media, radio, and television, where the available research dictates that age and gender demographics are the currency of a buy. They obscure an almost unlimited array of lifestyles, interests, and even media habits that are relevant to marketers if they want to deliver advertising to their best prospects. Today's media planning requires planners to identify smaller groups of product users and the media that

---

1.   Mediamark Research & Intelligence, LLC, Spring 2009.

best reach them. Online advertisers can use behavioral targeting to direct ads to people who visit related websites. Sponsored search on Google and many other venues allows delivery of advertising to people who, by definition, have shown an interest in a product or service.

Technology has made it economical to deliver program content that appeals to smaller and smaller groups of people. Audience fragmentation has become the dominant characteristic of media, especially television, in the 21st century. Today the average home can receive 119 channels, up from 61 channels in 2000.[2] Cable television networks, delivered either by wire or by satellite, can now be seen in 90 percent of U.S. households.[3] This proliferation of viewing choices has significantly eroded the audience to the traditional broadcast networks, but total hours of viewing have remained essentially constant.

The result is a splintering of the audience among channels whose content may or may not be relevant to advertisers. For example, marketers of vacation destinations will certainly advertise on the Travel Channel, but the majority of their customers never watch it. Although the target audience composition of the Travel Channel is very high (just about all the viewers are interested in travel), its coverage is very low—there are a great many travelers who never watch the Travel Channel. The planner's challenge is to develop a balanced plan that includes some vehicles that offer high coverage to ensure every product user will see the message, and others with high composition that will minimize waste. This coverage/composition trade-off will be a recurring theme throughout this book.

The expansion of video content to pre-roll commercials before streaming video on the PC, mobile cell phones, and other platforms will further fragment the audience into hundreds, if not thousands, of video sources that reflect the media equivalent of what has been called the Long Tail. The term was first coined by Chris Anderson in a *Wired* magazine article in October 2004. It expresses the concept, exploited by Amazon.com and other online retailers, that business can make a profit by selling relatively small quantities of a large number of items, versus the traditional model that relies on quantity sales of a relatively short product line. Applied to media, it means that an advertiser needs to spread the message across many small channels to reach the widely scattered audience. The typical cable advertiser will buy time on 20 to 30 cable networks in addition to schedules on the broader-reach broadcast networks.

---

2. Nielsen Television Audience 2007, updated June 26, 2009.
3. The Nielson Company, ADS Counts, March 2009.

EXHIBIT 1-1

Coors Light Beer's Use of Online and Mobile Internet
to Extend the Impact of Traditional Media

To kick off the summer, Coors Light used its status as the official beer of the NFL to connect the brand to the NFL Draft. The intent was to increase exposure during the off-season through TV, digital, mobile, outdoor, and on-site hospitality. So as the exclusive presenting sponsor of the draft on ESPN and the NFL Network, Coors Light ran NFL-themed creative and received in-program features and enhancements.

- Mobile alerts were created to provide customized content on players and teams, and they played a key role in keeping on-the-go fans informed while reinforcing Coors Light's official sponsor status.

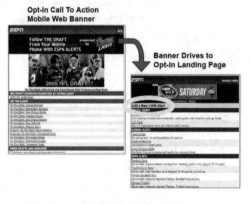

Source: MillerCoors LLC. Used with permission. Image quality is due to the requirements of the medium.

- Through NFL.com, ESPN.com, and Yahoo Sports, customized video features were deployed, reinforcing the branded messaging present across other media. These included out-of-home advertising placements, collateral materials in restaurants and bars, and the appearance of retired NFL players in drinking establishments to promote and drive traffic to the NFL-themed Coors Light website, while raising awareness of Coors Light's NFL Draft partnership.
- Hospitality events for distributors and retailers were hosted in New York, including a flag football game with retail partners as players and retired NFL athletes as coaches.

Source: MillerCoors LLC. Used with permission. Image quality is due to the requirements of the medium.

- Coors Light sponsored *ESPN: The Magazine* events and an EA Sports luncheon during the draft weekend, providing consumers access to Coors Light products, event tickets, and an opportunity to meet NFL players.
- At the NFL Draft event, Coors Light hosted interactive press conference booths on-site. For those not able to attend, remote events were hosted for the New York Giants and Jets, including watching parties at respective stadiums and several Dave & Buster's restaurants in the New York area as well as team training facility locations.

Results

The campaign was seen as a big success. Hundreds of thousands of individuals signed up to receive mobile SMS alerts, and millions of branded alerts were sent out over the draft weekend. In total, Coors Light received tens of millions of impressions across all NFL Draft–related media.

A regional manager of a major retail chain responded positively to the overall NFL Draft experience, "Wow, it was awesome. Everyone loved it and would love to do more things like this. It was by far the best thing we have done as a team in a very long time."

The Changing Role of Media Planners

As a result of technological advancements and audience fragmentation, the role of media planners has changed in advertising and media agencies. Today, media planning ranks in importance along with marketing and creative planning, but in the early days of advertising agency operations, media planning consisted of simple, clerical tasks. There were fewer media available in those days, and little research on media audiences had been done to guide planners in decision making.

Today, planning has become much more complex and important. Planners must have a greater knowledge base from which to formulate media plans. They not only must know more about media, which have increased tremendously in number over the past 10 years, but also must know how the media plan can contribute to the overall marketing plan. And most important, planners must have an almost intuitive sense of their target's life so they can select media that will expose the advertising at the most opportune time. This makes media planning today a more challenging, but also a far more creative, process than ever before.

Exhibit 1-2 presents a campaign created by McCann Erickson, Detroit, the ad agency for Travel Michigan (the state department responsible for promoting tourism to Michigan) as a good example of this. As part of a multimedia effort, the group ran advertising on the sides of tour buses in Chicago, knowing that people who visited the city would be good candidates for extending their vacation to include neighboring Michigan. Their marketing rationale follows:

> At the heart of the Pure Michigan campaign is a simple idea: Your time off should feel a world away from your everyday life. Applying the idea to out-of-home gave the state of Michigan a powerful tool for drawing a contrast between daily life and the idealized vacation getaway: putting a little piece of Pure Michigan right in the middle of the everyday world. Whether alongside a suburban interstate, on a city wallscape, or wrapped around a downtown Chicago tour bus, each out-of-home ad showcases a glimpse of Michigan's natural beauty. This startling contrast creates an oasis-like feel in the middle of an ordinary day—giving consumers a sample of what their Michigan vacation will feel like.

What brought about this need for a broader knowledge base? Foremost was the rise of the marketing concept, which changed media planning from an isolated activity to one closely related to marketing planning. In fact, one way to evaluate a media plan is to measure how effectively it helps attain the advertiser's marketing objectives. Another cause of the change was the development of new and more definitive media audience research techniques. As a result, more research is available to help planners choose from myriad alternatives.

EXHIBIT 1-2

Michigan Tourism Out-of-Home Tour Bus Advertising

Source: Travel Michigan. Used with permission.

The change is also due to the universal availability of the Internet and low-cost, high-speed computers that make routine the physical acquisition and manipulation of vast amounts of data. The Microsoft Excel spreadsheet is the workbench that planners use to compare and cost out media alternatives. Planners are expected to have a thorough knowledge of this tool, including the most commonly used functions and the four methods of database management (sort, filter, subtotal, and pivot table). Finally, the Microsoft PowerPoint presentation system is used to develop the presentation that will ultimately sell the plan to the client.

Media planning, then, is not so much a matter of being able to answer such relatively simple questions as where to place advertisements or how many advertisements to run each week. It is a matter of proving that optimal decisions were made under a given set of marketing circumstances. Advertisers demand such explanations, and media planners must be able to provide them. Today's media planners have changed as requirements for planning have changed. The new planner must have a breadth of knowledge, marketing understanding, research familiarity, computer literacy, creative planning awareness, and media acumen to do the job competently. It is within this framework that media planning now takes place.

Classes of Media

Planners like to separate media into various classes as a form of shorthand for the capabilities and characteristics that derive from their physical form. Typically, planners identify traditional media, nontraditional media, online media, and specialized media. However, even these distinctions break down with the convergence of media forms. Video is displayed on three screens: the television set, the personal computer in the form of streaming video, and the mobile platform that displays information and video on the cell phone. Magazines and even newspapers (their news content) are delivered electronically, posing a threat to the advertiser-supported business model that has sustained them for 100 years. Digital billboards vastly expand the capabilities of the oldest mass medium.

In the interest of convenience and common usage, we will stay with the four-way classification: traditional mass media, nontraditional media, digital media, and specialized media.

Traditional Mass Media

Mass media such as newspapers, magazines, radio, and television are especially well suited for delivering advertisements—as well as news, entertainment, and educational content—to a widespread general (or mass) audience. Planners find mass media valuable because (1) such media are able to quickly deliver large audiences at a relatively low cost, (2) they can deliver advertisements to special kinds of audiences who are attracted to each medium's editorial or programming, and (3) they tend to develop strong loyalties among audiences who return to their favorite medium with a high degree of regularity. Over the years, traditional mass media have developed systems and practices that respond directly and efficiently to the marketing needs of advertisers. They get the bulk of the advertising dollars, and they are the meat and potatoes of media planning. Online and the new digital media are joining them, but as of this writing, they have a long way to go before they will replace traditional media.

Television is the traditional mass medium that most people think of first. The digital revolution has resulted in a convergence of platforms on which people watch their favorite programs. While we may still call it television, *video* is a more appropriate term, with the only difference being the platform on which it is displayed. Nielsen refers to the "Three Screens" of video: conventional television, streaming video displayed on a computer screen, and mobile that displays video content on a cell phone screen. Although there may be little difference to the viewers, there are substantial differences in the way their audiences are measured and in the way advertising is planned and bought.

Media planners, however, also know that mass media have their limitations in delivering advertising messages. The most serious is that mass media audiences do not see, hear, or read a medium solely because of the advertising content. Media vary in their ability to expose both editorial and advertising material.

Broadcast media, such as radio and television, are seldom sought out by consumers for the advertisements alone. Broadcast commercials have an intrusive character, breaking into the play or action of a program and compelling some attention to the advertising message. Whether any given viewer will or will not watch a particular commercial is determined more by the ingenuity and value of the message than by its appearance on an interesting program.

As of March 2010, 36 percent of U.S. homes have a digital video recorder (DVR),[4] and on playback, most viewers skip the commercials of programs they have recorded. However, this negative consequence on ad exposure affects primarily scripted high-rated prime-time programs, daytime soaps, and late-night entertainment. Very few people record news, sports, most cable channels, and syndicated programs like "Oprah" and "Access Hollywood." And even for the highly recorded prime-time programs, the impact of DVRs has been greatly mitigated by the industry shift to the C3 rating, which reports the audience to the average commercial minute watched at normal speed live or within three days of telecast. Much more about this later on.

Newspapers have news, entertainment, information, and catalog values for their readers. A newspaper generally has excellent readership of local news editorial and advertising material, serving as a buying guide for readers who are looking for many different kinds of products. People often check newspaper ads immediately before their regular food shopping day to find the best grocery bargains. For frequently purchased products, where prices are prominently displayed, newspapers can be a very effective selling medium.

Surprisingly, newspaper circulation is up 7.4 percent according to the latest figures (2008 daily circulation: 50.7 million versus 47.2 million in 2000, according to the *Editor and Publisher International Year Book*). However, advertising revenue is down dramatically due to the shift of classified advertising to the Internet. As of summer 2009, ad revenue to local newspapers was 12.0 billion, down 2 percent from $12.2 billion in 2000, according to Nielsen Monitor-Plus. Flat revenue after 10 years of rising costs has forced bankruptcies, led to editorial staff cutbacks, reduced publishing days, and other problems. Despite this severe challenge to its business model, the newspaper remains a viable media option that continues to offer good

---

4. The Nielsen Company, April 2010.

value to advertisers. The medium will be presented in this book with the same capabilities as it has in the past.

Newspapers are relatively untargeted mass media. Magazines, on the other hand, are much more selective in their ability to precisely target advertising exposures. Some, such as fashion, home, and special-interest publications, are bought as much for their advertising as for their editorial matter. Other more general-interest publications, such as newsweeklies and personality and sports magazines, appeal to readers who are looking for interesting articles and stories rather than product information.

Billboards are the oldest form of traditional media. They offer the opportunity to reach consumers immediately before they enter a retail store, provide reminder advertising, and have been proven to create broad, immediate brand awareness of new products. Unfortunately, the medium has long suffered from inadequate measurement. The Traffic Audit Bureau, using GPS technology, aims to replace the old traffic count with modern measurement that they hope will allow the medium to be planned in a way similar to broadcast. We'll discuss this topic in more detail later.

Obviously, the creative quality of the commercial or advertisement affects its impact on the consumer and the numbers of consumers who will read, see, or hear it. This is true regardless of which medium is used.

Nontraditional Media

Traditional mass media all engage in one-way communication—from the source to great numbers of viewers, listeners, and readers using technology that has been around for decades. Almost any other innovative way of delivering ad messages to consumers is considered a *nontraditional medium*. These media disseminate advertising messages through means not usually called media. For example, the combination of magazines and sales promotion is sometimes called nontraditional media, even though sales promotion has not historically been categorized as a medium. Digital advertising, though certainly not traditional, is generally viewed in its own category.

Nontraditional media include the vast array of out-of-home venues where the advertising will stand out from its competition. In addition to providing a place for advertising, they also satisfy the need for additional revenue from companies that have exposure to the public and feel that their unique location offers an opportunity to sell advertising. The most commonly used nontraditional media include television screens in airport waiting areas, elevators, the top of gas pumps, in doctor's offices, and any other place where a video screen will display content to the public. Nontraditional media also include posters in health clubs, signage on a golf course, and banners at public events. Some locations, such as the walls of public restrooms, the floor of grocery stores, and overhead luggage bins of commercial airliners may be driven more by a proprietor's desire for additional income than by the advertiser's need for an alternative venue.

Many media planners recommend using nontraditional media, but there have been some problems in determining what the advertiser receives for the money. The problems are caused by the lack of continuing measurements of the audience delivered by these less-established media. In addition, what information does exist is typically provided by the media themselves, raising questions about its accuracy and objectivity. In most instances, planners have to guesstimate the sizes of audiences. The Digital Place-based Advertising Association (www.ovab.org) has developed measurement standards that are intended to resolve or at least mitigate these problems.

Online Media

The proliferation of online media options in the last 10 years justifies its own classification. It includes any communications medium where there is a real-time interaction between the user and the content producer via the Internet. The content is accessed with a Web browser or device functioning as a Web browser. So this includes conventional websites viewed on a personal computer; streaming video; social media such as Facebook or LinkedIn; search engine marketing (SEM) with Google, Bing, or others; Web-enabled cell phones; long-form high-definition video delivered to a television set functioning as a computer monitor; and other online forms that are sure to be developed after this book has gone to press.

The fundamental principles of online planning are the same as for traditional media, but there are two schools of thought regarding where it fits in the media department organization. One approach is to think of online as simply another medium to be planned by the traditional media planning group. This has the advantage of consolidating all media planning in the hands of a single person or group, allowing them to choose whatever media make the most sense for the advertiser (sometimes referred to as "media agnostic" planning). The downside of this approach is that online media and measurement tools change so rapidly that it takes full-time involvement to stay current. In the online world, six months is a long time.

The other approach is to create a separate online unit within the media department or even as an outside company specializing in online media planning and buying. Although this group might be organized by client, their day-to-day involvement with the medium and support from others in the group who can answer questions allow these specialists to do a better job of planning online display and search advertising than is possible by a generalist. On the other hand, specialists must guard against becoming narrow advocates of online in a world where advertisers are looking for the best media to meet their marketing objectives, regardless of which that turns out to be.

In the experience of David L. Smith, president of Mediasmith, the practice is evenly split: "Some have separate groups within a media department. Some are integrated and some are a separate company. Take your pick. There is no *most*."

Specialized Media

Special-interest consumer magazines appeal to specific reader interests such as skiing, money management, photography, or antiques. These magazines are read as much for their advertising as they are for their editorial content. Therefore, these magazines often attract readers who purchase the magazine not only for the editorial material, but also for information on the kinds of products advertised. Such media are often referred to as *niche media* because of their special-interest focus.

A large category of media also exists to meet the specialized needs of industrial manufacturers, service companies, wholesalers, retailers, and professional workers such as physicians, attorneys, and teachers. These media take the form of publications that contain editorial matter as well as advertising pertaining to the specialized market, but they also include films, trade shows, convention exhibits, CDs, and even flash drives containing a file with the promotional message and stamped with the advertiser's logo that can be used by the recipient long after the initial presentation. Business-to-business advertisers are typically the advertisers most interested in these forms of media.

Other specialized media exist exclusively for the purpose of delivering advertising messages. They carry no editorial matter and are not sought after by readers as are other forms of media. Such advertising-oriented media include handbills, direct mail, outdoor billboards, car cards that appear on buses or trucks, and freestanding inserts (FSIs) in newspapers.

Another specialized medium is the catalog. Although consumers often request catalogs, they look at catalogs less frequently than they do mass media. At the same time, many advertisers find catalogs productive because consumers use them as shopping guides. One form of catalog is the telephone book, which carries advertising but also carries editorial matter—telephone numbers. Plumbers, for example, might justifiably use telephone book advertising exclusively, because plumbers are not usually called until an emergency arises. On such occasions, the consumer will search ads in the Yellow Pages to find a plumber but probably will not notice such ads at any other time. Although still widely used today, the rise of the Internet and sources such as Craigslist have severely impacted the Yellow Pages and newspaper classified advertising, calling into question the long-term survivability of the medium.

General Procedures in Media Planning

Marketing considerations must precede media planning. Media planning never starts with answers to such questions as, "Which medium should I select?" or "Should I use television or magazines?" Planning grows out of a marketing problem that needs to be solved. To start without knowing or understanding the underlying marketing problem is illogical, because media are primarily a tool for implementing the marketing strategy.

As you will see in the hypothetical media plan presented in Chapter 2, the starting point for a media plan should be an analysis of a marketing situation. This analysis is made so both marketing and media planners can get a bird's-eye view of how a company has been operating against its competitors in the total market. The analysis serves as a means of learning the details of the problem, where possibilities lie for its solution, and where the company can gain an advantage over its competitors in the marketplace.

After analyzing the marketing situation, marketing and media planners devise a marketing strategy and plan that state marketing objectives and spell out the actions to accomplish those objectives. When the marketing strategy calls for advertising, the usual purpose is to communicate to consumers some information that helps attain a marketing objective. Media are the means whereby advertisements are delivered to the market.

Once a marketing plan has been devised, an advertising creative strategy must also be determined. This consists of decisions about what is to be communicated, how it will be executed, and what it is supposed to accomplish. A statement of advertising copy themes and how copy will be used to communicate the selling message is also part of that strategy. Media planning decisions are affected by the advertising creative strategy because some creative strategies are better suited to one medium than to any other. For example, if a product requires demonstration, television is the best medium. If an ad must be shown in high-fidelity color, magazines or newspaper supplements are preferable. Creative strategy also determines the prospect profile in terms of such demographic variables as age, sex, income, or occupation. These prospects now become the targets that the planner will focus on in selecting media vehicles. Modern channel planning software can aid in the process of selecting the best media channels. (See Chapter 10 for more on this subject.)

Up to this point, persons other than the media planner have been making decisions that will ultimately affect the media plan. The marketing or marketing research people are responsible for the situation analysis and marketing plan, although media planners are sometimes involved at the inception of the marketing plan. Copywriters and art directors are generally responsible for carrying out the creative strategy. Sometimes a marketing plan is as simple as a memorandum from a marketing executive to the media planner or even an idea in an advertising executive's mind. In such informal situations, media planning begins almost immediately, with little or no marketing research preceding it. Exhibit 1-3 summarizes the preplanning steps.

EXHIBIT 1-3

Scope of Media Preplanning Activities

Marketing Problem
All media planning starts with a problem in the context of national, local, or business-to-business marketing/advertising. Examples of the kinds of problems could be how much to spend for advertising next year, how to increase sales volume, or how to stop eroding market share.

Situation Analysis	Marketing Strategy Plan	Creative Strategy Plan
Purpose: To understand the marketing problem. A company and its competitors are analyzed on the basis of:	Purpose: To plan activities that will solve one or more of the marketing problems. Includes the determination of:	Purpose: To determine what to communicate through advertisements. Include the determination of:
1. Size and share of the total market	1. Marketing objectives	1. How product can meet consumer needs
2. Sales history, costs, and profits	2. Product spending strategy	2. How product will be positioned in advertisements
3. Distribution practices	3. Distribution strategy	3. Copy themes
4. Methods of selling	4. Which elements of the marketing mix to use	4. Specific objectives of each advertisement
5. Use of advertising	5. Identification of "best" market segments	5. Number and sizes of advertisements
6. Identification of prospects		
7. Nature of the product		

Media Planning

The media planner begins work as soon as a marketing strategy plan is in hand. This plan sets the tone and guides the direction that the media decisions will follow.

The first item to come out of such a plan is a statement of *media objectives*. These are the goals that a media planner believes are most important in helping attain marketing objectives. Goals include determination of which targets (persons most likely to purchase a given product or service) are most important, how many of those targets need to be reached, and where advertising should be concentrated at what times.

Objectives form the basis for media strategies. A *media strategy* is a series of actions selected from several possible alternatives to best achieve the media objectives. Media strategies will cover such decisions as which kinds of media should be used, whether national or spot broadcast advertising should be used, how ads should be scheduled, and many other decisions.

After the strategy is determined, the implementation of the media plan begins. Some planners call all these subsequent decisions tactics. Whatever they are called, many decisions still have to be made before tactics culminate in a media plan. As indicated in Exhibit 1-4, these decisions might include the selection of vehicles in which to place ads, the number of ads to be placed in each vehicle, the size of each ad, and the specific position within each vehicle that an ad will occupy.

A media plan is custom tailored—designed expressly to meet the needs of an advertiser at a given time for specific marketing purposes. A media plan should never be a copy of last year's plan with new costs, nor should it be simply a blank form with spaces that can be filled in quickly with selected dates or times for running ads. Each media plan should be different from preceding ones for the same product.

Plans are custom tailored because the marketplace is rarely the same from year to year. Competitors rarely stand still in their marketing activities. They change their messages, change their marketing expenditures, introduce new brands, or discontinue distribution of old brands. Consumers also change, moving to different geographical areas, getting new jobs, retiring, getting married, adopting different leisure-time activities, or buying new kinds of products. As a result, each marketing situation presents new opportunities as well as new problems.

Because marketing situations change, new approaches to planning are constantly needed to keep up with or ahead of competitors. Media planning is also affected by the new kinds of research or analysis needed to keep abreast of a changing business world. Media planning requires a great sensitivity to change. For this reason, even direct competitors may decide on very different media strategies. Exhibit 1-5 shows the allocation of calendar 2008 media dollars by the six leading vacuum cleaner companies.

EXHIBIT 1-4

Kinds of Questions That Lead to Decisions About Media Objectives and Strategies

The following is an overview of some of the many questions that lead to media objectives and strategies. Note that strategies grow out of objectives.

Media Objectives	Media Strategies
What action should we take as a result of media used by competitors?	Should we use same media mix as competitors? Should we allocate weight the same way as competitors? Should we ignore competitors?
What actions should we take as a result of our brand's creative strategies?	Which media/vehicles are best suited? Any special treatments (gatefolds, inserts)? Which dayparts?
Who should be our primary and secondary targets?	Which product usages patterns should we consider? Heavy/medium/light users? What distribution of strategic impressions? Which dayparts?
What balance of reach to frequency is needed?	What levels of reach and frequency? What levels of effective reach/frequency?
Do we need national and/or local media?	What proportions should go into national media?
What patterns of geographical weighting should we use?	Should we weight by dollars or GRPs? Where should we place weights? When should we weight (weeks/months)? What weight levels for each market?
What communication goals (or effectiveness goals) are needed?	Which criteria of effectiveness should we use?
Which kind of scheduling patterns suit our plans: continuity, flighting, or pulsing?	Should we use one or more? When should we weight more heavily?
Do media have to support promotions? Why?	What proportion of the budget should be used? What media mix?
Is media testing needed? How should it be used?	How many tests and in which markets? How should we translate (Little USA or As Is)?
Is budget large enough to accomplish objectives?	Do we need to set priorities? Which must we achieve, and which are optional? Do we need more money than is available?

EXHIBIT 1-5

Is There a *Best* Media Strategy?

	BRAND A	BRAND B	BRAND C	BRAND D	BRAND E	BRAND F
Network TV	60%	0%	0%	0%	18%	0%
Cable TV	19	79	44	0	24	1
Syndicated TV	4	8	0	0	32	0
Spot TV	0	2	0	2	6	0
National Magazine	17	1	53	63	0	99
Network Radio	0	0	0	20	0	0
Spot Radio	0	0	0	7	0	0
Internet	1	10	3	8	19	0
Total	100%	100%	100%	100%	100%	100%

Comments:

1. Media expenditures often provide more insight into strategy than any other data.
2. From the data, one can conclude that there is no one best media strategy for all advertisers, because each perceives the market in slightly different ways based on its own marketing needs. Some marketers want to increase market share—others want simply to maintain their present position. Such differences play a major role in media selection. Also, some advertisers see one medium as being more effective than others.
3. In this case, four of the six vacuum cleaner brands use television, but Brand B places almost 80 percent of its budget in cable TV, while Brand A concentrates in network TV. Brand C uses only cable TV with a strong consumer print campaign, while Brand D uses almost no TV, splitting its budget between national magazines, radio, and the Internet. Brand E uses television and the Internet. Brand F puts virtually the entire budget in national magazines. The 1 percent spending in cable TV is probably a test.
4. Occasionally, one sees all competitors using the same media, but the competitors in this seemingly routine product have widely differing views of the value of alternative media.

Principles for Selecting Media Vehicles

Of all the media decisions, one of the most important is selecting individual vehicles. Planners tend to select one or more vehicles that effectively reach the target audience prospects (1) with an optimum amount of frequency (or repetition), (2) at the lowest cost per thousand impressions, (3) with a minimum of waste (or non-prospects), and (4) within a specified budget.

These principles apply most when selecting vehicles for mass-produced and mass-consumed products such as food, clothing, or automobiles. Yet even though they are more difficult to execute, the principles should be the same in selecting vehicles for such products as noncommercial airplanes or yachts where prospects are distributed unevenly throughout the population. It may be less cost-efficient to reach those prospects than it would be to reach prospects for mass-consumed products, because planners must select vehicles that contain large amounts of waste to reach such selective markets. There are other times when the principles have to be modified. For example, if a creative strategy calls for producing TV commercials in high definition, then cost or waste must be disregarded in favor of meeting creative goals. Most often, however, these principles are followed consistently in planning.

When planners apply media selection principles, they use media delivery statistics as one piece of evidence that they have achieved the reach required. *Delivery* means simply the number of audience members reached by, or exposed to, a vehicle or a combination of media vehicles.

When the goal is to expose the greatest number of people possible for the available budget, the planner starts by looking among the many media alternatives that will reach prospects. A planner does this using media audience research data for individual vehicles. The data are in the form of numbers classified by audience types, and the numbers listed for each medium can be used as proof of audience delivery. In other words, the planner uses this statistical evidence to prove that the best vehicle(s) for reaching the targeted prospects has been selected. Obviously, there are other considerations in making this decision. Costs of media might be so high per prospect reached that the planner has to reject the first choice in favor of other media that reach smaller numbers of prospects but at lower costs.

Once audience delivery numbers have been found, they are related to the total number of prospects in the market. If a market consists of 35 million women in the United States who purchased a given kind of product within the last month, then the size of the market is 35 million. The planner might place the ad in an assortment of magazines that reach 17.5 million purchasing women, or 50 percent of the market. Is 50 percent enough? It depends on the marketing objectives. If 50 percent isn't enough, and if there is still money in the budget, the planner might place the ad in additional magazines to extend the reach of the print portion of the plan. Or the planner might decide that 50 percent reach of print, when added to the reach of the other media in the plan, satisfies the marketing objectives. Because no decision is made in a vacuum, the planner must also take into consideration the creative, promotional, and executional goals of the marketing strategy while evaluating the vehicle's ability to deliver prospects.

This discussion applies primarily to the traditional mass media. The selection of websites to carry digital advertising is based on some of the same criteria, plus additional measures that are unique to the online medium. So planners look at the number of prospects who visit the site, time spent on the site, the concentration of those prospects among all the site's visitors, the cost that the site charges for each thousand impressions delivered, and historical records of the number of visitors who click through the banner to the advertiser's own website. This represents a major change from traditional planning. Thus the media planner of the future needs to understand not only the traditional media planning techniques, but also the new ones that are now emerging.

Problems in Media Planning

Although media planning has become very important within advertising agency operations, it is not performed as efficiently as one might suppose. The planner faces many different kinds of problems that make it difficult to arrive at objective decisions.

Insufficient Media Data

Media planners almost always require more data about markets and media than are available. Some data never will be available, either because audiences cannot be measured or the data are too expensive to collect. For example, no complete and inclusive research service measures the audience exposure to outdoor advertising, to television viewing in hotel rooms, or to portable television viewing. Why? Because such media are too expensive to adequately measure, given their complexity and the amount of advertising revenue they produce. Both outdoor exposure and out-of-home TV viewing have been measured, but not on a continuous basis in all cities. There is also inadequate research showing the amount of money that competitors spend yearly for outdoor advertising, local cable TV advertising, regional sports TV networks, sponsored search advertising on Google, and many other advertising venues.

The Nielsen television rating service measures the audience size only in terms of individuals whose people meter button is pushed or who wrote in a diary that they are watching television. But even if there are people in front of the television set who say they are watching the program, there is no guarantee that they are paying attention to the commercials. Numerous studies have attempted to measure engagement with television programs, but have come up short, beginning with finding an acceptable definition for the term. Joe Plummer, the chief research officer of the Advertising Research Foundation (ARF), put forth this not entirely satisfactory definition, "Engagement is turning on a prospect to a brand idea enhanced by the surrounding context." A council of the ARF has been formed to study the question in more detail and issue reports of research findings on the subject.[5]

Another problem in television planning is that decisions about the future performance of television programs must be based on past performance. If the future is radically different from the past, then the data on which a decision is based may be worthless.

Although advertising impressions delivered on the Internet are counted with extreme precision, it takes a special effort to know if a banner ad actually appeared on the user's screen or if the viewer clicked away before it had a chance to come up, especially if the ad appears near the bottom of the page. Even then, it is impossible to know if any attention was paid to the ad. With click-through rates typically well below 1 percent, the impact of a banner ad is likely to be minimal. Greater attention is paid to the highly creative "rich media" that include streaming video, audio, animated cursor, and so on. But there is no data on "how much" more attention will be paid to this particular rich media execution.

The problem of obtaining sufficient information is especially acute for small advertisers, many of whom cannot afford to buy research data. They must rely on published guides, such as Mediaweek's *Marketer's Guide to Media*, that give an indication of costs and audiences, but they are typically a year or more old and lack the detail of a paid research subscription. They also may lack sales and marketing information, even about their own products, if they sell only to distributors or wholesalers. Since an advertiser's detailed sales information is highly confidential, often from their own agency, media planners typically must estimate the client's sales position from published sources or simply go without that information in the preparation of their plans.

Measuring how people read newspapers and magazines is another problem. How much of any given magazine or newspaper is read? How many advertisements are read? How thoroughly are they read? What is the value of placing an advertisement in one vehicle versus another? How does each vehicle affect the perception of an advertisement that it carries? What percent of the people who read a Sunday newspaper open up the *Parade* or *USA Weekend Magazine*?[6] Answers to these and

---

5. www.thearf.org/assets/engagement-council.

6. A 2003 MRI study reported that 75 percent of carrier newspaper readers read *Parade*, while 55 percent of the carrier paper readers read *USA Weekend*. There are no plans to repeat the study.

many other questions are not available on a continuing basis, so the media planner must make decisions without knowing all the pertinent facts.

Time Pressures

A problem that affects media planning in an entirely different way is that of the time pressure involved in making decisions. This is compounded by the universal availability of e-mail that leads to the expectation of an instant response. Gone are the days when a planner had a few days' grace from the time it took for a written response to be delivered by the postal system.

When the agency and advertiser are ready to start their advertising program, the planner often is faced with a lack of the most recent information needed to solve problems thoroughly. For example, in many cases the planner requires competitive media expenditure analyses showing how much each competitor spends in major markets throughout the country. Although modern systems can deliver the raw data in seconds, the systems for gathering the data from the television networks, magazines, radio stations, and so forth have not changed in decades. Today's planners must wait six to eight weeks to learn about the competitor's spending in these media.

Another time-related problem is the limited number of broadcast times and programs available to be purchased by advertisers at any given time. This problem is compounded if the client is slow to approve the budget, in which case the most desirable broadcast time periods and programs might be sold before the advertiser enters the marketplace.

In other situations, research data are so plentiful that there are neither personnel nor time to analyze them. This is especially true for the large amounts of computerized data on media audiences and brand usage. Computers are able to produce masses of cross-tabulations at lightning speeds, but often such data go unused because there is insufficient time to analyze them. This is especially true for online media research. Josh Chasin, the research director of comScore, said, "One of the consequences of being the most measurable medium is that the Internet ends up as the medium with the most measures." The online planner's challenge is to decide which of the many measures are most useful for selecting websites for an online campaign, or which measures are most relevant for the advertiser's marketing objectives.

Institutional Influences on Media Decisions

One of the less obvious external sources of influence on media decisions is the effect of client pressure to use or not use certain media vehicles or to use them in certain ways. Often these pressures are well known by everyone working on a client's account; the client continually reminds everyone of the restrictions. But there are times when these influences are known by relatively few persons, perhaps only those who regularly visit the client and are constantly communicating directly with him or her. Other subtle influences also affect planners. Directors or assistant directors in the media department or in account executive positions often influence decisions.

The problem with these institutional influences is that little or no information is available concerning the extent to which they exist or how much they affect decisions. These influences probably vary from client to client.

Lack of Objectivity

One of the continuing problems in media decision making is the sterility of thinking about strategy. Planners are not always objective. For example, an overdependence on numbers can affect objectivity. Media executives often think that when a decision is substantiated by numbers, such as television ratings, the decision must be valid because the numbers prove it so. It is often difficult to argue with decisions proved by numbers, yet the numbers can be misleading. The methods of measurement might be imprecise, the sample size might be too small, or the technique of measurement might be biased or too insensitive to really measure what it is supposed to. Or there might be a set of numbers of major significance that are not available to the media planner—all of which can affect the objectivity of the decision maker. Uncritical acceptance of numbers is a dangerous practice and can lead to decisions that common sense indicates are wrong.

Objectivity is also affected when a planner accepts relative data as absolute. For example, the sizes of television audiences reported through ratings are not absolute measurements. When a television rating service shows that 5 million homes tuned in to a given television program, this does not necessarily mean that precisely 5 million homes actually tuned in to the program. It is an estimate that is based on a sample. For this reason, there is a margin of error around the number that varies depending on the size of the sample and the size of the audience being measured— the smaller the sample and the smaller the audience, the larger the margin of error. Planners must be aware that there is no significant difference between two media vehicles that have almost the same audience. For example, a TV show with a 2.4 rating is not necessarily more popular than another show with a 2.3 rating. Rating services provide guidelines to help users know if the difference between audience estimates is significant. They also provide indications when the sample is too small to give statistically reliable ratings.

Although the audience ratings are only estimates, a planner cannot ignore the numbers and make decisions entirely on the basis of experience. Clients are certain to challenge the basis upon which media decisions are made.

Measuring Advertising Effectiveness

The effectiveness of direct response online advertising can be measured very accurately with the use of click-through rates and the number of leads generated. But for consumer package goods and the many other products whose advertising objectives go beyond an immediate response, there is no generally accepted way of measuring advertising effectiveness. This makes it difficult to prove the correctness of media decisions beyond the audience information reported in the research sources.

For many years, advertisers have attempted to measure the return on investment (ROI) that they get from their advertising dollars. This seemingly intuitive measure is complicated by the lack of clear definitions. Does it mean sales? Profit? Brand awareness? Trial? How is the return on the advertising investment differentiated from that of the entire marketing plan? The "investment" part of the metric is also ambiguous. Is it just the money spent in media? Or is it the money spent on promotions, coupons, packaging, sales incentives, and all the marketing expenses other than paid advertising?

Consequently, decision making has not advanced to the point where there is always substantive proof that one medium is much better than another. Often a media planner has biased preferences in favor of one media class over others and will favor the medium regardless of what statistics or other objective evidence might indicate. In this writer's experience, specialty agencies, particularly those dealing exclusively with online planning and buying, tend to be advocates of online media—a frame of mind that differs from generalist media planners who recommend whatever medium best meets the needs of the advertiser.

Notwithstanding these problems, decision making is improving and will undoubtedly improve as long as the people in charge realize there are problems and attempt to improve the situation.

CHAPTER TWO

Sample Media Plan Presentation

A *media plan* is the blueprint for how the advertising message will be delivered to the target audience. It is also a persuasive document that communicates the rationale behind a recommendation to spend significant amounts of money. To provide a broad overview of the media planning process and the topics of this book, this chapter presents a hypothetical plan along with explanations about why particular actions were taken.

Typically presented by the planner at a meeting with the advertiser, a media plan summarizes weeks or months of behind-the-scenes work—evaluating alternatives, meeting with media representatives, and developing the understanding of the consumer and marketplace that is necessary to produce the most effective media plan.

As a blueprint for action, a media plan must be organized so each set of actions flows smoothly in the readers' minds. Media plans have two main audiences: the clients (including the account executives) and the media buyers. Most likely the clients will be the first persons outside the agency to see the plan. They will probably pay most attention to determining whether the recommended media plan can do what it is supposed to do in solving the original marketing problem. The plan should also enable the buyers—who eventually have to implement the strategies—to proceed quickly and accurately. The media plan can help all this by being well organized, well written, and simply presented.

Although there is extensive backup documentation in a "leave-behind," the presentation itself is relatively straightforward, and not especially long—often only 10 to 15 minutes. It talks in human terms about the people the advertiser is trying to reach. The following pages show a typical (but hypothetical) media plan as it might be presented to a brand's marketing director. It is a simple, "plain vanilla" plan, yet it illustrates concepts that will be discussed in greater detail in the following chapters.

At the barest minimum, a media plan should include (possibly, but not necessarily, in this order) the following elements:

- Media objectives—what tasks the media is expected to carry out
- Competitive analysis—spending levels, media used, timing
- Target audience analysis and recommendation
- Media habits of the target audience
- Recommended media selection rationale—reasons for selecting the various media elements and vehicles
- Media strategy—how the media plan will accomplish the stated objectives
- Flowchart, budget, and expected reach and frequency

Depending on the particular situation, the media plan may also contain the following elements:

- Magazine selection rationale—cost, coverage, composition, and cost per thousand (CPM) of publications that were recommended and those considered but not recommended
- Spot market list and media dollar allocation rationale
- Product seasonality
- Detailed broadcast cost estimates
- Other media considered but not recommended
- Alternative print and broadcast plans considered but not recommended
- Detailed newspaper list
- Alternative plans at varying budget levels above and below established level
- Decision dates/cancellation flexibility
- Responses to earlier client questions
- Anything else the planner thinks may become a question or an issue during the presentation based on earlier discussions with the client and account group (either incorporated into the presentation or held in reserve in case the question comes up)

Background to Hypothetical Plan

Let's say that the fictitious RBB Sporting Goods Company has been a leading producer of sporting products for more than 20 years. In anticipation of baby boomer retirements, the company plans to expand into products for golfers, beginning with Power Flight golf clubs. These newly engineered clubs promise to improve the average golfer's game. The Power Flight's core is made of titanium dioxide, making it more flexible than other clubs. It is also lighter and stronger than other models. The product will be in full national distribution in time for golf season.

RBB will be hiring a new advertising agency to handle the Power Flight golf club introduction. They have told the agency to assume a total advertising budget of $11 million, of which $10 million is for working media, and they have asked for a recommended media plan. The account group says the creative department is working on 30-second television commercials and page-four/color (P4/C) magazine ads. The online creative team is developing banners to drive golfers to the company's website.

Media Objectives

Media plans typically begin with a statement of the *media objectives*—that is, what goals the media are expected to accomplish. In this case, the first and most important objective is to create awareness of the new golf clubs and sustain that awareness throughout the golf season.

Because the product will be sold nationally, there must be advertising everywhere in the country. If the client had said they needed additional weight in certain cities, that goal would be included as an additional objective. Similarly, if RBB had made plans for a professional golfer to demonstrate the product at a local country club, a media objective would be to announce this event with local media. If the clubs were going to be introduced at a trade show, there might be a need for advertising in the show's catalog. In short, the media objectives reflect the advertiser's marketing objectives.

Media objectives specifically identify the marketing target and how many times those people should see the advertising message during the introductory and sustaining periods. This reflects a balance between how many people will see the ads and how many times they will see it (i.e., a few people many times or many people a few times.) The need to balance trade-offs is a key recurring theme in media planning.

Finally, the client has indicated there is a strong technical story that explains how the Power Flight clubs improve golfers' accuracy. In addition to creating awareness, the media plan must effectively communicate this relatively complex message. The media objectives for the introduction of the Power Flight golf club are shown in Exhibit 2–1.

EXHIBIT 2-1

Media Objectives

- Within the $10 million budget, create national awareness of RBB Power Flight golf clubs prior to the start of the golf season.
- Following introduction, provide sustaining support through the remainder of the warm-weather months.
- Target advertising to regular golfers who play at least one a month.
- During the introductory period, reach 80 percent of target golfers an average of five times and 50 percent three or more times.
- Following the introduction, sustain awareness by reaching 30 percent of golfers at least once a month.
- Use media that can create awareness and effectively communicate the technical advantages of the Power Flight clubs.

Competitive Analysis

Knowledge of the competitive environment is critical to any media plan. The competitive analysis includes budgets, media selection, and timing of media delivery.

Budgets

First, knowing the planner has $10 million to work with is meaningful only when compared to the spending levels of RBB's competitors. Exhibit 2-2 shows how much money was spent by the leading brands and the whole golf club category in the previous year, 2008. It indicates that the budget should be adequate to do the job, but RBB will still trail two of the TaylorMade brands that together will have almost $24 million in TaylorMade exposure. The introductory $10 million will have to work hard to overcome this competitive noise

Media Selection

How much the competitors spent is only part of the story. The planner also needs to know which media the competitors used. Exhibit 2-3 indicates that the majority of the dollars were in network television and magazines. Backup charts show spending by medium for each advertiser. They show which television programs were used (mostly weekend golf tournaments) and which cable networks (mostly

EXHIBIT 2-2

Competitive Environment

Leading Golf Club Competitors

BRAND DETAIL	JAN. 2008–DEC. 2008 $ (000.00)
TaylorMade Golf Clubs Driver	$12,409.60
TaylorMade Tour Burner Golf Clubs Driver	11,400.50
Ping G10 Golf Clubs Iron	5,394.50
Titleist AP1 Golf Clubs Iron	4,892.50
Nike IC Golf Clubs Putter	4,639.80
Nike SQ Golf Clubs XLS/Driver	4,542.20
Cleveland Hibore Golf Clubs XLS/Driver	4,459.60
All Others (160 brands)	105,529.60
Total Golf Clubs	$153,268.30

Source: The Nielsen Company, Monitor-Plus. Used with permission.

EXHIBIT 2-3

Leading Competitors' Media Use

Golf club competitors concentrate spending in national consumer magazines and network television.

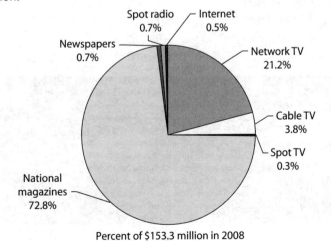

Percent of $153.3 million in 2008

Source: The Nielsen Company, Monitor-Plus. Used with permission.

ESPN). Backup charts also show which magazines were used and other details about competitors' plans.

Exhibit 2-4 shows how TaylorMade used display banners on the Internet to promote their clubs.

Exhibit 2-5 shows the websites where Callaway Golf Company bought links adjacent to the results of selected search terms. *Sponsored search* has become an important advertising medium because the ads appear only to people who have demonstrated an interest in the product.

EXHIBIT 2-4

TaylorMade Use of Online Display Advertising

SITE/SUBSITE	IMPRESSIONS	ESTIMATED SPENDING ($)
ESPN.com (General)	16,743,000	$138,700
Golf.com (All)	13,943,000	144,800
CBSSports.com (General)	13,858,000	101,600
PGA Tour (All)	1,866,000	15,900
CBSSports.com MLB	1,225,000	8,100
PGA (All)	593,000	2,300
ThatsRacin.com (All)	439,000	3,400
ESPN.com NFL	321,000	2,500
ESPN.com Baseball	317,000	2,100
NHL.com Network (All)	187,000	1,300
TheGolfChannel.com (All)	106,000	700
Total	49,598,000	$421,400

Source: The Nielsen Company, Nielsen Online AdRelevance. Used with permission.

EXHIBIT 2-5

Callaway Golf Company's Use of Online Sponsored Search Impressions

Impressions by company for Callaway Golf Company in consumer goods sports and exercise equipment industry during most recent month for sponsored search link ads.

COMPANY	IMPRESSIONS	SITE/SUBSITE	IMPRESSIONS
Callaway Golf Company	2,837,000	PGA (All)	1,739,000
Total	2,837,000	CNN (General)	411,000
		Yahoo! Search	242,000
		Google (General)	136,000
		About.com Sports	48,000
		AOL.com Search	30,000
		Shopzilla (All)	29,000
		MapQuest.com	24,000
		Epinions (All)	21,000
		BizRate.com (All)	19,000
		ConsumerREVIEW Network	18,000
		BNET (All)	18,000
		CNET Download.com	14,000
		All Other Sites	88,000
		Total	2,837,000

Source: The Nielsen Company, Nielsen Online AdRelevance. Used with permission.

Timing of Media Delivery

Timing of media delivery is critical, as well. In the case of golf, competitive advertising naturally follows the seasons, as shown in Exhibit 2-6. Note the peak in spending between March and June, as the weather turns warm and golfers start to think about the clubs they will use when the golf courses open for business. But also note that money is spent throughout the year, even in winter. This reflects the need to maintain awareness among golfers on warm-weather vacations. The continuation of advertising through December suggests advertising to support the purchase of golf clubs as a gift for the holidays.

Leading Competitors' Timing of Delivery

Golf club advertising is concentrated in the spring in preparation for the summer golf season.

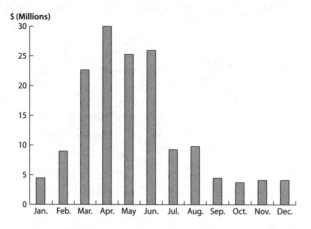

Source: The Nielsen Company, Monitor-Plus. Used with permission.

Target Audience Analysis

Another part of every media plan is an analysis of the target audience. RBB has said they believe their best prospects are "frequent golfers—those who play more than 12 rounds of golf a year." This reflects the advertiser's market research, but their studies typically provide little useful information about the consumer's *media* habits. For this purpose, ad agencies purchase syndicated research (one study that is sold to many different buyers, as distinguished from custom research tailored to a single company). This research provides information on product usage, demographics, and media behavior.

For example, Mediamark Research & Intelligence, LLC (MRI, www.mediamark .com), asks respondents about their personal participation in golf and more than 50 other sports, ranging from aerobics to whitewater rafting. Respondents are asked how often they engage in each activity: "two or more times a week, once a week, two to three times a month, once a month, less than once a month, or never." The planner makes the judgment that "once a month or more" is comparable to the client's "frequent" golfer. This definition yields a group that accounts for 5.08 percent of all adults—a small enough target to be selective, but large enough to be statistically valid. (See Exhibit 2-7.)

EXHIBIT 2-7

The Target Audience

11.4 million (5.08 percent) adults are regular golfers (play 1+ times/month). 79.8 percent of them are men. They tend to be 55–74 years old and college graduates, work in professional/managerial jobs, and earn more than $100,000/year.

	U.S. POPULATION		REGULAR GOLFERS (PLAY 1+ TIMES/MONTH)		
	(000)	(%)	(000)	(%)	INDEX
Total adults age 18+	224,899	100.00%	11,423 (5.08%)	100.00%	100
Men	108,644	48.30%	9,116	79.80%	165
Women	116,235	51.70	2,307	20.20	39
	224,900	100.00%	11,423	100.00%	100
Ages 18–34	68,760	30.60%	3,063	26.80%	88
Ages 35–54	86,599	38.50	4,184	36.60	95
Ages 55–64	32,911	14.60	2,064	18.10	123
Ages 65–74	19,414	8.60	1,375	12.00	139
Ages 75+	17,216	7.70	735	6.40	84
	244,900	100.00%	11,423	100.00%	100
College graduates+	59,704	26.50%	5,129	44.90%	169
Professional/ managers/ administrators	52,326	23.30%	3,836	33.60%	144
Employee income $100,000+	12,108	5.40%	1,839	16.10%	299

Source: Mediamark Research & Intelligence, LLC, Spring 2009. Used with permission.

Media Habits

In addition to demographics, MRI tells planners which television programs are watched by regular golfers. Although MRI data are not as timely or as detailed as the Nielsen ratings, they offer insights into the kind of programs that this group enjoys.

Exhibit 2-8 illustrates the concept of media selectivity. *Comp,* or *composition,* represents the percent of adults or program viewers who are regular golfers. As noted before, 5.08 percent of all adults are regular golfers. If the viewers of "The Tour Championship" were the same as all adults, we would expect 5.08 percent of them to be regular golfers. But the MRI research shows that 47.8 percent of them fall in this group. So, 47.8/5.08 = 9.42 × 100 = 942. By convention, the planner would say that the program's viewers are 842 percent (or 8.4 times) more likely to be regular golfers than the average adult. We subtract 100 from the calculated 942 to account for people who are as likely to be regular golfers.

EXHIBIT 2-8

Target Audience's Media Habits: Watching Golf on TV

	ADULTS	REGULAR GOLFERS (PLAY 1+/MONTH)		
	(000)	(000)	COMP	INDEX
Total Adults	224,889	11,423	5.08	100
The Tour Championships	4,927	2,357	47.8	942
Wachovia Championship	4,667	2,123	45.5	896
World Golf Championships—Accenture	4,839	2,148	44.4	874
Deutsche Bank Championship	4,143	1,803	43.5	857
World Golf Championships—Bridgestone	5,117	2,219	43.4	854
Memorial Tournament—Morgan Stanley	3,803	1,645	43.3	852
World Golf Championships—Mission Hills	4,217	1,799	42.7	840
Honda Classic	4,982	2,108	42.3	833
Senior PGA Championships	4,812	2,018	41.9	826
The Players Championships	9,199	3,844	41.8	823
BMW Championships	3,836	1,595	41.6	819
EDS Byron Nelson Championships	4,008	1,642	41.0	807
Senior British Open	4,410	1,786	40.5	797
LPGA Tour Championship	4,680	1,890	40.4	795
AT&T Pebble Beach National Pro-Am	8,922	3,559	39.9	785

Source: Mediamark Research & Intelligence, LLC, Spring 2009. Used with permission.

The media behavior analysis continues in Exhibit 2-9 by showing regular golfers' selectivity to other sports programs on TV. These analyses show which programs have concentrations of the target audience (regular golfers) and guide the planner in selecting the best media to reach them.

EXHIBIT 2-9

Target Audience's Media Habits: Other Sports on TV

	ADULTS	REGULAR GOLFERS (PLAY 1+/MONTH)		
	(000)	(000)	COMP	INDEX
Total regular golfers	224,889	11,423	5.08	100
Basketball—college games	55,407	6,170	11.1	219
Football—college games	73,448	7,739	10.5	207
Baseball	68,440	6,954	10.2	200
Tennis	34,024	3,417	10.0	198
Basketball—professional games	57,377	5,548	9.7	190
Football—Monday night professional	85,732	8,257	9.6	190
Bowling	23,679	2,255	9.5	187
Football—weekend professional	90,382	8,431	9.3	184
Soccer	31,438	2,701	8.6	169

Source: Mediamark Research & Intelligence, LLC, Spring 2009. Used with permission.

The same research can show us which websites are most visited by regular golfers. Clearly they are attracted to sporting sites, but they are also attracted to financial services. Exhibit 2-10 shows the top websites for golfers.

The same concept applies to golfers' readership of consumer magazines. Readers of *Golf Digest* are seven times more likely to be regular golfers than the average adult; readers of *Men's Fitness* are 77 percent more likely to be regular golfers.

Although composition is important, planners must also consider *coverage*—the percent of the target that reads a magazine, watches a TV show, or uses other media. *Golf Digest,* for example, is read by 2,295,000 regular golfers. Expressing numbers in thousands, 2,295,000 readers/11,423,000 golfers = 20.1 percent. We say that *Golf Digest* "covers," or is read by, 20.1 percent of regular golfers. Composition shows the percent of the magazine's readers who are in the target. In this case, 40.9 percent of *Golf Digest* readers are regular golfers. (Total *Golf Digest* readers are not shown on this report.) *Sports Illustrated* covers virtually the same number of golfers, but its low 10.1 percent composition indicates there would be a great deal of waste if this magazine was selected. (Because 89.9 percent of its readers are not regular golfers, they would have little interest in ads for the new Power Flight clubs.) This need to find a balance between coverage and composition is a recurring theme in media planning and is even more relevant when we consider the Internet.

Top Websites Visited by Regular Golfers

Target: Golf Sports Personally Participated 1+ Times a Month
Population: 11,423,000

	AUDIENCE (000)	COMP.	COVERAGE	INDEX
Regular Golfers (1+/month)	11,423	5.08%	100%	100
USAToday.com Sports	307	15.5	2.6	293
The History Channel Websites	213	13.6	1.8	258
CBS College Sports Network	554	12.4	4.7	234
Motley Fool	384	11.6	3.3	220
PGA Tour	188	11.6	1.6	220
FT.com	201	11.5	1.7	217
USAToday.com Money	212	11.0	1.8	208
CBS Sports	995	10.9	8.4	206
Wall Street Journal Online	792	10.9	6.7	205
SI Digital Sales	677	10.7	5.7	202
FNFL.com	203	10.5	1.7	198
CNBC.com	283	10.4	2.4	196
Bloomberg.com	408	10.1	3.5	191
NFL Internet Network	442	10.1	3.7	190
ESPN	1,763	9.9	14.9	187
NASCAR Online	381	9.7	3.2	184
CNNMoney	803	9.7	6.8	183
NHL.com	315	9.7	2.7	183
CBSSports.com	439	9.6	3.7	182
NHL.com Network	326	9.5	2.8	180

Source: The Nielsen Company NetViews, MRI Media Fusion + Product (5-09/F08), 2009.
Used with permission.

Planners must also consider the cost-efficiency of the media they select. This is typically evaluated as *cost-per-thousand* target people exposed, or CPM. A page in *Golf Digest* costs $110,080 and is read by 2,295,000 regular golfers. To find the cost per thousand, divide the cost by the number of target readers: CPM = $110,080/2,295 = $47.97 per thousand golfers.

Exhibit 2-11 illustrates the trade-offs that media planners must make among coverage, composition, and media cost-efficiency.

EXHIBIT 2-11

Target Audience's Media Habits: Magazines

	AUDIENCE (000)	COMP	COVERAGE	INDEX	4C COST	4C CPM
Regular Golfers (1+/month)	11,423	5.08%	100%	100	—	—
Golf Digest	2,295	40.9	20.1	806	$110,080	$47.97
Golf Magazine	2,198	39.2	19.2	772	159,000	72.34
PGA Tour Partners	516	32.9	4.5	647	40,545	78.58
Forbes	645	11.7	5.7	230	114,509	177.53
BusinessWeek	489	10.4	4.3	205	112,000	229.04
Sports Illustrated	2,119	10.1	18.6	198	320,000	151.01
Kiplinger's Personal Finance	271	12.6	2.4	274	67,970	250.81
Fortune	456	11.6	4.0	228	159,600	350.00
Money	811	10.3	7.1	203	192,200	236.99
Men's Fitness	680	9.0	6.0	117	84,640	124.47
Popular Mechanics	772	8.8	6.8	173	125,770	162.91
U.S. News & World Report	779	8.0	6.8	158	154,448	198.26
Newsweek	1,241	7.0	10.9	138	215,800	173.89

Source: Mediamark Research & Intelligence, LLC, Spring 2009. Used with permission.

Media Selection Rationale

Planners are theoretically free to choose any mass medium (television, radio, magazines, newspapers, outdoor, Internet), but in practice the choice reflects a general understanding of the category by the advertiser, the agency's account team, and media management. Because the decision in this example has been made to start the creatives working on 30-second television commercials and full-page four-color magazine ads, the plan is expected to reflect these media. To a large extent, the rationale for selecting the primary media is obvious and reflects the media/marketing objectives and the competitive practices of the category.

Although the broad media to be used may be predetermined (in this case, TV and consumer magazines), the planner needs to show the rationale for selecting different vehicles and components. For television, this includes program types, dayparts, cost-efficiencies, the reach and frequency of alternative weight levels, and the scheduling options considered. In the stand-up presentation, the media planner will provide this rationale by referring to the preceding charts on media habits as well as more detailed analyses.

For magazines, the plan needs to show publications that were considered and those that were and were not recommended. This latter information can be useful to advertiser and agency management if they need to explain to sales representatives why a given magazine did not get the order. Again, this information is provided by the chart that shows the target's readership and cost-efficiencies of the candidate and selected magazines. (Note that an actual plan would show many more publications than this sample.)

Creative Media Options

In the Power Flight example, television and print are the meat-and-potatoes media that—in an academic setting—would earn a grade of C. But advertisers expect something more: a creative fillip that will separate them from their competitors. This is an opportunity for planners to show their initiative and imagination. They might recommend an unusual use of conventional media, such as, in this case, a multipage insert in golf magazines to give a detailed explanation of the new club's technical advantages. Or because one of the objectives of the Power Flight media plan is to create awareness, planners might recommend placing introductory ads on the hood of golf carts or in the hitting area of practice facilities. See www.pinpointgolf.com for a broad range of media directed to golfers. A full listing can be found in the Out-of-Home Advertising Source from SRDS (formerly known as Standard Rate & Data Service). Interestingly, these golf course advertising venues have virtually no ads for golf products; instead, they carry primarily financial services, business consultants, international airlines, and other advertisers who want to reach an upscale target.

While not in the final plan, the planning group also considered running the commercial as preroll video on Hulu, NBC.com, and the many Internet sites that offer streaming video of popular programs or clips.

Creative media are generally less expensive than mainstream media, and they add interest and excitement to the plan. Also, they mark the planner as a person who gives more than just what is expected.

Media Strategy

The plan now draws on the background material presented to lay out the proposed strategies that will accomplish the stated media objectives, as shown in Exhibit 2-12. Television will be the primary medium to create awareness. A media objective is to direct advertising to regular golfers, but the Nielsen program ratings that are needed by time-buyers count audiences only in terms of age and gender. From the targeting

---

EXHIBIT 2-12

Media Strategy

- Use television as the primary medium to create awareness.
  —Target men 35 to 64 years of age.
- Use network and cable television golf and weekend sports programs to achieve broad national reach of target regular golfers.
- Concentrate introductory weight in February and March to lead the golf season.
  —Purchase TV golf tournament sponsorships to achieve high frequency during the introduction.
- Provide sustaining support in cable and network weekend sports programs throughout the warm-weather golf season.
- Use golf-oriented consumer magazines and selective newsweeklies to communicate the technical advantages of Power Flight golf clubs and to maintain awareness during the holiday season.
- Use RBB's website to provide additional technical details about the Power Flight clubs. Highlight the website's Internet address in print and TV.

---

analysis, it is clear that the most selective target is men age 35 to 64 years of age. The strategy identifies the recommended dayparts and program types that will be selected. It indicates the general timing of the introductory and sustaining weight, but specifics will be presented later in the flowchart. Finally, the strategy identifies consumer magazines and RBB's website on the Internet as the recommended media to deliver the technical information about the Power Flight golf clubs.

Flowchart and Budget

The last key element of a media plan is the flowchart. This single document, shown in Exhibit 2-13, summarizes the action elements of the media plan. It shows what media will be used, how the ads will be scheduled, how much weight will be given to each, the reach and frequency of the plan, ad sizes, and the cost of each element that adds to the total budget. Each of these is an *estimated* cost that will not become final until the negotiations are complete. Buyers are expected to purchase each medium for the stated cost, plus or minus 10 percent, but the bottom line total can never exceed the $10 million budget authorized by the advertiser.

EXHIBIT 2-13

Media Plan Flowchart

RBB Sporting Goods
Power Flight Golf Clubs
Introductory Media Plan

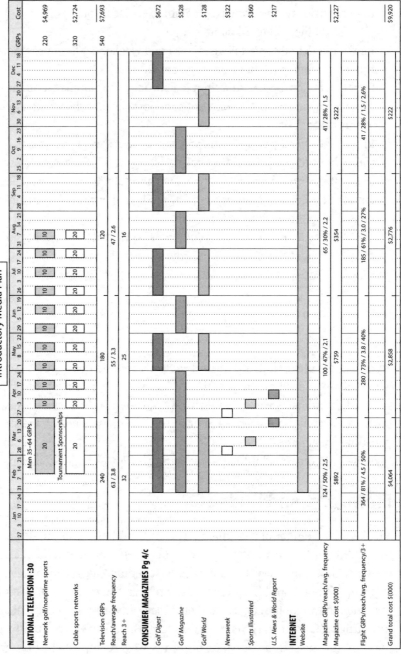

Post-Buy Evaluation

At some time after the advertising has run, the planner and buyer prepare a post-buy evaluation that reports the number of television rating points that were actually delivered according to the Nielsen ratings, and the final price that was paid. These numbers are then compared to the originally planned goals. The post-buy evaluation is generally prepared as a top-line report, but may include detail down to the individual telecast level if the actual buy greatly over- or underdelivers the planned goal, in which case an explanation from the buyer is required.

For magazines, the post-buy report shows on what page each ad appeared (to ensure that the advertiser got a fair rotation when there was more than one insertion in a given magazine), presence of any neighboring competitive advertising, right-hand or left-hand page, adjacency to compatible editorial material, and other characteristics that the advertiser and agency consider important. In addition to advising the client, this report is used as background for future negotiations with the publications.

Note that the media post-buy evaluation is a numerical analysis of the way the media buy was executed versus what was planned. It typically does not deal with the larger issues, such as whether awareness was actually created or the campaign was successful. These relate to the effectiveness of the whole advertising program, which is the shared responsibility of the creative agency, the media planning and buying group, the advertiser, and everyone else associated with the business.

CHAPTER THREE

The Relationship Among Media, Advertising, and Consumers

T his chapter addresses the relationship among media, advertising, and consumers. This relationship affects the manner in which consumers perceive media as well as advertising. It also affects the manner in which media is measured, planned, and delivered. This chapter sets the stage for Chapter 4, "Basic Measurements and Calculations."

How Consumers Choose Media: Entertainment and Information

Most advertising is delivered to consumers by mass media such as newspapers, television, magazines, or radio. Audiences are not, however, waiting for mass media to come to their doors. They have many other activities that compete for their time and interest, such as business, family, church, and leisure.

Audiences become interested in certain subjects because a need or want is developed. They choose the television programs they watch and the magazines they read because they expect to see certain subjects that satisfy their interests quickly. For their favorite TV shows, they will set their digital video recorder (DVR) to record or will watch at their leisure from their cable system's video on demand (VOD) or online from Hulu or another video service. Sometimes they are willing to waste a bit of time watching television programs of little interest while waiting for their favorite programs to come on or leafing through a newspaper or magazine casually as they wait to go on to some other activity, but they probably pay less attention to these intervening media than they do to their favorites.

What audiences usually want from media is either entertainment or information. To what extent does any media vehicle provide what audiences want? The degree of intensity among audiences in evaluating media content depends on several variables, including those discussed in this section. This difference in intensity will most likely affect the degree of attention paid to the medium itself or to advertising placed therein.

Strong Feelings

Many audience members have strong or weak feelings about a medium. They express some of the feelings using adjectives that describe what they like, such as being a leader, authoritative, provocative, warm, cold, strong, or weak. Some media are difficult to describe, suggesting that the relationship between audience members and the media is confusing, negative, or indifferent. When media images are measured, feelings often show up for some media. Media that take political stands are usually perceived to have clear images. An image represents feelings, attitudes, opinions, and facts about a medium.

Loyalty

Audiences often like some media so much that they develop loyalties that go beyond economic constraint. An April 2009 study by the Pew Research Center found that 52 percent of the people questioned rated a television set as a necessity, slightly ahead of a home computer (50 percent) and a cell phone (49 percent).[1]

Loyalty to certain media, however, does not necessarily mean that the loyal audience will perceive media advertisements similarly or buy more of the advertised products. Other factors affect buying, including the need to have more information about a brand. If the audience already has a great deal of brand knowledge, the audience might respond to the advertising. Generally, when changes have been made in the brand or there have been changes in the content or creative style of advertising, then the message will influence buying behavior to some extent.

Media Usage and Subsequent Behavior

Advertisers who buy space in a magazine generally assume they are reaching all readers of that particular periodical, but some subscribers do not read each issue

---

1. Pew Research Center's Social & Demographic Trends survey, April 2–8, 2009.

immediately and many have back issues at home they have not even opened. The Audience Accumulation study by Mediamark Research & Intelligence, LLC, (MRI) found that as many as 10 percent of a magazine's audience can occur six months after the issue date.[2] If asked why they have not read magazines they are paying for, they might respond that they do intend to read them when they have some free time. The potential for reaching these people exists, but it takes a long time for some magazines to achieve their ultimate potential audience.

There is a widespread assumption that television sells better than print media because television is intrusive and its audiences tend to react to the medium more regularly than they read magazines. Television programs featuring famous persons or interesting national events do draw huge audiences. Yet audience response varies greatly to ads carried in these programs. Some advertisers seem to sell their products well; others don't.

For example, in 2000, at the height of the new technology bubble, the Super Bowl featured 19 dot-com advertisers—accounting for almost one-third of all the commercials in the game. A year later the majority of these companies were bankrupt due to poorly thought-out business plans and the general decline of the technology sector. Only four online companies placed ads in Super Bowl 2001. By 2010, Super Bowl XLIV had 9 dot-com advertisers out of the total 75 commercials.[3] All of this suggests that there is more to a successful advertising campaign than selecting media vehicles that deliver large audiences.

It is difficult, however, to assess the effectiveness of one media vehicle's ability to sell the advertised products on the basis of the size of its audience or the number of advertisements it carries. Large audiences do not automatically buy more than smaller audiences. In the end, the quality of an ad's creative message and how memorable it is has more influence on the ad's ability to sell products than any inherent qualities of the medium that delivers it.

Consumers simply do not pay attention to commercials if they do not need the brand or product and they already know a lot about the brand. They have developed the ability to see and hear a message and then forget it. Perhaps this is caused by an overload of communication, known as *semantic satiation*. Furthermore, sometimes audiences pay attention to commercials or print ads but don't respond immediately.

---

2. Julian Baim, Martin R. Frankel, and Joseph Agresti, "Magazine Audience Accumulation: Development of a Measurement System and Initial Results," Worldwide Readership Research Symposium, Florence, 1999.
3. The Nielsen Company, Monitor-Plus.

Interactive Television

Interactive television has been talked about for many years and is a reality today on cable television or online streaming video. In the context of media planning, it is an advertising message in conventional television that allows the viewer, with the click of a button on the remote, to order a product, request additional information, or initiate other communication with the advertiser. The leading supplier of this service is TiVo, the first and now the largest branded user interface with DVR. Cable services like Comcast have their own generic interface, but TiVo is the most widely known branded service.

Interactive advertising appears in the form of a small graphic, or tag, that appears on the screen during commercials in specially prepared programming or during long-form infomercials for such products as automobiles, vacation destinations, financial services, and so on. By clicking on the tag, viewers notify the advertiser of their interest in the product. Because their name, address, and other contact information are registered with the cable company or TiVo, the information or further entertainment is automatically forwarded.

In February, 2010, Canoe Ventures (www.canoe-ventures.com) introduced its Request-For-Information (RFI) interactive platform that allows cable network viewers to interact with commercials using their remote control. For an additional charge, advertisers can add a banner on the bottom of the screen where viewers can respond to opinion polls; request additional information; receive coupons, discounts, or promotional giveaways; or provide other feedback to the advertiser.

Exhibit 3-1 shows how one local cable system uses interactive TV to promote a series on one of its channels.

Varied Relationships Between Audiences and Media

Relationships between audiences and media run the gamut from casual to intense. When sports teams are playing, the reason for watching any game depends on the team's chance of making the play-offs. If the team has a good chance, the audience will return each week with a sense of loyalty and anticipation for the game. Die-hard Chicago Cubs fans notwithstanding, if a team has a losing record, then the number of viewers will most likely drop because the relationship with the event is not as strong.

Even if a vehicle has a large and interested audience, the numbers might not be the critical determination of its effect. Relationships today are not strong, especially among certain demographically defined audiences. For example, teenagers seem uninterested in reading newspapers, and all the techniques that have been used to attract them still have not changed the very loose relationship between the two.

EXHIBIT 3-1

Charter Communications Uses Its Interactive
Capability to Promote a TV Series

Charter Communications in Los Angeles has been a pioneer in the field of interactive television, offering the service to its 300,000 digital subscribers since 2002. In the fall of 2008, they created an interactive microsite containing video and other materials that would enhance the viewing experience of History Channel's "Cities of the Underworld" series. One industry observer commented, "It's the ability to have interactivity with a series . . . the different information on the different pages of the microsite give you a different perspective on the show . . . it's all about giving the consumer that 360-degree experience, being a part of it, instead of just being a voyeur."[*]

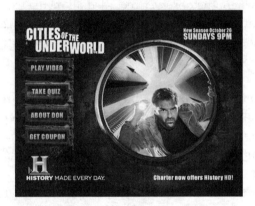

Source: Charter Communications. Used with permission.

Advertisers using interactive television must be aware of technical and business model differences among the various cable companies, be sensitive to privacy concerns, ensure that interactive responses come from responsible adults, control the geographical distribution of the requests, and ensure that the interactive content does not interfere with the television program.

[*] Mark Garner, VP for Distribution, Marketing, and Business Development at A&E Television. Quoted on http://www.cable360.net/blog/?p=56.

Mass media today tend to be rejected by some media planners in favor of more specialized media with smaller, more selective audiences. Data from single-source research often indicate that small market segments account for a large proportion of sales. This is the Long Tail phenomenon referred to earlier. The relationship between audiences and media, however, is more important: If the relationship is casual, then advertising may not be as effective. If the relationship is close, then smaller audiences will account for a large proportion of sales, although this requires purchasing advertising on a large number of vehicles. With the fragmentation of the television audience across more than 80 measured cable networks, advertisers with broad targets typically buy time on more than 20 cable channels in addition to buying the major broadcast nets.

Video Consumer Mapping Study

In 2009, the Nielsen-funded Council for Research Excellence published the largest study to date that was specifically designed to provide a broad understanding of video media. The Video Consumer Mapping study[4] is based on a 24-hour period of direct observation (in the person's home, at work, in the car, etc.) using a specially designed portable computer where the observer recorded all media exposure in 10-second increments. The study was built on pioneering methodological research by Ball State University's Center for Media Design, called the Middletown Media Studies.[5]

There were 10 key findings:

1. Although the composition of consumers' screen media time varied across age groups, their total screen time was strikingly similar, except among those 45–54, whose screen time was highest.
2. The degree of concurrent screen media exposure (multitasking) was equivalent for all age groups under 55.
3. The study confirmed that more than 99 percent of Nielsen's three-screen time is TV. Even among those 18–24, TV represented more than 98 percent.
4. Live TV leads all video time by a large margin, followed by DVD, with DVRs third.
5. The study suggests that computing has displaced radio as the number-two media activity. Radio is now number three, and print is number four.
6. New HDTV ownership (first and second set) led to higher TV exposure, though some of this increase appeared to be temporary.
7. Early DVR owners spent much more time with DVR playback than new DVR owners.
8. A higher percentage of TV time was spent as sole medium compared to computers, print, or audio. DVR playback time was even more likely than live TV to be a sole medium.
9. TV users were exposed to, on average, roughly an hour a day of live TV ads and promos.

---

4. www.researchexcellence.com/vcmstudy.php.
5. www.bsu.edu/middletown.

10. Serious caution needs to be applied in interpreting self-reported data for media use. TV was substantially underreported, while online video and mobile video usage was overreported.

How Consumers Perceive Digital Advertising

The Internet has greatly expanded the ability to sell products by providing virtually unlimited information to the prospective buyer. It has blurred the line between advertising as pure salesmanship and advertising as a provider of product information. This is especially true for high-cost, considered purchases such as automobiles, travel services, computer systems, and financial services, where a vast amount of information is needed to make a reasoned decision. Even advertising for food products can include detailed recipes and nutritional values. The Internet can then go beyond salesmanship to take the order, collect payment, and arrange shipping. According to MRI, by spring 2009, 85.9 percent of adults had access to the Internet, 72.6 percent went online every week, and 35.3 percent had bought something online in the last 30 days for personal or business use.[6] Also, according to MRI, 63.5 percent of U.S. homes access the Internet via a high-speed broadband connection, a penetration that is likely to grow to near total coverage over the life of this book. Given this broad penetration, a number of retailers, including the Best Buy consumer electronics chain, consider the Internet their largest store.[7]

For this reason, the Internet must be seriously considered for every media plan. Despite this, the Internet has yet to challenge traditional media as the primary advertising venue. In 2008, digital advertising accounted for only 6 percent of total measured media spending. Television continues to dominate, capturing 62.2 percent of media dollars with national consumer magazines second at 13.5 percent.[8]

How Audiences Process Information from Media

Much of the information received from media is stored in people's short-term memory. Such information, like the last few words of a sentence just heard or read, or a telephone number found in an online search, can be recalled for only a short time. Advertisers have observed that audiences who want to remember some part of an advertising message can do so by spending time and effort in rehearsing

---

6. Mediamark Research & Intelligence, LLC (MRI), Spring 2009 survey.
7. www.gomez.com/download/cs_best_buy.pdf.
8. The Nielsen Company, Monitor-Plus, 2008.

the message. They can repeat it mentally until it is learned. Then the message is remembered longer, because it has been transferred to long-term memory.

The point is that media often do not do any more than deliver advertising to consumers. Media planners are sometimes called on to help consumers remember a message by buying media vehicles repeatedly within a given period. If audiences are not interested, they will not pay attention and the repetitions will be wasted. Audiences can be very selective in what they hear or see.

Can a media planner do any more to deliver advertising messages? There is a widespread disagreement among media professionals about this question. Some say much can be done by strategic media planning. By careful media selection and timing, by placing ads in markets where sales opportunities are best, by repeating the advertising, and by other strategic activities, a planner can help the advertisers achieve their goals. Others say that a media planner's job is done when the message is delivered to the right targets, at the right time, and in sufficient quantities.

It is clear that media work with the creative message and the appeal of a product to get the message through to consumers. When the audience wants or needs a product for any reason, they tend to pay attention to an ad for that product. They may not notice an ad the first time it is broadcast or printed, but their attention will presumably alert them to find that ad inevitably. Audiences are not waiting for an ad to appear; however, creative effort can take ordinary ideas and dramatize them to such an extent that the audience will pay attention to the ad for a short time at least.

Audiences accept commercials as a necessary evil they must put up with to view free program content. However, the growth of DVRs and their ability to fast-forward through commercials shows that people will gladly avoid commercials if given the tool. Although estimates vary, there is agreement that more than 70 percent of the people watching a program via DVR playback skip through the commercials. On the national television venues of network broadcast, cable, and syndication (not local spot TV), this is accounted for in the C3 ratings that show the number of people watching a TV program and its commercials at normal speed live or within three days of telecast. Because of this metric, advertisers get what they are paying for and have avoided the dire consequences that were predicted when the DVR first came out. There will be more about this in Chapter 4.

Yet great creative efforts do not necessarily translate into positive results in the marketplace. For example, in the late 1990s, widely viewed advertising for the Taco Bell restaurant chain featured a talking Chihuahua whose signature *"¡Yo Quiero!"* became a national icon. The campaign was dropped in 2001 after marketers realized that it was not effectively driving customers into the restaurants. It was a popular and creative success, but a marketing failure. This runs counter to the general belief that any product can be sold by clever advertising.

The Media's Importance in the Buying Process

It is assumed that the power of media advertising to influence sales depends on where in the purchasing process a consumer happens to be. The classic Engel/Kollat model of the buying process tells us that the order of purchasing is as follows:[9]

1. *Problem recognition*—For example, an auto needs new tires, or an individual wants a new suit of clothes.
2. *Search for alternatives* to solve a problem—For example, a consumer reads, hears, or sees advertising; talks to a friend about the problem; or goes shopping for a product or brand.
3. *Alternative evaluation* of different brands—For example, a consumer has found two or three brands that could solve a problem. The consumer is deciding which one to choose.
4. *Purchase made* through a choice of a brand—This is the buying action.
5. *Postpurchasing evaluation*—After buying, the consumer evaluates whether the product and brand meets his or her expectations for solving the problem.
6. *Feedback* about how satisfying the purchase was—Unsatisfactory purchases can be returned, or the consumer might keep the product and look for confirmation that he or she made a good buying decision. Frustration about the quality of the purchase can result in anger against the brand or the store where the purchase was made.

If consumers do not perceive that they have a problem, then presumably they will not react much to either media or advertising. On the other hand, when consumers do have a problem, they are receptive to both. Some problems are simple, such as finding that there is no ketchup in the house when hamburgers are being served. Others, such as buying a new home, are complex.

---

9. James F. Engel, Roger D. Blackwell, and Paul W. Miniard, *Consumer Behavior*, 8th edition (Hinsdale, IL: Dryden Press, 1997).

Media Planning and the Marketing Mix

It is important for anyone studying media planning to understand the relationship between media planning and the marketing mix. The *marketing mix* is a group of elements that a firm uses to sell a product. This mix was once called the "four Ps": product, place (or distribution), price, and promotion. It has been suggested that the four Ps are dead, but the marketing mix is as important as ever. It has always taken more elements than the four Ps to describe the marketing process. A fuller account is listed in Exhibit 3-2.[10] Marketing strategy is discussed more fully in Chapter 6, "Marketing Strategy and Media Planning."

Although media are not always considered to be a fundamental element of the marketing mix, they play a significant role in the selling process when advertising is required. The key to understanding the relationship between media and the marketing mix is that media do not work alone; they are part of a team of selling variables. Planners often get so involved with the complexity of their work that they forget this. In addition, media's role is important because it controls the efficient delivery of advertisements to those who will probably buy.

EXHIBIT 3-2

The Four Ps of Marketing

PRODUCT	PLACE	PRICE	PROMOTION
Quality	Distribution channels	List price	Advertising
Features	Coverage	Discounts	Copy and art
Options	Locations	Allowances	Media
Style	Inventory	Payment period	Personal selling
Brand name	Transportation	Credit terms	Sales promotion
Packaging			Public relations
			Direct marketing
			Integrated marketing
			Event marketing
			Local area marketing

10. Modified from Philip Kotler, *Marketing Management* (Englewood Cliffs, NJ: Prentice-Hall, 1984): 69.

Therefore, targeting prospects correctly is one way that the media/marketing team effort is fulfilled. Inefficient targeting means wasted effort and money. Media adds a qualitative value to an advertisement because of some quality in the medium. An example is *Good Housekeeping*'s "Seal of Approval," which is given after advertised products pass various quality tests in the company's laboratory, and which is intended to give the reader more confidence in their quality. Other qualitative values exist for specialized media that contribute to the medium's integral role in the advertising message.

Exposure: The Basic Measurement of Media Audiences

Industry leaders have chosen a measurement of media audiences—exposure—that is less than perfect, but that can differentiate media vehicles on the basis of their audience sizes. Audiences also can be measured and compared with competitive media at a reasonable cost. Exhibit 3-3 shows many other means of measuring media audiences.

EXHIBIT 3-3

Ways That Media Audiences Could Be Measured

MEDIA MEASUREMENT	WHAT IT MEASURES	WHAT IT MEANS
Vehicle exposure	Exposure to TV or print media (not ads)	Open eyes facing a vehicle (or opportunities to see ads)
Print media circulation	Numbers of copies distributed	People/families receiving newspaper vehicles (no exposure counted)
Advertising exposure	Number of ads exposed per issue or per TV program	A gross (or crude) counting of total number of ads exposed in a vehicle
Advertising perception	Number of ads that consumers remember having seen in a vehicle	The smallest amount of communication remembered of ads in a vehicle
Advertising communication	The total amount of recalled material from ads in a vehicle	Feedback from ad messages in vehicles
Response function: media effectiveness	The number of responses to specific advertising in a vehicle	The effects of advertising on consumers of responses such as sales, brand awareness, attitude change, and recall of messages

Technically, *exposure* means "open eyes (or listening ears) facing the medium." However, the research that measures (quantifies) exposure is different for each medium. So the meaning of an exposure is different. In magazines, for example, a person is counted as a reader if he or she says it was read or just looked into during the most recent publication period (month for monthlies, week for weeklies, etc.). Persons exposed to a television program are counted only if they press their own designated button on a measuring device known as a people meter. Of course, not every home has such a device, and even when the device is available and a person is watching a program, the failure to press the button will mean that a viewer is not counted. In midsize and smaller local markets, television viewing and radio listening are measured when people fill in a diary. In the larger markets, radio listening is recorded on the Portable People Meter (PPM) that counts stations within earshot of the radio's loudspeaker. On the Internet, exposure occurs when the user is served an ad banner, pop-up, or a page of content from a website.

People who are not acquainted with measurements of media audiences are always surprised when they are told that audience numbers obtained from the media research such as Experian Simmons, MRI, or The Nielsen Company are based on the average issue of a magazine or telecast of a TV program and not the number of people who are exposed to the individual advertisements in the vehicles. Even some experienced professionals forget or never knew that media exposure measurements do not show how many persons have read advertisements. Also, it cannot be assumed that a large audience for a media vehicle automatically means a large number of individuals saw a client's advertisement. The exception, as noted earlier, is the audience to the three national television venues, network, cable, and syndication, where the audience is reported as the number of people watching the average commercial minute, including all DVR playback at normal speed for up to three days after the initial telecast. Local television, including markets using the Local People Meter (LPM), continues to be measured in terms of the average quarter-hour audience.

Magazine audiences are reported in terms of the number of people who read the average issue, regardless of whether they saw the ads or not. In 2009, MRI offered a new service called AdMeasures that adjusts the average-issue audience by a factor that accounts for the number of people who read each specific issue, and then further adjusts that audience by the number of people who recall "noting" each ad. This yields the number of people exposed to each specific advertisement in a magazine. The AdMeasures service must be purchased as another product of the MRI research company.

Its availability illustrates the dilemma facing advertising and media agencies that must decide whether the substantial additional expense of this new research tool is justified by the additional precision it offers, and more important, whether that additional knowledge can be applied to future plans. The industry has gone from a situation in past years where the information simply didn't exist, to the present time when research companies are offering a growing list of innovative research products for sale, forcing the agencies to decide if they are worth the cost.

Need for Better Media Vehicle Measurements

Despite all the new data coming from the research companies, planners continue to need better tools to help them find the best medium or vehicle for their client's advertising messages. If it could be shown that one medium sells more of a brand than any other medium, and if the cost were not prohibitive, then that medium would be the one in which to place advertising.

Unfortunately, no measurement available today can provide precisely that kind of information. Some planners have conducted customized research to guide them in finding a medium that has the greatest sales potential. The problem with that kind of research is that it is difficult to parse out each individual medium's contribution to a sale because after all, media are not the only factors contributing to sales. Every element of the marketing mix contributes a little, and some contribute a great deal. For example, sometimes the factor that is most responsible for selling a product is a reduced price; media that carry news of the price reduction in an ad play a secondary role in the sale. Other media mix factors that contribute to a sale are distribution, positioning, personal selling, sales promotion, public relations, and packaging. And the most important elements in the selling of a brand generally are its product quality and uniqueness.

Many planners are dissatisfied with using exposure for media comparison purposes. They argue that media are not passive carriers of ads; rather, each medium has some power to affect an audience in some way, and this power should be measured.

The problem is that advertisers have been unable to separate the effect of the medium from the effect of the quality of the creative message. Research companies can measure the persuasive power of individual commercials and compare the results to the average (norms) of all the commercials that they have ever measured. But these tests are conducted after the commercials have been created. Some score high, some score low. In the end, developing persuasive advertising is far more an art than a science.

To be effective, a commercial must be seen—it must reach the target. But seeing an ad only once is not enough. To be effective, a commercial or magazine ad must be seen a number of times. Determining how many times a person needs to see an ad for it to elicit the desired response is one of the basic challenges of media planning.

Response Function

A *response function* quantifies the perceived ability of multiple exposures of an ad to elicit a response from the viewer. If we broadcast a commercial 20 times, some people will see it only once, others will see it 5 times, others 8 times, and a few might even see it all 20 times. The response function shows what percent of the people who are exposed to an ad varying numbers of times are expected to respond to that ad. For instance, we might say that only 10 percent of the people who see a commercial once will respond, but 50 percent of the people who see it eight or more times will respond. Exhibit 3-4 illustrates a sample response function. It reads, "10 percent of the people exposed to the ad once will respond; 25 percent of the people exposed twice to the ad will respond," and so on.

EXHIBIT 3-4

Sample Response Function

NUMBER OF EXPOSURES	PERCENT RESPONDING
1 time	10%
2	25
3	35
4	40
5	44
6	47
7	49
8+	50

Media research can tell the planner with great accuracy how many people are exposed to a campaign different numbers of times. But deciding what percent of those people will respond is a subtle judgment that depends on the product being sold, the ad's creative quality, the medium in which the ad appears, and a variety of other factors. We will go into this subject in more detail in Chapter 6. Exhibit 3-5 shows the hypothetical gauntlet that a marketing communication must run before it results in a sale.

EXHIBIT 3-5

How Consumers Could React to Media and Advertising

How can a planner think about the effect of a media plan in terms of the ultimate sales response? One answer is to estimate what happens after the ads appear in the media vehicles. The following is a hypothetical example of such an estimate:

		TARGET AUDIENCE
Number of targets in the United States		10,000,000
Percent of U.S. targets exposed to media vehicles	50%	5,000,000
Percent of those reached who saw any ad in vehicles (ad exposure)	25	1,250,000
Percent of targets who saw any ad and who read our ad(s)	25	312,500
Percent of those who read our ads and who bought our brand because of our ad(s)	10	31,250
Percent of those who bought our brand once and who bought it a second time (a rough measure of brand loyalty)	10	3,125

Measuring Audiences to Advertising Vehicles

Some media planners believe that vehicles are nothing more than passive carriers of ads to consumers. A simple measurement such as exposure, therefore, is considered adequate for comparing media vehicles. In other words, identifying the vehicle that delivers the largest number of the target audience is a good enough way to select media. But cost-efficiency is equally important. This requires that the media selected reach the largest number of prospects at the lowest cost. *Cost-efficiency* simply means that audience size must be related to media costs. Measuring this efficiency is done through cost per thousand, cost per rating point, or both.

Cost per Thousand
The statement, "Potatoes: $2.00" is meaningless until it is expressed as "Potatoes: $2.00/pound." To compare the cost-efficiency of different media options, the cost of an ad is expressed in terms of the cost-per-thousand targets exposed. Specifically, *cost per thousand (CPM)* is the cost to deliver 1,000 people or homes. It is calculated by dividing the cost by the audience delivered and multiplying the quotient by

1,000. The audience base can be circulation, homes reached, readers, or number of audience members of any kind of demographic or product usage classification.

CPM is a comparative device. It enables planners to compare one medium or media vehicle with another to find those that are the most efficient. It can be used for either intramedia or intermedia comparisons.

Following are various formulas that can be used to compare vehicles or media on the basis of cost per thousand:

1. *For print media (when audience data are not available):*

$$CPM = \frac{\text{Cost of 1 page} \times 1{,}000}{\text{Circulation}}$$

CPM circulation tells planners how much it costs to deliver 1,000 copies of the print ad, but it tells them nothing about the people who read those copies. It is used as a fallback measure to evaluate publications that do not have audience research.

2. *For print media (when audience data are available):*

$$CPM = \frac{\text{Cost of 1 page} \times 1{,}000}{\text{Number of prospects reached}}$$

3. *For broadcast media (based on homes or audience reached by a given program or time):*

$$CPM = \frac{\text{Cost of 1 unit of time} \times 1{,}000}{\text{Number of homes or persons reached by a given program or time}}$$

4. *For newspapers:*

$$CPM = \frac{\text{Cost of 1 ad} \times 1{,}000}{\text{Circulation}}$$

Wherever precise demographic classifications of the audiences are available, these data should be used in the denominator of the formula.

The procedure for using any of the preceding formulas is to compare media on the basis of the two variables: audience and cost. The medium with the lowest CPM is the most efficient, other things being equal. Since each medium is measured differently, CPM analysis is most typically applied to vehicles within a single medium, that is, one magazine versus another or one television program versus another.

Media planners should be cautious about automatically accepting or rejecting media vehicles on the basis of slight differences in CPM; a difference of 10 percent one way or another is meaningless. And people such as David Poltrack, director of research at CBS, note that the range of error in television sample audiences is so great that a true calculation of the room for error would tell us that even a CPM variation of a dollar or more might not be real.[11] Unfortunately, planners often ignore this advice in day-to-day practice.

Generally, the media vehicle with the lowest CPM is selected, but not always. If the advertiser requires a special kind of target audience and few or no media reach them exclusively, then the CPM comparisons are ignored. Rather, media selections are based on the principle of reaching the largest number of targets, regardless of cost.

For example, the target audience sometimes is individuals with annual incomes of more than $100,000. A few media vehicles reach a small proportion of these audiences, but even if many such vehicles were used, the total number of persons reached might be relatively small. On the other hand, a very large number of these persons might be reached with mass media such as a network television program or a national magazine. It is obvious that either of these two media would also include a large amount of waste because of the low target audience composition. Therefore, when the CPMs are computed, they will seem unduly high. Yet the waste and the high CPM might have to be ignored to maximize the size of target audiences reached.

Mass-produced and mass-consumed products, such as fast food, breakfast cereals, and automobiles, usually have target audiences for whom media are selected primarily on a CPM basis. Specialized products such as yachts, private airplanes, and international travel have specialized target audiences. Selecting media to reach them requires less attention to cost-efficiencies and more to audience sizes. The concepts of coverage (how many people are exposed to the medium) and composition (the percent of all exposed people who are in the target) will be discussed in more detail in Chapter 4.

Cost per Rating Point

Another method of comparing the cost-efficiency of radio and television vehicles is the *cost per rating point (CPP)*. Essentially, CPP measures the cost of one household or demographic rating point in a given market. It is calculated by dividing the cost per commercial, or spot, by the rating. In television, a *rating* is the percent of the

---

11. Erick Larson, "Watching Americans Watch TV," *Atlantic Monthly* (March 1992): 72.

target audience in a market that is tuned in during the average minute or quarter hour of a program. A *market* is the geographic area that can receive the program; it can range from the entire United States down to a local market called a *designated market area (DMA)*. This will be discussed in more detail in Chapter 4. Both CPM and CPP are measurements of relative value, but each uses a different base. The formula for calculating CPP is as follows:

$$CPP = \frac{\text{Cost of a commercial}}{\text{Rating}}$$

For example, if the cost of a prime-time network TV commercial is $200,000 and the national women 25–54 rating for that announcement is 4 (that is, 4 percent of all the 25- to 54-year-old women in the United States were watching during the average minute of this program), then the CPP would be $200,000/4 = $50,000.

How does a CPP compare with a CPM for the same station and commercial? The following example shows the differences as they might relate to a local market:

Population: women 25–54 = 900,000
Program's women 25–54 viewers: 36,000
Cost of a 30-second commercial: $1,100

DMA Rating
Viewers × 100/population = rating
36,000 × 100/900,000 = 4.0

CPM = Cost × 1,000/Viewers
Cost of 30-second commercial: $1,100
Number of women ages 25–54 delivered at 8:00 P.M.: 36,000
$1,100 × 1,000/36,000 = $30.56

Cost Per Point (CPP)
Cost/rating
Cost of 30-second commercial: $1,100
DMA rating at 8:00 P.M.: 4.0
$1,100/4.0 = $275.00

Is there any preference for using one measurement method over the other? Generally, CPM is used to compare the efficiency of individual vehicles, while CPP is the tool most often used to calculate the cost of an entire broadcast plan.

Is There a Better Way of Measurement?

We use CPM to compare media efficiency because we have to. Advertisers would much prefer to compare media on the basis of their ability to generate sales. Unfortunately, no one has been able to correlate the size of a medium's audience with the number of additional sales that an ad produces, because advertising is only one of many factors that determine how much of a product will be sold. Researchers cannot measure sales, but they can measure the number of people exposed to the ad, allowing planners to evaluate the cost per thousand people exposed.

The Internet provides a much more direct link between exposure and action by reporting back to the advertiser the number of people who are exposed to the banner ad as well as the number who click through a banner to the advertiser's website. It also allows an advertiser to know exactly how many sales were generated for products and services that can be sold online. This is a dramatic leap forward, but for the majority of day-to-day low-interest products, advertisers will continue to evaluate media in terms of CPM.

The Top Five Perennial Questions That Media Research Cannot Answer

Up to now we have discussed the general concepts and methodologies of media research and the concepts that are unique to each of the major media. The methodologies that are based on a random sample have a statistical margin of error. All methodologies have nonsampling error caused by the real-world challenges of producing research. But these sources of error can be identified and accounted for. In the course of a planner's work, other questions come up for which there are no simple answers. These are the most important questions in media because they involve subtle judgments about what is best.

The following frequently asked questions cannot be definitively answered, because they depend on what is happening in the mind of each consumer. They are presented here as "impossible" questions to sensitize planners to the inevitable day when one of these questions comes up in the course of their work, and to provide something to say and ways to think about helping the advertiser make a reasonable judgment.

1. How Much Is Enough?

This is the most common question, and it takes many forms. What is the least I can spend and still have an effective campaign? If I have X number of gross rating points (GRPs) against my primary target, am I delivering enough weight against the secondary target? My last campaign was wildly successful. I ran *XX* number of GRPs and actually had to turn away customers. Next time, how much weight can I cut back and still be successful?

Several approaches will put the advertiser in the ballpark. If the advertiser has competitive sales and spending information, it is common to match the share of voice to the share of market. An advertiser with a 10 percent share of a market should be spending at least 10 percent of the media dollars spent in that industry.

Certainly an advertiser should look back at the experience with comparable products. For example, some industries have a historic advertising-to-sales ratio.

An industry rule of thumb is that an ad must be seen three or more times for it to be effective. While this sounds like a reasonable prescription, it evades the question, "How many people can I afford to reach 3+ times?" In the end, and unfortunately, many advertising budgets are simply what remains after all other costs have been accounted for.

2. Which Medium Is Most Effective?

Effective at doing what? Different media have different strengths. Effectiveness depends heavily on the creative quality. Many people think television is the most effective medium, but this question comes up when television is not appropriate or affordable. There are virtually no independent, public domain studies of cross-media effectiveness. Advertisers who do conduct these studies treat the results as highly confidential. The publicly available research that does exist comes from industry associations whose studies are designed to promote the value of their medium. As they say, "Don't ask your barber if you need a haircut." The best advice is to ensure the advertiser has matched the strength of the media to the marketing objectives.

3. What Is the Best Environment?

This question assumes there is a rub-off effect between the medium and the advertising message. However, as noted earlier, numerous studies have failed to quantify that effect or even to confirm that it exists. We know that high-rated television programs attract more light viewers, but these iconic programs have a heavy cost premium. The first position in a commercial break has a larger audience than midbreak positions, but pod position is usually beyond a buyer's control. In magazines, an ad on the back cover is more likely to be read than one inside the book, but advertisers pay a premium for that position. Some advertisers believe a magazine ad near the front of the book is preferable, but since most insertion orders request "far forward, right-hand page," these assumed-to-be desirable positions are more likely to be given to advertisers running a heavy schedule. At the least, planners should ensure that multiple ads are given a fair rotation.

4. Which Is Better: Flighting or Continuity?

This age-old question concerns how a limited advertising budget should be scheduled over the year: in short bursts of heavy media weight followed by hiatus weeks of no activity, or continuous advertising at low weight. If the budget allows the advertiser to buy 1,600 GRPs a year, should they be scheduled in 4-week flights (total 16 weeks on-air) of 100 GRPs per week? Or would it be more effective to run for 40 weeks at 40 GRPs per week?

For products that are sold more or less evenly throughout the year, advertisers are guided by the *recency theory* of advertising that was proposed by media guru Erwin Ephron. In contrast to the theory that three exposures are needed, the recency theory is based on research that shows a single exposure close to purchase is most effective. Since there is a steady demand for nonseasonal products, the advertiser should maintain a continuous presence on-air. The goal should be to maximize the total weekly reach points (the annual sum of each week's reach points). This is achieved by continuity scheduling.

However, this ignores the effect of a competitor's advertising that may be flighted. Also, synergy is needed between the advertising and seasonal consumer or trade promotions.

Finally, there is a reluctance to go below a perceived minimal level of about 50 GRPs per week. Most advertisers appreciate the importance of continuity, but given this minimum, they find continuity scheduling to be an ideal that is beyond their brand's budget.

5. When Is My Commercial Worn Out?

It is hard enough to know what a commercial "does" when it is fresh. Commercial wearout is really a variation of the "How much is enough?" question. An industry rule of thumb is that a commercial is worn out when the heaviest viewers are exposed 26 times—somewhere around 1,000 to 1,500 GRPs. This has become a benchmark for judging a given situation, but many questions remain. Does that rule apply to a single execution or to an entire campaign of similar but different creative executions? Over what period of time? What is the effect of hiatus periods? Does this guideline refer to demographic target rating points (women ages 25 to 54) or household points, which are usually larger?

One researcher sees a political agenda behind the question. The agency wants to make a new commercial and the advertiser doesn't, or vice versa. People who are closely involved with the lengthy creative process may be so close to the commercial that they will think it is worn out when in fact it hasn't even been on air.

It should be clear by now that there is no simple answer to these "How much is enough?" questions of effective frequency, flighting versus continuity, minimum GRP levels, maximum hiatus weeks, media effectiveness, wearout, and so forth. Research can provide guidance, but in the end, it requires agency and advertiser judgment to apply these general findings from the past to specific plans for the future.

CHAPTER FOUR

Basic Measurements and Calculations

This chapter describes and explains the basic measurements and calculations used in media planning. These explanations serve as the foundation for understanding media strategy decisions, which will be discussed in Chapter 6. The measurements and calculations discussed in this chapter are by no means all that are available. They represent only those used most often.

It is vital to understand how media audiences are measured and what those measurements mean. Media planners can, and sometimes do, make strategy decisions without using measurement data as a guide, but such decisions are difficult to defend because they tend to be too subjective. Measurement data, on the other hand, provide a degree of objectivity that is hard to refute.

How Media Vehicles Are Measured

Most media audiences are measured through sample surveys, using data about a small group to find out about a larger universe's exposure to a particular medium. The research companies take a sample because measuring the entire audience (a census) is generally not practical. Sample sizes can vary from as few as 200 to as many as 26,000 individuals for single-source services such as Mediamark Research and Intelligence, LLC (MRI), and Simmons. Online samples and samples using TV set-top boxes (STBs) can run in the hundreds of thousands or even millions, but even these immense samples have limitations that will be discussed later.

Given the widespread availability and use of the Internet, researchers have been tempted to shift away from traditional telephone and direct-mail sample recruitment to obtain the necessary sample. However, while an Internet survey may be acceptable for some purposes, it is not representative enough for audience estimates that must reflect the total population. As noted in Chapter 3, 85 percent of people have access to the Internet, meaning that the viewing habits of 15 percent cannot possibly be accounted for. Statisticians call this sample frame bias. In addition, the sample is limited to people who volunteer to participate. Their media behavior is likely to be different from those who do not sign up, but there is no way to know or quantify the difference. This is called response bias. So-called representative samples or quota samples keep recruiting until the researchers have enough people of each age and gender cell to match the U.S. population. But the relatively few young adults who do accept may not have the same media habits as the great many in their cohort who refuse. A random sample based on household addresses, where everyone has an equal chance to be included and where extra effort is made to recruit those who initially refuse, is the best methodology for research used as "currency" by the billion-dollar broadcast and print media.

Some research, such as Nielsen's national television ratings, are ongoing and report the audience to every program 24/7/365. Most others are made at specified intervals and produce reports annually or several times a year. Changes in measuring technology are continually being made as new ideas or methods are developed, and planners are always looking for better ways to measure audiences. The methods presented in this chapter simply represent those used most often today.

Nielsen Television Ratings

Nielsen is currently the primary supplier of television ratings that are used as the currency of advertising sales. It uses three methodologies:

1. Nielsen People Meter (NPM)—for national television and the largest local markets
2. Integrated set meter/diary—midsize markets—due to be replaced by the People Meter
3. Diary only—small markets

The NPM is the most precise and accurate method for measuring television audiences. The Nielsen Company (http://en-us.nielsen.com) employs a single sample of more than 18,000 homes that are equipped with a people meter to produce all national (network, cable, and syndicated program) television ratings and local ratings in the top 26 markets, called designated market areas (DMAs), covering 50 percent of the population. These 26 markets are referred to as Local People Meter (LPM) markets.

The NPM consists of two parts. The human interface is a small box that sits on top of each set in the house that has a screen five inches or larger (see Exhibit 4-1). Household members use this or a remote control to record who is watching. Each person is assigned a button, and there is a place on top where visitors can enter their age and gender. A row of lights on the front blinks red when the set is first turned on.

Household members are instructed to push their button when they are "watching television." So when Dad watches the football game, he punches his button and his light changes from red to green. Mom, who may be in the room but is doing something else, does not punch hers. Her looking up from time to time, and even watching a commercial, would not be recorded. From the moment when someone's button is pushed, every channel the set is tuned to is recorded. The meter reports viewing in one-minute increments, allowing Nielsen to report the number of viewers in the average minute of the program (the AA rating).

EXHIBIT 4-1

The Nielsen People Meter

Source: The Nielsen Company, the Nielsen People Meter. Used with permission.

The second part of the people meter is another, larger box off in a closet somewhere that identifies which channel the set is tuned to and sends the data by telephone line to Nielsen's computers in Florida. This is a challenge in today's 500-channel television environment. The Active/Passive (A/P) Meter identifies the station being watched with an inaudible code imbedded in its audio signal (the active part). A wire carries the signal from each set's loudspeaker or audio output jack to the meter. Passive digital signal matching is used to identify channels that are not encoded. Together they achieve almost 100 percent accuracy in identifying what the viewer is watching. The A/P Meter was specifically designed to handle today's digital environment, including cable boxes, satellites, digital video recorders (DVRs) like TiVo, high-definition television (HDTV), video games, PC viewing, and other forms of video delivery that have not even been invented.

In an initiative called "TVandPC," by the end of 2010 Nielsen will have installed meters on all the personal computers in a 7,500 home subset of the people meter sample. Users will sign in to their computer in the same way that they push their people meter buttons. Then all online activity will be recorded, including watching news, sports, or entertainment TV programs via Hulu or other Internet video services. With this information, Nielsen will be able to report the total audience to programs, whether that viewing occurs on the television set or on the PC. The viewing data will be carefully monitored to ensure that the addition of computer tracking will not affect Nielsen's ability to recruit its people meter sample.

In the 26 largest markets, television audiences are measured with the people meter and are known popularly as local people meter (LPM) markets. The hardware and all of the procedures are identical to the way Nielsen measures national television. The only difference is that the sample is weighted to represent the local market's population instead of the nation's. The LPM has minute-by-minute granularity that would allow reporting the average minute (AA) audience, but by long-standing practice all spot markets, even LPM markets, continue reporting the average-quarter-hour (AQH) audience. In addition to providing local ratings, the people meters in these markets are included in the sample for the national ratings, although they are then reweighted to the national population.

While the largest DMAs are measured with the people meter, in 31 midsize markets (20 percent of the country), audiences are measured with a combination of meters and diaries. A device called a Recordimeter provides continuous data on what programs the set is tuned to. A diary is used to record demographic data (see Exhibit 4-2). This meter-diary integration is the same methodology that has been used since 1956 and is scheduled to be replaced with the A/P Meter by 2012, at which time local television in 70 percent of the United States will be measured with the modern people meter technology.

Nielsen is working on simpler, less expensive versions of the A/P Meter for markets ranked 57 to 125. But until it is released, and indefinitely for markets ranked 126 and higher, all viewing will be captured in a diary. Respondents write down what station and program they are watching in quarter-hour increments, causing ratings to be defined in terms of the number of viewers during the AQH of a program or daypart.

While researchers are quick to admit that Nielsen's diary is the least accurate methodology, especially in today's world, it is also the least expensive. Like all media research, the bulk of the cost is borne by the media that use the data to support their sales efforts. Buying agencies pay relatively little. In the smaller markets, the fixed cost of research becomes a heavy burden on stations that have limited ability to raise their ad rates. So although the diary methodology is deeply flawed, it is all that stations in the smaller markets can afford.

EXHIBIT 4-2

Nielsen TV Viewing Diary

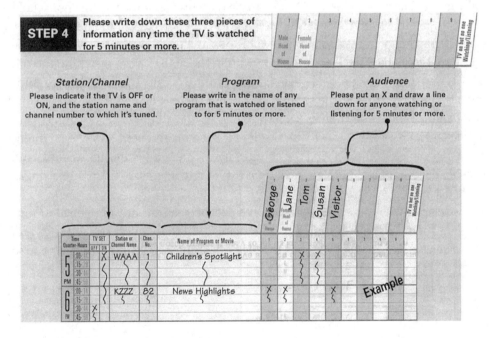

Source: The Nielsen Company, Nielsen Station Index. Used with permission.

Copyrighted information of The Nielsen Company, licensed for use herein.

On the other hand, the diary has the advantage of providing a direct link to the viewers in the form of written comments on the last page. These are a popular source of information for station managers who make an annual visit to specially provided reading rooms in Nielsen's Technology Center near Tampa, Florida. For more information about how TV ratings are produced, go to http://en-us.nielsen .com/tab/product_families/nielsen_tv_audience.

Proposed Set-Top Box (STB) Alternatives for Measuring Television

Researchers are constantly looking for ways to improve television measurement, and in the process, they are developing a service that would compete with Nielsen. The international research firm of Taylor Nelson Sofres (TNS) is developing a service that would use the set-top cable or satellite box to record television viewing. TiVo (the DVR company)[1] and Rentrak, a multimedia measurement company,[2] are also developing STB systems. Not to be left out, Nielsen is working on a way to incorporate STB measurement into its rating service.

Cable and satellite television systems now serve 90 percent of the United States,[3] opening the possibility of tapping the STB to learn what programs are being watched. This has the advantages of accessing an exceptionally large sample, potentially in the tens of millions, and total passive measurement: the viewing household doesn't need to do anything for its viewing to be reported. On the negative side, since 10 percent of homes do not have cable or satellite, their viewing would not be accounted for. The STB doesn't identify who in the household is watching the set, so this measure doesn't provide demographic rating points. It is a measure of tuning, not viewing—that is, the set may be on, but there is no certainty that anyone is watching. Since many homes keep the cable box on all the time, researchers are forced to estimate when the TV set itself is turned on and being watched. Finally, the many cable systems serving the country have different technical standards and varying degrees of cooperation, making it difficult to aggregate them into a single, unified sample.

Whether any of these will replace or even become sufficiently developed to supplement the people meter remains to be seen. Until these questions are resolved, the television ratings used for the currency of buying and selling will continue to be measured with a sample.

---

1. www.tivoadvertising.com.
2. www.rentrak.com.
3. The Nielsen Company, Nielsen Answers, July 2009.

Arbitron Radio Ratings

There are more than 270 radio markets in the United States because the geographic areas measured are smaller than television DMAs. Because of its low cost, radio has traditionally been measured with a seven-day diary. Since 2001, the Arbitron Company has been deploying a pager-sized personal meter that responds to special codes in the radio station's audio signal. Because it is totally passive, this Portable People Meter (PPM) not only greatly improves radio audience measurement, but also changes the definition of *audience* from people who consider themselves "listening to the radio" to people who are within earshot of the loudspeaker, regardless of whether they are paying attention to the set. Following exhaustive tests, Arbitron is replacing the diary with the PPM. As of December 2009, they expect to have it operational in 33 radio markets, representing 47 percent of the United States.[4] The remaining markets will continue to be measured with a diary. The PPM potentially could be used to measure television viewing, but a series of technical and operational difficulties have prevented that from happening. Nevertheless, it remains a possible methodology in the future.

Although Nielsen is primarily known for its television audience ratings, it is moving into the radio measurement business with a diary that uses stick-on labels to identify which stations are being listened to. Nielsen is starting out in 50 small to midsize markets, but if successful, they are expected to expand the service to larger markets, providing significant new competition to Arbitron.

Radio has traditionally been thought of as an entertainment medium delivered by local stations that are licensed by the Federal Communications Commission (FCC). The growth of broadband Internet has led to another medium: streaming audio, sometimes called Web radio. According to Arbitron/Edison research,[5] by summer 2009, 49 percent of adults had ever listened to Web radio, and 17 percent had listened to the medium in the last week. Content is mostly an online feed from terrestrial stations that may or may not include the advertising. As of this writing there is no ongoing national measurement, but that is expected to change if interest in the medium increases.

National satellites provide yet another venue for delivering audio content. Sirius XM Satellite Radio has more than 180 channels that can be accessed from anywhere in the continental United States. This pay service is available online, but the majority of its subscribers listen in their car. Measurement has proven to be a challenge because the satellite audience is so fragmented that no single channel amasses

---

4. Arbitron, estimate as of September 2009 at www.arbitron.com.
5. *AdweekMedia*, July 20, 2009.

enough listeners to be reportable, and advertisers are reluctant to scatter their message across the whole demographically diverse network. Unless the company can survive on subscription fees, the lack of measurement may undermine the advertising business model of what, on the surface, is an attractive media option.

Magazines and Newspapers

At least three different techniques are commonly used to measure magazine and newspaper audiences: recent-reading and frequency-of-reading techniques for magazines, and the yesterday-reading technique for newspapers.

Recent Reading

MRI is today the sole user of the recent-reading technique. In this method, interviewers visit a national random sample of adults. Each interviewer has the black-and-white logotypes of more than 200 magazines printed on individual cards. These are screened to about 12 to 15 magazines that the respondent claims to have read or looked into within the last six months. For these magazines, respondents are shown the cards one at a time again and asked if they have read or looked at the magazine within the last month, week, or other publication period, which includes browsing a magazine while waiting in the checkout line of a grocery store. Those who say they are "sure they have" are considered readers of the publication. After this questioning, respondents are asked for demographic information about themselves and their family. The interviewer then leaves behind a 115-page questionnaire booklet that asks respondents to fill out details about various products they have used and how often they used them. This booklet includes virtually every consumer product and service sold in America. Upon completion, the interviewer returns, collects the booklet, and gives the respondent a modest check as thanks for participating in the survey.

Today, the recent-reading technique used by MRI is the most widely used source of magazine audience estimates. It is considered single-source research because it captures media behavior, product usage, demographics, and attitudes, all from a single sample. This technique has the advantage of being able to quickly survey a large number of publications with a reliability that has been proven in more than 30 years of practice.

There are several disadvantages. First, by showing just the logo, the respondents may become confused about which magazine they have read, especially if the title is similar to other magazines (e.g., *Parents* versus *Parenting*). Also, since just the logo is shown, readership could apply to any issue of a magazine, inflating the overall readership of the publication (a source of error called "telescoping"). Finally, this technique is more costly than mailed surveys because it must be administered in person by the interviewer. Nevertheless, the readership estimates are consistent from year to year, and because every magazine is treated equally, this technique is viewed as the best measure of the relative audience size of different magazines.

Frequency of Reading

The *frequency-of-reading technique* is the most commonly used method for determining the number of people who read a magazine. In this procedure, the respondent is shown a list of magazine logotypes or cover pictures and is asked to record for each magazine the number of copies they have read out of the last four issues—one out of four, two out of four, and so on. It is the least expensive methodology because the survey can be conducted through the mail.

The frequency-of-reading technique is used by Simmons Research, a division of the Experian Company. It offers single source research that is similar to, and in fierce competition with, MRI. Simmons's National Consumer Survey measures the same behaviors, but its survey is conducted entirely by mail. These methodological differences—MRI in person, Simmons by mail—give each service different strengths and weaknesses that agency media researchers must account for. Most media planners use MRI's service as the primary source for magazine audience estimates. Simmons is stronger in its measurement of demographic segments such as Hispanics and gay/lesbian populations. Simmons has traditionally had more detailed psychographic information. A more detailed comparison of the two services is beyond the scope of this book.

Yesterday Reading

In the *yesterday-reading technique,* respondents in a selected sample are asked which newspapers they read yesterday. The procedure is much the same as the recent-reading technique for magazines. Because relatively few newspapers are read in any given market, this interview is quite short.

Internet

Nielsen Online (www.nielsen-online.com) and comScore Media Metrix (www.comscore.com) are the two most widely used companies that measure the number of visitors to Internet websites. Both services maintain a large nationally representative sample of Internet users who allow the researchers to place software on their computers that record every site visited. In addition to determining the number of unique visitors, the services can tell how long people stay with each page, how deeply they go into a site, and the number of times they return. Both services are considered "passive" measures because the data are collected automatically, without any conscious effort by the respondents. This allows them to report on many more sites than would be possible in a survey that relies on respondents' memories.

In addition to the basic demographics of people who visit different websites, advertisers want to know which sites are best for users of the advertiser's products. comScore provides this information, as it asks its respondents which products they use. This information is linked to the sites they visit as they browse the Web. Nielsen Online has a competing service called @Plan, which asks respondents which products they use and then electronically tracks which websites they visit.

Mobile Internet Measurement

In addition to their Internet measurement services, both Nielsen and comScore have systems that measure Internet browsing on smart cell phones. comScore reports that more than 22.4 million people access the Internet every day via their mobile phones.[6] As mobile usage expands and changes, the measurement systems are forced to change with it, raising the business question, "Is there enough advertiser demand for the medium to justify the cost of measuring it?" This cost-benefit analysis for producing the research is a constant challenge throughout the rapidly evolving media landscape.

Data Fusion

To supplement the @Plan service, Nielsen has an agreement with MRI to create a fused database that combines the Nielsen Online and MRI samples based on key demographic hooks. Each Nielsen Online respondent is matched to an MRI respondent with the same age, gender, income, presence of children, Internet usage, and other demographic variables. The result is a single record that consists of every website the Nielsen respondent visited and every product the MRI respondent used.

Fusion is necessary because it is not humanly possible for a single respondent to provide all the information contained in both the Nielsen Online and the MRI surveys. Fusion has been used for many years in Europe and is now becoming widely accepted in the United States. The result is a system that can tell the user which websites are visited. Exhibit 2-10 shows which websites are visited by regular golfers—information that would not be possible without the fused database. On the other hand, users must keep in mind that fusion relies on the accuracy and, more important, the relevance of the demographic hooks that link the online and product usage behavior. The "one size fits all" demographic hooks used by syndicated services are less relevant for individual products than more specific characteristics.

---

6. http://searchenginewatch.com/3633213.

So for websites visited by frequent business travelers, occupation would be a better hook than income.

Out-of-Home

Outdoor audiences are measured by the Traffic Audit Bureau (TAB) (www.tabon line.com), which counts the number of cars passing each billboard on the average day. This is translated into "daily circulation," which is the basis for media sales. In 2009–2010, the TAB introduced their new Eyes On system, which combines auto and pedestrian traffic counts with route destination surveys and in-person interviews to report the number of people likely to see an advertiser's message. This enables outdoor audiences to be segmented according to demographics, including age, gender, race, and income, based on people who actually see the ads. Because this is a totally new way of thinking for both media buyers and sellers, the TAB expects it will take time to be adopted.

Other out-of-home media such as ads on buses, airport posters, signage in baseball stadiums, and mass-transit advertising estimate their audience with a variety of techniques ranging from ticket sales to proprietary surveys. Because these studies generally are conducted by the media themselves, they are considered less reliable than research conducted by independent companies such as the TAB, Nielsen, and MRI. The Digital Place-based Advertising Association (DPAA, www.ovab.org) is a new organization created to develop guidelines and best practices for measuring the many forms of out-of-home media.

How the Data Are Interpreted

All audience measurement techniques involve interacting with a sample of people who live in the geographic area being measured, whether that is a local market such as Chicago or the entire United States. Researchers calculate the percent exposed by dividing the number of sample respondents who read a magazine, watched a TV show, or were exposed to an Internet banner by the total number of people in the sample. Then they project this percentage to the total population by simple multiplication.

For instance, if the NPM sample has 18,000 households, and if 370 of those homes watched "30 Rock" on a given Thursday night, the percentage is 370 divided by 18,000, which equals 2.1 percent. This is the *household rating* of the program. To find out how many households this represents nationwide, multiply the 114,900,000 U.S. television households by 2.1 percent to get 2,412,900 households. The 18,000-home sample has been projected to the 114.9 million U.S. homes that have a working television set. About 1 percent of homes do not have television, and so are not included in the ratings. This same process is used for demographics by simply substituting the appropriate number of viewers and population base.

General Uses of Vehicle Audience Measurements

One of the most significant problems facing media planners is deciding in which medium to place advertisements, because there are so many options—and the numbers of available media keep growing. The size and cost of reaching target audiences in these alternative media are important measurements for comparison purposes.

The result of all these attempts at measurement is a large volume of numerical data, produced at regular intervals. However, the effect of such a quantity of data on media planners and others involved in marketing/media operations sometimes produces a sense of confidence that is perhaps unwarranted. Despite the quantitative aspect, media planning is not scientific in the same manner as, say, physics is.

Media audience numbers are the best that can be attained at a reasonable cost, but they do not represent the kind of measurement data planners would ideally like to have, such as information about which media vehicle produces the most sales. Because the numbers often take on undue importance, users of measurement data are warned that the numbers are only rough estimates for interpretive purposes, not absolutes.

Planners should also understand that the numbers are, in fact, the manufactured product of the research companies. Like all companies, they must sell their numbers and make a reasonable profit for their investors. As a result, there is a constant stream of new research services that all purport to give planners a better understanding of the media they are planning and buying. So on the one hand, planners are faced with salesmen offering new and better research for a price, and on the other, they face the practical constraints of their own budgets and the reality that in the end, all media planning decisions are judgments. In this book we will focus on the core metrics that every planner must know, recognizing that although other measures are available that provide supplemental information, they are too numerous to be considered here.

Planners use audience measurement and product usage data for the following comparative purposes:

1. To learn the demographics of product or brand users
2. To learn the audience demographics of various kinds of media vehicles—who reads, sees, or hears the vehicles
3. To learn the way purchasers use a product or brand (How many are heavy, medium, or light users?)

4. To learn whether audience members of a particular media vehicle are heavy, medium, or light users of the product
5. To learn how many people were exposed to vehicles

All of this information has one basic goal: to help planners and buyers match media with target markets.

Two main concepts guide planners in their use of measurement data. The first is to find vehicles that reach the largest numbers of prospects for a product category or a brand within that category. But planners do not always select the vehicle that delivers the largest number of prospects. Sometimes they choose a second concept, which is finding the vehicle that delivers the greatest concentrations of prospects, even if there are relatively few of them.

Various Concepts of Audience Measurements

One difficulty in matching markets with media is that no single measurement can be used to determine the audience sizes for all media. Therefore, it is difficult to make intermedia comparisons (such as comparisons between the audience sizes of a television program and a magazine). As is apparent from the previous discussion of methodologies, audience size numbers do not mean the same thing from medium to medium, even when they are measured on the same base. A *base* is a demographic group, such as total women or men ages 35–49. All media can be properly measured against the same base, but the methodology and the meaning of exposure is different for each medium. The audience numbers mean different things because the measurement methodology is different, not because they are measured against different bases.

Actual or Potential Audience Size Measurements

Those who use media audience research should be careful not to confuse data that show the actual size of a vehicle's audience with other data that look similar but show only potential audience size. The division of audience measurement data into classifications of *actual* versus *potential*, or *vehicle distribution* versus *vehicle exposure*, depends on how the audience is measured.

Before statistical sampling was widely accepted, media owners simply used distribution counts of their vehicles as evidence of audience size. Circulation of print media (number of copies printed) is one of these older measurements. It represents only potential audience size of the measured vehicle, because it does not measure how many people will actually read a given copy of the periodical. In the last 30 years, as media research techniques have become more sophisticated, print media have been able to define their readership in terms of numbers of people who actually read the publication, in addition to pure circulation or distribution counts. The VISTA Service from Affinity Research (www.affinityresearch.net) and the AdMeasures service from MRI go beyond readership of the magazine and report the number of people who actually read the advertising. Nevertheless, the starting point and the core metric for most planners is the number of people who read the average issue, or the average issue audience.

Print Circulation Measurements

Circulation measurements are available for most newspaper and magazine vehicles, but these data are of limited use in selection decisions. Although they tell how many copies were printed and distributed, they do not provide the planner with information about the number of readers. One unit of circulation means one copy of a periodical distributed, but for every copy distributed, there could be as many as six different readers. Needless to say, this can be confusing. Furthermore, circulation data tell the planner nothing about the demographics of the audience, such as the readers' age, gender, household income, education, and other crucial pieces of information that are needed to select vehicles that will reach precise marketing targets.

As a result, circulation data are seldom used alone in selecting magazines in which to place ads. However, such data are often used in making decisions about newspapers because they are chosen primarily for their ability to reach a certain geographic area. Also, generally the demographics of newspapers, as a true mass medium, are well-known.

When circulation data must be used, the most reliable are measurements verified by the Audit Bureau of Circulation (ABC, www.accessabc.com). The accuracy of ABC audits is widely accepted throughout the advertising industry. They are the legal basis for a magazine's rate. That is, a magazine charges a certain amount of money to carry a page of advertising with the guarantee that it will deliver a certain number of copies, as reported by the ABC. If the magazine falls short of this "rate base" circulation, it owes the advertiser a rebate. So while MRI is used to compare the readership of alternative magazines, the ABC audit is the legal and financially accountable underpinning of the medium. The ABC is a nonprofit, cooperative association of about 1,100 advertisers and advertising agencies and 2,100 daily and weekly newspapers, consumer magazines, business publications, and farm publications in the United States and Canada. It audits and reports the circulation of these publications at regular intervals.

In addition to total circulation, ABC data include circulations categorized for newspapers by city zone, trading zone, and outside areas. Circulation is also categorized for newspapers by metropolitan statistical areas (MSAs) and television DMAs, making it possible to determine how the distribution of copies matches the selling and marketing areas of advertisers.

Magazine data from ABC show circulation categorized by size of metropolitan areas, by states and regions of the United States, and by other geographic divisions, all aimed at helping the planner choose the medium that best reaches geographic targets. No demographic data about the reading audience are available from ABC.

The ABC releases the publisher's statement twice a year (June and December) as "the Pink Sheet." It has a wealth of information about the magazine, including single copy sales, cover price, circulation by issue, public place copies, five-year circulation trend, and other statistics about the magazine. A full description of the Pink Sheet and extensive free tutorials are available on the ABC website.

Many planners think of the Pink Sheet as an audit, but it is not—it is the publisher's claim of how many copies they distribute. After the Pink Sheet is released, the ABC auditors physically travel to the magazine's offices and audit the books to verify that the publisher's statement is correct. Their findings are released as the Audit Report. It lacks the detail of the Pink Sheet, but it validates the total circulation that is used as the basis for the publication's rates. A short report, referred to as the white audit, is released showing only those magazines whose audit is more than 2 percent different from the publisher's statement. In the event of a shortfall, advertisers have the right to go back and claim a rebate, but only for publications that guarantee their rates. Some publications avoid this risk by not stating a rate base. Also, since the white audit may not be available for more than a year after the issue date, planners need to keep a record of insertions and make an effort to claim the rebate when it is deserved.

Audience Accumulation

Audience accumulation is the buildup of total audiences over time (usually a month). A major part of the accumulation concept is that audience members are counted only once, no matter how many additional times they are exposed to a particular vehicle or commercial. The number of different people who see an ad at least once is called *reach.* Some people who are reached will see an ad only once; others will see it many times. The number of times the average person who was reached sees the ad is called *frequency.* The concepts of reach and frequency apply to all media and will be discussed in more detail in Chapter 5.

It is of utmost importance to know that the vehicle exposure is not about advertising, per se. Its main purpose is to learn how many persons looked at something inside the magazine. When the planner wants to know how many persons saw advertisements, then a different measurement based on number of reading days, number of issues read, and percent of pages opened can be used. This measure is called *advertising page exposure*, but there is disagreement among planners about the validity of the estimates. So exposure is a broad measurement of the vehicle. The point is that when a vehicle is seen, it has potential for selling through ads.

Audience Accumulation in Magazines In magazines, audience accumulates in three ways:

1. When advertising is placed in successive issues of the same magazine
2. When advertising is placed in the same month's issue of different magazines
3. Over the issue life of the publication, as the magazine is read by more and more people, passing it along from one reader to another

In 2000, MRI released the first modern study of how quickly a single issue of a magazine accumulates readers. As expected, it revealed that a time-sensitive magazine such as *TV Guide* accumulates virtually all of its audience within a week, while newsweeklies such as *U.S. News and World Report* take almost a month to reach 90 percent of their total readership. Monthly magazines take almost three months to accumulate the same readership level.[7] This study is updated with each MRI survey.

Within a magazine's total audience, researchers distinguish between *primary readers* (those who either have purchased the magazine themselves or are members of the purchaser's household) and *secondary*, or *pass-along, readers* (those not in the purchaser's household). Typical pass-along readers are the purchaser's friends and people reading in doctors' offices, beauty salons, or on airplanes.

In addition to the type of reader, syndicated research companies also provide data showing where people read magazines. MRI cites in-home and out-of-home readership for all the publications in their reports. Several isolated research studies have indicated that the in-home reader, whether a primary or pass-along reader, reads more pages of a magazine and spends more time reading than the person outside of the home. Media planners sometimes use this information to give different values, or weights, to each type of reader to compare one media vehicle to another.

Audience Accumulation in Broadcast Although the concept of reach accumulation is the same in broadcast as with magazines, the mechanics differ widely. This is because once a TV or radio program is broadcast, it is finished (unless it is recorded). Those people who viewed or listened to the show are the only audience

---

7. Mediamark Research, Inc. "Magazine Audience Accumulation: Development of a Measurement System and Initial Results," 2000.

the program will have; there is no pass-along audience as with magazines. Time is a major element in broadcast accumulation.

Nevertheless, TV and radio programs do accumulate audience in three ways:

1. Within the program audience while it is being broadcast
2. With successive airings of the same program within a four-week period
3. With the airing of different programs within the same four-week period

Viewers are counted by the NPM if they press the buttons designating themselves as viewers of a given program. If new viewers watch a program after the first telecast, they are added to those who viewed it previously. Radio listeners are so designated if they write in a diary that they listen to five minutes or more of the programming. If they are carrying a PPM in one of the markets using that methodology, they are counted if they are within earshot of a loudspeaker carrying a radio program. Each week that a program is aired, new audience members will tune in for the first time, and thus the program's reach grows. Another way accumulation grows is by advertising on different programs or radio stations that appeal to the same audience, such as women ages 18–49.

In the real world, people tune in and tune out programs at different times during the program broadcast. Ten people might tune in a particular program in the first five minutes, but some of them will tune out, and some new people will tune in. This phenomenon occurs throughout the program.

Exhibit 4-3 shows how the accumulated total audience of a single episode varies for several programs compared with the audience who viewed the program during an average minute. In every case, the tuned-in audience is greater in number than

EXHIBIT 4-3

Comparison of Program Ratings:
Average Minute Versus Total for Entire Program

PROGRAM	PROGRAM LENGTH	DAY OF TELECAST	HOUSEHOLDS VIEWING (%)	
			AVERAGE MINUTE	TOTAL PROGRAM
"American Idol"	60 min.	Tuesday, May 19, 2009	14.1	19.5
"30 Rock"	30 min.	Thursday, May 21, 2009	2.4	3.0
"60 Minutes"	60 min.	Sunday, May 24, 2009	5.4	8.3

Source: The Nielsen Company, NTI Pocketpiece, May 18–24, 2009. Used with permission.

those who tuned out. In other words, the bucket is being filled faster than it is being emptied. This results in a gradual buildup of audience over the entire program.

Coverage

Audiences can be analyzed in two broad ways: in total numbers of people (e.g., the evening news audience) and as a percentage of the demographic universe of which they are a part (e.g., all women ages 35–49). One might compare the audience size of 10 magazines or television programs on the basis of which delivers the greatest number of people in a target audience or on the basis of which delivers the highest percentage of the total population in that target audience. Either method will reveal the same relative differences between the media vehicles.

Coverage is a convenient term planners use to assess the degree to which a media vehicle delivers a given target audience. The higher the coverage, the greater the delivery—the more people who will be exposed to the medium and presumably the advertising. Coverage is usually expressed as a percentage of a market population reached.

To calculate coverage, researchers divide a given medium's delivery of a specific demographic group (or target audience) by the total population of that demographic group (the market size, or *universe*). For example, suppose a magazine is read by 2.5 million women ages 25–54, and the total population of women ages 25–54 is 62.9 million. Then the magazine has a 4 percent coverage of that target audience (i.e., 2.5 million divided by 62.9 million).

Unfortunately, the term *coverage* can be confusing, because it is used in different ways for different media forms (see Exhibit 4-4 for a summary). The term is most typically applied to magazines. For example, according to MRI, 56.1 million adults in the United States live in a household that owns cats,[8] and 11.4 million of them read *People* magazine. So a planner would say that *People*'s coverage of cat-owning adults is 20.4 percent (i.e., 11.4 million divided by 56.1 million). This 20.4 percent represents actual exposure to the vehicle. Put simply, an ad in *People* would be delivered to about a fifth of all cat owners. In newspapers and television, coverage represents only the potential for exposure, not actual exposure (or reach). Because *coverage* can mean a number of different things, it is important for anyone who uses this term to know and understand its alternative meanings. Following is a discussion of how coverage is defined in specific media.

Newspaper Coverage *Newspaper coverage* is the number of copies circulated compared to the number of households in the circulation area. Most newspapers mea-

---

8. Mediamark Research & Intelligence, LLC, Spring 2009.

EXHIBIT 4-4

Different Meanings of the Term *Coverage*

KIND OF COVERAGE	MEANING	USES
General concept (more accurately called "market coverage")	The number of prospects delivered (exposed) by a given medium. Coverage expressed as a percentage of the universe of prospects.	Serves as a goal in planning. Used to determine whether media selected are delivering enough prospects.
Newspaper coverage	The number of circulation units as a percentage of the number of households in an area. If the readers of newspapers in a local market are measured, then coverage is the number of readers in a demographic segment (such as men ages 18–24) as a percentage of all men 18–24 in the local market.	For local markets. A goal to determine whether enough households are reached with one or more newspapers. This represents potential audience size.
Magazine coverage (sometimes called "reach")	Same as the general concept. Prospects are demographically defined.	Same as the general concept. This represents estimated actual audience size.
Spot TV and radio coverage (local market)	The number of TV (or radio) homes within the signal area of station that can tune in to that station.	Serves as a basis for potential delivery in planning. Indicates the maximum size of the potential audience of radio or TV homes.
Spot TV coverage for a national campaign (also for spot radio)	Total number of TV homes in selected markets that are part of a campaign, that can tune in (or can be reached).	It can show the percentage of U.S. TV homes that may be potentially delivered by a spot plan. Maximum number and percentage of potential exposure.
Network TV program coverage	The number and percentage of U.S. TV homes for all stations in a network carrying a given program, compared to total TV homes in the United States.	An indication of the maximum potential of TV homes that a TV program can reach.
Outdoor advertising and transit coverage	The number of people who pass and are exposed to a given showing of billboards in a local market, expressed as a percentage of the total people in the market.	To determine the size of an audience that might look at each showing of billboards.
Cable TV channel coverage	The number and percentage of U.S. TV homes that can receive a given cable channel from any source: wired cable, direct broadcast satellite, apartment cable system, or other system.	An indication of the maximum audience that can be reached by an individual cable network.
Internet coverage	All members (two years of age or older) of U.S. households that currently have access to the Internet. Some services define coverage as the percent of persons who used the Internet or other digital media at home, work, or college in the last 30 days.	Provides the maximum number or percent of persons who can be exposed to an Internet ad campaign.

sure the number of copies sold or distributed and call this *circulation.* This is the number audited by the ABC.

If the circulation of a newspaper is 500,000, and the number of households in the area (the household universe) is 2,000,000, then the coverage is 25 percent. The assumption is that each unit of circulation equals one household covered. Newspaper coverage represents potential rather than actual exposure, because not everyone in a household that receives a copy of a newspaper actually reads it; exposure to the medium is not necessarily assumed. Therefore, coverage based on circulation is only a rough measure of newspaper audience size related to the total number of households in that area.

When using newspaper coverage, planners sometimes suggest that a minimum coverage level in any individual market should be at least 50 percent. If it can be assumed that not all persons in all households will be exposed to any given edition of a newspaper, then 50 percent is the lowest level that seems practical. Perhaps only two-thirds of that 50 percent will be exposed. Some media planners set much higher limits on local market coverage, such as at least 70 percent. In such situations, it may take a number of newspapers in that community to attain 70 percent gross coverage (i.e., double-counting homes that subscribe to two or more papers as opposed to net coverage that counts each home only once).

When a newspaper has research of its readership and provides a breakdown of that audience by demographic segments, then coverage will mean something different. In this case, it will mean the number of individuals exposed to newspapers compared to the total number of individuals (rather than households) in the market. Because such measurements are not always available on a regular basis, newspaper coverage usually means potential exposure. Scarborough Research (www.scarborough.com) is the primary source of newspaper readership in more than 80 DMAs. In addition to newspaper readership, Scarborough provides information about local sports teams, shopping malls, movie theaters, community events, and even product usage. Scarborough can be thought of as a local market MRI.

Magazine Coverage   *Magazine coverage* is simply the number of prospects who read a publication divided by the size of a target market. This is sometimes referred to as a magazine's *average issue audience.* The concept is directly comparable to a broadcast rating; however, the standard methodology used by the research companies cannot measure the audience to each issue. Hence the need to report the numbers of readers to the *average* issue.

Another way to look at magazine coverage is to look at total users of a given product class. For example, as shown in Exhibit 4-5, MRI reported that 31,981,000 adults were dieting to maintain their weight or physical fitness. This figure represents the size of the total market of such consumers. If 7,279,000 readers of *People* magazine are controlling their diet, that number represents 22.8 percent market coverage by *People* (7,279,000 divided by 31,981,000).

EXHIBIT 4-5

Magazine Coverage and Composition

	NUMBER (000)	COVERAGE	COMPOSITION	INDEX
Total adults dieting for weight control	31,981	100.0%	14.2%	100
High-Coverage Magazines—Low Composition				
People	7,279	22.8	16.7	117
AARP The Magazine	5,921	18.5	16.6	117
Reader's Digest	5,186	16.2	16.3	115
Parade Carrier Newspapers	10,875	34.0	15.0	105
High-Composition Magazines—Low Coverage				
First	908	2.8	29.9	210
Shape	1,558	4.9	28.8	203
Self	1,529	4.8	25.2	177
Working Mother	498	1.6	24.3	171
Fitness	1,266	4.0	22.7	160

Source: Mediamark Research & Intelligence, LLC, Spring 2009. Used with permission.

Earlier in this chapter, we discussed the ways that researchers determine how many people read a given magazine. But the number of readers, as a number by itself, is of little value until it is put into context as a percent of both the target (coverage) and of the medium's total audience (composition.)

Exhibit 4-5 illustrates the concept. Mass magazines, such as *People*, are read by such a large percent of the whole country that they can't help also being read by a large percent of target dieters. They offer high coverage, but there is a great deal of waste; more than half the circle of *People* readers is outside the target audience. In this case, we would say that *People* has high coverage of our target but low composition.

Small, selective magazines such as *Fitness,* on the other hand, cover only a relatively small part of the target, but a larger percent of the magazine's (few) readers fall within the target. There is far less waste. We would say *Fitness* has low coverage but high composition.

Exhibit 4-6 shows the differences in coverage and composition for magazines that might be used to reach this dieting target audience. The indices quantify the target audience selectivity of each magazine.

EXHIBIT 4-6

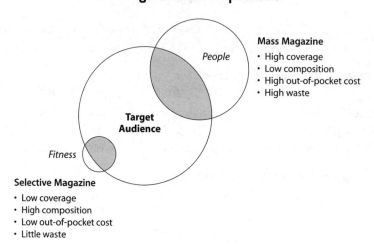

Coverage Versus Composition

People

Mass Magazine
• High coverage
• Low composition
• High out-of-pocket cost
• High waste

Target Audience

Fitness

Selective Magazine
• Low coverage
• High composition
• Low out-of-pocket cost
• Little waste

Planners must be careful to avoid either extreme. This balance between coverage and composition is a key trade-off in all media, especially in view of today's heavily fragmented environment. Using only high-coverage mass magazines, prime-time television programs, or website portals will certainly reach the target, but a significant part of the budget will be wasted on people who have little or no interest in the advertised product. On the other hand, using only high-composition magazines, selective cable networks, and niche websites runs the risk of missing people who buy product but who do not happen to be attracted to the highly selective media vehicles. Planners typically use a mixture of high-coverage and high-composition media to ensure adequate reach while minimizing waste.

Local Television and Radio Coverage For local radio and television, coverage means the number (or percentage) of homes that can physically receive a usable television or radio signal over the air. This technical definition applies primarily to radio stations and to the 10 percent of homes that do not subscribe to cable or satellite. Furthermore, the coverage area of television stations was defined using the old analog signal that could provide an acceptable, if snowy, picture to fringe areas. Since the June 2009 conversion to digital television, over-the-air reception is all or nothing, changing the size of the area where a station provides acceptable service.

Although the signal strength contour is important for the licensing of broadcast stations, for media planning purposes the coverage area of stations in a given market is defined by viewing patterns, not engineering signal coverage.

Spot Radio and Television Coverage in Multiple Markets An advertiser who buys spot announcements in a number of markets located in various geographic regions of the United States will be interested to know what percentage of all television (or radio) homes in the country the commercial could potentially reach. Perhaps a planner has selected 50 of the largest markets in the country in which to advertise. To determine the percentage of coverage, it is only necessary to add the percent of the United States represented by each of the 50 markets. Exhibit 4-7 lists the percentage coverages for the largest U.S. markets.

For example, by buying spot announcements in the largest 50 markets, planners can potentially reach 67.8 percent of the television homes in the country. The planner then knows that the maximum audience size (expressed in terms of homes that can tune in to a station's signal) is no larger than 67.8 percent.

EXHIBIT 4-7

Coverage of Top U.S. Markets Using Spot TV

MARKETS	U.S. COVERAGE
Top 10	29.4%
Top 20	43.8
Top 30	53.4
Top 40	61.7
Top 50	67.8
Top 60	72.8
Top 70	77.0
Top 80	80.6
Top 90	83.8
Top 100	86.6

Source: The Nielsen Company, *U.S. TV Household Estimates*, September 2008. Used with permission.

Network Television Coverage In network television, coverage is defined as the number and percentage of all U.S. television households that are able to receive a given program. Generally speaking, the degree of coverage is affected by the number of stations in a network lineup. The more stations, the more coverage. Exhibit 4-8 indicates the coverage of several network programs. Although these statistics are of interest to the television networks, which want to see their programs carried on as many stations as possible, buyers and planners are typically not concerned with such data, because coverage is automatically accounted for in a program's rating.

EXHIBIT 4-8

Network Program Coverage

NETWORK	PROGRAM	HOUSEHOLD COVERAGE	NUMBER OF STATIONS IN NETWORK LINEUP
ABC	"20/20"	98%	381
NBC	"30 Rock"	98	379
CBS	"Old Christine"	98	389
FOX	"24"	98	373
Univision (Hispanic)	"Sabado Gigante"	80	93
MNT	"Jail"	87	250

Source: The Nielsen Company, *NTI Pocketpiece*, May 18–24, 2009. Used with permission.

Cable Television Coverage Cable coverage is defined as the percent of U.S. households that can receive a cable network by any means, including cable, large satellite dish, direct broadcast satellite, microwave, or other distribution methods.

Unlike network television signals, which are carried by broadcast stations that can reach all television households, individual cable networks must secure clearance on thousands of local systems. Although some can offer hundreds of channels, others are limited to only a few dozen, resulting in strong competition to secure clearance. Large, established channels, such as ESPN, CNN, and USA Network, are carried by virtually all cable systems (and so report near 90 percent coverage of U.S. television households), but newer channels must fight for every household—many cover less than 25 percent of the United States.

Because cable channels must compete with the broadcast networks for advertising dollars, they prefer to report their ratings as a percent of the households in their coverage area, instead of the total U.S. For example, a cable channel that can be seen in 20 million homes may have a program that is seen in 500,000 households. This is only 0.4 percent of the 114.9 million U.S. TV households. It makes a stronger sales story to say that the program has a 2.5 percent rating in its coverage area (to the base of the 20 million coverage area households).

Internet Coverage By 2009, more than 86 percent of all adults had access to the Internet at home or at work, and 73 percent go online in the average month.[9] Like cable networks, Internet websites prefer to express their audience as a percent of these active Internet users, rather than of the larger total U.S. population. Internet websites also promote their coverage in terms of the number of unique visitors per month. This can be a useful relative statistic, but it is meaningless to planners who buy a fixed number of impressions that represent only a small fraction of what is available on the site. Planners must be careful not to apply the assumptions of traditional mass media where advertising impressions equal the media audience, to the Internet where advertising impressions are determined by how many the planner wants to buy.

Out-of-Home Media Coverage Out-of-home media include all media that are located outside a person's home, such as billboards, posters in shopping malls, advertisements in and on buses, and so forth. Coverage for out-of-home media is the percentage of the population that passes one or more out-of-home media in a given period of time. Coverage for out-of-home media, therefore, represents the potential for advertising exposure.

Out-of-home media are generally purchased by advertisers on the basis of *daily showing,* or *gross rating points (GRP).* A gross rating point is a measure of the total (duplicated) number of people delivered by an advertising vehicle or vehicles. Suppose a market has 200 different billboards erected in and around the city, each of which is passed by an average of 1,000 cars each day, which is the *daily effective circulation (DEC).* If an advertiser purchases 50 of these billboards, a total of 50,000 cars will pass one or more of these boards each day (50 multiplied by 1,000). If the market has a population of 100,000, then these 50 boards would constitute 50 GRPs/day, or a 50 showing. We call the data "gross" or "duplicated" because a car that passes 2 of the 50 boards will be counted twice. Other showing sizes can also be purchased, such as a 100 showing (comprising twice as many exposures as in a 50 showing), a 25 showing (half as many exposures), and so on. They can also be expressed as 100, 50, and 25 GRPs/day.

Since DEC is based on the number of cars passing the boards, the outdoor companies have never been able to clearly define these GRPs in terms of a demographic

9. Mediamark Research & Intelligence, LLC, Spring 2009.

target or with the kind of precision that planners are accustomed to receiving from other media. The TAB's new Eyes On research is intended solve this problem by providing daily target audience impressions, GRPs, reach, and frequency. It will take time to convert the outdoor industry, both buyers and sellers, to this new metric, from a start in 2009. Visit www.eyesonratings.com to get the latest information about this new way of measuring the outdoor audience.

An outdoor medium is able to generate very high coverage, and therefore high reach, over time. Exhibit 4-9 shows an estimate of accumulated reach over a 30-day period for different sizes of outdoor showings using the traditional DEC methodology.

EXHIBIT 4-9

Reach of Outdoor Showings

100 SHOWING		50 SHOWING		25 SHOWING	
REACH	FREQUENCY	REACH	FREQUENCY	REACH	FREQUENCY
91.5%	27.9	90.6%	14.3	87.4%	7.7

Source: Simmons Market Research Bureau, 1991. Used with permission.

Households Using Television (HUT)

One important television measurement is *households using television (HUT)*. This can also be expressed as *persons using television (PUT)*. HUT/PUT represents the total percentage of homes or people in a market that are watching television at a given point in time. Because it includes a time consideration, HUT/PUT can be classified as a measurement of net potential audience size.

Remember that coverage data in television represent only audience potential. If a station covers (i.e., is watched in) 1,410,000 TV homes, this does not mean an advertiser will reach all of those homes with a commercial on that station. But what determines how many homes will be reached? To a great extent, the HUT at any time of day provides a clue to the possible tune-in. As a measure of the net potential audience, HUT indicates what percentage of households with a television set have it turned on at any given time of day, such as morning, early afternoon, late afternoon, prime time, or late evening.

Television viewing is affected by living habits. In the morning, tune-in tends to be low, with many men and women at work and children in school. Primary viewers are stay-at-home parents and small children. When children return home from school at about 4:00 P.M., the tune-ins rise dramatically. After 6:00 P.M., when many people have returned home from work, the rise in tune-ins is even greater. After 10:00 P.M., viewing drops again. Exhibit 4-10 indicates the variations in viewing for different time periods, as well as by seasons of the year.

Media planners can study HUT data and estimate potential audience size better than by studying coverage figures alone. In the evening hours, more viewers are available than at any other time of day, because both children and adults are usually at home. But variations in viewing occur not only during a single day, but also during a given week and month. During the summer, for example, when people spend more time outdoors, television viewing is lower in early fringe (4–6 P.M.) and prime time than it is in winter. Despite these variations, television is still able to reach well more than 90 percent of the population each week in summer because viewing of the other dayparts is relatively constant over the year. As we will see, the cost of advertising varies from daypart to daypart, with prime time being the most expensive. Most television plans include a mixture of dayparts, washing out

EXHIBIT 4-10

Variations in TV Viewing by Daypart and Season

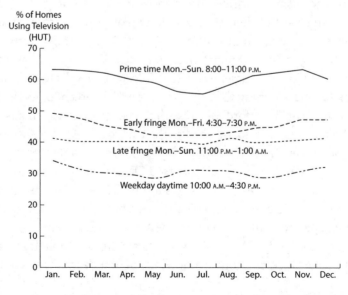

Source: The Nielsen Company, *Households Using TV Summary Report*, 2nd Qtr., 2009. Used with permission.

the differences among them. Many schedules on cable television are bought "run of station" (ROS), meaning the spots rotate through all the dayparts.

Broadcast Impressions and Ratings

These key concepts begin with the *impression*: a single person watching television, listening to the radio, or otherwise exposed to the medium during the average minute or quarter hour of the program. So if one million people were watching a program that carries our commercial, the program (and presumably our commercial) would have delivered one million impressions. Since millions are hard to work with, a more useful way of handling them is to divide the impressions by the population. The result is a rating.

A *broadcast rating* (television or radio) represents an estimate of the percent of people who view a program or have tuned in during a specific time period. This rating is determined through sampling procedures. It is financially and physically impossible to measure the viewing habits of every person in the United States, but it is possible to measure a small sample of viewers. This information, however, is only an estimate of the size of the actual viewing audience.

These estimates are reported in the form of percentages of the demographic universe being considered. For households tuned in to a network television program, the base figure usually includes all households in the United States that have at least one television set. The geographic area for local television stations is based on the time residents spend watching stations of a given market, or DMA.

Nielsen research shows which city (and which TV stations) the residents of each county spend most of their time watching. For example, this research shows that the residents of Cook County, Illinois, spend 51 percent of their weekly viewing hours watching stations that are licensed to the Chicago television market.[10] Accordingly, Cook County is assigned to the Chicago DMA. DeKalb County spends 43 percent of its time watching Chicago stations and 5 percent of its time watching stations in neighboring Rockford. Because the majority of its viewing is to Chicago stations, DeKalb County is also assigned to the Chicago DMA. Boone County, however, spends 36 percent of its time watching Rockford but only 6 percent watching Chicago. Thus, it is assigned to the Rockford DMA. Nielsen uses this procedure to assign every county in the United States to one DMA or another. Each of these counties spends 40 to 50 percent of their time watching the national cable television stations, which does not figure into their DMA assignment. Exhibit 4-11 shows the counties of the Chicago DMA bounded by a heavy line. Although fringe counties may shift from one DMA to another following Nielsen's annual review, the general

---

10. The Nielsen Company, 2008 County Coverage Study.

outlines of each market are relatively constant. The counties in the Chicago DMA have not changed from 2001 when the last edition of this book was written.

Ratings are made for both households and individuals. The universe for network, cable, and syndicated programs consists of all persons of a given age group living in national television households. For example, for women ages 18–49, the broadcast network program base would be all women ages 18–49 in television households in the United States. A rating for women ages 18–49 in the Chicago DMA would be based on the women of that age group who live in any of the counties that make up the Chicago DMA.

Local television and radio ratings are expressed as the percent of the DMA's population who are watching or listening to the average quarter-hour of a program or daypart. This is different from the national audience that is expressed as the audience to the average minute. Television ratings reflect the percent of people in the DMA who are tuned in; radio ratings reflect the percentage of the people in the MSA—essentially the largest counties in the market. Exhibit 4-11 identifies the counties in the DMA and the Radio Metro Area (RMA).

Rather than talk about a rating of 5 percent, it is common practice to talk about a program having a 5 rating. This custom assumes the understanding that a rating is a percentage. Because the audience is so fragmented, the rating of most cable net-

---

EXHIBIT 4-11

Counties of the Chicago DMA

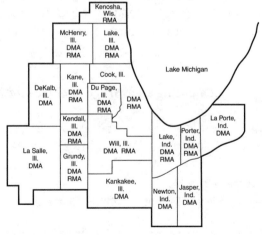

TV DMA—16 counties
Radio Metro Area (RMA)—11 counties

Source: The Chicago DMA Television Market. Copyright: The Nielsen Company, 2009.

works is less than 1.0, and very frequently, less than 0.5 percent—less than one-half of 1 percent of the target population.

Average Audience Rating For national broadcasts on network, cable, and syndicated programs, The Nielsen Company provides an *average audience rating*, which represents the percentage of homes (and people) tuned in to the average minute of a program.

To learn how many households (or people) have tuned in to a program, one need only multiply the rating by the total number of TV households in the United States. This is called a *projection*. For example, if a program had a 3.0 average audience (AA) rating, and the total number of households in the United States was 114,900,000, then 114,900,00 × 0.03 = 3,447,000 households tuned in. A commercial on that program would develop 3,447,000 impressions, typically expressed as 3.4 million impressions. Exhibit 4-12 illustrates the method by which the average audience rating is calculated for a 15-minute segment of a program. On a local market level, the base would be relatively smaller, but the procedure for projection would be the same. Also, local demographic ratings are expressed in terms of *average quarter-hour audience* because of limitations in the diary where viewing is recorded.

The average minute audience reported for national television is referred to as the *program audience* because it is the average of all the minutes in a program—those with entertainment and those that have advertising.

The Three-Day Commercial Audience (C3) Rating In February 2010, household penetration of the DVR was 37 percent and was still growing at a rate of about 1 percent per month.[11] Recording is heavily concentrated in the high-rated scripted prime-

---

EXHIBIT 4-12

Computing an Average Audience Rating

MINUTES IN A PROGRAM	1	2	3	4	5	6	7	8	9	10	11	12	13	14	15
Percentage tuned in	30	30	30	31	31	31	31	32	32	32	33	33	33	33	33

Total tuned in for 15 minutes = 475

Average percentage tune-in for 15 minutes = 475 ÷ 15 = 31.7

---

11. The Nielsen Company, Npower.

time programs such as "Desperate Housewives," "30 Rock," "The Office," "Lost," and others. Daytime soap operas and late fringe entertainment are also heavily recorded. Conversely, there is virtually no recording of live sports events, news, and most cable network programs.

Numerous studies have shown that more than 70 percent of the viewers watching a prerecorded program on their DVR fast-forward through commercials, yielding a much smaller audience to the commercials than to the average minute of the entire program. Other research showed that 85 percent of the recorded programs were played back within three days of the original telecast. This includes a substantial amount of viewing within an hour of the telecast, caused by viewers starting to play back a program half an hour after it starts, and then fast-forwarding through the commercials—the so-called near-live phenomenon. Exhibit 4-13 shows the dramatic effect that this fast-forwarding during the commercials has on the minute-by-minute audience.

The program in Exhibit 4-13 was watched by 1.98 percent of adults ages 18–34 who live in a household with a DVR during the average minute of the program, including any playback within three days of the telecast. But the normal-speed audience to the average commercial minute was only 1.53.[12] Some advertisers want an even more precise measure—the number of viewers to their particular 30-second

---

EXHIBIT 4-13

C3 Ratings Versus Live+3 Program Rating

1.53% of A18–34 in DVR households watched the average commercial minute.

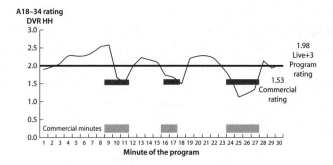

Source: The Nielsen Company, Npower. Used with permission.

---

12. The Nielsen Company, Npower.

commercial—not just the average commercial minute. While such a precise measure is technically possible, for all practical purposes the C3 rating has become the industry standard for national television.

Advertisers demanded to pay only for viewers during the commercial minutes that were being played back at normal speed within three days of the original telecast. This led to the C3 rating, which has become the standard metric for national television ratings. The audience to each minute of the telecast is multiplied by the percent of seconds devoted to commercials that are played back at normal speed. This commercial audience for each minute is totaled and divided by 60 to get the number of viewers to the average commercial minute. Exhibit 4-14 shows how the C3 rating is calculated.

Exhibit 4-15 shows the effect of DVR recording. It compares the live audience (average of all minutes in the program, including entertainment) with the total audience (live + DVR playback) on the same day (a few minutes delay), after one day (live+1), after two days (live+2), after three days (live+3), after seven days (Live+7), and with the audience after three days to just the minutes with a commercial played at normal speed (the C3 rating). This not only illustrates the dramatic effect of DVR playback, but also shows how the C3 rating compensates for fast-forwarding through the commercial and so is an accurate measure of how many people will be effectively exposed to the advertising.

Spot television ratings, even in LPM markets, remain tied to the average quarter-hour audience, including all playback up to seven days after telecast. This greatly inflates the audience to the commercial minutes, but as of this writing, that is how the audience is reported. Since local news is the most important program to the stations and there is virtually no DVR recording of the news, the effect of this overstatement is probably minimal.

Share of Audience *Share of audience* reflects the percentage of homes tuned in to a program based on only those homes that had their sets turned on. This is used as a measure of program popularity that is not affected by the seasonal changes in HUT we saw earlier. The sum of the shares is 100 percent, just like the total of all the slices of a pie. The relationship between rating, HUT, and share is expressed by the following simple equations:

$$\text{Rating} = \text{HUT} \times \text{Share}$$

$$\text{Share} = \frac{\text{Rating}}{\text{HUT}}$$

$$\text{HUT} = \frac{\text{Rating}}{\text{Share}}$$

EXHIBIT 4-14

How the C3 Commercial Audience Is Calculated

The commercial audience is the audience to each minute multiplied by the percent of seconds that have a commercial.

MINUTES OF PROGRAM	A18–34 RATING IN DVR HH	A18–34 AUDIENCE IN DVR HH	COMMERCIAL AUDIENCE		
			COMMERCIAL SECONDS IN EACH MINUTE	(000) × COMMERCIAL SECOND / 60	CALCULATION DETAIL
1	1.91	317,632	0	—	
2	1.97	327,519	0	—	
3	2.06	342,799	0	—	
4	2.29	380,888	0	—	
5	2.28	378,117	0	—	
6	2.28	378,925	0	—	
7	2.37	394,100	0	—	
8	2.54	420,940	0	—	
9	2.58	428,556	16	114,282	428,556 × 16/60 = 114,282
10	1.68	279,330	60	279,330	
11	1.52	251,650	44	184,543	
12	2.00	332,158	0	—	
13	2.23	369,650	0	—	
14	2.17	359,542	0	—	
15	2.11	350,071	0	—	
16	1.74	289,401	47	226,698	
17	1.67	276,967	43	198,493	
18	1.50	248,224	0	—	
19	2.21	366,082	0	—	
20	2.27	377,273	0	—	
21	2.28	378,208	0	—	
22	2.20	364,631	0	—	
23	1.96	325,244	0	—	
24	1.66	274,781	26	119,072	
25	1.12	185,882	60	185,882	
26	1.22	201,952	60	201,952	
27	1.36	225,510	4	15,034	
28	2.14	355,683	0	—	
29	1.94	321,645	0	—	
30	2.04	338,194	0	—	
	1.98 Program Rating		360 sec	1,525,286/6 minutes = 254,214 viewers to average commercial minute	
			6 minutes	254,214 / 16,602,000 (A18-34 in DVR HH population) = 1.53 commercial rating	

Source: The Nielsen Company, Npower. Used with permission.

EXHIBIT 4-15

Comparison of Program and C3 Ratings

ADULTS 18–34 AVERAGE MINUTE RATING

PROGRAM	PROGRAM LIVE	PROGRAM LIVE + SAME DAY	PROGRAM LIVE + 1	PROGRAM LIVE + 2	PROGRAM LIVE + 3	PROGRAM LIVE + 7	COMMERCIAL LIVE + 3
Total A18–34							
"Desperate Housewives"	3.2	4.1	4.6	4.8	4.9	5.1	3.8
"Scrubs"	2.0	2.5	2.7	2.8	2.9	2.9	2.1
"24"	2.7	3.4	3.7	3.8	3.8	4.0	2.9
"Grey's Anatomy"	4.3	5.3	5.8	6.1	6.3	6.6	4.8
Adults 18–34 in DVR Households							
"Desperate Housewives"	3.4	6.3	7.8	8.5	8.8	9.3	5.8
"Scrubs"	1.5	2.9	3.8	4.0	4.1	4.3	2.3
"24"	2.4	4.8	5.7	5.9	5.9	6.5	3.6
"Grey's Anatomy"	4.2	7.2	8.8	9.7	10.7	11.5	6.2

Source: The Nielsen Company, NPower, week of Jan. 12, 2009. Used with permission.

The relationship among these three is illustrated in Exhibit 4-16. It shows that in 40 percent of the homes, the TV set was not turned on—the people were not at home, they were reading a book, or they were doing something else with their life besides watching television. Conversely, 60 percent of the homes were using television. The viewers were divided among the various broadcast stations and cable networks, with each program getting its share of the pie. The sum of all the shares is 100 percent; the sum of the ratings equals the HUT, or 60 percent. The share statistic enables the media planner to compare the relative popularity of two programs that compete for viewers at the same time of the day. Since the HUT for a given month and daypart is relatively stable year to year, media buyers use the share to calculate the estimated future rating. More about this later when we talk about buying television.

EXHIBIT 4-16

The Relationship Among Rating, HUT, and Share

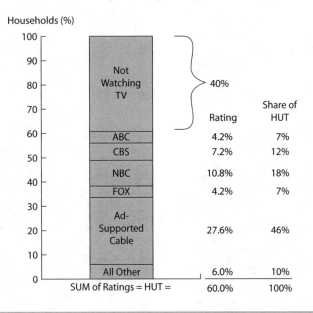

Households (%)

	Rating	Share of HUT
Not Watching TV	40%	
ABC	4.2%	7%
CBS	7.2%	12%
NBC	10.8%	18%
FOX	4.2%	7%
Ad-Supported Cable	27.6%	46%
All Other	6.0%	10%
SUM of Ratings = HUT =	60.0%	100%

Exhibit 4-17 shows sample pages from Nielsen Television Index to illustrate the various kinds of ratings used by media analysts. Note the average audience and share for each program listed. The Pocketpiece has been largely replaced by computer access to the ratings with extensive detail by demographic group. However, the basic information is the same as pictured in Exhibit 4-17.

It is important to remember that although ratings can be reported for households, planners most often use ratings for people viewing programs. Such ratings usually are broken down by various age and gender demographic groups that have been cross-tabulated with other demographics such as household income, head-of-household education, number of children, and so on. These cross-tabulations allow a media planner to have a better understanding of who views each program and thus better match markets with media.

Although ratings, HUT, and share help planners understand broad patterns of television usage, these audience statistics are used most commonly by media buyers

EXHIBIT 4-17

Sample National Nielsen TV Audience Estimates

A-16

NATIONAL *NielsenTV* AUDIENCE ESTIMATES   EVE.SUN. AUG.30, 2009

TIME	7:00	7:15	7:30	7:45	8:00	8:15	8:30	8:45	9:00	9:15	9:30	9:45	10:00	10:15	10:30	10:45	11:00	11:15
HUT	51.5	52.4	53.5	55.3	57.6	58.8	59.9	61.0	62.6	63.1	63.3	62.8	61.6	60.5	58.2	56.5	51.1	47.1

ABC TV — AMER FUNN HOME VIDEOS (R) → — EXTREME MAKEOVER-HM ED-8P (R) → — SHARK TANK → — DEFYING GRAVITY →

HHLD AUDIENCE% & (000): 3.7 / 4,200 ... 3.9* ... 3.5 / 3,990 ... 3.7* ... 3.1 / 3,530 ... 3.1* ... 1.9 / 2,160 ... 1.9* ... 5.4*
T/4% AVG. AUD. 1/2 HR: 5.8 / 3.4* ... 5.5 ... 6.* ... 4.9 ... 3.0* ... 3.1 ... 1.9* ... 1.0*
SHARE AUDIENCE: 3.7 ... 3.6 ... 3.9 ... 5.6 ... 3.3 ... 3.2 ... 4.1 ... 5.* ... 3.4 ... 3.0 ... 2.0 ... 1.7 ... 1.9 ... 4.5
AVG. AUD. BY 1/4 HR: 3.3 ... 4.0 ... 3.2 ... 3.1 ... 3.4

CBS TV — 60 MINUTES (R) → — BIG BROTHER 11-SUN → — THERE GOES NEIGHBORHOOD → — COLD CASE (R) →

HHLD AUDIENCE% & (000): 6.5 / 7,430 ... 6.7* ... 4.7 / 5,410 ... 5.0* ... 2.3 / 2,630 ... 2.4* ... 3.8 / 4,380 ... 3.5* ... 4.2*
T/4% AVG. AUD. 1/2 HR: 10.2 / 6.3* ... 12* ... 6.6 ... 5.* ... 3.6 ... 2.4* ... 5.6 ... 3.6* ... 1.9*
SHARE AUDIENCE: 12 ... 6.8 ... 5.4 ... 4.7 ... 2.5 ... 2.3 ... 3.2 ... 3.8 ... 4.0 ... 4.3
AVG. AUD. BY 1/4 HR: 6.0 ... 2.1

NBC TV — DATELINE SUN-7PM → — SIMPSONS (7:59-8:30)(R)(PAE) — SIMPSONS-SUN 8:30P — NBC NFL PRE-SEASON 8:30 CHICAGO AT DENVER (8:30-11:18)(PAE) →

HHLD AUDIENCE% & (000): 3.1 / 3,500 ... 3.0* ... 6.5 / 7,460 ... 6.0* ... 7.0* ... 7.5 ... 7.2* ... 6.3* ... 5.8*
T/4% AVG. AUD. 1/2 HR: 5.6 / 3.1* ... 5.* ... 17.7* ... 1.1* ... 1.2* ... 1.2* ... 1.0* ... 1.0*
SHARE AUDIENCE: 3.3 ... 3.0 ... 2.8 ... 5.7 ... 6.4 ... 6.9 ... 7.0 ... 7.6 ... 8.0 ... 6.3 ... 5.4 ... 6.2 ... 6.0 ... 5.7 ... 4.5

FOX TV (1) — AMERICAN DAD-SUN7:30P (7:29-7:59)(R)(PAE) — FAMILY GUY (9:00-9:31)(R) — AMERICAN DAD (9:31-10:00)(R)(PAE)

HHLD AUDIENCE% & (000): 1.3 / 1,660 ... 1.4 / 1,660 ... 2.5 / 2,910 ... 2.8 / 3,250 ... 2.9 / 3,350 ... 2.5 / 2,880
T/4% AVG. AUD. 1/2 HR: 1.6 / 2.0* ... 3.3 ... 3.6 ... 3.8 ... 3.2
SHARE AUDIENCE: 1.4 ... 1.2 ... 1.7 ... 2.5 ... 2.6 ... 2.8 ... 2.9 ... 3.0 ... 2.5 ... 2.6
AVG. AUD. BY 1/4 HR: 1.3

CW TV — LIVE FROM THE RED CARPET → — 36TH ANNUAL DAYTIME EMMY →

HHLD AUDIENCE% & (000): 0.9 / 1,030 ... 1.0* ... 2.0 / 2,310 ... 1.9* ... 2.0* ... 2.1* ... 2.1*
T/4% AVG. AUD. 1/2 HR: 1.6 / 0.8* ... 2* ... 4.8 ... 1.1* ... 3* ... 3* ... 3*
SHARE AUDIENCE: 0.8 ... 1.0 ... 1.8 ... 1.9 ... 2.0 ... 2.0 ... 2.1 ... 2.0

UNI TV — HISTORIAS PARA CONTAR8:00 — VIVA EL SUENO-SUN (8:00-10:05)(PAE) — QUIEN TIENE RAZON? EE- SUN (10:05-11:00)(PAE) —

HHLD AUDIENCE% & (000): 0.7 / 850 ... 0.8* ... 1.2 / 1,400 ... 1.2* ... 1.3* ... 1.3* ... 1.3 / 1,220 ... 1.6* ... 1.1*
T/4% AVG. AUD. 1/2 HR: 1.4 / 0.1* ... 1* ... 2.4 ... 1.2* ... 2* ... 2* ... 1.6* ... 1.2* ... 1.1*
SHARE AUDIENCE: 0.7 ... 0.9 ... 1.0 ... 1.1 ... 1.2 ... 1.3 ... 1.4 ... 1.3 ... 1.1 ... 1.1

ION TV — SUNDAY 7PM MOVIE THE DEAD POOL → — SUNDAY NIGHT MOVIE THE ENFORCER →

HHLD AUDIENCE% & (000): 0.5 / 550 ... 0.4* ... 0.5* ... 0.6* ... 0.7 / 770 ... 0.6* ... 0.6* ... 0.6*
T/4% AVG. AUD. 1/2 HR: 1.2 / 0.3* ... 1* ... 1* ... 1* ... 1.4 / 7* ... 1* ... 1* ... 1*
SHARE AUDIENCE: 0.3 ... 0.4 ... 0.5 ... 0.6 ... 0.7 ... 0.8 ... 0.7 ... 0.6
AVG. AUD. BY 1/4 HR: 0.3 ... 0.4

PRIMER IMPACTO EXTRA-SUN: 0.3 / 390, 0.5*, 0.3, 0.4

For explanation of symbols, See page B.

Estimates include Live-7

U.S. TV Households: 114,500,000
(1) TIL DEATH-SUN 7P FOX(7:00-7:29)(R)(PAE)

Source: The Nielsen Company, Pocketpiece, August 24–30, 2009. Used with permission.

who must decide on which specific program to place the ads. In this context, the ratings provide a critical measure of the media value received for the cost of the ad. In essence, ratings are the "currency" of broadcast negotiation and buying worth more than $60 billion per year. To ensure the quality of these estimates, the survey methodology and execution are closely scrutinized by an independent industry organization, the Media Rating Council (www.mediaratingcouncil.org), which reports its findings to the users.

CHAPTER FIVE

Advanced Measurements and Calculations

The preceding chapter introduced the concept of audience accumulation, along with other measurements of a single telecast or print insertion. But broadcast commercials and print ads are repeated many times to develop sufficient weight to achieve the advertiser's marketing goals. This chapter introduces the more advanced numerical tools used to manage this weight and develop media plans: gross rating points (GRPs), gross impressions, reach, frequency, and effective frequency. These tools answer the most commonly asked questions about a media plan, such as the following:

- How many people will see the ad? (Reach)
- How often will they see it? (Frequency)
- How many people will see it at least three times? Four times? N times? (Effective reach)

Reach and frequency are parts of strategy planning and to an extent can be manipulated to help attain certain marketing and media objectives. Generally, when the advertiser needs broad message dispersion, high levels of reach will be planned. To achieve a great deal of repetition, the plan will call for high frequency or effective frequency levels. Sometimes a plan will have to attain both high reach and high frequency.

GRPs

Recall from Chapter 4 that when planners want to know the audience size for a single TV program, they use either a program rating or a calculation of the number of viewers exposed to the program. For a single ad in a magazine, they use either a target audience measurement in thousands or a percentage that represents coverage of the market. Internet planners want to know how many different people will be exposed to a banner or pop-up ad that is presented after a given number of impressions on a certain website. Planners typically speak in terms of the weekly or even the total campaign weight across all the media vehicles they use. To do that, they simply add ratings or audience size numbers from each time the commercial is broadcast and disregard the duplication that results. *GRPs* are the simple addition of ratings each time the commercial is shown. The sum of audience sizes, generally reported in thousands, is called *gross impressions*. Both numbers are duplicated—that is, they are sums of measurements that can overlap.

Using GRPs or gross impressions allows the planner to use a single number that describes the quantity of message weight. *Message weight* is a number that quickly tells the planner the duplicated audience for many programs within a given time period. Planners often deal with the number of GRPs per week or per month. But one also can discuss the message weight of an entire year, using either GRPs or gross impressions. The user of these numbers, however, must always remember that they represent duplicated audiences.

When using GRPs, it is important to specify the demographic group that they apply to. Without that qualifier, it is like saying you went to the store and bought 10 pounds. It is far more meaningful to say you bought 10 pounds of potatoes. So when referring to GRPs, the planner would say 100 women 25–54 GRPs, 125 men 18–49 GRPs. Fast-food advertisers typically run more than 200 adult 18–34 GRPs per week.

Some planners use GRPs when they refer to household rating points and use target rating points (TRPs) when referring to demographic points. Both terms are correct, but whichever is used must include the applicable demographic base to be meaningful.

GRPs in Broadcast Media

In planning for television, GRPs are often used to describe the message weight delivered each week or month, although they could be used for any number of weeks or months. Following is an example of commercials that constituted 120 adult 18–34 GRPs a week:

4 commercials in a program with a 5 A18–34 rating	=	20 A18–34 TRPs
15 commercials in a program with a 2 A18–34 rating	=	30 A18–34 TRPs
20 commercials in a program with a 1.5 A18–34 rating	=	30 A18–34 TRPs
40 commercials on a cable network with a 1.0 A18–34 rating	=	40 A18–34 TRPs
Total weekly weight	=	120 A18–34 TRPs

These are percentages, so when adding GRPs, they must always refer to the same demographic. Five percent of adults 18–34 plus 5 percent of women 35–64 isn't 10 percent of anything.

GRPs in Other Media

In recent years, planners have extended the GRP concept to other media such as magazines, newspapers, and outdoor. In magazines, for example, GRPs equal the percentage of market coverage of a target audience times the number of ad insertions, as in the following example:

People magazine's coverage of target dieters: 22.8 percent
Number of ads to be placed in *People*: 5
Dieter GRPs (22.8 × 5): 114.0

Another way to use GRPs for magazines (or newspapers) is to add the target coverage for one insertion in a number of different magazines.

One last way to calculate GRPs is to multiply reach times frequency for a given time period. For example, a schedule that reaches 60 percent of the target an average of five times will have 300 GRPs (60 × 5).

For outdoor, the Outdoor Advertising Association of America (www.oaaa.org) adopted the "showing" as the basic unit of sale. It reflects daily GRPs, so a *100* showing delivers 100 GRPs per day and is the number of poster panels required in each market to produce a "daily effective circulation" equal to its population. Other units of sale are expressed as fractions of the basic unit: a 75 showing equals 75 GRPs daily, a 50 showing is 50 GRPs daily, and so on. This change in no way alters the 30-day period of sale and measurement. The new Eyes On measure of outdoor advertising promises to change the unit of sale to demographic GRPs.

Gross Impressions

Gross impressions is the same concept as GRPs, with the exception that the audience is expressed in terms of thousands of viewers instead of as a percent of the population. So gross impressions is the simple addition of the viewing audience in thousands each time the commercial is shown. Assuming we are talking about a national schedule, the previous example for 120 A18–34 GRPs would look like this. Note that the adult 18–34 population is 68.1 million.

Note the calculation. For 20 TRPs, 0.2×68.1 million = 13.62 million impressions:

4 telecasts in a program with a 5 A18–34 rating	= 20 TRPs =	13.62 MM Impr
15 telecasts in a program with a 2 A18–34 rating	= 30 TRPs =	20.43
20 telecasts in a program with a 1.5 A18–34 rating	= 30 TRPs =	20.43
40 telecasts on a cable network with a 1 A18–34 rating =	40 TRPs =	27.24
Total weekly A18–34 weight	= 120 TRPs =	81.72

There are two methods of calculating gross impressions. One method is to multiply GRPs by the target audience base. The other is to add the target audience impressions delivered by each vehicle.

The same math applies to each of the programs. So, again using this example, each telecast of the program with a 5 adult 18–34 rating is watched by 3.405 million viewers ($0.05 \times 68.1 = 3.405$). So four telecasts multiplied by a 5 rating equals 20 TRPS, which equals 13.62 million impressions (4×3.405).

In short, GRPs or gross impressions are the simple addition of the ratings or impressions each time the ad appears. Because they do not account for duplication, GRPs can, and frequently do, exceed 100. Heavy campaigns for movies and political campaigns often run much higher than 500 GRPs per week. The rating each time the commercial appears is added to the total points for the week.

The concept of GRPs is central to media planning because it is the basis for determining the cost of a broadcast campaign. In this example, if a planner wishes to run 120 A18–34 GRPs per week, and if the cost is $2,000 per GRP, the campaign will cost the advertiser $240,000 per week ($120 \times \$2,000$). This will be discussed in more detail in Chapter 6.

The use of gross impressions for print media is much the same as it is for broadcast. Exhibit 5-1 shows how total gross impressions would be calculated for three magazines with varying numbers of ads to be purchased. The number of impressions delivered by a media plan usually runs into the millions. Because the number is so large, it is called a *boxcar figure*. (This expression is used from time to time

Total Gross Impressions for Three Magazines

MAGAZINE	NUMBER OF TARGETS REACHED AT LEAST ONCE		NUMBER OF ADS TO BE PURCHASED		GROSS IMPRESSIONS
A	5,000,000	×	5	=	25,000,000
B	2,100,000	×	3	=	6,300,000
C	7,000,000	×	2	=	14,000,000
Total gross impressions					45,300,000

to indicate that we are using big, coarse, crude measures of media "tonnage"—numbers so large as to be almost meaningless in human terms but impressive to the unsophisticated—like when politicians talk about "trillions of dollars.") Alone, gross impressions have limited meaning. But if (rarely) they can be related to some measure of campaign effectiveness such as sales volume, brand awareness, or competitive media plan effectiveness, they can be used to compare media.

Gross impressions also are useful in comparing the weight given to geographic areas or demographic segments of a market. For example, if the planner wants to be sure a given media plan reaches a number of different geographic areas in the correct proportions, the gross impressions could be added for each vehicle in the plan, and then the proportions of each could be compared with a weighted goal. Exhibit 5-2 shows an example of how this works. This table indicates that the gross impression distribution of the vehicles selected comes fairly close to the goals set for the plan in terms of percent of impressions by county size. It might not be worth the extra effort to make the gross impression totals come any closer to the stated goals.

There is one more thing to remember: when working with different geographic areas, it is correct to add impressions. So 1 million A18–34 impressions in Los Angeles plus 500,000 A18–34 impressions in San Diego equals 1.5 million total impressions. Los Angeles's A18–34 population is 4,376,000; San Diego's is 716,100. So the 1 million L.A. impressions equals 22.8 TRPs (1,000,000/4,376,000). The 500,000 San Diego A18–34 impressions equals 70 TRPs (500,000/716,100).

Because these are percentages of different bases, planners cannot add the GRPs. 22.8 percent of Los Angeles plus 70 percent of San Diego isn't 92.8 percent

EXHIBIT 5-2

Distribution of Gross Impressions in Media Plan for Brand X

COUNTY SIZE	VEHICLE 1	VEHICLE 2	GROSS IMPRESSIONS DELIVERED (000) VEHICLE 3	TOTAL	TARGET	GOAL FOR PLAN
A	308,582	246,972	471,342	1,026,896	47.0%	51.0%
B	276,980	151,370	153,981	582,331	26.7	24.1
C	187,752	72,764	78,796	339,312	15.5	17.3
D	156,150	60,016	18,796	234,962	10.8	7.6
TOTAL				2,183,501	100.0%	100.0%

of anything. The correct method is to add the impressions and then divide by the sum of the populations (4,376,000 + 716,100 = 5,092,100). Then 1.5 million/5,092.1 million = 29.5 combined market A18–34 TRPs.

Reach

Reach is a measurement of audience accumulation. Reach tells planners how many different prospects will see the ad at least once over any period of time the planner finds relevant. Reach is usually expressed as a percentage of a universe with whom a planner is trying to communicate. If the universe is women ages 18–49, then all women ages 18–49 represent the universe.

Note also that reach differs from GRPs because it is an unduplicated number: each person is counted only once. To understand the difference between GRPs and reach, consider that a popular weekly television program might have an A25–34 rating of 4.5. That is, the average minute of the program is watched by 4.5 percent of adults ages 25–34. An advertiser who buys one spot on this program each week over a four-week period delivers 18 A25–34 GRPs (4.5 × 4 = 18). But the GRP statistic double-counts people who see the commercial several times. Reach takes out duplication to tell the planner how many *different* people will see the commercial at least once. A special analysis on Nielsen computers could tell us these commercials have a four-week reach of 12 percent (or 12). Reach, as a percent of the target, can never exceed 100 percent, while GRPs can continue building without limit.

Why Audience Is Counted Only Once

The reason audience members are counted only once in a reach measurement lies in the history of media research. When early planners were trying to decide which kind of measurement to use to count the size of a vehicle's audience, some believed an audience member would have to be exposed several times to an ad before it would have any effect. Other planners disagreed, saying it could not be known how many exposures would be required. Planners decided to compromise and count one exposure to a vehicle as evidence of reach, because whether or not the ad was seen, there was a significant difference between being exposed and not being exposed. To be exposed at least once means that audiences then had an opportunity to see ads within the vehicle. There obviously would be no opportunity to see ads if there were no exposure.

Another historical reason for the development of reach concerned the invention of a statistic for radio and television that would parallel the audience reach of a monthly magazine. Planners realized it would be unfair to compare a one-week broadcast rating with the reach of a monthly issue of a magazine. Obviously, the magazine reach would be higher, but by using a four-week reach for broadcast media, the planner now had a statistic that was fairly comparable to that of a monthly magazine in terms of audience size.

Exhibit 5-3 illustrates the measurement of reach using a sample of 10 persons. The sample size for measuring reach is actually much larger, but using 10 simplifies the concept. Four weeks is the usual measuring period, but reach can be measured for almost any period of time. Four weeks happens to have become a standard measuring unit, easily conforming to a monthly accounting period.

Exhibit 5-3 is interpreted this way: Viewers 3, 5, 8, and 9 saw the program in week 1, so the one-week rating is 40 percent (4 out of 10). Because viewers are counted only once, the one-week reach is the same as the one-week rating. In week 2, only one new person was added to the audience (Viewer 7), so the second-week rating was 10 and the two-week reach was 50 (or 40 for week 1 and 10 for week 2). In week 3, only one new viewer was added (Viewer 6), so the rating was 10, but the three-week reach was 60. In week 4, again, only one new viewer was added (Viewer 10), and the four-week reach was 70. Note that Viewers 3, 5, 6, and 9 viewed the program more than once in the four-week period but were counted only once for the purpose of calculating reach. Also note that the one-week rating is unduplicated, so

EXHIBIT 5-3

A Four-Week Reach Measurement for Program X

VIEWER	WEEK 1	WEEK 2	WEEK 3	WEEK 4
1	—	—	—	—
2	—	—	—	—
3	⊗	×	—	×
4	—	—	—	—
5	⊗	—	×	—
6	—	—	⊗	×
7	—	⊗	×	—
8	⊗	—	—	—
9	⊗	×	—	×
10	—	—	—	⊗
Ratings each week	40	30	30	40

For a weekly evening program: × = Viewed the program;

⊗ = Counted only in reach measurement.

GRPs = 140, reach = 70, frequency = 2.

it would be correct to call that rating the one-week reach, although common practice usually refers to it as a rating.

Kinds of Reach

There are two ways of looking at reach in broadcast planning:

1. The four-week reach of an individual vehicle, such as a television program
2. More commonly, the combined reach of dozens of television programs and cable networks that would be bought in an ad campaign

No matter how reach is defined, the same principle applies, namely, that audience members are counted only once, no matter how many times they see the vehicle within a four-week period. If four television programs are being considered for one campaign package, some audience members will be exposed three or four times to only one television program, and other audience members will be exposed to all four television programs a different number of times. But if they see any one of the four programs at least once, they are counted as having been reached in a four-week period. In either case, the concept of exposure is the same. We don't know whether those exposed to the vehicle saw the ads (or our ads), so we can only say that *reach* means "opportunities to see" ads, not ad exposure.

Suppose, for example, the reach of four programs was 35 million men ages 18–34. If the planner places a commercial in each of the four television programs, it is estimated that 35 million men ages 18–34 will have an opportunity to see at least one of those four vehicles and, the planner hopes, one of the four commercials within the vehicle. The word *hope* is a reminder that reach is concerned only with vehicle exposure, not exposure to a given commercial. The Nielsen NPower program can be used to give the reach to a campaign of specific commercials, but this report is available only after the ads run.

Exhibit 5-4 shows another way how the concepts of GRPs, reach, frequency, and frequency distribution apply to a schedule of four television programs. Six homes viewed one of the four programs at least once in the measured week. A home or person is counted only once, regardless of how many programs were viewed. Therefore, the first home has received two impressions (one from "America's Got Talent" and one from "The Office") but is counted only once toward reach. The second home didn't see any of the telecasts. The third home was exposed once, the fourth home three times, and so on.

At the end of the one-week schedule of four telecasts, 6 of the 10 homes have been reached one or more times. Other terms that are sometimes used to describe the net reach of four television programs are *cumulative audience, audience accumulated by four television programs,* and *net unduplicated audience.* Each term is correct, but in popular usage people are more likely to say, "The reach of these four programs is 60 percent." Note how GRPs and reach increase with each telecast. *Average frequency* (the number of times the average home saw a commercial) is calculated as GRPs divided by reach.

Relationship Between Reach and Coverage

It can be confusing to know whether to use the term *coverage* or *reach* when referring to audience accumulation data. The terms can be interchangeable because *coverage* sometimes is synonymous with *reach.* A better answer is that coverage and reach are quite different, because coverage could mean potential to be exposed to the advertising, and reach refers to those people who actually are exposed.

Popular usage of these terms provides the basic answer. Coverage usually refers to potential audience for broadcast media and to actual delivered audience for print

EXHIBIT 5-4

Reach/Frequency of a TV Schedule

	"HOUSE" 6/22 8:05 P.M.	"AMERICA'S GOT TALENT" 6/23 10:14 P.M.	"THE OFFICE" 6/25 8:23 P.M.	"LAW & ORDER: SVU" 6/28 10:45 P.M.	TOTAL IMPRESSIONS
🏠		✓	✓		2
🏠					0
🏠				✓	1
🏠	✓	✓	✓		3
🏠	✓			✓	2
🏠			✓		1
🏠					0
🏠	✓		✓		2
🏠					0
🏠					0

	"HOUSE"	"AMERICA'S GOT TALENT"	"THE OFFICE"	"LAW & ORDER: SVU"	Freq. distribution
Ratings	30%	20%	40%	20%	Not exposed: 40%
GRPs	30	50	90	110	Exposed once: 20%
Reach	30%	40%	50%	60%	Exposed twice: 30%
Frequency	1.0	1.25	1.8	1.83	Exposed 3+ times: 10%

media. Reach always refers to the audience actually delivered by any advertising vehicle. Exhibit 5-5 summarizes the distinction.

How Reach Builds Over Time

Reach for television programs accumulates, or builds, in a fairly consistent pattern over time as a commercial is broadcast over and over again. The first time a

---

EXHIBIT 5-5

How to Use the Terms *Reach* and *Coverage*

Use *reach* to express a whole number or percentage of different people actually exposed only once to a media vehicle or combination of vehicles.

> **Example:** Television program X reaches 9 million men ages 18–34 within a four-week period.

> **Example:** Magazine Y has a reach of 25 percent of men ages 18–34 with an average issue.

Use *coverage* to express the potential audience of a broadcast medium *or* the actual audience of a print medium exposed only once.

> **Example:** A network television program has a coverage of 95 percent of TV homes in the United States.

> **Example:** Magazine Y has a 25 percent coverage of men ages 18–34. (Means the same as *reach*.)

---

commercial is telecast, it accumulates the largest number of viewers. The second time it is telecast, most of the viewers are repeat viewers, although some new viewers are added. The third and subsequent telecasts accumulate even fewer new viewers. Exhibit 5-6 shows the classic pattern of diminishing returns as a commercial is repeated and GRPs are added across many programs on many broadcast and cable networks.

In this illustration, after 500 GRPs have been delivered, approximately 68 percent of viewers will have seen the commercial at least once. Does reach ever level out over a year? No. The curve is asymptotic to the maximum reach—that is, the curve is never perfectly horizontal, but it comes close after about 2,000 GRPs.

Reach in Print Media

Whereas the telecast of a commercial is the basic advertising unit in broadcast media, in print media the basic unit is an issue of a magazine or newspaper. One does not usually speak of the four-week reach of a magazine, although there are measurements that estimate audience accumulation over time for the average issue of a magazine. Generally speaking, monthly magazines have a longer issue life than

EXHIBIT 5-6

The Relationship Between GRPs and Reach in Prime Time

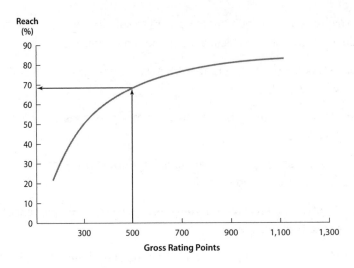

Source: DRAFTFCB, Reach-2007. Used with permission.

weeklies, and general-content magazines have a longer life than news-oriented magazines.

Magazine reach can be expressed in a number of ways:

- The total number of people who read the average issue of a magazine, also called the *average issue audience* of a magazine like *Newsweek*
- Target audience reach of multiple issues of the same magazine (e.g., the reach—or *net unduplicated audience*—of the July 1, July 8, July 15, July 22, and July 29 issues of *Newsweek*)
- Target audience reach of single issues of different magazines within the same month (e.g., the reach—or net unduplicated audience—of the July issues of *Oprah, Real Simple, Cooking Light,* and *Better Homes & Gardens*)
- The reach of single or multiple issues of different magazines occurring throughout the advertising campaign (e.g., the reach of *Popular Mechanics* in June and August, *Field & Stream* in July and August, and *Sport* in June and July)

Because a reach measurement can express many qualities, knowing them all becomes important. Exhibit 5-7 summarizes these qualities.

EXHIBIT 5-7

Meaning of *Reach*, Summarized

Reach is

1. A measurement of audience accumulation over a specified period
2. An unduplicated statistic
3. Measured, although it can sometimes be estimated
4. Measured for a single vehicle or a group of different vehicles
5. Measured for subsequent issues of the same magazine (e.g., the seven-issue reach of *TV Guide* is . . .)
6. Reported for a four-week period of television watching
7. Reported for almost any period in broadcast measurements
8. Reported by the issue in print media
9. Reported either as a raw number or as a percentage of some universe
10. Reported for households or for individuals in a demographic category
11. Another term for coverage in print media
12. Measured on the basis of exposure to a vehicle or vehicles
13. Not routinely measured for exposure to specific ads in vehicles. Possible with custom analysis of TV and print schedules.
14. A measurement that tells how many different people had an opportunity to see ads in vehicles
15. A media strategy that shows dispersion of audiences

Combined Reach of Multiple Media

Planners are frequently asked to show the combined reach of all the media in a plan. For example, if 65 percent of the target was reached by the television commercial, and 54 percent of the target saw the magazine ad at least once, what percent of the target saw either one or the other? In short, what was the total reach of the campaign?

In a sense, this common question asks planners to mix apples and oranges, because each medium is measured differently. The 65 percent reach of the television campaign represents people who actually saw the commercial that week. The magazine reach, on the other hand, represents all the people who ever saw the issue, even if that readership occurred many weeks later from an old copy at the barber shop or doctor's office. Note also that the TV rating is the percent who saw the average minute of the program or the average commercial minute (the C3 rating), while the magazine audience is the percent who read the issue, not necessarily the particular page where the advertiser's ad appeared.

Despite these technical issues, advertisers want to know the net reach of the campaign, and planners are expected to create fruit salad out of these different media elements.

Random Duplication Numerous studies have shown that duplication between different mass media is random. Using the previous example, assume the reach of the TV commercial was 65 percent and the reach of a magazine campaign was 54 percent. Random duplication assumes that if 65 percent of the target saw the TV commercial, then 65 percent of the people who saw the magazine ad also saw the TV. Some saw only the TV commercial, some saw only the magazine ad, and some, the duplicated piece, saw both the TV and the magazine advertising. This last section must be subtracted so we don't count them twice.

The basic equation, sometimes called the Sainsbury model, is:

$$\text{Reach} = a + b - (ab)$$

where a = reach of the first medium (expressed as decimal)

b = reach of the second medium (expressed as a decimal)

Reach = decimal percent of the target exposed to either of the two media

So in this example: Reach = $a + b - (ab)$

Reach = TV + Magazines − (TV × Magazines)
Reach = 0.65 + 0.54 − (0.65 × 0.54)
Reach = 1.19 − 0.351
Reach = 0.839 × 100 = 84%

Even though we carried the math out to three decimal places for the calculation, the final reach should be reported to the client as a whole number (84 percent, not 83.9 percent). This indicates that reach is an estimate and avoids giving the impression of greater precision than is warranted. To get frequency, add the GRPs and divide by the reach. Assume there were 120 TV GRPs and 177 magazine GRPs.

TV GRPS: 120 + Magazine GRPs: 177 = 297 total GRPs
Frequency = GRPs / Reach
Frequency = 297 / 84
Frequency = 3.5

The campaign reached 84 percent of the target audience, and the average person who was reached saw the ad (either the TV commercial or the magazine ad) an average of 3.5 times.

For three or more media, calculate the reach of the two highest-reach media. Then repeat the process, using this calculated reach and the third-highest medium, and so on. This is true for broad media: prime-time television, broad Internet websites, radio across multiple stations. So the net reach of Google and Bing can be calculated with random duplication, while the net reach of SI.com and ESPN.com would involve more than random duplication. If there is 20 percent more duplication, the equation would read:

$$a + b - 1.2(ab)$$

We would subtract 20 percent more than the random *ab* combination. Note that the exact level of duplication has to come from a computer system. There is no way for a planner to estimate nonrandom duplication.

Duplication Between Media Vehicles Planners are frequently asked to provide the duplication between different media vehicles, especially magazines. First it is important to remember that duplication analysis is only possible between two magazines. As Exhibit 5-8 shows, even with three magazines there are seven possible answers; the possible combinations of more than three magazines are mind-boggling.

EXHIBIT 5-8

The Seven Pieces of Three Magazine "Duplication"

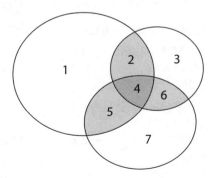

For multiple magazine schedules, planners use conventional software to obtain the net reach—the percent of the target that sees at least one of the vehicles. The magazine names are entered as rows and as columns.

Duplication is frequently calculated for two magazine combinations. But even this can be confusing. Exhibit 5-9 illustrates duplication between *Good Housekeeping* and *Real Simple* magazines for women ages 25–54. Note that 34.4 percent of *Real Simple*'s readers read *Good Housekeeping*, while only 14.9 percent of *Good Housekeeping*'s readers read *Real Simple*. What is the duplication? 34.4 percent or 14.9 percent?

The best way to calculate duplication is to show the percent of people who read *either* magazine who have read both. From Exhibit 5-9, a straight cross tab, we know that 12,129,000 women ages 25–54 read *Good Housekeeping*, 5,252,000 read *Real Simple*, and 1,806,000 read both. The calculation is:

$$\text{Duplication} = \frac{\text{Readers of both Magazine A and Magazine B}}{\text{Readers of Magazine A} + \text{Readers of Magazine B} - \text{readers of both}}$$

So in this case,

EXHIBIT 5-9

Two Magazine Duplication

WOMEN AGES 25–54		TOTAL WOMEN 25–54	GOOD HOUSEKEEPING	REAL SIMPLE
Totals	(000)	64,062	12,129	5,252
	Vertical %	100	100	100
	Horizontal %	100	18.9	8.2
Good Housekeeping	(000)	12,129	—	1,806
	Vertical %	18.9	—	34.4
	Horizontal %	100.0	—	14.9
Real Simple	(000)	5,252	1,806	—
	Vertical %	8.2	14.9	—
	Horizontal %	100.0	34.4	—

Source: Mediamark Research & Intelligence, LLC, Spring 2009. Used with permission.

$$\text{Duplication} = \frac{1{,}806 \text{ readers of both}}{12{,}129 \, GH \text{ readers} + 5{,}252 \, RS \text{ readers} - 1{,}806 \text{ both}}$$

$$\text{Duplication} = \frac{1{,}806}{15{,}575} = 11.6\%$$

This calculation allows the planner to report duplication as a single number: 11.6 percent of the women 25–54 who read either *Good Housekeeping* or *Real Simple* actually read both.

Frequency

Frequency is the companion statistic to reach. It tells the planner the number of times that the average person who was reached saw the advertising campaign, generally within a four-week period. Some of the people who were reached saw the ad only once, while others were reached many times. Frequency tells the planner how often the average person saw it. Reach is a measure of *message dispersion,* indicating how widely the message is viewed by the target universe. Frequency is a measure of *repetition,* indicating to what extent audience members were exposed to the same vehicle or group of vehicles. Both reach and frequency are valuable decision-making tools, because they give the media planner different options for arranging message delivery in a media plan.

The basic equation is:

$$\text{GRPs} = \text{Reach} \times \text{Frequency}$$

$$\text{Frequency} = \frac{\text{GRPs}}{\text{Reach}}$$

$$\text{Reach} = \frac{\text{GRPs}}{\text{Frequency}}$$

Let's apply this to an example in broadcast. Suppose a Taco Bell commercial is telecast 80 times in a given week on programs whose commercials had an average adult 18–34 rating of 1.5. Some telecasts were on special-interest cable networks where the rating is 0.4 or even less; other telecasts ran in prime time on the broadcast networks where the rating might be 2.5 or higher. In short, the commercial appeared in 80 telecasts across many different programs whose average commercial rating was 1.5, giving a total of 120 GRPs. This schedule had a four-week reach of 55 percent. (Note that this number comes from Nielsen research or computer models; it cannot be calculated by hand.) The average frequency is calculated from the equation:

$$GRPs = Reach \times Frequency$$

$$Frequency = \frac{GRPs}{Reach}$$

$$Frequency = \frac{120}{55}$$

$$Frequency = 2.2$$

To summarize, the advertiser ran the commercial 80 times that week across a broad range of programs on broadcast and cable television. The commercial was watched by 1.5 percent of adults ages 18–34 on the average telecast, yielding 120 A18–34 GRPs. By the end of the week, 55 percent of this target had seen at least one of the 80 telecasts, and the average person who was reached saw the commercial 2.2 times. Some saw it more often than that, some saw it less, but the average person who was reached saw it 2.2 times.

Conversely, 45 percent of adults 18–34 were not reached: they never saw the commercial and wouldn't have anything to say if their friend asked, "What did you think of that new Taco Bell ad?"

For print, the calculations are similar. Suppose Magazine Y has a reach of 54 percent after six consecutive issues. The average issue of the magazine is read by 29.5 percent of the target (its average issue audience). First calculate GRPs; then use that value to find average frequency:

$$GRPs = 29.5 \times 6 = 177$$

$$Frequency = \frac{177 \, GRPs}{54 \, Reach} = 3.3$$

Again, the average issue audience (29.5) and the six-issue reach (sometimes called "cumulative audience" or "cume") comes from computer models and cannot be estimated by hand. Also, because reach is an estimate, it is usually displayed as a whole number.

Frequency Distribution

Media planners sometimes forget that frequency is an average, not an absolute number. It is subject, therefore, to the characteristics of all statistical averages. Averages, for example, are affected by extreme scores in a distribution. A few very high numbers can bring up the average of the scores, and a few very low ones can drag down the average. The only way to guard against being deceived by a frequency statistic is to look at a frequency distribution and see whether some segments of a sample are getting disproportionately more frequency than others.

Exhibit 5-10 shows a sample divided into fixed quintiles and each group's reach and frequency. (*Fixed quintiles* means that the sample of audience members exposed was divided into five equal groups, each with 20 percent of the total number exposed.) The distribution of frequency is obviously unequal in Exhibit 5-10. Some of the quintiles received much more frequency than others. This phenomenon is known as *skew*.

Exhibit 5-11 dramatizes the skew by showing the frequency distribution in graphic form. Daily Program X had a 5.2 average frequency, but some segments were receiving more frequency than others. The average frequency of 5.2 does not indicate the disparity. The planner could be deceived by the average frequency level of Program X, thinking every home in the sample tuned to the program 5.2 times during a four-week period. The illustration shows otherwise. Frequency distributions with a large skew are called *unbalanced*.

EXHIBIT 5-10

Quintile Analysis of Tune-Ins for Program X

DIVISIONS OF VIEWER SAMPLE	REACH	FREQUENCY	GRPS
Heaviest 20%	17%	11	187
Next 20%	17	6	102
Third 20%	17	5	85
Next 20%	17	3	51
Lightest 20%	17	1	17
Totals*	85%	5.2 avg.	442

*Reach of entire sample, 85; frequency of entire sample, 5.2; GRPs, 442.

EXHIBIT 5-11

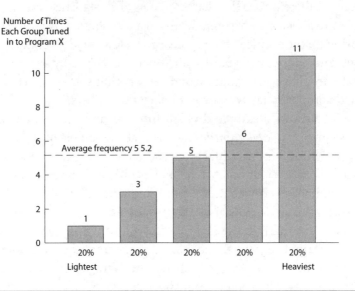

Frequency Distribution for Program X

Frequency distributions can be arranged according to quintiles, but they can also be arranged according to single increments of exposure, giving the planner a more detailed picture of exposure. Exhibit 5-12 shows a frequency distribution of exposure for all media in a given plan. Subtracting the number reached from the universe size shows that 8,227,000 of the universe of 29,356,000 did not see any of the vehicles used. Some 3,125,000 were exposed only once out of the 12 opportunities for exposure, and 2,269,000 were exposed to any 2 out of the 12 exposures. The number exposed at any frequency is unduplicated, meaning that these people are counted only once. A person receiving 12 exposures would not be counted at any other frequency level.

Frequency distributions therefore provide planners with a method of determining the pattern of repetition that the plan provides. Alternative plans will provide more or fewer repetition patterns. More important, however, is that the distribution will show whether repetition is spread widely or among only a very few prospects.

The example in Exhibit 5-13 shows how a frequency distribution can help a media planner decide among alternative plans. Plan A has a 4.0 average frequency and Plan B a 3.6. If the frequency is important, then Plan A would seem to be the better plan.

EXHIBIT 5-12

Frequency Distribution of Media Plan

		FREQUENCY OF EXPOSED	NUMBER EXPOSURES (000)
Reach	72%	0	8,227
Frequency	4.01	1	3,125
Gross impressions	84,749	2	2,269
Number reached	21,129	3	3,632
Universe	29,356	4	5,236
		5	2,474
		6	1,201
		7	1,462
		8	771
		9	622
		10	135
Calculations		11	104
21,129 ÷ 29,356 = 72%		12	98
84,749 ÷ 21,129 = 4.01			21,129

EXHIBIT 5-13

Four-Week Reaches and Frequencies of Two Media Plans

FREQUENCY OF EXPOSURE	PLAN A REACH		PLAN B REACH	
1	24%		20%	
2	16		15	
3	9		12	
4–5	6		13	
6–8	5	30%	10	40% 3+ reach
9–12	5		4	
13+	5		1	
Average frequency	4.0		3.6	
Total reach	70%		75%	
Reach at 3+ frequency	30%		40%	

Upon studying a frequency distribution such as the one in Exhibit 5-13, however, the planner learns something that could change the decision: Plan A delivers more audience members at exposure levels 1 and 2, but for exposures 3 through 8, Plan B is superior. Plan B reaches more persons than does Plan A at the 3-or-higher exposure level. If the advertising effort requires that people receive high levels of exposure (higher frequency), then Plan B is the obvious choice. Approximately 75 percent of the target will see the commercial at least once, while 40 percent will see it three or more times.

Weighted Frequency Distribution Planners often decide that the likelihood of a message being communicated depends on how many times the viewer is exposed. They believe that a single exposure doesn't do much good, making the people who are exposed only once worth less than those exposed more times. They may also believe that after a certain number of times, additional exposures won't be any more effective, that the 12th exposure is as good as the 10th.

They handle this by weighting the frequency distribution. Suppose in the preceding example the planner decides that people exposed only once are worth 25 percent of the maximum, people exposed twice are worth 50 percent, people exposed three times are worth 75 percent, and with four exposures or more, all are equally and maximally effective with a weight of 1.0.

Exhibit 5-14 shows that same analysis with frequency weighting taken into account. Plan B, with 49.5 percent weighted reach, is still the preferred plan, but now the decision reflects a more complete view of the value of each exposure. As

EXHIBIT 5-14

Weighted Frequency Distribution Reflects Communication at Different Levels of Exposure

FREQUENCY OF EXPOSURE	PLAN A REACH	WEIGHT	WEIGHTED REACH	PLAN B REACH	WEIGHT	WEIGHTED REACH
1	24	0.25	6.0	20	0.25	5.0
2	16	0.5	8.0	15	0.5	7.5
3	9	0.75	6.8	12	0.75	9.0
4–5	6	1	6.0	13	1	13.0
6–8	5	1	5.0	10	1	10.0
9–12	5	1	5.0	4	1	4.0
13+	5	1	5.0	1	1	1.0
	70%		41.8	75%		49.5

with so much of media planning, the weight that should be applied to each frequency level is the planner's judgment, taking into account the creative message, the objectives of the advertising, and all the other factors that go into the communications plan.

Note that the frequency distribution that planners see on their computer runs is not a real count of the number of people exposed varying numbers of times. Instead, it is produced by a computer model—mathematics—that takes for its input the number of units bought, the GRPs, and the average frequency. For this reason, a planner cannot do much to alter the 2+ or 3+ effective reach or the quintile analysis, which are directly calculated from the frequency distribution. These numbers become a fact of life, a characterization of the media plan that does little more than help the planner understand its delivery to different audience segments.

Relationship of Reach to Frequency

It is necessary to understand that reach and frequency occur at the same time but at different rates and in an inverse relationship. Within a given number of GRPs, as one goes up, the other goes down. To understand how these companion terms relate to each other, let us first look at the mathematics:

$$\text{Reach} \times \text{Frequency} = \text{GRPs}$$

According to this equation, an advertising schedule composed of a 50 reach with a 2.0 frequency yields 100 GRPs. If these same 100 GRPs were obtained in a different mixture of media, the reach might increase, but the frequency would decline. Conversely, a 100 GRP schedule in still other media mixtures might produce higher frequency, but less reach.

In a classic explanation, Seymour Banks, formerly vice president of Leo Burnett Company, discussed the dynamics of reach and frequency relative to rating size and number of telecasts:

> Reach is not directly proportional to either ratings or the number of telecasts. Rather, as ratings increase or as the number of telecasts used increases, reach also rises but at a decreasing rate. This is more easily understood when we consider that the companion of reach is frequency. When the rating or the number of telecasts increases, some of this increase goes towards boosting reach, while some of it contributes to an increase in frequency.[1]

---

1. Seymour Banks, *"How to Estimate Reach and Frequency"* (Leo Burnett Company, 1960): 5.

Up to a certain point, it is relatively easy to build reach. By selecting different day-parts in which to place commercials, it is possible to reach different kinds of people. But there is a point of diminishing returns, where each attempt to build more reach by selecting more and different kinds of programs results in reaching the same persons over and over again, with an increase in frequency rather than in reach. Some homes may never tune in their television sets over an entire month, so they are impossible to reach with TV in that month. Reach will increase as ratings and number of telecasts increase, but it will begin to decline in rate (not total) over time.

The point of diminishing returns can be seen in Exhibit 5-15, which illustrates reach accumulation among adults 18–49. It shows, for example, that when 500 GRPs are split evenly among prime time, late fringe, cable, and syndication, the plan will reach 78 percent of target adults one or more times. This includes 53 percent of target adults who are reached three or more times, and 38 percent five or more times. We see that 1+ reach rises rapidly until about 400 GRPs (74 percent reach), and that additional weight beyond this point produces proportionately less reach and more frequency. The percent exposed 3+ and 5+ times continues to rise, but at some point, these curves too will flatten in the same manner as the 1+ curve.

EXHIBIT 5-15

Effective Reach Versus GRPs and Cost

Even mix: prime time, late fringe, cable, syndication

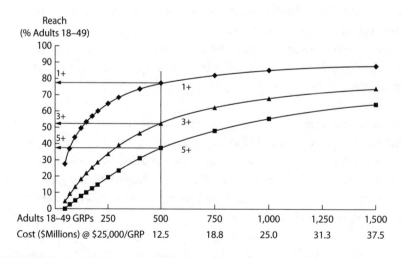

Source: DRAFTFCB Reach, 2007. Used with permission.

The challenge for planners comes when they must relate the desired reach to the cost of buying the GRPs necessary to achieve that reach. In Chapter 3 we discussed the concept of cost per rating point (CPP). In this example, the average cost per adult 18–49 rating point for 30-second commercials is $25,000, with weight split equally among prime time, late fringe, cable, and syndication. Using this price, it will cost $25 million to buy 1,000 points. Note that the CPP and the shape of the reach curves are different for each demographic target and daypart or combination of dayparts.

To summarize, reach and frequency are inversely related, but at a changing rate. When a campaign starts out, very few people have seen the advertising. Each new telecast reaches mostly people who have never seen it before, and reach rises quickly. As the campaign becomes more mature, there are fewer and fewer new prospects to expose. Reach rises more slowly with additional rating points. Meanwhile, the number of people exposed more than once increases, and frequency increases. That frequency can be expressed either as average frequency (GRPs/reach) or as the percent of the target exposed at least a certain number of times.

This latter form is used to show the "effective reach" of a campaign. If planners decide their commercial must be seen at least three times to be effective, then in the preceding example, a planner would say, "At 500 GRPs, 53 percent of the target is reached effectively at 3+ times." This takes a more realistic approach to describing the delivery of a campaign than using the 78 percent 1+ reach, which includes many people who will not see the commercial often enough to be effectively exposed. Most media plans will show all four numbers when describing media weight: GRPs, 1+ reach, average frequency, and reach at the recommended effective frequency level.

In the context of the weighted frequency distribution described earlier, for a 3+ reach the people exposed once or twice would be given a weight of 0—worthless— while every frequency level from three and beyond would be given a weight of 1.0. This way of setting the frequency distribution weights could be viewed as simplistic, but in the absence of better data, it may be more practical than arbitrarily setting a different weight for each frequency level.

Effective Frequency

Effective frequency can be defined as the amount of frequency (or repetition) the planner judges to be necessary for advertisements to be effective in communicating. The underlying assumption, of course, is that the average frequency statistic used in most media plans does not tell enough about a plan's delivery to be useful. Therefore, effective frequency can represent a great improvement over the ordinary 1+ reach and average frequency numbers used in traditionally created media plans.

Another problem with reach and frequency analysis is that it doesn't tell the planner anything about the effectiveness of the media plan or the adequacy of alternatives. The 1+ reach simply represents the *opportunity* to see advertisements. There is no guarantee that those who are reached actually see any of the ads. The C3 rating, while better than the average program minute, doesn't account for people not paying attention to the TV set even if they are physically in the room when the commercials are run. Put another way, although reach shows how many people are exposed to the ads, it does not tell the planner whether the ads will lead to increased sales or other desired results of the ad campaign. Ordinary frequency generated by a plan is the average number of times the target audience is exposed to the campaign. Average frequency, too, is not related to the plan's effectiveness.

Planners who use effective frequency attempt to correct for both situations by estimating the number of repetitions that are needed to attain communication goals. Those goals might be achieving brand awareness, attitude changes, brand switching, and recall of messages, to name a few. For example, if someone sets a communication goal of building 70 percent brand awareness, a media planner should ask, "How much repetition will help accomplish the task?"

Response Curves and Effective Frequency

The number at which frequency can be called "effective" depends on ideas of how much repetition is needed to communicate with consumers. Media planners find or estimate this number by observing what happens at varying repetitive levels. The analysis is common for digital advertising, where the number of exposures delivered to a given computer and the resulting click-throughs are easy to track. It is much more difficult to observe for traditional media.

Over many years, practitioners have hypothesized about how advertising works. Most believe that advertising does not work immediately. According to Herbert Krugman, author of the "three hit" theory, audiences may respond to their first perception of an advertisement by raising questions about the brand, such as, "What is it?" After audiences have perceived the same ad a second time, they will ask, "What of it?" On the second exposure, consumers then react to the commercial and begin to compare alternative brands. The third exposure is a reminder of the other two and the beginning of a time where consumers tune out the additional exposures. Krugman hypothesized that when audiences are in the market to buy a product, they will respond to that second repetition.

Therefore, effective frequency begins after the second repetition, but only when a consumer is ready to buy a given product. Many other practitioners have hypothesized that audiences begin to respond to advertising at about the third repetition. Beginning with the third repetition, the number of responses begins to grow with each additional repetition, but at a declining rate. If this hypothesis is plotted on a graph, it will have an *S* shape (see Exhibit 5-16). The first two repetitions are a threshold that audiences have to pass before advertisements become effective.

However, most researchers of advertising response curves have not found the S-shaped curve to occur very often. In fact, they have more often found a different kind of curve, often called a convex curve (see Exhibit 5-17). Many media planners who have adopted the concept of effective frequency believe that a convex curve represents a graphical picture of how repetition works in advertising. This curve is similar to the reach accumulation curve in Exhibits 5-6 and 5-15.

EXHIBIT 5-16

S-Shaped Response Curve

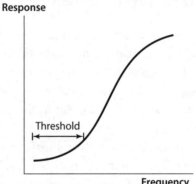

EXHIBIT 5-17

Convex Response Curve

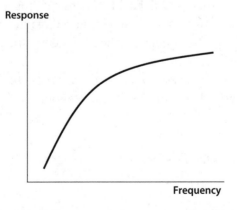

Effective Reach: The Other Side of the Coin

Once an effective-frequency level has been decided on, the planner needs to know *effective reach*—that is, the percent of the target audience exposed at the frequency level that is effective in the planner's judgment. If the planner thinks three exposures is enough to be effective, then the plan will need to show what percent of the target is exposed at this level. Saying, "We want to reach the target at least three times" is meaningless, compared to saying, "We want to reach 55 percent of the target at least three times." Typically, a planner wants to reach as many people at this level as possible within the authorized budget. Exhibit 5-15 is a useful way to show the relationship between cost and effective reach.

Brief History of Effective Frequency

To this point, effective frequency has been discussed as a simple numerical concept. In fact, it relates to a far subtler question: How many times does a person need to see an ad before "getting" the message? The answer depends on the nature of the product, the creative message, the advertising objectives, the medium being used, and a wide variety of other marketing factors. But in the end, the answer requires a judgment, because it really depends on what happens in the mind of the target consumer. Over the years, numerous research studies have been conducted to help planners make this judgment. The two most important are Michael Naples's seminal work on effective frequency and Erwin Ephron's Recency (Shelf Space) Model of Media Planning.

Naples Study

Probably the greatest impetus to establishing the concept in the United States was the publication of *Effective Frequency: The Relationship Between Frequency and Advertising Awareness,* by Michael J. Naples.[2] Published by the Association of National Advertisers, this book became required reading for almost every U.S. planner. The concept spread throughout the media departments of U.S. advertising agencies and is still widely used.

After presenting many research studies that supported the idea of effective frequency, Naples arrived at some conclusions about the implications for media planners:

---

2. Michael J. Naples, *Effective Frequency* (New York: Association of National Advertisers, Inc. 1979).

- One exposure of an advertisement to a target consumer group (within a purchase cycle) has little or no effect.
- Because one exposure is usually ineffective, the main thrust of media planning should be on emphasizing frequency rather than reach.
- Most of the research studies suggested that two exposures within a purchase cycle are an effective threshold level.
- Three exposures within a purchase cycle, however, are felt to be optimal.
- After three exposures within a purchasing cycle, advertising becomes more effective as frequency is increased, but at a decreasing rate. If this were drawn on a graph, it would appear as a convex curve rising from a zero point.
- Wearout of an advertising campaign is not caused by too much frequency, per se. It is caused by copy and content problems.
- Generally, small and lesser-known brands will benefit most from increased frequency. Larger, well-known brands might or might not be helped by increasing frequency, depending on how close they are to advertising saturation levels.
- Different dayparts on television are affected by different frequency levels. A similar idea applies to thin versus thick magazines, with the thinner ones having better response effects than the thicker ones.
- Frequency responses are affected by the amount of money an advertiser spends as a percentage of the product category total. Brands with the greatest proportion of exposures within their categories should also gain great effect when frequency is increased.
- The responses due to increased frequency are not affected by different media. What is true for one medium is true for others.
- Each brand might require a different level of frequency of exposure. One cannot generalize from a given brand's experiences to some other brand. Specialized research is required to find the unique frequency level for a brand.
- Two brands spending the same amount of money for advertising can have different responses to their frequencies.

Questions Regarding Effective-Frequency Research

As time has passed, planners have challenged this effective-frequency research. These concerns are summarized and discussed in the following paragraphs.

Is There a Need for Product Category Differentiation? One major problem of effective-frequency research was that most of it failed to show much difference between frequency effects for various product categories. This lack of differentiation tended to mislead planners into thinking that effective frequency is the same for all product categories. Now a growing number of planners are saying this idea cannot be correct. Frequency levels should vary from one product category to another.

Unfortunately, no measurements exist to show just which levels are needed for different kinds of products. Until this problem is resolved, media planners will have to make subjective decisions about how much frequency is enough. There is, however, some speculation that high-involvement products need less frequency and low-involvement products need more. The same idea applies to frequency levels of interesting and uninteresting products. The role of frequency then might be to help break through consumers' perceptual inertia for certain kinds of products.

Is There a Threshold? Another problem with the concept is determining whether a threshold exists before consumers begin to respond to advertising messages. Most of the research on the subject has suggested there are relatively few responses to the first few impressions of an advertising campaign. Advertising in these studies began to work with the second or third impression. Those who believed in the three-plus frequency concept believed that advertising began to be effective with the third impression. But many direct-marketing practitioners objected, noting that in their business, the first impressions often drew tremendous responses. Gus Priemer, then director of advertising service and media at S. C. Johnson & Son, Inc., also noted that in his experience of new-product introductions, the first impression had been able to generate noteworthy responses.

Attendees to a "Symposium on Effective Frequency" held in April 1986 at Northwestern University also questioned whether a threshold was realistic. The consensus at that meeting was that most response curves are convex, not S-shaped. The S-shaped curve was the one that indicated there was a threshold. Nevertheless, many planners still believe in a threshold. (The 1986 conference is cited here to illustrate that these perennial questions are as relevant today in the 21st century as they were more than 20 years ago.)

What Is the Relationship Between Good Advertising and Effective Frequency? A great many questions have been asked about whether effective frequency could be influenced by the quality of advertising messages. Why, for example, should the ad message not play a more important role in determining how much frequency is effective? Dull, uninteresting copy could require a great deal more frequency than scintillating creative messages. Since advertising agencies are expected to always produce top-quality creative product, they have little incentive to precisely define any relationship between creative quality and sales, assuming that was even possible.

Does Advertising Wear Out When There Is Too Much Frequency? Some of the research cited by Naples showed that negative responses occurred after using too much repetition. Some consumers will even forget an advertising message if frequency is too high. The research of Valentine Appel and L. Jacobovits (also reported in Naples's book) suggests that the shape of a wear-out curve looks like an inverted U. But among media planners, there seems to be no wide-ranging concern about this potential problem.

The effective-frequency concept for media planners relates most importantly to this point: How much media vehicle frequency is necessary to achieve the advertising exposure frequencies found in most of the research studies? Radio and television ratings and magazine audience exposures represent only exposures to vehicles. To go beyond vehicle frequency, we need research that either relates vehicle frequency to advertising frequency or directly shows the effects of vehicle exposure frequency to a given response. Some research studies have tried to do the latter, but more research is necessary.

Recency and the Shelf-Space Model of Media Planning

The subject was explored in detail at the Effective Frequency Research Day conducted by the Advertising Research Foundation in November 1994 and from which the following highlights were drawn.[3] Using Nielsen Household Panel data from the early 1990s, Professor John Philip Jones of Syracuse University challenged the conventional wisdom that three exposures are necessary for an ad to be effective. He said, instead, "Effective frequency is provided by a single exposure . . . one exposure generates the highest proportion of sales."

Although Jones found differences from one campaign to another in the incremental effectiveness of the second, third, and subsequent exposures, in all cases the first exposure had the largest effect on sales. He concluded, "Additional exposures add very little to the effect of the first." Media consultant Erwin Ephron expressed the concept more colloquially:

> If you tell a kid, "Remember to wash your hands before each meal" three times at 11 A.M., you are using frequency to teach. If you tell him once, right before dinner, you're using presence to remind. A reminder at the right time is a more effective way to influence behavior.
>
> Being there with a message for the consumer who is ready-to-buy, and being there continuously is what I call "presence"—the media equivalent of "renting the

---

3. "Effective Frequency Research Day Proceedings," Advertising Research Foundation, November 2, 1994.

shelf." . . . Not being there with a message when the consumer is ready-to-buy is the advertising equivalent of being out of stock—which is why I call this the "shelf-space model of media planning."[4]

Ephron relates this concept to media planning. Each week of the year, people are shopping and buying; they should be continuously exposed to a brand's message. Therefore, media plans should be evaluated in terms of weekly reach points delivered. The familiar convex curve of "diminishing returns" shows that reach builds rapidly at first, but beyond a certain point, additional GRPs yield mostly (wasted) frequency. Ephron compares two ways of scheduling 2,600 GRPs:

Plan 1
100 GRPs/week for 26 weeks
Weekly reach: 50 percent
Total reach points: $26 \times 50 = 1,300$

Plan 2
67 GRPs/week for 39 weeks
Weekly reach: 40 percent
Total reach points: $39 \times 40 = 1,560$

Both plans cost the same, and both deliver 2,600 total GRPs, but Plan 2 delivers 20 percent more weekly reach points. This, according to Ephron, is the most effective way to schedule weight—*if* we assume one hit is enough.

The recency model would suggest that consistent advertising is preferable to concentrating weight in flights. Taken to the extreme, the planner would simply divide the available budget by 52 weeks, then purchase as many GRPs per week as the budget permits. But this approach runs up against the long-standing belief that there is a threshold, a minimum number of GRPs per week that are necessary to be effective. A study of media plans by Helen Johnston, former vice president and director of media analysis at Grey Advertising, found minimum levels in the range of 70 to 100 GRPs per week:

There was no relationship to budget. All planners felt there was a level below which advertising would be ineffective. Compromises were affected by limiting

---

4. Erwin Ephron, "The Shelf Space Model of Advertising," February 1, 1995, www.ephron onmedia.com.

hiatus lengths. The average hiatus was 2.7 weeks, and there was an average of 7.6 hiatuses. As a result, only the richest brands attained true continuity or 52 weeks of advertising.

In summary, planners have a formidable task of weighing alternatives when they schedule media. Our task is not to persuade them of the importance of continuity. They fully appreciate that importance. However, they believe continuity to be an ideal that is beyond their brand's means.[5]

Despite these shortcomings, the shelf-space theory has become the starting point for media plan scheduling for sustaining support of existing brands:

- Begin assuming continuity scheduling for as many weeks as possible at whatever the planner thinks is the minimum number of TRPs per week.
- Then adjust the plan to reflect seasonality, promotional opportunities, product enhancements, and anything else you can specifically identify as bearing on the effectiveness of the campaign.

Recent Studies of Effective Frequency

Research companies like TRA (www.traglobal.com) can link the number of times a household is exposed to a campaign with product purchase from grocery store frequent-shopper cards. But no matter how sophisticated, these studies are always based on past behavior from the past creative and the past media plan. Advertisers question the actionability and the value of this expensive research.

Nielsen's Project Apollo attempted the same thing by linking television exposures to product purchase from their Homescan panel that records sales by asking panelists to scan the UPC code as products are brought home from the store. The study received support from the largest package goods advertisers, including Procter & Gamble and S. C. Johnson. It was viewed as the first serious attempt to answer advertising's perennial questions. However, because of the cost and the limited ability to act on the data, the study failed to progress beyond the pilot stage.

The key point is that it is difficult to prove the relationship between effective frequency and brand awareness, sales, or any other advertising or marketing objective. The relationship is subtle, not a simple cause-and-effect relationship.

---

5. Helen Johnston, "Research and Media Scheduling," *Journal of Advertising Research*, Nov./Dec. 1995: RC2–4.

Summary

It should be clear from this and from the five perennial questions described in Chapter 3 that there are no simple answers to these "How much is enough?" questions of effective frequency, flighting versus continuity, minimum GRP levels, maximum hiatus weeks, response function shape, and the like. Research can provide guidance, but in the end, planners must use judgment to apply these general findings from the past to specific plans for the future.

Finally, it should be noted that these concepts apply mainly to traditional mass media where the relationship between GRPs, reach, frequency, and frequency distribution is well known. They are largely irrelevant for online search advertising, where the goal is to present the ads to people who are looking for information about certain key words. They are equally irrelevant for the many nontraditional out-of-home media that lack research about frequency of exposure. Online banner campaigns that use behavioral targeting (e.g., sending ads for children's products to people whose browsing behavior indicates they are parents) are effective at reaching the target, even though the reach and frequency to an age/gender target audience such as women 25–54 may be quite low. It is important to understand the concepts, but planners are cautioned not to apply them wholesale to all the new media opportunities.

CHAPTER SIX

Marketing Strategy and Media Planning

There are many ways to start the media-planning process, but the best way is by analyzing the situation of a brand in the marketplace. The reason for making such an analysis is to learn how successful a brand has been against its competition, with the objective of finding opportunity areas to exploit or problem areas to correct. Ultimately, the findings of a situation analysis should lead to the establishment of marketing objectives and strategies, which in turn lead to the establishment of media objectives and strategies.

Although the responsibility for conducting a marketing situation analysis seldom rests with a media planner, someone from the agency's media department, such as a media researcher, is often involved to some extent in the research activities. Media planners often are involved in the marketing situation analysis, particularly an examination of the consumer, the competitive weight, and geographic and seasonal sales.

What a Media Planner Needs to Know

Every media plan is built around a brand's most important marketing problem. That's what marketing plans exist for: as a prelude to media/marketing planning. Other research about competitors and the market itself will be done later. However, recognizing the main problem is a problem in itself. Problems can come in all degrees of importance for a brand of product or service. If many interrelated problems are facing a planner, finding a solution could require a detailed situation analysis.

To help a brand achieve solutions, a planner must do a number of things. A good first step is to carry out a situation analysis. The following examples illustrate a few of the problems that could be critical for media planning:

- Sales are declining in the Southwest for Brand X.
- Consumers like Brand B better in the Southwest because they say it is lighter.
- The newest brand on the market has reduced its price below ours in the Southwest.
- The kinds of people who formerly used our brand have switched to Brand D.

Once the main problems have been identified, other details of the situation analysis should be decided on. Each can help the planner make significant decisions.

Along with the main problems, planners need to assess other elements of marketing, such as product quality, product uses, pricing, distribution methods, packaging, sales promotion use, personal selling activities, public relations, and advertising. From a practical standpoint, the planner does not need to know every detail, but only those items that are thought to contribute to product sales. These are elements of a situation analysis.

Situation Analysis

A *situation analysis* is research prepared in document, Excel spreadsheet, or PowerPoint presentation format to provide the background for a media planner to prepare a plan. It provides perspective on where a brand has been and where its potential lies in the future. Here are essential parts of a situation analysis:

- **History of the market.** This deals with sales of all brands in the market, including the brand for which planning is to be done. The analysis includes geographic sales distribution, market size in dollars and units, market shares, seasonal effects, and price effects. The goal is to find out where brands are now in terms of market share and how they got there. An important item, for example, might be pricing history. What happened to prices for various brands over the years, and how did these price manipulations affect sales? Another concern might be an analysis of cost history and profit related to sales, both for the brand under consideration and for competitors' brands, if known.
- **Distribution channels.** The objective here is to learn how a brand and its competitors distribute products. This includes the following information about each distribution channel: shelf-facings, inventories held, out-of-stock

situations, methods of selling, display and advertising allowances, and how and why promotions are used. Problems of selling are sometimes caused by poor distribution, not advertising. Distribution information often affects media strategy because it can help the planner decide where to advertise.

- **Consumer of the product.** A profile of users of the generic product type includes personal demographics such as age, gender, income, and occupation, as well as geographic location. Psychographics—lifestyles and attitudes—also should be included. A consumer profile of those who buy a specific brand versus those who buy competing products is important as well. Buying habits also should be analyzed in terms of when products are purchased, in which kind of retail outlets, and which sizes, models, and colors are purchased most often. How and when consumers use these products also should be known. Finally, it would be helpful to know about the buyer, the user, and the persons who motivate buyers and users. All of this "attitude and usage" information helps the media planner select targets for media. A thorough understanding of the target includes a feeling for their lifestyle and interests that can lead to media opportunities. Exhibit 6-1 shows an online branding campaign for Taco Bell that is directed to their core adult 18–34 target audience.
- **Product.** A history of the product and how it was developed is included in the product section of the analysis. When and why product changes were made and the effects of such changes on each competitive brand could be important. Consumer perceptions of the values of various brands also are important background information for the media planner.
- **Advertising and media analysis.** Probably the most important information for a media planner is an analysis of media expenditures for competing brands. This includes media classes used, names of individual vehicles, creative size, number of creative executions, gross rating points (GRPs) in total and by daypart, flighting patterns, when advertising ran during the year, dollar and percentage allocated to each medium and market, and many other factors that help the advertiser understand the competitor's marketing strategy.

Marketing Strategy Plan

Once a situation analysis has been completed and the problems of a brand in the marketplace have been identified, the next step is a search for selling opportunities. Opportunities are marketing facts that exist and, without much money or effort, sell the product naturally. Here are some examples of selling opportunities for Brand X:

EXHIBIT 6-1

Taco Bell's Feed the Beat™ Campaign

Taco Bell has the marketing objective of reinforcing brand awareness created by the television advertising to their adult 18–34 target audience. The Internet is a natural medium to reach this group, and music is a central part of their life. The marketing team created the Feed the Beat™ website, which allows visitors to listen to music that has been uploaded by the top 100 independent bands as nominated by fans or chosen by Taco Bell. Fans also had the option to vote for their favorite bands as part of the "Virtual Battle of the Bands." An online campaign drives visitors to the www.feedthe beat.com website and further reinforces awareness of Taco Bell. In the 2008 campaign, more than 180,000 votes were received.

The following is a sample banner and landing page of the campaign.

Source: Taco Bell Corp. Used with permission.

TACO BELL, TACO BELL LOGO and FEED THE BEAT are trademarks of Taco Bell Corp.

- Example 1: Brand X is outselling competitors by a wide range in key markets but spends less for advertising than the next three competitors. Is it possible that with a budget equal to or greater than any other single competitor in those markets, our sales and share can be considerably enhanced?
- Example 2: Brands C and D are manufactured in smaller packages, which consumers tend to buy more often than Brand X's larger package. Can we produce our brand in smaller sizes without expending much money or effort?

In contrast to opportunities, problems demand some action to correct the situation. A problem area might be a situation in which a brand does not have a competitive advantage or one in which a brand has been steadily losing its share of market for any number of reasons. Finding the causes for the decline is a first step toward changing the situation. Most situation analyses turn up more problem areas than opportunities, but the delineation of each problem area is a necessary preliminary step to marketing and media planning. Some advertisers call this phase a SWOT analysis: strengths, weaknesses, opportunities, and threats.

Marketing strategy planning consists of planning marketing actions that will solve the major problems and take advantage of the opportunities. In effect, a marketing strategy and plan is a blueprint for action geared to selling the product, with the ultimate goal of gaining an advantage over a competitor.

Perhaps the weakest part of many advertising campaigns is the lack of a sound selling strategy. Arthur Tatham, formerly chairman of the board of Tatham-Laird & Kudner, once said, "Brilliant copy and art will never make a weak selling strategy succeed. But . . . once there is a sound selling strategy, then good copy and art will multiply its effectiveness." Tatham's statement also applies to media selection and use. Without a sound selling strategy, media planning represents wasted effort. Media planning does not exist as an activity unrelated to marketing; it is a service function of marketing and selling. The fact that media are often selected and used without being based on a sound selling strategy demonstrates poor logic and inefficient modes of operation. Selling strategy is the heart of a marketing strategy and plan.

In summary, the major goals in a strong marketing strategy and plan are as follows:

- Setting objectives that will help solve existing problems and take advantage of opportunities
- Deciding how the product should be sold

- Determining to whom the main selling effort (the selling strategy) should be directed
- Determining what role various elements of the marketing mix should play in the sale of a brand
- Determining what adjustments should be made in package shapes or sizes
- Determining how much should be spent

Most often, the marketing plan is written by someone other than the media planner. Yet even if the latter is not directly involved in drawing up the plan, there are a number of reasons why the marketing strategy plan is a significant document to media planners. The foremost reason is that the marketing plan serves as a unifying and organizing force for all activity within an agency on a given brand's marketing and advertising plans.

This means that the account planners, account executives, and creative people, as well as media planners, must all be working from a single source of information. Coordinating the various disciplines can be a challenge when the advertising functions are split between the creative and the media agency. And giving the responsibility for online planning and buying, especially online display and search, to yet another organization further complicates the job of coordinating the marketing effort.

Once the plan has been written, it becomes easier to visualize the whole scheme of operations for a given brand. All proposed plans should be evaluated for their logic and completeness to avoid information gaps or contradictions. If a marketing plan exists only in someone's mind or in bits or scraps of memoranda, then errors are hard to locate, because no one has an overview of the entire operation.

Perhaps the key to the success of a marketing plan is the degree to which it spells out all tactics. Marketing consultant Herbert Zeltner long ago cautioned that many marketing plans are "either glossed over in the rush of hammering together a marketing program, or merely slapped together as a collection of ponderous clichés." In words still applicable today, he noted:

> To be truly useful, the market strategy statement should not merely reflect some happy generalities about an increase in volume or share of market for the coming fiscal period.
>
> But establishing the requirement that a specific percent volume increase is to be achieved—through the expenditure of a precise sensible sum of money—and that this increase can most realistically be expected through more aggressive development of certain stated territories or segments of the market . . . is the type of state-

ment which gives a properly astute media planner the challenge he needs to create both a perspective and workable media recommendation.[1]

The media planner needs specific direction, explicitly stated, to begin making decisions. The media plan grows directly out of the marketing strategy whenever it requires advertising to be used. The various segments of the strategy statement, however, are not all equally significant to the media planner. Foremost in importance are the marketing objectives, the basic selling idea, sources of business, overall sales strategy, and spending strategy. Each of these will be discussed in more detail on the following pages. Exhibit 6-2 shows an outline of a basic strategy statement.

Marketing Objectives

The marketing goals that the company and agency agree upon should, if achieved, result in the solution of a marketing problem. Marketing goals are measurable in most cases and provide a means of determining whether the strategy employed has been effective. For the media planner, the objectives will undoubtedly affect the kinds of media selected and the ways media are used. In a sense, then, marketing objectives serve as controls for media planning.

Most marketing objectives relate directly to achieving share of market for a brand; others relate to communication objectives. Here is a sample of marketing objectives for different brands (taken from various strategy statements):

- To increase share in an expanding segment of the X market
- To regain lost volume—increase sales a maximum of 5 percent and, in turn, shoot for a 14 percent share of market
- To acquire a 20 percent share of market the first year after national introduction, 25 percent the second year, and 30 percent the third year
- To introduce the product so that we have at least 5 percent share in each sales division
- To increase share of market and increase the morale of the sales force in the face of many competitive new-product introductions
- To find and persuade new customers for our product
- To maintain national coverage
- To provide regional and local impact where two-thirds of sales are made
- To increase the overall visibility of the product name against the potential customers and the trade across the country

---

1. Herbert Zeltner, "Marketing Strategy Statement," *Media/Scope* (August 1964): 10.

EXHIBIT 6-2

Outline for Basic Marketing Strategy Statement

I. Major Strategy
This should be the briefest possible statement of the major one or two strategies recommended for the planning period, with just enough statement of the problem to explain the strategy. If you can write this section in one or two sentences or paragraphs, do so. If it takes you more than a single-spaced page, it is probably too long.

II. Basic Objectives
A. Short term (next fiscal 12 months, unless otherwise stated):
1. Increase share of total market
2. Arrest decline in share
3. Develop added volume
4. Increase total market
5. Achieve profit goal
6. Reduce losses

Translate objectives into approximate sales and/or profit goals.

B. Long term (any prescribed period beyond the next planning period):
1. Increase share of total market
2. Increase total market
3. Increase profits
4. Position goal, i.e., gain leadership
5. Develop and establish a brand or corporate image
6. Expand line of service or products

Translate objectives into approximate sales and/or profit goals.

III. The Basic Selling Idea
A one- or two-sentence statement of the key selling idea. This is the base from which the creative strategy evolves.

IV. Presentation of the Basic Selling Idea
The creative strategy in its briefest form

V. Use or Uses for Which the Product Will Be Advertised
A. Major
B. Minor

VI. Sources of Business and Relative Importance of Each
A. Consumer sources—What are the characteristics of the people who are the best prospects?
1. Regional factors
2. City size
3. County size
4. Income groups

5. Age of homemaker
6. Occupation of head of household
7. Family size
8. Seasonal
9. Gender—men, women, children
10. Who is principal purchaser?
B. Dealer sources—What is the relative importance of various types of outlets?
C. Competitive sources—Important competitive brands or companies: national, regional, local

VII. Overall Sales Strategy
A. Relative importance of price
 1. To the consumer
 2. To the trade
B. Relative importance of personal selling
C. Relative importance of dealers
D. Relative importance of advertising
E. Relative importance of promotion
F. Relative importance of publicity

VIII. Product Strategy
A. The need for product improvement—Analysis of product superiorities and weaknesses compared to competitive products
B. The need for related products
C. The need for adding new sizes or deleting unprofitable sizes
D. The need for improving
 1. Packaging
 2. Package design

IX. Spending Strategy
A. Is there a need for higher or lower margins? What effect will this have on price, quality, and quantity of the product?
B. What is the proper amount to spend
 1. On introduction?
 2. On reintroduction?
 3. On an ongoing basis?
C. Is an extended payout plan indicated, and if so, what is the optimum time?

X. Facts and Documentation
The pertinent facts needed to define the problems and to document the strategies outlined in the strategy sections

Whenever marketing objectives require advertising in specific geographic areas, then the planner must select media that best reach those areas. Sometimes the objectives call for added promotional effort in a geographic region such as the West Coast. Or the objectives might call for a special advertising effort in a given market, such as Los Angeles or Portland. Such objectives will limit media choices, because desired media vehicles may not be available in some areas. The marketing objectives give the planner direction in selecting media, but it is up to the planner to find media that best deliver the target audience specified. These marketing objectives provide critical input to computerized "channel planning" systems, which will be discussed later in this chapter.

Occasionally, objectives deal with some area other than market shares (e.g., to increase the image of authority among adults). In this situation, the planner might feel that adults, especially those aged 21–34, are good prospects, yet they are not buying the product. Media habits of the target audience become the key factor in the selection of media channels and media vehicles. Online and social media would be seriously considered for a plan directed to this target given their above-average use of these media.

Marketing Mix and Strategy

The tools that marketers use for implementing strategy were discussed in Chapter 3. Recall that each element of the mix is a selling tool. A good product that meets consumers' wants and needs is one of the best selling tools. Price is a selling tool, as is distribution. If a grocery store does not carry a given brand of product, many customers will ask for some other brand instead. They usually will not go to some other store in search of the brand. Promotion in general, and sales promotion specifically, are each selling tools. Other forms of promotion are public relations (including event marketing), direct marketing, advertising copy and art, and media.

The idea of a marketing mix is that it takes a number of different marketing mix elements to sell a product. Selling bottled water requires a good product as well as price, distribution, advertising, and sales promotion. But selling automobiles requires a different mix: product, price, distribution, sales promotion, public relations, and advertising. In short, the idea of a mix is important in terms of finding the optimum elements for selling. The use of many marketing mix communication elements usually requires integration, because each element could convey a different message and thereby reduce the effectiveness of communication. *Integrated marketing communications (IMC)* is one buzzword for this age-old concept. Another buzzword for the process is *cross-channel communication*, where the advertiser uses a combination of conventional television, video advertising on the personal computer, and video on mobile devices such as smart phones. Although each is, technically, just another screen on which to display video advertising, the planning and buying process is quite different for each.

Budget

Once the marketing objectives have been stated, it is necessary to know how much money will be available to attain them. It is not realistic to make a grandiose marketing plan and then find that the advertiser is unwilling or unable to provide sufficient funds to make the plan successful. (Budgeting and allocations to markets and media will be discussed in Chapter 13.) At this point, the media planner can be called in to help estimate the costs of the media strategy, even before the main portion of the plan has been started. If enough money is not available to accomplish a given set of objectives, then the objectives must be reduced or revised.

Estimating the cost of a marketing plan usually involves two separate activities: estimating media costs and estimating production costs. Media costs are obtained from research services that provide this information, such as SQAD for radio and television costs[2] and SRDS[3] for the cost of magazine and newspaper advertising. Planners should also talk to professional broadcast and online buyers who know the latest costs and ultimately are responsible for buying the planned rating points and online impressions within the specified budget. Production costs are estimated either by arbitrarily allocating a given percentage of the total budget for that purpose or, if the advertising is relatively simple, by obtaining estimates on specific kinds of production pieces that are needed, such as artwork, typography, videotape, or film. Generally, the media planner is responsible for estimating only the media cost portion of the marketing plan.

Planners are sometimes asked to estimate how much money needs to be spent in media to achieve a given marketing objective or sales target. This is, frankly, an unfair question because sales are dependent on a constellation of factors that go far beyond the media plan—creative quality, product performance versus its competitors, distribution, price to the consumer, promotion, and all the other factors that go into the marketing plan. This is another variation of the perennial question, "How much is enough?"

A planner can tell the advertiser how much money the competitors are spending in order to identify the cost of entry into the competitive set. Media planners can also share their experience with other brands and products. But planners should never imply that a given expenditure will result in a certain level of sales. At best, a planner can estimate the awareness of a new product that will be generated from

---

2. www.sqad.com.

3. www.srds.com.

a given amount of media weight, but it is beyond the planner's ability to say how many of those who become aware of a new product will go on to try it. The planner is even less able to say how many of those who tried the product will become repeat purchasers.

Market-mix modeling companies use mathematical models based on past history to estimate the effect of various spending levels. Experience might show, for example, that an advertiser increased its national share of market by three percentage points by spending $10 million. It could then be roughly estimated that it would cost $3.3 million to raise the share one percentage point. This linear relationship of spending and share of market, however, is seldom witnessed in the real world. And any reference to experience is open to the challenge that "this situation is different."

Sometimes the competitive spending analysis shows that the amount of money needed to compete in the category is beyond the means of the advertiser. The revenue produced by the expected sales (even the most optimistic estimate) will not support the media spending needed to be competitive. In such cases, either the objectives have to be changed, or the advertiser must realize that spending the available dollars will not produce the desired results. The planner's role is to present the documentable facts and avoid implying that budget X will produce sales Y on the grounds that media spending is only one of the many factors that influence sales.

Creative Strategy

A major part of the marketing strategy plan is an explanation of how the product will be sold: the creative platform that is generally developed by the account planning group. From that basic selling idea comes the creative strategy, possibly the single most important influence on the planner during the media selection process. The creative strategy often directs the planner to choose one medium over another or to select a combination of media.

A creative strategy in which color is an integral part requires magazines, direct mail, newspaper supplements, television, streaming video, or other media that offer quality color. Newspapers accepting freestanding inserts (FSIs) offer additional alternatives to the media planner. Where the creative strategy calls for the use of cartoon characters, then either comic strips or television will be most appropriate. Again, the creative strategy gives direction to the selection process and input to the channel planning system.

Where a strategy calls for demonstration, one might first think of television. However, it is possible to demonstrate the use of a product in print advertisements with sequential panels showing the various steps in using the product. Radio also is capable of demonstration through the use of words, sound effects, and music, which play on the listener's imagination. Sometimes the creative strategy calls for the use of an announcer or salesperson who can exude a feeling of warmth and sincerity. Either television or radio is required here, because each excels at conveying emotional impact.

If the creative strategy calls for music, media choices are limited to radio or television. An alternative is to record the music and advertising message on a CD and have it inserted into magazines. In this case, however, the creative strategy must give way to the budget, which might not accommodate the expense of recording and inserting the CD.

Occasionally, creative strategy calls for large illustrations. This suggests billboards to the media planner, although direct mail or a two-page spread in newspapers or magazines might be equally acceptable.

Some advertising messages seem to have more impact on consumers in one medium than they do in another. However, impact is a hazy concept. It is generally assumed to mean that advertising does something to audience members, such as make the message memorable, change attitudes toward the brand, impart significant bits of information, or perhaps serve as a motivating factor in buying. The assumption is not always valid, because there is often little proof that what is claimed to happen actually does. In any case, where creative strategies call for traditional media because of their perceived impact, the planner might find it difficult to break with tradition—essentially the agency and client's expectations of what media should be used, coupled with their inherent desire to avoid risk.

The media planner for a consumer package good (CPG) that had traditionally used primarily television recommended putting the entire budget in print, converting a weak but conventional television plan into a very strong but unconventional print plan. After many long meetings the client eventually accepted the change, but when sales in the first quarter of the plan were a little below expectations, the unconventional media plan was blamed (fairly or unfairly). All the remaining money was moved into television.

The creative strategy also influences the role of online display advertising and search (the purchase of advertising adjacent to selected keywords in search engines such as Google and Bing). For some products, such as hotels, travel, automobiles, and financial services, the role of online is obvious. For others, such as low-interest consumer package goods, online media is another way to extend the brand message to light users of traditional media. Regardless of its role, the online creative must incorporate the same creative message as the traditional media.

Dealers and Distribution

A major factor in media decision making is the product's geographic distribution, as it makes sense to limit advertising to areas where the product is sold. To do otherwise is to waste effort and money. There are, of course, exceptions, such as when a manufacturer will advertise in an area where the product is not distributed, in an effort to "force" distribution on the dealers in that area. Perhaps dealers have refused to handle a new brand because they feel they already have too many similar products on their shelves. Some grocery chains even practice a one-for-one policy, in which they refuse to take on a new brand unless the manufacturer removes an existing brand from the shelves. By advertising in an area where a product is not yet distributed, the manufacturer hopes to create such a demand for the product that the dealers and distributors will be forced to carry the brand. This strategy, however, sometimes backfires because consumers who seek the brand and cannot find it might be alienated as future consumers of the brand.

For most products, however, advertising is limited to areas where the product is distributed and, even then, only to the markets that produce the most sales or have the greatest potential for sales.

Because dealers are important sources of business, the ability to select media that best communicate with dealers represents another aspect of that planner's job. For Business-to-Business (B2B) advertising, the trade press is the most frequently used medium, but a planner could also choose to communicate with dealers through direct mail, trade shows and conventions, or even mass media.

Dealers also influence media decisions because they are so important in selling at the local level. They are on the firing line and often know which medium works best in their markets. At times they may communicate with the agency indirectly through distributors, wholesalers, or salespeople. Their influence can be very important for their own markets. Furthermore, they often dislike agency media choices, feeling that the media planner is too distant from the scene of action to know which local or national medium works best. In any case, the media planner must pay a great deal of attention to dealers and to the importance of distribution in the media plan.

Overall Sales Strategy

The media planner should examine each element of the marketing mix to determine how it might affect media selection and use. Foremost, of course, is the role to be played by advertising. Although one can conceive of a situation where sales promotion, for example, might be more important in attaining objectives, advertising usually plays a significant role in the marketing strategy, and its role should be defined. The more specific this definition is, the better the media planner can plan strategy. Generally, advertising is assigned a communication task that must be accomplished before a product can be sold effectively.

When pricing tactics are important in marketing strategy, a special media effort might be needed either to announce the price or keep the news in front of the consumers. Special prices to dealers may require special trade media selections and use.

Sales promotion, too, has special significance to media planners. Many promotions call for inserts, such as coupons, booklets, or sample CDs, in magazines or newspapers. All of these inserts require careful planning, especially in estimating their cost and timing. Marketing or creative plans might also require gatefolds, die cuts, or special inks, all of which require additional media considerations such as cost, production lead time, and availability. Furthermore, the media planner must often select media to announce and keep a special promotion in front of consumers. Contests, cents-off deals, and premiums can lose their impact if consumers do not notice them. To maintain the desired impact, the general media strategy is to buy media so as to get the largest reach possible.

For other promotions, it is necessary to tie in local store information with national advertising so the audience in any given market knows where to buy an advertised national brand. The names and addresses of stores carrying the product are usually listed at the end of commercials or next to or near newspaper or magazine ads. The local dealers are expected to split the cost with the national advertiser in a cooperative arrangement, or "co-op" advertising.

Other parts of the marketing mix, such as personal selling, public relations, or packaging, are of less importance in media planning. But the planner should know as much as possible about the whole marketing strategy to maximize the effectiveness of media decisions.

Test Marketing

Whenever a marketing strategy plan calls for test marketing, there is likely to be media involvement. For example, a test-marketing situation might use three markets to test whether the following objectives can be attained:

- To gain a substantial share of each market's sales
- To determine whether the total market for the product can be expanded
- To determine how many repeat purchases will be made
- To accomplish the first three objectives within a reasonable length of time at a reasonable profit (this requires special media planning)

To carry out the test, the company would introduce the new brand in the three markets, using different marketing tactics in each test market. For example, in Market A, 50 percent of the households would be given a free sample. In Market B, 100 percent of the households would be given a free sample. And in Market C, local newspapers would carry a coupon redeemable for a free sample at local stores. Each test market requires local advertising to call attention to the offers, especially to the coupon offer. Sales in each market would then be measured and compared to see which performed best.

As another example, test marketing could affect media planning if media weight varied in each of the three test markets. Market A might receive 100 television GRPs per week; Market B, 150 per week; and Market C, 200 per week. Sales would then be measured to see how the different weights affected volume.

Still another way to test media weights in several markets would be to give each market a specified advertising weight for a limited time. Sales would be measured for that period, then a heavier weighting might be applied to each market equally or in different proportions, and sales would again be measured. (Test-marketing strategy affects media planning in ways ranging from simple dissemination of advertising to special testing situations within all or portions of the test markets. For more details on test marketing, see Chapter 14.)

In summary, the marketing strategy affects the media planner's operation in many ways. The media plan itself grows out of a marketing plan. It is inconceivable for the media planner to operate without first having some kind of marketing strategy as a basis on which to select and use media. The ideal situation occurs when the marketing strategy is written and available for all personnel who work on a product or brand within the agency. The plan then serves as a unifying force and directs action toward a common goal.

Competitive Media Expenditure Analysis

Once the planner understands the marketing strategy that determines how media will be involved, it is time to consider the kinds of media and the way they are used by the competition.

Identifying the competitors is an important and often subtle marketing judgment. A regional fast-food restaurant certainly competes with McDonald's, but knowing that McDonald's spends hundreds of millions of dollars a year on national television is not relevant to their small regional budget. Wal-Mart is the leading seller in many product categories, but should an advertiser even try to compete directly with that retail giant? A company that sells automobile insurance competes with larger companies for whom auto is just one of many policy lines. Should the competitive analysis focus on these competitors' automobile insurance or on the brand awareness created by advertising their whole line of products?

In short, identifying relevant competitors is just one of the many marketing judgments that inform a media plan. Most planners will look at the top five spenders individually and a single line that adds up all the remaining competitors in order to see total category spending.

Once the competitors are identified, it is easy to find out how much they spend in each medium if the advertiser or agency subscribes to the syndicated research sources that provide this information (discussed later in this chapter). But when such research services are not purchased, it is a challenge to discover who the competitors are and how much they are spending. Some information can be obtained from news in the trade press about competitive media expenditures, but products produced and sold locally might not be identified very well, especially products that are not advertised much. Other sources of information are local media salespeople, media representatives, local media research departments, and the company's own sales staff.

In determining the effect of competitors' media plans and devising strategies to counter such effects, the key piece of information is the share of market held by each competitor as compared with the advertiser's brand. Brands that lead or are close behind the advertiser pose a threat. As far as media planning is concerned, the question is, Should we use the same media our competitors use or make special efforts to use different media? Another question is, How much advertising should we put into a market to counter competitors' advertising effects?

The answers to these and other questions about competitors depend greatly on an advertiser's marketing objectives and an evaluation of what effect competitors will have in preventing the attainment of such objectives. Each situation is different. Whether to use the same media that competitors use might not be as important as identifying which medium or combination of media most effectively reaches the kind of prospects who are likely to buy the advertiser's brand. These media might happen to be identical to the media used by competitors. The media planner should consider what the competitors do but should not necessarily imitate them simply because they happen to have a larger share of market.

Planners should try to assess weaknesses in competitors' media tactics. Perhaps a competitor is not using a medium properly, or has dissipated advertising money in too many media, or is missing an important segment of the market. These errors represent opportunities in media selection and use, and such opportunities should be exploited. Marketers do not analyze a competitor's activities and their effects on a brand in order to copy the competitor's tactics, but rather to assess its strengths and weaknesses in light of the marketing objectives. Plans for attaining objectives are based on problem as well as opportunity situations.

In essence, the planner must know at least the following information about competitors before making plans:

- What are the total advertising dollars spent by the industry, and how has that changed over the past five years?
- How much money and what share of total industry spending comes from the largest competitors?
- Which media are used, and how much is spent in each medium?
- How is the advertising weight distributed over the year?
- In which markets are media concentrated?
- How much weight in GRPs is placed nationally and in each market? What TV dayparts? What commercial lengths?
- Based on their media selection (cable networks, magazines, websites carrying display and search advertising), who is their likely target audience in terms of age and gender?

Principal Sources of Expenditure Data

Media spending information can be obtained by subscription to the two most widely used reporting services: Kantar Media Intelligence and Nielsen's Monitor-Plus. For additional information, see www.kantarmediana.com and http://en-us .nielsen.com/tab/product_families/nielsen_monitorplus. These services do not provide a perfect picture of competitive media expenditures, however, because it is economically unfeasible to measure every dollar spent in every medium for every product. Expenditure analyses are therefore never quite complete for several reasons:

- The expenditures reported do not incorporate negotiated discounts on the purchase of space or time. There may be large variations between what the syndicated services report and what buyers actually spend, especially for online media.
- It takes time for the information to be gathered and processed. The delay varies depending on the medium. Television occurrences (date, time, and program) can be available within a week for the standard reports or overnight as a custom request. Television GRPs are available in a few weeks, but expenditures can take as much as two months to be reported, again depending on the medium.
- Some widely used media are not reported, such as spending for spot cable TV and regional sports networks. At this writing, both Nielsen and Kantar Media

have plans to add local cable expenditures to their services in the next few years. The services do not report spending for online search because prices are set by auction and can change hourly. The services do report the number of impressions and the websites that carry them.

The best way to assess the accuracy of competitive media reports is to compare the findings of these reports to the actual media used for the product you have planned and placed in media. But when preparing a competitive expenditure analysis, always show the reported spending for your product, never the actual. That way, whatever biases or shortcomings exist in the data will apply equally to your product and to the competitors'.

It is important to keep in mind that accuracy depends on the level of granularity—how close you look. The photo of a teenager's face taken five feet back looks terrific. A close-up reveals all the acne and other blemishes typical of that age. So the report of a brand's annual spending in television is generally within 10 percent of actual because the measurement errors over the year tend to cancel each other out. Spending by the same brand in Cleveland during the week of May 4th could be wildly out of line as compared to the actual.

These limitations simply mean that competitive media expenditure data are not to be interpreted literally. Nevertheless, coupled with other marketing and media information, such data provide a more complete picture of a competitor's spending activities.

Kantar Media and Monitor-Plus both measure competitive media expenditure data for the following 17 major media, with some variations in source comprehensiveness between the two services:

1. Network TV
2. Spot TV
3. Cable TV networks
4. National syndication TV
5. Hispanic network TV
6. Hispanic cable TV
7. Network radio
8. Spot radio (nationally placed)
9. Spot radio (locally placed)
10. National consumer magazines
11. Local consumer magazines
12. Sunday supplements
13. Local newspapers
14. National newspapers

15. Outdoor

16. Free-standing inserts (FSI)

17. Online display advertising (for search, impressions only)

Both services also monitor business-to-business advertising. Spending for online display advertising (banners, rich media, GIF/JPEG graphics, flash) is reported by Kantar Media's Evaliant and Nielsen Online's AdRelevance service. These feed spending data to their multimedia services while providing additional information on websites used, impressions, and display of the advertising itself.

Nielsen Monitor-Plus Syndicated Reports

Now let's examine each of the 17 media reported by Monitor-Plus. Kantar Media and Monitor-Plus are fiercely competitive services, especially because most agencies subscribe to only one. And once a service is chosen, agencies tend to stay with it for many years, even decades, because switching from one to the other is highly disruptive.

Kantar Media's heritage goes back 50 years, and today has the largest number of subscribers. Monitor-Plus links seamlessly with a variety of other Nielsen services. Each service has strengths and weaknesses, but there are no deal breakers. Put another way, this service has whistles, that one has bells. This one has dandruff, that one has bad breath. An agency contemplating the purchase of a competitive research service must do a thorough comparison of their respective capabilities, cost, and appropriateness for the agency's client mix. Our analysis focuses on Monitor-Plus for the simple reason that it is the service my agency, DRAFTFCB, now subscribes to.

Monitor-Plus data are delivered with two online computer programs: Ad*Views provides highly granular information about a competitor's television schedule, including spot-by-spot detail, GRPs by daypart, commercial length, weight by market, and so on. It even provides a second-by-second storyboard of the commercial with audio. Similar granularity, including pictures of the ads, is available for magazine campaigns. In short, Ad*Views provides as much granularity as a planner might need.

A second system, Quick*Views, provides a top-line summary of the spending information by advertiser, by medium, by month—the same dollars as Ad*Views, but no GRPs, no detail by market, no information about ad size, just spending and number of units. This is usually the first place a planner should go to learn about the competitive environment. Then as questions arise, Ad*Views provides the additional needed detail. For the Kantar Media service, the comparable software is StrADegy.

An overview of the Monitor-Plus service is available online at http://en-us .nielsen.com/tab/product_families/nielsen_monitorplus. The following summarizes the information currently available from the service:

National TV
- 10 broadcast networks: ABC, CBS, FOX, NBC, UPN, WB, PAX, MNT, CW, ION
- 89 general market cable networks
- 200+ syndicated programs
- Five Hispanic broadcast networks: Telemundo, Univision, Telefutura, Azteca, MTV Tr3s
- Six Hispanic cable networks
- 24/7/365 monitoring
- Local clearance available by market (the audience and estimated value of the weight delivered to each market by the national television networks)
- Monitored since 1992
- Ratings are available in terms of Live, Live+Same Day, Live+7, and C3

The delivery schedule varies by media type. For television, occurrence information (date, time, and advertiser, but no spending or audience information) generally is available within two weeks after the end of the monitored week or overnight as a custom report. National ratings are reported 21 days after the end of the week, and national dollars come in six to eight weeks after the end of the month. It takes that long because the information comes from the networks, which don't begin totaling expenditures until the month is over. They take four weeks to pull the numbers together and send to Nielsen, which then takes another two to three weeks to process and load the data late Sunday night. Since the occurrences and ratings are completely under Nielsen's control, they are delivered sooner. The complete calendar is available to Ad*Views subscribers in the "Data Availability" section of the software.

For all television venues, Monitor-Plus identifies and tracks commercials with its video signature technology. In simple terms, think of the TV picture as made up of tens of thousands of dots, pixels, that each second are either on or off. By recording the on-off status of a pixel each second, Nielsen creates a 30-byte binary number: on, on, on, off, on, off = 111010 . . . and so on. The actual code is made up of 128 such pixel identification points. Professional television coders look at each commercial to identify the product being advertised. Once a commercial (and its electronic fingerprint) has been coded, it will be accounted for wherever the commercial appears: on network TV, on any of 89 cable networks, in any market, or on any syndicated program.

To estimate brand spending, Monitor-Plus assigns a dollar value to each program and applies this rate to each monitored brand's television commercial. Broadcast-network cost estimates are developed from information provided by the networks. Syndicated program rates are based on cost data supplied by the SQAD company (see www.sqad.com) and proprietary models. Cable costs are based on the Nielsen rating multiplied by the cable network's cost per rating point furnished by SQAD.

Spot TV
- 210 television markets—in 128 markets, Nielsen monitors all announcements; in the remaining markets it electronically reports commercials previously recorded in another market or nationally
- Ratings in terms of Live+7
- Spot TV costs obtained by multiplying the program's rating times the SQAD average cost per GRP
- Monitored occurrences, spending, and ratings available 14 days after the end of the week
- Monitored since 1992

Network Radio
- Service includes three radio sales networks (Citadel Media [formerly ABC], Premiere, and Westwood).
- Spending only, based on calendar month—dollars assigned to first day of the month
- Reports available eight weeks after the end of the month

Spot Radio
- 39 markets monitored 24/7/365, approximately 20 stations per market
- Airplay detected and identified by a patented and automated recognition process
- Expenditures estimated from Arbitron radio rating × SQAD average cost per GRP

Consumer Magazines and Sunday Supplements
- National measurement of 200+ consumer magazines based on analysis of subscription copies from various markets across the country
- Five national Sunday supplements—*New York Times Magazine, Los Angeles Times Magazine, Parade, USA Weekend,* and *Wall Street Journal Magazine* (Saturday)

- Data available eight weeks after end of the month
- Magazine costs estimated using the published rates, adjusted for corporate frequency discounts (does not include special negotiated rates)

Local Newspapers
- 157 daily and Sunday newspapers in 59 DMAs
- Reports available 8 to 10 weeks after the end of the month

Actual measured advertising is multiplied by the one-time rate (Standard Advertising Unit [SAU] open rate per column inch) adjusted by an advertiser's volume discounts for each newspaper measured. Costs also reflect rates for premium-space portions of a newspaper, such as group supplements, preprinted inserts, color comics, and rotogravure and color advertising.

National Newspapers
- *New York Times*, *Wall Street Journal*, and *USA Today*
- Reports available eight weeks after the end of the month

Outdoor
- Expenditure information is provided by outdoor advertising companies and includes all outdoor advertising, such as posters, painted bulletins, transit, kiosks, and so on.
- Data available 8 to 10 weeks after the end of the quarter

Digital Advertising
- Online expenditures are provided by Nielsen's online division, which produces the AdRelevance competitive tracking service.
- AdRelevance dollars and display advertising impressions are reported by the AdRelevance software. Dollars are also fed over to the Monitor-Plus division's software and are incorporated into the Ad*Views reports. For search advertising, AdRelevance reports only impressions, not spending, because the auction market for search does not have a fixed rate card.
- Nielsen Mobile provides competitive expenditure information for display advertising on mobile platforms.

Custom Competitive Reports
Often an advertiser needs more detail than is provided by these standard reports. These include advertising in community newspapers, detailed advertising for a product category such as cell phone carriers, advertising for local retail stores in one

neighborhood, advertising on local cable television, ethnic media, and so on. The largest supplier of custom competitive information is Competitrack.[4]

Online Buzz

Advertisers need to keep up with consumer attitudes as expressed in blogs, newsgroups, social networks, YouTube videos, and any other place where consumer opinions are posted. Nielsen Buzzmetrics[5] was created to monitor these postings and report to its subscribers. This service can be especially useful during public relations challenges, new-product introductions, or any other time when it is important to know what is being said in the blogosphere. Numerous other services are becoming available that provide similar analyses of consumer-generated content.

Gathering and Assembling the Data

Studying competitive expenditures involves two major tasks. The first of these tasks is to gather and assemble the data. The second is to analyze the data.

What kinds of data should the media planner seek? The first thing is to determine how much each competitor spends annually in each medium and the five-year trend of spending. Such data provide a bird's-eye view of the industry and the key competitor's media activities. To make such data more meaningful, the planner should analyze expenditures for individual brands, rather than total expenditures for a company. Because each brand is competing with others for a share of total market sales, specific expenditures by brands are most meaningful.

A good starting point is a three-way analysis:

- Five-year trend of total spending in the category by advertiser
- Last year's spending by medium by advertiser
- Last year's spending by month by advertiser

Exhibit 6-3 shows this analysis for the top seven restaurants in the QSR (Quick Serve Restaurant) category. There is a remarkable amount of information in these three tables:

- How category spending has changed over the past five years
- Who the leaders are, and how much of category spending they account for
- Which QSRs are increasing their spending and which are decreasing
- Which QSRs are using Hispanic national television, and which are not

---

4. www.competitrack.com.

5. http://en-us.nielsen.com/tab/product_families/nielsen_buzzmetrics.

EXHIBIT 6-3

Sample Report from Nielsen Monitor-Plus Quick*Views

SUBSIDIARY	JAN. 2008–DEC. 2008 $(000)	JAN. 2007–DEC. 2007 $(000)	JAN. 2006–DEC. 2006 $(000)	JAN. 2005–DEC. 2005 $(000)	JAN. 2004–DEC. 2004 $(000)	5-YEAR TOTAL $(000)	PERCENT OF 5-YEAR TOTAL
McDonalds	$813,561	$746,041	$841,168	$757,545	$677,825	$3,836,138	19.7%
Subway	420,968	383,496	409,807	362,912	334,900	1,912,084	9.8
KFC	291,081	294,279	316,558	305,893	264,276	1,472,087	7.6
Wendy's	276,392	293,569	371,781	379,238	360,104	1,681,084	8.6
Burger King	271,618	233,646	282,306	278,259	313,338	1,379,167	7.1
Pizza Hut	262,513	230,182	250,070	266,364	233,441	1,242,570	6.4
Taco Bell	258,028	238,956	271,459	244,463	209,244	1,222,151	6.3
All Other QSR	1,535,973	1,322,089	1,384,625	1,326,176	1,142,430	6,716,293	34.5
Total Category	$4,130,135	$3,747,258	$4,127,773	$3,920,850	$3,535,558	$19,461,574	100.0%

SUBSIDIARY	2008 TOTAL $(000)	NETWORK TV $(000)	CABLE TV $(000)	SYNDICATED TV $(000)	SPOT TV $(000)	SPANISH-LANGUAGE NETWORK TV $(000)	SPANISH-LANGUAGE CABLE TV $(000)	NATIONAL MAGAZINE $(000)	OUTDOOR $(000)	NETWORK RADIO $(000)	SPOT RADIO $(000)	INTERNET $(000)	ALL OTHERS $(000)
McDonald's	$813,561	$232,031	$78,073	$21,870	$236,562	$52,350	$3,108	$27,842	$76,701	$3,168	$61,138	$16,561	$4,157
Subway	420,968	132,483	66,982	4,461	152,272	19,350	2,233	14,793	5,064	6,302	12,339	3,015	1,672
KFC	291,081	99,816	56,938	--	115,878	11,219	--	679	1,737	--	3,211	1,105	1,177
Wendy's	276,392	133,542	59,435	5,427	30,940	19,730	1,686	--	4,899	35	17,587	2,104	329
Burger King	271,618	105,096	66,669	9,484	23,733	21,806	2,275	8,446	8,169	860	22,914	2,008	159
Pizza Hut	262,513	80,308	76,329	5,394	83,096	11,603	784	--	2,488	507	839	2,988	433
Taco Bell	258,028	109,809	63,903	--	57,924	--	39	8,524	232	--	10,194	4,848	299
All Other QSR	1,535,973	126,307	268,258	3,473	980,034	31,812	4,454	6,909	45,945	7,367	42,848	9,569	8,497
Total Category	$4,130,135	$1,019,391	$737,086	$50,110	$1,680,438	$167,871	$14,579	$67,193	$145,235	$18,239	$171,071	$42,199	$16,723
Percent of total	100.0%	24.7%	17.8%	1.2%	40.7%	4.1%	0.4%	1.6%	3.5%	0.4%	4.1%	1.0%	0.4%

SUBSIDIARY	2008 TOTAL $(000)	JAN. 2008 $(000)	FEB. 2008 $(000)	MAR. 2008 $(000)	APR. 2008 $(000)	MAY 2008 $(000)	JUN. 2008 $(000)	JUL. 2008 $(000)	AUG. 2008 $(000)	SEP. 2008 $(000)	OCT. 2008 $(000)	NOV 2008 $(000)	DEC 2008 $(000)
McDonald's	$813,561	$60,066	$61,847	$62,944	$64,469	$68,087	$77,854	$66,072	$97,426	$65,200	$64,863	$62,272	$62,460
Subway	420,968	40,451	37,501	39,519	30,781	29,369	28,914	42,568	38,996	30,622	34,164	34,725	33,357
KFC	291,081	23,650	27,840	31,580	26,987	28,882	25,945	22,408	26,273	25,113	21,049	13,629	17,725
Wendy's	276,392	21,621	17,354	26,706	29,148	19,311	20,219	22,280	22,680	29,226	22,471	24,452	20,923
Burger King	271,618	19,951	15,492	22,436	32,129	21,316	19,885	21,925	16,365	23,923	26,386	26,061	25,699
Pizza Hut	262,513	21,574	19,487	24,990	27,181	19,872	16,826	19,197	23,364	20,961	19,296	29,667	20,098
Taco Bell	258,028	29,537	23,338	21,421	18,490	22,579	22,023	19,445	14,584	20,381	28,200	21,852	16,178
All Other QSR	1,535,973	119,255	101,176	139,521	157,244	142,724	133,837	114,847	101,299	126,123	136,620	138,992	124,285
Total Category	$4,130,135	$336,106	$304,035	$369,117	$386,479	$352,191	$345,503	$328,742	$340,988	$341,548	$353,050	$351,649	$320,726
% of total	100.0%	8.1%	7.4%	8.9%	9.4%	8.5%	8.4%	8.0%	8.3%	8.3%	8.5%	8.5%	7.8%

Source: The Nielsen Company, Monitor-Plus. Used with permission.

- How online spending compares to traditional media
- Which months have above-average spending and which have below

These data are the raw material for virtually unlimited additional analysis keyed to an advertiser's needs. For instance, a competitor's target audience can be revealed from its GRP weight by cable network and its selection of Internet websites. It is best to download the data in this raw form and then calculate shares and other percentages on the spreadsheet.

In gathering expenditure data by brand, it is always advisable to include the planner's brand as well as all the competitive brands in the category, so all are compared on the same research basis. Even though planners may know actual spending for their own brand, it should never be compared with the measured activity of their competitors. As stated earlier, planners should always compare measured spending for their own brands to that of the competitors.

The study of total national expenditures is only one approach to analyzing competitors' marketing and media strategies. If you see a substantial amount of spending in local media (spot TV, spot radio, local newspapers, or outdoor), it would be useful to compare the media weight of a brand with its competitors on a market-by-market basis. Since the dollars spent in a market will vary depending on the size of the market, planners must run an Ad*Views report showing GRPs to understand strategic differences. In Chicago, $500,000 will have a very different consumer impact from $500,000 in Rockford, Illinois. That difference will be revealed by the GRP delivery, which in turn can be used to estimate the reach and frequency of a competitor's campaign.

Finally, it is important to know how much was spent in each medium during each month of the year. Most brands have peak selling seasons and vary the weight of their advertising accordingly. This kind of analysis helps establish timing and scheduling plans for the media selected later in the planning process.

Analyzing the Data

One worthwhile use of media expenditure analysis is to examine spending by advertisers who lead in share of market. Those with smaller shares might want to learn which media, markets, and audiences are most important to the leaders. Sometimes it is possible to find that leading competitors ignore one or two media entirely. In such a case, it is possible for advertisers with lesser shares to preempt a medium for themselves. For example, if all of the share leaders emphasize network television, then a planner can select radio as a medium in which a brand could be significant. We saw this earlier in Oreck vacuum cleaner's use of radio. The planner should keep in mind, however, that a competitor's avoidance of a medium might signal the possibility that the medium is not appropriate for the product's advertising. Furthermore, as noted earlier, an advertiser may not want to risk a radically different media strategy, even one that may make sense to the planner.

Competitive expenditure analysis is helpful as a means of knowing what competitors have done, but not necessarily as a means of knowing what to do as a result. These analyses might show, for example, that a competitor is test-marketing a product, calling for a revised market strategy to combat the situation.

Probably the greatest danger in analyzing expenditure data comes from simply copying the leaders blindly. If a leading competitor places 10 percent of its budget in Market A, then other competitors often follow the leader. But the followers' products and market strategies might not lend themselves to such weight in Market A. Furthermore, the share leader might establish its weight proportions for reasons quite different from those that followers should use.

The best use of an expenditure analysis is as part of an organized intelligence system that includes other kinds of marketing information to tell a clear story of the competitors' strategies. Although some advertising agencies tend to deprecate the use of expenditure analysis as not being worth the investment in money or time, most large agencies find it valuable if used properly as an indication of spending strategy. When used intelligently, expenditure data are well worth the time and money invested.

Using Competitive Media Expenditure Analyses

Following is a list of uses of a competitive media expenditure analysis devised many years ago by the staff of *Media Decisions*.[6] It reviews the most important uses and values to be obtained by completing such an analysis:

1. The expenditure figures can show you the regionality and seasonality and how these factors are changing for all competitive and potentially competitive brands.
2. The data can give you a fix on ad budget size and media mix, market by market.
3. You can use the data to spot new-product tests and to track new-brand rollouts.

---

6. "Do You Know Your Competitive Brand Data?" *Media Decisions* (August 1975): 60.

4. You can infer from where the money is being spent how competitors view their target audiences, how they profile their brands, and where they seek to position themselves in your marketplace.

5. You can watch spending patterns of the opposition—TV flighting, radio station rotation, position practices in magazines, or day of week in newspapers.

6. Once you have complete knowledge of what your enemies are up to, you can make better decisions about where to meet them head-on and when to outflank them.

7. In new-product and line-extension planning, expenditure data are essential to estimate how much it will cost to get into a market, who is already there, and which competitive product types are growing fastest in the new product's market segment.

International Competitive Analysis

Competitive spending analysis in the United States is relatively straightforward, whether from Nielsen Monitor-Plus or Kantar Media. All the major media are measured, the services routinely cover all products advertised in those media, and the information is delivered to the planner's desktop with easy-to-use software. Both services can be expected to give the planner a complete picture of the competitive landscape, with only minor differences in emphasis, convenience, and quality.

International competitive analysis is quite different. Where the U.S. services are standardized, international competitive analysis is completely customized. Three companies provide international competitive analysis: Nielsen Global Ad*View,[7] Kantar Media,[8] and Xtreme Information.[9] No single service covers the entire world, so a multicountry report requires piecing together the capabilities of the three monitoring services. Typically the order is placed with one of the services, which acts as the coordinator, drawing on its capabilities in countries it measures and working with "partner" suppliers in the countries that it lacks.

An important service is harmonizing the reports from the different countries. There is no country-by-country coordination among the researchers who compile the data. Each may give a slightly different name to the same international advertiser. So a report on advertising by aircraft manufacturers in the UK might show spending by "Airbus Corporation," spending in France may be reported for "Airbus Corp," in Germany it may be "Airbus," and in Spain "Airbus-Aircraft." These are

7. http://nl.nielsen.com/products/documents/NielsenGlobalAdView_000.pdf.

8. www.tnsglobal.com/media.

9. www.xtremeinformation.com/services.htm.

all the same company, but because the words are presented with slight differences, they must be reexpressed in a single form to allow rolling up to a multicountry total in an Excel spreadsheet.

Planners seeking an international competitive report need to prepare a *request for proposal* from the three services, listing the countries, inclusive dates, report frequency (annual, quarterly, monthly), the media to be reported, and the advertisers or the product category to be tracked. Note if the report is to include specific media vehicles as well as the total by medium and if you require examples of the creative executions—the print ads, TV commercials, and so on. Keep in mind that each element will add to the cost, which can be substantial—many tens of thousands of dollars, depending on how much detail is needed and how many countries. Often the proposal will be presented as a lump sum, without the country-by-country cost detail. Specify the form of the report (an Excel spreadsheet and pivot table is best). Once the contract is signed, assume it will take several months to deliver the report after the end of the report period (the report for January activity would be delivered in March or April).

Finally, there is no such thing as a worldwide estimate of spending. That would require a competitive report covering many dozens of countries at a cost of hundreds of thousands or even millions of dollars. The three suppliers can provide an estimate of worldwide spending, but it will represent only the countries they individually monitor and only for the most commonly used international product categories such as financial services, airlines, hotels, etc.

Managing Media Planning and Buying

Most simple media plans are laid out in an Excel spreadsheet. Its infinite flexibility makes it an ideal platform. But this same strength is problematic for large advertisers that have multiple brands and large planning groups that need a single cost database, common words to describe each medium (one planner's "Network Prime Time" would sort differently in a corporate roll-up with another planner's "Net Prime"), an organizational structure that reflects different divisions or product groups, password-controlled security, and the ability to customize flowchart display and reporting to the needs of an individual advertiser. Advertisers often want online access to the plans for internal reports (but not to change the numbers!).

The two leading providers of these systems are Workhorse Software (developers of Mediatools)[10] and Nielsen-IMS (developers of Brandfx), http://en-us.nielsen.com/tab/product_families/nielsen_ims. Both systems have been in use for many

---

10. www.workhorsesoftware.com.

years, serving the largest and most complex advertisers. While lacking Excel's infinite flexibility, their structure and discipline will pay benefits that well justify their cost.

These flowchart computer programs are different from the housekeeping systems that manage the three functions of all media buying: estimating (the listing of what has been purchased), billing (documentary support for the media agency's bill to the advertiser), and paying (the database that validates invoices from the media and supports their payment). The two companies that provide this service are Donovan Data Systems[11] (the oldest and most widely used service) and MediaBank[12] (a more recent entry into the field, but still with decades of experience). Since these housekeeping systems tie directly into the agency's financial management programs and affect the day-to-day work of virtually every department, the buying decision should involve the entire agency.

Sources of Marketing Data

Size and share of market for a brand and its competitors, and other information contained in a situation analysis, can be obtained from a number of syndicated research services. Other data can be obtained from periodicals, association reports, government, and media. The following paragraphs provide brief descriptions of the major syndicated services and other sources of data, including Internet addresses, when available. Many of these companies maintain websites that provide limited but often highly useful data in exchange for a no-charge registration.

Major Data Services

The most widely used syndicated research services are those of The Nielsen Company; Information Resources, Inc.; Mediamark Research & Intelligence, LLC (MRI); and Experian Simmons. Numerous other research companies provide specialized lifestyle and other marketing information.

The Nielsen Company (www.nielsen.com) In 2002, when the previous edition of this book was published, A. C. Nielsen market research and Nielsen Media Research were two separate companies. Even within the companies, their divisions operated as independent silos with few if any direct contacts. Since then, all of the divisions

---

11. www.donovandata.com/index.html.

12. www.mbxg.com.

and marketing services have been combined into a single worldwide organization, The Nielsen Company, with a universally known name, international scope of operation, and a mandate to integrate its many services in whatever way possible to meet the marketing needs of its clients. It is safe to say that if there is a research need, Nielsen has a product or division that deserves to be considered. Media planners will primarily use the TV ratings. The full range of services can be found on its website.

Information Resources, Inc. (IRI) The InfoScan Census offered by Information Resources, Inc. (www.infores.com), is a syndicated tracking service for grocery industry data at the national, local market, and chain store levels. It integrates scanner sales, feature ad, coupon, display, and price data from more than 45,000 supermarkets, drugstores, and mass merchandisers with scanner panel data from 90,000 households. The InfoScan Census database comprises weekly feedback on 3.2 million products from stores representing the total movement of some 70 percent of all commodity volume in the United States. Data are available for more than 190 retail chain and market geographies in addition to the retail trading areas of participating accounts. For additional detail on IRI's test-market capabilities, see Chapter 14. Like Nielsen's market research division, IRI sells data only to advertisers.

Single-Source Research Two services, MRI and Simmons, provide product and media usage data from a single survey. Each company uses its own nationally projectable sample that lets a planner identify the demographics, attitudes, and behaviors of heavy, medium, and light product users. Since the two services are fierce competitors for the agency's research business, each has written their own description.

- **Mediamark Research & Intelligence, LLC (MRI).** Since 1979, MRI has been the dominant voice in media and consumer research in the United States. No other organization—not even the Census Bureau—knows more about American consumers. MRI's Survey of the American Consumer™, used in most media and marketing plans in the country, is the primary source of audience data for the consumer magazine industry and the most comprehensive and reliable source of multimedia audience data available. The survey's multidimensional database provides marketers with a view of audiences of all major media, their demographics, lifestyles, attitudes, and product usage information on close to 6,000 brands, covering more than 500 categories. MRI conducts in-depth personal interviews with more than 26,000 adults ages 18 and older from an area probability sample covering 26,000+ individual house-holds throughout the United States. The sample is refreshed every six months to provide unique insights into the media consumption and product usage behavior of U.S. consumers. Go to www.mediamark.com.

- **Experian® Simmons^{SM} (Simmons).** The former Simmons Market Research Bureau is now a division of Experian, the multinational consumer information and credit reporting company. Simmons provides, four times per year, syndicated reports on consumer behavior, including media use, brand purchases, frequency of purchases, and an array of psychographic, opinion, and attitudinal measures. Simmons measures the full-spectrum of consumers, reporting on adults (18+), teens (12–17), and kids (6–11) and provides detailed information concerning Hispanic consumers. SimmonsLOCAL is the localized version of the flagship National Consumer Survey (NCS) that reports on virtually all of the variables contained within the NCS for every DMA in the country. In addition, Simmons has custom measurement capabilities that provide direct linkage from proprietary research or customer databases to the syndicated products. With Experian Simmons, planners can understand brand use, consumer attitudes and opinions about categories, products, and media, and determine the best media choices for reaching the desired audience.

Zip Code Marketing. There are two major providers of zip-code-based lifestyle data: Nielsen Claritas, at www.claritas.com, and Experian Mosaic (www.experian.com). Both provide marketing data at every microgeographic level, including zip codes, census tracts, census block groups, compiled list cells, and postal carrier routes. These services, too, are fiercely competitive. Following are their self-descriptions:

- Nielsen Claritas PRIZM is the industry-leading consumer segmentation system that yields the richest, most comprehensive, and precise insights available. Nielsen PRIZM combines demographics, consumer behavior, and geographic data to help marketers identify, understand, and target their customers and prospects. PRIZM defines every U.S. household in terms of 66 demographic and behavior types or segments to help marketers discern those consumers' likes, dislikes, lifestyles, and purchase behaviors. Used by thousands of marketers in Fortune 500 companies, PRIZM provides a common language for marketing in an increasingly diverse and complex marketplace.
- ExperianMosaic® USA, classifies all American consumer households and neighborhoods into one of 60 segments and 12 groups to help understand the multiple dimensions of their socioeconomics, behaviors, and preferences

driving their lifestyles. Mosaic USA is available at the household, Zip+4, Block Group, and Zip Code levels to allow matching to whatever market approach is required to help target the best audience.

Other Sources of Data

The sources of data just described provide specific and pertinent data for a situation analysis but are relatively expensive. The cost might be too high for many small manufacturers or agencies, so it becomes necessary to find substitute sources of data. There are a number of relatively inexpensive sources, although they do not provide the same amount of detail, especially about competitors' sales and distribution practices. When the information is incomplete, advertisers must make assumptions about the missing data. Astute observers can, however, check these assumptions by taking note of the marketing actions of their own company and competitors. The following paragraphs, meanwhile, identify major sources of data for the situation analysis.

***Sales & Marketing Management* Survey of Buying Power** Marketing and media planners often use this survey (www.salesandmarketing.com) as a convenient source of three kinds of data about markets:

1. Population and household data for all major geographic markets in the United States
2. Effective buying income and spending statistics about markets
3. Retail sales data by broad product classes: (a) food stores; (b) eating and drinking places; (c) general merchandise stores; (d) automotive dealers; (e) furniture, home furnishings, and appliances; (f) drugstores; (g) apparel and accessory stores; (h) gasoline service stations; (i) building materials and hardware stores

No individual brand sales are shown, and the only classifications of consumers are by population and income. However, the report is convenient in locating and evaluating geographic markets by state, by metropolitan statistical area, by county, or by city. Furthermore, the three factors (population, income, and retail sales) have been combined into a multiple-factor index number for each market, which simplifies comparisons among markets.

Convenient tables ranking markets by sales potential also facilitate comparisons by each of the nine retail product categories. A user trying to find and evaluate markets for a drug product, for example, will find a table that ranks markets from best to poorest on the basis of sales of drugs. *Sales & Marketing Management* publishes its Survey of Buying Power annually. This publication is now part of Nielsen Business Media. Additional information is available at their website.

SRDS SRDS (www.srds.com) publishes media rate books for all major media. In its local media books (newspaper, spot radio, and spot television) are market data sections similar to those in the Survey of Buying Power. SRDS also shows geographic markets by state, metropolitan statistical area, county, and city, but not in as much detail as the Survey of Buying Power. Local media rate books are published monthly, and the market data are revised annually.

SRDS publishes a quarterly TV and cable source, which contains a market profile for each local TV market in the United States, including demographics, sales data, and local media data. It also provides a reference for information on TV station representatives, owners of multiple TV stations, network TV personnel, commercial TV stations, TV syndicators, national and local cable TV representatives, and TV trafficking specifications. Since radio and television rates are negotiated, there are no prices in SRDS.

In addition to the hard-copy books, SRDS makes available some of its information on the Internet. Subscribers receive one password for each paid subscription. As of this writing, SRDS makes online reports available on the following topics: consumer magazines, Internet, business-to-business magazines, radio, newspapers, out-of-home, TV/cable, and the *International Media Guide*, which includes business magazines, consumer magazines, and newspapers worldwide.

Marketer's Guide to Media Every year Mediaweek publishes a handy reference resource titled *Marketer's Guide to Media*, which includes current rates and audience estimates for the major media. This guide describes trends in total advertising expenditures, costs, and audiences for network, cable, syndication, and spot television; radio; out-of-home; magazines; newspapers; and online services. It can be bought online at www.adweek.com/adweek/news_stand/directories.jsp.

TV Dimensions Another annual, *TV Dimensions*, provides advertisers, ad agencies, and the media with a 500-page analytical and reference tool that covers all aspects of the television medium. Sections include a history of television; the growth of cable, VCR usage, and the Internet; program type appeals; reach and frequency; qualitative factors regarding viewer interest and attentiveness; commercial exposure and impact; and intermedia comparisons. There are similar publications for magazines, Internet, intermedia comparisons, and radio. They can be bought online at www.mediadynamicsinc.com.

Census Data The Census Bureau (www.census.gov) of the U.S. Department of Commerce publishes many census analyses that are helpful in marketing planning. Most useful have been the Census of Business and Census of Population. But other census data, too numerous to list here, are available for special industries. The *Statistical Abstract of the United States*, published once a year, has been considered helpful as a quick source of data for media market planning. It is available online at the Census website.

Media Studies of Special Markets Often local and national media conduct special market studies that are helpful resources for learning about geographical as well as special markets. Although the purpose of these reports is to show a given medium in a favorable light, the researcher should not assume that all such studies are biased. Often a medium will sponsor a study that represents a significant contribution to the understanding of markets and media. Sometimes the only research available on a special market or medium is these studies.

Advertising Trade Publications A number of publications offer market and media data on a regular basis. The most useful ones are *Advertising Age* (www.adage.com), *Adweek* (www.adweek.com), *Mediaweek* (www.mediaweek.com), and *Broadcasting & Cable* (www.broadcastingandcable.com). Information can be obtained by using search tools in the publications' websites to locate studies published in their past issues, which can be purchased online.

Associations Many trade associations report market data for their members. In some cases, these data show sales by brands, but others tend to be rather general. Because there are so many different trade associations, it is advisable to determine whether the associations in a particular industry can be of aid in compiling the situation analysis.

Miscellaneous Sources Yet other sources of data are available at relatively low cost to the market/media planner. Federal, state, and local governments all produce various kinds of research that can be helpful. Federal data can be found by contacting the Government Printing Office in Washington, D.C. (www.gpo.gov) or by inquiring at a government depository library.

Chambers of commerce, both national and local, can be helpful in finding the right kinds of data needed for marketing situation analyses. Obviously, data from these sources will be rather general, but the information might be useful for preliminary portions of the analysis.

Finally, for analysis of products and product values, *Consumer Reports* (www .consumerreports.org), which is published by Consumers Union, provides monthly and annual publications for a small cost. *Consumer's Digest*, published six times a year, is a similar source. The magazines also produce an annual buyer's guide. Both of these organizations put various brands of products through tests to determine quality and the best buy for the money. Not all brands or models are tested, but many of the most popular brands on the market are analyzed. Ordinarily, this kind of information is difficult to obtain except by special research services, so these two publications make the job of finding product values relatively easy.

CHAPTER SEVEN

Strategy Planning I

Who, Where, and When

O nce the advertiser has an overall marketing strategy, a media strategy can be developed. The first three parts of the strategy answer three questions:

1. *To whom* should we target our advertising?
2. *Where,* geographically, should we advertise?
3. *When* should we advertise?

The answers to these questions will drive other decisions made later in the development of a media strategy. For example, if it has been agreed that advertising should be directed primarily to women 18–34, then media alternatives such as sports magazines or TV programs directed primarily to men would not be appropriate. (Obviously, there are some exceptions—but not many.) Because they will affect every aspect of the media plan, decisions about the target market must be made early. The remaining parts of the media strategy—weighting, reach, frequency, and continuity—will be discussed in Chapter 8.

Sometimes the media planner makes these decisions alone, but more often the process includes input from creative, the account group, and marketing planners, as well as from the client. Most often, the decision making is a team process.

Answers to each of the three big questions rely most heavily on numerical analysis of marketing and media data, but they also involve judgment and subjective appraisal. Numbers that are evaluated literally are subject to error. One must know where the numbers came from, that is, how they were obtained or calculated. The best planners know the value of research methodology as well as how to analyze the numbers. The search for objectivity in planning requires both abilities.

Target Selection

A media plan's *target audience* is the group of people whom the advertising is attempting to influence. Most typically, advertising is directed to current users of the product or service. Although targeting information is available for products that appeal to specialized markets such as upper-income households, which are surveyed by IPSOS/Mendelsohn,[1] and teens, who are surveyed by Teenage Research Unlimited,[2] the most commonly used services are Experian Simmons[3] and Mediamark Research & Intelligence, LLC (MRI).[4] Both studies begin with a survey of product usage and media behavior from a random sample of homes in the 48 contiguous states, and cover virtually every product or service sold in America. Exhibit 7-1 shows the MRI survey's question dealing with the use of bottled water and seltzer.

The results of the survey are made available to subscribers on a computer database that allows custom cross tabulation of the data. Exhibit 7-2 shows the format of these tabulations. Although this example is from MRI, it illustrates the universal concepts of horizontal (percent of the medium's audience in the advertiser's target), vertical (percent of the advertiser's target in the medium's audience), and selectivity index that compares the product's users to the average adult. In the analysis of media vehicle audiences, "vertical" equates to coverage; "horizontal" equates to composition.

The goal is to identify and define the targets—those who are most likely to buy the product or service. Targets are defined on the basis of one or more demographic characteristics of consumers who have purchased the product or brand in the past. Purchasers are typically described in terms of age, income, occupation, education, and so forth. Custom research can provide this kind of information, but it is usually quite expensive and time-consuming. The services listed earlier are known as "syndicated" research because they cover a broad range of products and services with a single questionnaire, spreading the cost across multiple buyers. Virtually every advertising agency subscribes to these services as a cost of doing business.

One of the first media-planning action steps is to decide whether to concentrate on all users or a narrower product usage category. A great deal depends on whom the advertiser wants to reach. This is a marketing as well as a creative and media decision. Most likely, the creative personnel, the account planning team, the agency

---

1. www.ipsosmediact.com/media/mendelsohn.aspx.
2. www.teenageresearch.com.
3. www.experiansimmons.com.
4. www.mediamark.com.

EXHIBIT 7-1

MRI Survey on Bottled Water and Seltzer

BOTTLED WATER & SELTZER	You Personally:	
	Drank in last 6 months	Drinks or glasses/ last 7 days
	134	
TOTAL:	☐ _____	00
TYPES:		
Flavored	☐ _____	01
Non-Flavored	☐ _____	02
KINDS:		
Sparkling	☐ _____	03
Non-Sparkling	☐ _____	04
FORMS:		
Sweetened	☐ _____	05
Unsweetened	☐ _____	06
BRANDS:		
Acquafina	☐ _____	07
Arrowhead	☐ _____	08
Calistoga	☐ _____	09
Canada Dry Seltzer	☐ _____	10
Clearly Canadian	☐ _____	11
Crystal Geyser	☐ _____	12
Crystal Springs	☐ _____	13
Dannon Water	☐ _____	14
Deer Park	☐ _____	15
Evian	☐ _____	16
Great Bear	☐ _____	17
Hinckley & Schmitt	☐ _____	18
Ice Mountain	☐ _____	19
La Croix	☐ _____	20
Mountain Valley	☐ _____	21
Natural Mineral Water	☐ _____	22
Naya	☐ _____	23
New York Seltzer	☐ _____	24
Ozarka	☐ _____	25
Perrier	☐ _____	26
Poland Springs	☐ _____	27
Schweppes Seltzer	☐ _____	28
Seagram Seltzer	☐ _____	29
Sparkletts	☐ _____	30
Utopia	☐ _____	31
Vermont Pure	☐ _____	32
Vintage Seltzer	☐ _____	33
Zephyrhills	☐ _____	34
	☐ _____	999

OTHER (Write In)

Do you receive home delivery of bottled water? Yes ☐1   No ☐2   135-0

Source: Mediamark Research & Intelligence, LLC. Used with permission.

account representative, and certainly the advertiser will all have an opinion of who they believe can be convinced to buy the brand. Sometimes the goal is to convince consumers to switch brands; other times it will be to convince persons not using the product category to try it. But once the buying category has been decided, the targets will then be found by studying demographic and lifestyle data. Planners use indexes to show how the demographics of product users compare to the population as a whole.

EXHIBIT 7-2

Demographics of Medium/Heavy Bottled Water or Seltzer Users

BASE: ADULTS		TOTALS	MEDIUM/HEAVY BOTTLED WATER OR SELTZER— LAST 7 DAYS
Total adults	(000)	224,899	107,113
	Vert%	100.0	100.0
	Horz%	100.0	47.6
	Index	100	100
Men	(000)	108,664	48,895
	Vert%	48.3	45.7
	Horz%	100.0	45.0
	Index	100	94
Women	(000)	116,235	58,218
	Vert%	51.7	54.4
	Horz%	100.0	50.1
	Index	100	105
Ages 18–24	(000)	28,550	14,433
	Vert%	12.7	13.5
	Horz%	100.0	50.6
	Index	100	106
Ages 25–34	(000)	40,210	21,160
	Vert%	17.9	19.8
	Horz%	100.0	52.6
	Index	100	110
Ages 35–44	(000)	42,681	22,186
	Vert%	19.0	20.7
	Horz%	100.0	52.0
	Index	100	109
Ages 45–54	(000)	43,918	22,807
	Vert%	19.5	21.3
	Horz%	100.0	51.9
	Index	100	109
Ages 55–64	(000)	32,911	15,111
	Vert%	14.6	14.1
	Horz%	100.0	45.9
	Index	100	96
Ages 65+	(000)	36,629	11,416
	Vert%	16.3	10.7
	Horz%	100.0	31.2
	Index	100	65

There are 224,899,000 adults in the United States.

There are 107,113,000 medium/heavy bottled water users.

47.6% of adults are M/H bottled water users (107,113/224,899).

There are 28,550,000 adults ages 18–24 in the United States.

12.7% of all adults are ages 18–24 (28,550/224,899).

There are 14,433,000 18–24-year-old M/H bottled water users.

13.5% of M/H bottled water users are ages 18–24 (14,443/107,113).

50.6% of 18–24-year-olds are M/H bottled water users (14,433/28,550).

Adults 18–24 are 6% more likely to be M/H bottled water users than the average adult. (13.5/12.7–1).

Adults ages 65+ are 35% less likely to be M/H bottled water users than the average adult. (10.7/16.3 –1).

Source: Mediamark Research & Intelligence, LLC, Spring 2009. Used with permission.

Case Study 7-1 shows a corporate advertising campaign whose target audience was opinion leaders, both in government and across the country. The advertiser used a multimedia campaign of television, magazines, and online media with high-impact, large creative units (60- and 90-second television, spreads, online rich media), concentrated in the media vehicles used by this target.

CASE STUDY 7-1

The Dow Chemical Company "The Human Element" Campaign

Background
In the past, Dow Chemical was a faceless company. The true story needed to be told—the story of a company that is helping create solutions for affordable and adequate food supply, decent housing, improved personal health and safety, and sustainable water supplies.

Marketing Goals
The three specific marketing goals were to:

1. Forge new and unlikely relationships with key influencers, educators, current and potential employees, and the general public.
2. Increase overall awareness and knowledge of Dow and its policies, products, and initiatives.
3. Improve Dow's reputation among key stakeholders.

The Concept
The big idea was the understanding that change lies at the intersection of chemistry and humanity. The most important element of all was missing from the standardized periodic table of elements. This was the "Human Element." When you have that, anything is possible.

The Media Plan
The media plan was designed to reach the marketing target in a variety of selective venues with a mixture of traditional and digital media. The message was carried by 90-, 60-, and 30-second spots on NBC broadcast television and 16 cable networks including CNN, National Geographic channel, Fox News, Discovery, and the History Channel.

CASE STUDY 7-1 **The Dow Chemical Company**
"The Human Element" Campaign *(continued)*

In print, the campaign ran in high-impact two- to six-page spreads, gatefolds, and barn-door ads in 28 opinion leader magazines such as *The Atlantic*, *Fortune*, *The New Yorker*, *Time*, *Newsweek*, *The Economist*, and *National Geographic*.

Online advertising followed the same pattern, with banner ads and rich media creative units on 16 online sites such as BusinessWeek.com, CNN.com, NewYorkTimes.com, WallStreetJournal.com, NationalGeographic.com, Forbes.com, and Time.com.

Results

The campaign resulted in dramatic progress in building relations with Congress as well as with nongovernmental organizations involved with energy, climate change, and the global water supply. Key influencers have publicly recognized Dow, proving that the campaign not only was being seen by the target but also impacted perceptions in a positive manner.

This is an example of the campaign's local print creative:

Source: The Dow Chemical Company. Used with permission.

In addition to demographics and product usage, MRI and Simmons have classified their respondents according to various lifestyles based on the products they use and their attitudes. Simmons segments include GreenAware, Tipping Point, Waistband, Political Persona, and others. MRI has Consumer Innovators, Leisure Styles, Diet Control Attitude, Civic/Political Engagement, Financial Attitude, and other groups.

Index Number Analysis

In analyzing numerical data, there are three commonly used bases: raw numbers, percentages, and index numbers. Raw numbers are used least often because they are so large and because it is difficult to compare the raw numbers of one brand with those of another brand, each of which can have radically different bases. Percentages are a means of equalizing the bases of numbers from two or more companies, so they are usually preferred over raw numbers for making comparisons. Index numbers are the ratio of two percentages and are most preferred for comparisons.

An *index* is a number that shows a relationship between two percentages or between two raw numbers. Generally, index numbers are printed as whole numbers. The value of an index is that it relates sales or product usage to population demographics, enabling one to have a convenient common method for comparison. If the population segment is considered to be "average," then an index number for sales tells how much above or below average sales are, in absolute terms. An index number of 100 is equal to the average; 125 is 25 percent above average, and 80 is 20 percent below average. Exhibits 7-3 and 7-4 provide an example of using index numbers.

EXHIBIT 7-3

Medium/Heavy Users of Bottled Water by Age Segment

AGE SEGMENT	NUMBER OF ADULTS IN UNITED STATES (000)	PERCENTAGE OF U.S. ADULTS	NUMBER OF M/H BOTTLED WATER USERS	PERCENT OF ADULT USERS
18–24	28,550	12.7%	14,433	13.5%
25–34	40,210	17.9	21,160	19.8
35–44	42,681	19.0	22,186	20.7
45–54	43,918	19.5	22,807	21.3
55–64	32,911	14.6	15,111	14.1
65+	36,629	16.3	11,416	10.7
Total adults	224,899	100.0%	107,113	100.0%

Source: Mediamark Research & Intelligence, LLC, Spring 2009. Used with permission.

EXHIBIT 7-4

Calculating Index Numbers (Based on Exhibit 7-3)

AGE SEGMENT	CALCULATION	INDEX
18–24	13.5÷12.7	106
25–34	19.8÷17.9	110
35–44	20.7÷19.0	109
45–54	21.3÷19.5	109
55–64	14.1÷14.6	96
65+	10.7÷16.3	65

Source: Mediamark Research & Intelligence, LLC, Spring 2009. Used with permission.

Which demographic segments should be selected as target markets for media to reach? The usual answer is to select those demographic segments with the largest volume of sales or the largest number of users. In other words, advertise where the brand has a history of success. The 25–34 age group accounts for 19.8 percent of users and 17.9 percent of the population. Using the 110 index (19.8/17.9), we see that people this age are 10 percent more likely to use bottled water than the average adult. While this age group is the most selective, we see that the 35–44- and the 45–54-year-old age groups have a 109 index, which is statistically identical to 110. We also see a clear fall-off in usage by the 55–64 and 65+ age groups. Obviously, income, occupation, education, and other demographic categories would also have to be checked before a final decision could be made.

In this example, we compared the percentage of usage in each age segment to the percentage of population in that segment. (One could compare the raw numbers of usage and population distribution in each segment, but such comparisons are more difficult than those made using percentages.) When the percentage of usage is compared with the percentage of population distribution in each segment, an index number can be calculated to make the comparisons easier to analyze. The formula for calculating such numbers is as follows:

$$\text{Index number} = \frac{\text{Percentage of users in a demographic segment}}{\text{Percentage of population in the same segment}} \times 100$$

Using the formula to calculate index numbers for the data in Exhibit 7-3 yields the index numbers in Exhibit 7-4. The index numbers in Exhibit 7-4 show how much the product is being used compared with the potential (or population proportion) in each segment. An index number below 100, as seen in the 55–64 and 65+ age groups, indicates lower than average usage. So even though the groups together account for almost one-fourth of all users, they represent less than would be expected, given the size of the 55+ population. Clearly the younger age segments represent the best prospects—both because they account for the largest percent of users and because they are far more likely to use bottled water than the population as a whole. In this sense, index numbers more accurately indicate potential for usage or sales. One cannot easily see this kind of relationship, however, without first calculating the index numbers. Given the demographic skew shown here, the advertiser would probably make adults 25–54 the primary target, with a secondary target of women 25–54.

It is helpful to think of index numbers as measures of central tendency, just as averages or means are in the statistical world. An average does not describe any one person in a group, only the group as a whole. Likewise, an index number higher than 100 means that the usage of the product is proportionately greater in that segment than one that is average (100) or below average (any number below 100). Segments with index numbers higher than 100 do not necessarily have numerically more users in them than in other segments; they might only have proportionately more. Theoretically, the segment with the highest index number represents the best potential for usage. In analyzing marketing data, one should calculate index numbers for all demographic groups, such as age, sex, income, occupation, and education. As is shown in Exhibit 7-3, tables should always show 100 percent at the bottom to tell the user that these numbers do add up to 100. It is a good idea for planners to double-check to be sure the numbers do, in fact, add to 100 when appropriate. Some tables, such as presence of children by age, add to more than 100 because households with both young and older children will, correctly, be double-counted.

While looking at the demographic profile, planners should concentrate on indexes that are greater than about 110 or less than about 90. Indexes of 98 or 102 are so close to the average that they might be caused by statistical bounce. Planners should also look for a pattern in the numbers. Here, bottled water users are concentrated in the 25–54 age group. The 55–64 age group is slightly below average, and the 65+ group is well below average. Products with above-average usage by people ages 25–54 can be expected to have children and larger than average households. These patterns help the planner identify the product user's lifestyle.

Although the technique of calculating index numbers shown in Exhibit 7-4 can be used, there is a simpler way to compute the numbers, shown in Exhibit 7-5. Briefly stated, the method starts with a measurement of the total number of users in a market. A percentage of the universe is then computed. This percentage indicates that, of the total population, x percent are users. The number of users is divided by the number of individuals in each population segment, and percentages are calculated. Finally, each of these segment percentages is divided by the total percentage of users to obtain an index number. Note that the index numbers obtained by this method are identical to those obtained in Exhibit 7-4.

EXHIBIT 7-5

Another Method of Calculating Index Numbers

Step One: Find the total number of users compared with the total population in the market:

Total number of users in all segments (000): 107,113
Total number of adults in the United States (000): 224,899
Percentage of total adults who are users (users/adults): 47.6

Step Two: Divide to find the percent of users in each demographic segment.

AGE SEGMENT	NUMBER OF USERS (000)	POPULATION SIZE	USERS/ POPULATION
18–24	14,433	28,550	50.6%
25–34	21,160	40,210	52.6
35–44	22,186	42,681	52.0
45–54	22,807	43,918	51.9
55–64	15,111	32,911	45.9
65+	11,416	36,629	31.2
Total adults	107,113	224,899	47.6%

Step Three: Divide each of the percentages in Step Two by the percentage in Step One.

AGE SEGMENT	USERS/ POPULATION	USERS/ ADULTS	INDEX
18–24	50.6%	47.6%	106
25–34	52.6	47.6	110
35–44	52.0	47.6	109
45–54	51.9	47.6	109
55–64	45.9	47.6	96
65+	31.2	47.6	65
Total adults	47.6%	47.6%	

Source: Mediamark Research & Intelligence, LLC, Spring 2009. Used with permission.

Be careful not to be misled about index numbers: the demographic segment with the highest index number does *not* always represent the best potential. Aside from the fact that one segment might have some other qualification of great marketing value, it is also possible that a segment with a high index number has a low degree of product usage or sales or a low population size for that segment. If so, the segment with the highest index number would not represent the best potential for continued usage.

To illustrate, Exhibit 7-6 shows marketing data for a fictitious brand. Although the 18–24 age segment has the highest index (134), it also has the lowest percentage of product usage and the lowest population percentage of any segment. It would not be very meaningful, therefore, to limit the selection of media to those reaching the 18–24 segment and ignore the other segments, especially because 85 percent of the usage is in the 25-and-older segment. First examine the volume of usage or sales in each demographic segment to determine whether the volume warrants inclusion as a media target. Only then will index numbers help locate good potential target segments.

Lifestyle Analysis

Demographics paint a general picture of the target and are needed for buying broadcast media, but by themselves, these dry statistics mask the human side of product users. To add some personality, media planners also analyze product users' *lifestyles*—that is, how they spend time and money. Following are the most commonly used lifestyle analysis tools that give planners a more intuitive understanding of their target.

Storyfinder The previous example of an MRI cross tabulation (or *cross tab* for short) showed demographics, but it is also possible to cross tabulate product usage

---

EXHIBIT 7-6

An Example of Misleading Index Numbers

AGE SEGMENT	POPULATION IN EACH SEGMENT	PRODUCT USAGE IN EACH SEGMENT	INDEX
18–24	11.1%	15.0%	134
25–34	19.3	17.8	92
35–49	30.2	29.2	97
50+	39.4	38.0	96
Total	100.0%	100.0%	

with all of the answers in the survey. A Storyfinder ("Golddigger" in MRI software) is essentially a large cross tab. The column represents the product user that the planner is studying, and the rows (more than 3,000 of them) reflect every product and service that is measured. The planner then sorts the analysis by index to identify the most selective behaviors that might shed light on the user's lifestyle. In setting up the computer run, the planner also excludes behaviors that have fewer than 50 respondents and so are statistically unstable.

Exhibit 7-7 shows the results of a Storyfinder for adults who are medium–heavy users of bottled water and seltzer. It is clear from these activities that the target users enjoy an active and energetic lifestyle, use the Internet, are concerned about their health, and have the financial resources to enjoy the finer things in life. These insights are not apparent from demographic analysis alone.

In this table, the "Unwgt." column is the unweighted sample size—the number of people (respondents) who actually filled out the questionnaire. Note that some of the groups are so small that the data are unstable and should be used with caution. The asterisk indicates that the sample consists of fewer than 50 respondents. This represents the practical limit to a planner's ability to fine-tune the target, although samples of less than a few hundred should be viewed as providing directional information.

Psychographics Both MRI and Experian Simmons ask respondents a series of questions about their attitudes toward various products, services, and aspects of their life. Exhibit 7-8 shows the most selective psychographics ("Agree Mostly") for medium–heavy users of bottled water or seltzer. This analysis tells planners that their target is technologically savvy, is willing to try new products, and wants to be perceived as a person who reflects the latest fashion.

Leisure Styles and Consumer Innovators The Storyfinder is a simple cross tab of every measured behavior, although it fails to combine a number of behaviors that may, taken together, signal a lifestyle or consumer interest. MRI's Leisure Styles and Consumer Innovators codes were developed from a factor analysis of the MRI database. Like the psychographics, these groupings can offer insights into the consumer, but they are seldom used to select specific media vehicles. Experian Simmons has similar segmentations that group people by a broad range of behaviors and attitudes.

Exhibit 7-9 shows the selectivity of MRI's Consumer Innovators and Leisure Styles for medium–heavy bottled-water users. They are above average in all of the Innovator groups (30 percent more likely than the average adult to be a "Super Innovator"). They also score significantly above average in the Leisure Style groups:

EXHIBIT 7-7

Storyfinder Analysis of Medium–Heavy Bottled Water or Seltzer Users

Total Sample
Target: Medium–Heavy Bottled Water or Seltzer Users
Population: 107,113 (000)

	UNWGT.	(000)	VERT%	HORZ%	INDEX
TOTALS	12,764	107,113	100.00	47.63	100
Bought instant-developing camera in last 12 months	52	433	0.40	79.89	168
Bought pasta machine in last 12 months	21	299*	0.28	78.07	164
Heavy user of meal/dietary/weight-loss suppl.	148	1,399	1.31	76.95	162
Ordered baby accessories by mail in last 12 months	121	1,085	1.01	76.19	160
Used home/herbal remedy to treat muscle ailments	75	667	0.62	73.95	155
Bought last 35mm point & shoot camera in last 12 months	53	485	0.45	73.60	155
Bought sport watch as gift in last 12 months	131	1,178	1.10	72.31	152
Participated in casino gambling in Caribbean	146	1,159	1.08	72.26	152
Referred to Internet Yellow Pages for home improvement in last 12 months	118	1,017	0.95	70.92	149
Referred to Internet Yellow Pages for professional counselor services in last 12 months	86	780	0.73	70.46	148
Used a branded prescription to treat ailments	77	672	0.63	70.00	147
Participated in casino gambling in Connecticut	177	1,205	1.12	69.90	147
Referred to Internet Yellow Pages for copier (electrical equipment) in last 12 months	101	992	0.93	69.86	147
Heavy user of prepared mixed drinks with liquor	181	1,679	1.57	69.78	147
Referred to Internet Yellow Pages for music stores (leisure/equipment) in last 12 months	180	1,512	1.41	69.17	145
Bought receiver-amp audio equipment in last 12 months	104	961	0.90	68.45	144
Referred to Internet Yellow Pages for personal care products and services (child) in last 12 months	159	1,421	1.33	68.42	144
Bought low-ticket sports & recreation equipment (elbow/knee) in last 12 months	90	631	0.59	68.29	143

*Projections relatively unstable—use with caution.
Source: Mediamark Research & Intelligence, LLC, Spring 2009. Used with permission.

EXHIBIT 7-8

Selective Buying Styles and Psychographic Attitudes of Medium–Heavy Bottled Water or Seltzer Users

Base: Adults
Target: Medium–Heavy Bottled Water or Seltzer Users
Population: 107,113 (000)

	"AGREE MOSTLY" WITH STATEMENTS		
	VERT%	HORZ%	INDEX
TOTALS	100.0	47.6	100
Text messaging is an important part of my daily life.	16.3	56.7	119
Others ask my advice about vacation travel.	7.0	56.1	118
I often spend more money than expected on my fashion purchases.	13.3	54.3	114
I like to live a lifestyle that impresses others.	7.3	53.7	113
I often try different ways to style my hair.	10.7	53.4	112
I am willing to pay more for a flight on my favorite airline.	6.4	53.3	112
I'm willing to use the Internet to shop for fashion products.	15.4	53.3	112
I often find myself in a leadership position.	18.6	53.1	111
Others ask my advice when it comes to food.	11.1	52.9	111
I buy new clothes at the beginning of each season.	7.8	52.6	111
I would rather book a trip over the Internet than meet a travel agent.	22.7	52.6	110
I consider my fashion style to be trendy.	7.7	52.4	110
I advise when others are buying technology/electronics products.	8.0	52.3	110
I enjoy customizing the look and sound of my cell phone.	10.4	52.3	110
I consider myself sophisticated.	9.1	52.3	110
My goal is to make it to the top of my profession.	15.9	52.1	109
If I find a food product I like, I recommend it to others.	19.5	51.8	109
I'm among the first of my friends to try new technology products.	6.4	51.6	108
I purchase products to help organize my life.	14.9	51.4	108

Source: Mediamark Research & Intelligence, LLC, Spring 2009. Used with permission.

Sports Enthusiasts, Outdoor Speedsters, and Collectors, confirming the earlier observations of their active lifestyle seen in the Storyfinder.

Focus Groups While not a statistical tool, media-oriented focus groups can provide insights into the target that are unavailable from questionnaire-based research.

Using DRAFTFCB's "Mind, Mood and Moment" process, media planners talk to target consumers in their natural surroundings (e.g., men drinking beer in a bar). This relaxed but carefully structured meeting probes the target's daily life patterns—these consumers' interests, what they do for fun, what frustrations they experience, their social life, their goals for the future. Of special importance is a discussion about their involvement with and attitudes toward the media.

EXHIBIT 7-9

Consumer Innovators and Leisure Styles of Medium–Heavy Bottled Water or Seltzer Users

Target: Medium–Heavy Bottled Water Users
Population: 107,113 (000)

	UNWGT.	(000)	VERT%	HORZ%	INDEX
TOTALS	12,764	107,113	100	47.63	100
Consumer Innovators					
Super Innovators (3+ of above segments)	888	6,275	5.86	61.74	130
Electronics	1,753	14,716	13.74	61.62	129
Food	2,130	17,239	16.09	58.89	124
Leisure	1,152	8,926	8.33	54.25	114
Home Appliance	1,203	9,511	8.88	52.72	111
Personal Care/Health	2,543	20,975	19.58	52.79	111
Financial	1,886	12,411	11.59	49.30	104
Leisure Styles					
Sports Enthusiasts	853	7,408	6.92	56.70	119
Outdoor Speedsters	400	3,573	3.34	54.93	115
Collectors	831	6,693	6.25	52.35	110
Cultured Nesters	2,217	15,018	14.02	50.37	106
Outdoor Adventurers	767	5,647	5.27	49.30	104
Puzzles and Games	1,271	11,311	10.56	48.04	101
Hunters and Fishers	378	3,726	3.48	45.76	96
Passives (May not participate/partic-ipates at lower levels)	6,047	53,738	50.17	44.94	94

Source: Mediamark Research & Intelligence, Spring 2009. Used with permission.

For example, a Mind, Mood and Moment session on behalf of a state tourism association revealed that respondents look forward to the weekends when they can get away from their busy and hectic weekdays. This observation led to a campaign that suggested weekend automobile trips to points of interest in the state. Media weight was concentrated on Thursday and Friday evenings when people were planning their weekend activities, as well as Sunday newspaper ads that contained specific travel directions.

The use of focus groups illustrates the value of understanding the marketing target's human side, as well as the cold statistical characteristics of these consumers.

Where to Advertise

The question of where to advertise has a number of answers. The simplest, of course, is to advertise wherever the brand is distributed. Obviously, advertising in a geographic market where the brand is not distributed is usually a waste of money. Occasionally, however, the objective might be to "force" distribution by creating a demand for a brand through advertising, even though the brand is not yet distributed in the market. When the planner has this objective, it makes sense to advertise before distribution is available.

However, beyond the obvious answer is the question of whether it is better to advertise in geographic markets where sales for a given brand have been good or to advertise where sales have not been good. Some planners believe that to advertise where sales have been good is a solid defensive strategy. One should protect what one has and also try to build on it. Additionally, one should ask, Have sales in the good markets been fully exploited? If not, it could make sense to spend more money there, rather than going to some other market where the risks would be greater. After all, many customers like the brand well enough to buy it repeatedly, and their word-of-mouth influence could well prompt sales to people who have not purchased the brand in the past. Also, distribution and retail acceptance of the product are well established.

Choosing where to advertise is really a matter of risks. Despite the observation that "it is always good sense to fish where the fish are," is an advertiser missing productive new markets by placing most advertising in the best markets? Conversely, can the advertiser afford the risk of losing the best markets to sound out new, unknown markets? The "defensive strategy" minimizes risks and maximizes potential.

Advertising in markets where a brand's sales are low is called an "offensive strategy," because success will require heavier advertising expenditures than previously used. Again, the risks must be carefully weighed. If competitors have been selling well in these markets but the brand in question has not, the question is why?

Are the poor sales a result of poor distribution? Or have advertising expenditures in the market been insufficient? Are there other reasons? Can these problems be corrected?

A planner selecting a market with a low sales history should be able to answer the following question: is there any evidence that increased advertising in this market will produce a corresponding increase in sales? This question is difficult but necessary to answer. Students in practice exercises often want to increase advertising because they believe "advertising sells." But they usually cannot find any other strong reason for doing so except that competitors are selling well in the market. One must understand, however, that once a competitor becomes entrenched in a market with a good brand that meets the needs of consumers, consumers might not see a reason to switch brands. In fact, getting them to switch brands might be impossible, unless the new brand has some superior attribute. The risks of trying to exploit such a market are great, and the likelihood of success is, at best, indeterminable.

Finally, the greatest risk is to select new markets where neither the designated brand nor competitive brands have been exploited through advertising. These markets might have great sales potential, but they could also be difficult places to sell a given product. It also might be assumed that if these markets really had great potential, competitors would have known about it, too, and would have made efforts to exploit that potential.

Aside from these basic guides for market selection, other factors should be considered, such as selecting one or perhaps more markets in each of the client's sales territories. Almost all companies with nationally distributed products divide the country into sales territories, and these in turn are usually subdivided into small groups. The names of such territories vary from company to company. Some use the terms *divisions* and *districts*; others use *regions* and *divisions*, or other designations. No matter what the territories are called, it might be necessary to include at least one market in each of these divisions, depending on the needs of the company. The weight (or amount of advertising used) in these areas will vary, however, so the better markets receive more dollars of advertising than the poorer markets.

Planners should be careful to understand the exact area of an advertiser's sales territory. The author once presented a plan for San Francisco and was asked, "What about Sacramento?" This meeting with the client was not a good place to learn that the San Francisco sales territory included all of Northern California.

To answer the question of where to advertise, planners study distribution, sales records, or brand and product usage. Simmons and MRI provide data on users. Nielsen and similar companies provide advertisers (but not their agencies) with data on sales.

Classification of Geographic Areas

Sales should be analyzed by different geographic patterns, from the largest—that is, regions of the country—to the smallest neighborhoods possible. (In some situations, analysis by neighborhood is impossible because of the lack of research data.) The idea behind geographic analysis at all levels is to learn precisely where prospects live. This information guides media selection. The following geographic categories are the most commonly used:

- Regions
- States
- TV market delineations such as DMAs
- Metropolitan or nonmetropolitan areas
- Counties

In studying marketing and media research data, the analyst will find a number of different methods used to divide the country geographically. The U.S. Census Bureau divides the country into four regions and nine divisions. The Nielsen Company uses a division consisting of six geographic territories, although it will divide the country in almost any way most suitable for a specific client. Exhibit 7-10 compares these divisions. Exhibit 7-11 maps the states in Nielsen's six territories.

EXHIBIT 7-10

Comparison of Geographic Divisions

4AS MEDIA AUDIENCE RESEARCH COMMITTEE DIVISIONS	TELEVISION INDEX NIELSEN'S TERRITORIES	CENSUS BUREAU'S NINE DIVISIONS	CENSUS BUREAU'S FOUR REGIONS
1. North East	1. Northeast	1. New England	1. Northeast
2. North Central	2. East Central	2. Middle Atlantic	2. Midwest
3. South	3. West Central	3. East N. Central	3. South
4. Pacific	4. Southeast	4. West N. Central	4. West
	5. Southwest	5. South Atlantic	
	6. Pacific	6. East S. Central	
		7. West S. Central	
		8. Mountain	
		9. Pacific	

Nielsen Television Index Territories and Time Zones

Source: The Nielsen Company. Used with permission.

What is a local market to a media planner? A *market* is a group of people living in a certain geographic area who are likely to buy a given product or brand. But that definition is unsatisfactory for planners when it comes to determining the nature of a local market, because definitions vary depending on the research company providing the data for a given area.

Different research companies define markets differently to meet the needs of their users. A local retailer advertising exclusively in newspapers in a given city might prefer to think of its market as a retail trading zone, which includes the central city and surrounding suburbs. But a national advertiser using all media might prefer that a market be defined in terms of the entire metropolitan area and might use a government-defined area. Another manufacturer using television almost exclusively might prefer to use Nielsen's DMA. Each of these local market definitions is somewhat different.

As a result, it becomes important for the planner to know the various definitions of what constitutes a local market when planning media. Which definition is most suitable? Some media planners have asked for standardizing definitions, but without much success. Until standardization becomes acceptable, the differences should be clearly understood. Explanations of the definitions used most often follow.

Designated Market Area (DMA) The designated market area (DMA) is The Nielsen Company's definition of a television market. There are 210 DMAs in the United States. A DMA is an exclusive geographic area consisting of all the counties in which the home market television stations hold a dominance of total hours viewed. Since a DMA is based on viewing habits, the counties of a DMA do not necessarily have to be contiguous. The Denver DMA includes counties in Wyoming that are distant from the block of Colorado counties that make up most of the market. These Wyoming counties happen to spend the largest share of viewing hours watching Denver stations.

Each county is assigned to one DMA, except where a mountain range or other geological feature divides viewing. In California, Contra Costa East spends most of its time watching Sacramento stations while Contra Costa West watches San Francisco.

Core-Based Statistical Area (CBSA) This data set contains the boundaries for metropolitan and micropolitan statistical areas in the United States. The data set contains information on location, identification, and size. The database includes metropolitan and micropolitan boundaries within all 50 states, the District of Columbia, and Puerto Rico.

Metropolitan and Micropolitan Statistical Area (MSA and μSA) "The United States Office of Management and Budget (OMB) defines metropolitan and micropolitan statistical areas according to published standards that are applied to Census Bureau data. The general concept of a metropolitan or micropolitan statistical area is that of a core area containing a substantial population nucleus, together with adjacent communities having a high degree of economic and social integration with that core. . . . The 2000 standards provide that each CBSA must contain at least one urban area of 10,000 or more population. Each metropolitan statistical area must have at least one urbanized area of 50,000 or more inhabitants. Each micropolitan statistical area must have at least one urban cluster of at least 10,000 but less than 50,000 population."[5]

The following analysis is shown to better explain how these designations look for Chicago. The Chicago Primary Metropolitan Statistical Area (PMSA) consists of the following Illinois counties, according to the 2000 census:[6]

---

5. www.census.gov/population/www/metroareas/aboutmetro.html.

6. www.december.com/places/chi/cmsa.html.

Cook	Kendall
Du Page	Lake
Grundy	McHenry
Kane	Will

The Chicago-Gary-Kenosha CMSA consists of the following principal metropolitan statistical areas (PMSAs):

Chicago, IL PMSA
Kankakee, IL PMSA
Gary, IN PMSA
Kenosha, WI PMSA

City Zone and Retail Trading Zone   Newspapers define their markets in terms of city zones and retail trading zones. A *city zone* represents the corporate city limits plus heavily populated areas adjoining a city in which the newspaper is sold, as designated by an agreement between the publisher and the Audit Bureau of Circulations (ABC). A *retail trading zone* is an area beyond the city zone from which retailers draw sufficient customers to warrant spending advertising dollars to reach them. This area is also determined by an agreement between the publisher and the ABC.

Newspaper Designated Market   Another newspaper classification, a *newspaper designated market* covers the geographic area in which the newspaper provides primary editorial and advertising services. The ABC, in consultation with the publisher, decides which areas to include and the boundary lines. Newspapers can also define markets by counties in which coverage percentages are computed. Data show where newspapers have at least 50 percent coverage, 20 percent coverage, and so forth. The circulation of every ABC-audited newspaper in every county is reported in the annual SRDS publication, *Circulation (2010).*[7]

To illustrate how market definitions vary, even within one geographic market, Exhibit 7-12 shows different definitions in the city of Chicago and outlying areas. The DMA includes 16 counties in Illinois and Indiana. The Chicago MSA (which is the same area as the PMSA) covers 8 counties. And for the *Chicago Tribune*, the newspaper designated markets include 8 counties in Illinois and Indiana.

For practical purposes, spot-market media plans are generally based on the DMA when television is the primary medium and on the MSA when radio is used.

---

7. www.srds.com.

When newspapers are the primary medium, the coverage area is defined by the area of each newspaper's regional sales editions.

Sales Analysis

Gathering data about the sales volume of a brand and its competitors makes it possible to start deciding where to advertise. One approach is to select geographic markets on the basis of sales or market share produced in the past. In this situation, the deciding factor is the volume of past sales, rather than the index of potential sales. Without a doubt, the volume of sales produced by a geographic market in the past must be the first consideration in making the selection. The question of whether to go to high-index potential markets depends to some extent on whether sales have been optimized in the existing high-volume markets. Perhaps an increase in advertising in current markets will result in an equivalent increase in sales.

Exhibit 7-13 shows the sales of a company and its competitors reported on the basis of seven regions plus three large metropolitan areas: New York, Chicago, and Los Angeles. The index numbers in this table were computed by comparing sales percentages for each brand with total industry sales by region.

Does Exhibit 7-13 tell the planner precisely where to advertise? No, but it tells where the brand is doing well relative to competitors: in East Central, West Central,

EXHIBIT 7-12

DMA, MSA, and Newspaper Designated Markets of Chicago by County

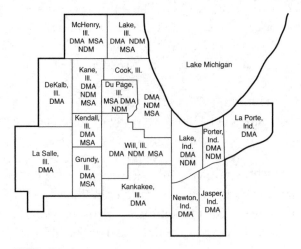

TV DMA—16 counties
MSA-PMSA—8 counties
Newspaper Designated Markets (NDM)—8 counties

Chicago, Los Angeles and remaining Pacific. The planner needs to obtain and understand this kind of information before proceeding to more specific information that will help pinpoint markets in which to advertise.

When information is available, sales analysis by regions is usually followed by a county analysis, which provides another dimension for the media planner to consider in selecting the best media to reach these markets. To deal with county sizes conveniently, Nielsen classifies them with an A, B, C, D system:[8]

- A counties—All counties belonging, as of June 30, 1999, to the largest metropolitan areas, which together account for 40 percent of U.S. households according to the 2000 census
- B counties—All counties in the next largest set of metropolitan areas, which together account for 30 percent of U.S. households

---

EXHIBIT 7-13

Sales of Brand X and Competitors, by Region

REGION	U.S. HOUSEHOLDS	SALES	INDEX	BRAND X SALES	BRAND X INDEX	BRAND Y SALES	BRAND Y INDEX	BRAND Z SALES	BRAND Z INDEX
New England	5.8%	3.4%	59	3.5%	60	3.5%	60	2.4%	71
New York	8.4	5.0	60	4.6	92	4.5	90	6.5	130
Middle Atlantic	11.4	10.8	94	11.0	102	10.1	94	12.9	119
East Central	15.8	17.6	111	19.5	111	16.8	95	18.3	104
West Central	14.0	16.0	115	17.5	109	16.2	101	16.4	103
Chicago	3.7	5.4	144	7.1	131	5.4	98	5.3	98
Southeast	15.7	13.3	85	13.1	98	12.1	91	14.0	105
Southwest	9.9	8.8	89	9.4	104	9.2	105	7.5	85
Los Angeles	5.1	7.0	138	4.7	67	9.1	130	5.8	83
Remaining Pacific	10.2	12.7	124	9.6	76	13.2	104	10.9	86
Total	100.0%	100.0%		100.0%		100.0%		100.0%	

Source: Data provided by a major advertiser.

---

8. Nielsen National Reference Supplement, 2008–2009.

- C counties—All counties in the next largest set of areas—including both metropolitan areas and nonmetropolitan counties, which account for 15 percent of U.S. households
- D counties—All remaining counties

Exhibit 7-14 shows a sales breakdown by county size for liquid and powdered forms of a given product. For the total market, county size C has the best potential. For the liquid market segment, county size A shows the best potential, followed closely by C counties. For the powdered market segment, C counties have the best potential. Once again, note the potential for sales shown by index numbers and the actual sales volume shown for the total market and its segments. In all cases, county size A has the highest percentage of sales. The decision should weigh both volume and potential.

Product Usage by DMA The major syndicated services are primarily designed to provide product usage, media behavior, demographics, and all the other services on a national basis. Product usage at the DMA level is available from Scarborough, which has respondents in the top 81 markets. Their competitor, Media Audits, provides similar measures in 86 markets. These are the only sources for information about local sports teams, local retailers, local newspapers, and so on. MRI estimates product usage in all 210 DMAs from a combination of regional usage, county size, and metro/nonmetropolitan city classification. But since it is modeled from the broad area usage, it is not able to provide information about local retailers or other detail. MRI does provide sample-based product usage in the top 10 markets. Simmons provides similar information in the top 14 DMAs.

EXHIBIT 7-14

Sales of Brand X and Competitors, by County Size

COUNTY SIZE	POPULATION DISTRIBUTION	TOTAL MARKET		POWDERED MARKET SEGMENT		LIQUID MARKET SEGMENT	
		SALES	INDEX	SALES	INDEX	SALES	INDEX
A	41.4%	42.3%	102	39.1%	94	45.4%	110
B	27.2	26.9	99	27.6	101	26.2	96
C	16.3	19.2	117	20.6	126	17.9	109
D	15.1	11.6	76	12.7	84	10.5	70
Total	100.0%	100.0%		100.0%		100.0%	

Source: Data provided by a major advertiser.

Addressability Media tend to cover large areas: total U.S., broad regions, or complete DMAs. Recent technology has allowed advertisers to focus local cable television weight on communities or even individually addressable television sets. This would allow an advertiser to run different creative executions in different parts of a market, reflecting local habits or demographic characteristics. But there have been bumps in the road. One system, Canoe Ventures, planned to deliver advertising to communities via six large cable operators. It was forced to scrap the service due to operational flaws. Another company, Invidi, has technology that can target individual households served by cable companies or satellite. At this writing, the service is too experimental to be called an operational medium. But as technology advances, addressability could add a significant capability to the television medium and greater responsiveness to advertisers' marketing needs.

Heavy-User Data

Although a geographic analysis begins to answer the question of where to advertise, an examination of data about heavy users will provide additional insights. Often, a small percentage of heavy users account for the largest percentage of product usage. This is true for many product categories, but not for all.

Studying heavy users gives a different dimension of a market's location. If the marketing strategy calls for heavy users, then their whereabouts becomes important. Exhibit 7-15 shows that medium–heavy users of bottled water or seltzer strongly tend to live in metropolitan areas. Stated more specifically, medium–heavy users of bottled water are slightly (3 percent) more likely to live in CBSA metropolitan areas than is the average adult. The significant below-average index in the non-CBSA (rural) areas is another indication of the young, active, upscale lifestyle of bottled-water users.

EXHIBIT 7-15

Total Versus Light and Medium–Heavy Users of Bottled Water by Type of CBSA (Index to Total Adults)

	INDEX TO TOTAL ADULTS		
	TOTAL USERS	LIGHT USERS	MEDIUM– HEAVY USERS
Metropolitan CBSA	103	103	103
Micropolitan CBSA	87	84	88
Non-CBSA	76	91	72

Source: Mediamark Research & Intelligence, LLC, Spring 2009. Used with permission.

Buying Power Indices

Another method for determining where to advertise is to use buying power indices. These indices help a planner evaluate sales and product usage or general sales potential in certain geographic areas. Buying power indices include the brand development index (BDI) and category development index (CDI), as well as weighted BDIs and CDIs.

Brand Development Index (BDI) One useful tool available for helping a media planner decide where to advertise is the *brand development index (BDI)*. This index measures the number of cases, units, or dollar volume of a brand sold per 1,000 population. It is calculated from data for each individual market in which the brand is sold, according to the following formula:

$$BDI = \frac{\text{Percentage of a brand's total U.S. sales in Market A}}{\text{Percentage of total U.S. population in Market A}} \times 100$$

Following is an example of how the BDI would be calculated for a brand in Seattle:

$$\frac{\substack{\text{Sales of the brand in} \\ \text{Seattle (\% of U.S.)}}}{\substack{\text{Population in Seattle} \\ \text{(\% of U.S.)}}} \times 100 = 3.09/1.58 \times 100 = 1.96 \times 100 = 196$$

The BDI is an index number representing sales potential. It conforms to the same basic characteristics of index numbers discussed earlier. The larger the sales in a market relative to its population percentage, the higher the BDI in that market.

Category Development Index (CDI) The *category development index (CDI)* is similar to the BDI, except that it is based on the percentage of sales of a product category, rather than a brand, in a given market. The method of calculating the CDI is as follows:

$$CDI = \frac{\substack{\text{Percentage of product category's} \\ \text{total U.S. sales in Market A}}}{\substack{\text{Percentage of total U.S.} \\ \text{population in Market A}}} \times 100$$

An example of the CDI in Seattle would be set up as follows:

$$\frac{\substack{\text{Category Sales in} \\ \text{Seattle (\% of U.S.)}}}{\substack{\text{Population in Seattle} \\ \text{(\% of U.S.)}}} \times 100 = 2.71/1.58 \times 100 = 1.72 \times 100 = 172$$

Both the BDI and CDI are useful in decision making. One tells the planner the relative strengths and weaknesses for the brand, and the other the relative strengths and weaknesses for the category. These indices should be calculated for any market where the brand is sold. As summarized in Exhibit 7-16, the following results are possible:

- High BDI and high CDI—This kind of market usually represents good sales potential for both the brand and the category.
- High BDI and low CDI—Here the category is not selling well, but the brand is. This is probably a good market in which to advertise, but surely one to watch to see whether the brand's sales decline in time.
- Low BDI and high CDI—This kind of market shows potential for the category but demands that someone study the reason why the brand is not doing well here. Is it because of poor distribution? Not enough advertising dollars, GRPs, or reach in the market? To advertise in this market without knowing the answer would be a risk.
- Low BDI and low CDI—This kind of market represents a risk for any brand. Here, too, a planner might want to know why the category does not sell well. Such a market would probably not be a good place to advertise under most circumstances.

In using BDI/CDI data for each market in decision making, the planner has a number of ways to proceed. One is to set arbitrary criteria for each market. For example, a planner could decide that for a market to be selected, it would have to meet at least one of the following requirements:

EXHIBIT 7-16

BDI/CDI Relationships

	HIGH BDI	LOW BDI
High CDI	High share of market Good market potential	Low share of market Good market potential
Low CDI	High share of market Monitor for sales decline	Low share of market Poor market potential

- A BDI of 125 or greater
- A BDI at least 10 points higher than the CDI
- A certain percentage sales increase over a previous year in that market, a sales volume of x dollars in the market, or both

Market selection on such a basis might seem arbitrary, but it could be based on the experience of a planner who, over a period of years, simply knows which market characteristics have been the most profitable.

Weighted BDIs and CDIs   Another method of selecting markets might be to weight the BDI and CDI to arrive at a single combined index. Before this weighting is done, however, a marketing strategy decision must be made to guide the media planner in the proper weighting of the two indices. A marketing strategy that calls for x dollars of advertising spending in direct proportion to sales (a basically defensive posture) requires that the percent of brand sales component of the BDI be used exclusively in allocating media expenditures to each market. At the other extreme, if a marketing strategy requires that brand advertising be allocated only on the basis of category development (a basically offensive posture, generally used for new brands without a sales pattern), the media planner would have to use only the percent of category sales component of the CDI in deciding spending by market.

Any mixture of these two strategies requires a mixture of weights for the BDI and the CDI. For example, suppose the marketing strategy states that brand sales should be protected in all high-sales areas but that spending should be increased where category development is high and brand development is low. In that situation, the planner might elect to weight the BDI 75 percent and the CDI 25 percent (weights must add up to 100 percent). The following example illustrates how that calculation would be made in a typical market:

Weighted BDI = $165 \times 0.75 = 124$
Weighted CDI = $140 \times 0.25 = 35$
Weighted BDI + Weighted CDI = 159

All markets would be evaluated on the basis of a similar weighting, and only those that reach a certain level would be selected.

Weighting is risky, however, unless the planner knows exactly what each weighting signifies. A safer procedure would be to weight BDI and CDI 50 percent each and then combine them. Nevertheless, some kind of arbitrary decision would have to be made. The cutoff point might be set at 125—that is, any market indexed at higher than 125 would be selected and any less than 125 rejected, at least until experience dictates otherwise.

Using Buying Power Indices Sometimes an advertiser does not know a product's sales volume in each geographic market, possibly because the advertiser sells through distributors and wholesalers. Although many manufacturers in the food, drug, and appliance fields know, from their own records, how large their sales are to wholesalers or distributors, they often do not know how well sales are going at the retail level, or there is a long time lag between wholesale and retail sales. Furthermore, even if a manufacturer should eventually learn how consumer sales are going, this information might not be indicative of a brand's share of total sales compared to its competitors.

The best these advertisers can do is examine the number of wholesale shipments into each market and prepare their media plans on such a basis. However, these data could be misleading because of shipments to regional distribution centers operated by large retail chains. As a result, the number of shipments by a manufacturer into a given market might not be equivalent to the sales potential of that market. Lack of sales volume and share, market by market, handicaps the media planner in deciding where to place advertising.

The retail sales division of The Nielsen Company, and its competitor, Information Resources, Inc. (IRI), survey retail sales throughout the country and sell the resulting data to virtually every large package goods advertiser. Typically, these advertisers will make the critical numbers available to their ad agencies. Nevertheless, many small advertisers simply cannot afford to purchase this sales volume and share data from the syndicated research services. They have to use shipments or sales potentials determined through other ways.

One source available to all advertisers and agencies is *Demographics USA* (www .tradedimensions.com), which can help determine the sales potential of geographic markets. This book is published annually and is available at a relatively low cost. The data are based on census measurements plus updated projections. The survey computes a multiple-factor index for every major U.S. metropolitan area. A factor is a market quality that affects sales. Therefore, it is possible to examine the general sales potential of every geographic market. Generally, the more people there are in a market, the greater the sales potential, so population is a factor. Another factor is effective buying income, based on total income after taxes (similar to disposable income). A third factor in the survey's index is total retail sales. The three factors are judgmentally weighted to indicate that some factors are more important than others in making sales. Population could be weighted double, total retail sales weighted three times, and effective buying income weighted five times. When added together, the result is a single number reflecting these judgments that can be used for market selection.

On the one hand, the indices described help the planner determine the relative value of each market. These values in turn can be used to determine budgets or media weights. On the other hand, the indices might be too general for certain kinds of products. Some specialized products will need additional or more specific marketing data. However, the information in *Demographics USA* can be used with data from other sources to provide a better and more selective index. Taking the market for air conditioners as an example, the planner could combine survey data with information on average maximum annual temperature and average annual humidity to create a special index number for each market. Furthermore, factors could be weighted in any way necessary to get a better perspective of the relative value of each market. One can use the buying power indices for a quick evaluation of alternative geographic markets.

The question of where to advertise is based on an analysis of sales and product usage or general sales potential, plus consideration of the marketing objectives. The users of the buying power data will find that the index numbers are an easy way to compare a large number of categories. If raw numbers or percentages are needed, they are usually provided so that users need not make any further preliminary calculations.

Cutoff Points

In selecting markets for advertising, it is often difficult to judge at which point to drop markets at the bottom of the list. The place at which the list is divided is called the *cutoff point.* One way to establish a cutoff point is to select markets on the basis of some arbitrary number, usually in multiples of 10, 25, or 50. This is a widespread practice in the industry. Using this method, whatever markets are listed as number 51 or lower are eliminated. Yet most media planners would agree that there is not always much difference between the 50th market and the 51st market.

A more logical way to set the cutoff point is to determine how much weight (in terms of dollars) should be assigned to the best markets. Once these dollars have been allocated, then all remaining money is distributed to the poorer markets based on a weighting system. Usually such weighting would be based on spending a minimum amount of money in a market. If a market's potential does not justify such an expenditure, then advertising to that market might not be worthwhile. Weighting systems divide markets into groups titled A, B, C, and so on. An A market might receive a given number of dollars of advertising per thousand population. The B markets receive somewhat less, and C markets receive much less.

At times, a system of gross rating points (GRPs) is used to determine how much money will be spent in a market. The money is allocated from the top of the list down, until it runs out, thereby automatically establishing the cutoff point. In many cases, media planners and client representatives have, through experience, developed a minimum number of markets that must be on any list. Then they add markets with whatever money is left after allocating money to the basic list.

One problem in establishing cutoff points is that often a few markets account for a large percentage of sales. For example, 25 markets might account for 75 percent of a brand's sales. The next 25 largest markets might account for only 8 percent additional sales. Usually media planners prefer to have fewer markets and spend enough money on each to fully exploit the selected markets.

Often, too, marketing objectives affect the length of a list. For example, if an objective is to protect the brand's share of market from inroads of competitors, then more money might be put into markets where competitors are trying to sell against the brand. Usually a brand has its best markets, so the list has to be reduced somewhat to allocate extra money at the top of the list.

The process of selecting markets and determining cutoff points is not the sole responsibility of the media planner. Usually, the account executive and a client representative share this responsibility. In such cases, decisions are made by compromise as well as by logic. In a personal conversation, one media planner once explained the situation this way:

> This give-and-take process between the account executive, the client, and myself is often logical, but sometimes ludicrous. For example, I'll have both Rochester and Albany on my market list. The account man may take Albany off but leave Rochester in. But the client puts Albany back in and removes Rochester. Why? Well it could be that we can't afford both, or the client feels that he has to back a stronger sales force at Albany. But the whole process of selecting markets is an "editing" operation, in which we each edit the others' recommendations until a market list takes shape.

In summary, market lists and cutoff points are established on the basis of subjective factors as well as objective criteria. The most important criteria are the sales goals and the money needed to attain them in each market. Experience, compromise, and some arbitrary factors also influence the process at various times.

When to Advertise

Decisions about when to advertise depend on a number of important considerations, including the following:

- Monthly sales patterns
- Budget constraints
- Competitive activities
- Specific goals for the brand

- Product availability
- Promotional requirements

Each of these points deserves individual discussion, but one point underlies them all: advertise when people tend to buy the product in question. It is difficult if not impossible to make them buy at any other time. Studying sales by product category over a period of 20 or more years shows that buying takes place at fairly regular intervals and not capriciously. Therefore, it is important to learn when people tend to buy and to capitalize on these buying habits.

Monthly Sales Patterns

The most important consideration in deciding when to advertise is to know when sales peaks occur for the product category compared with when sales peaks occur for the brand. Exhibit 7-17 shows category sales indexed to brand sales by month. Sales for the category in question tend to be rather flat month by month, but the brand tends to have rather clear-cut highs and lows. Theoretically, the brand should advertise more heavily in months when its sales have been higher.

EXHIBIT 7-17

Category and Brand Sales, by Month

MONTH	CATEGORY SALES	BRAND SALES	INDEX*
January	8.2%	6.8%	83
February	7.7	6.5	85
March	8.5	8.2	96
April	8.2	7.5	91
May	8.5	8.9	105
June	8.2	8.9	109
July	8.5	9.4	110
August	8.5	10.3	121
September	8.2	8.2	180
October	8.5	8.8	103
November	8.2	7.6	93
December	8.5	9.5	112

*Brand sales ÷ category sales × 100

The answer is not always so clear-cut, however. Perhaps the category sells well in a particular month, but the brand does not. Thus the dilemma: should the brand advertise more heavily in months when the category is selling well or in months when the brand is selling well? Usually, one would advertise more heavily in the months when the category is selling well. Although other considerations can require a change in this strategy, some planners use only category sales as their guide in planning.

Usually a monthly sales analysis for a product category will indicate a seasonal effect. Thus, in studying monthly sales records, a planner should keep in mind the effect of certain seasons on sales. Back-to-school or graduation months certainly influence the sales of certain kinds of products, as do Christmas or Easter. January and August have become the "white sale" months to sell bed linens, towels, and tablecloths. If a brand belongs to a category that is affected by seasons, then monthly sales should be more carefully studied so as not to miss an opportunity.

Budget Constraints

Often the advertising budget is not large enough to permit year-round advertising. In such a situation, the planner will probably allocate the advertising dollars to the best selling months. Whether to maintain continuity (continuous advertising all year long) or flights (periodic advertising interspersed with no advertising) depends on the recency theory discussed in Chapter 5 as well as other considerations that will be discussed later.

Competitive Activities

In planning a media schedule, it is important to consider when competitors advertise. If their timing pattern is different from that of the overall category, then the planner will have to decide how important the difference is. Does it put the planner's own brand in a weaker position? If so, the planner will want to copy a competitor's timing. Most often, however, competitors tend to follow category sales patterns fairly closely.

Specific Goals for the Brand

At times, a marketing or media objective is to react aggressively to competitive strategies. Perhaps such a strategy will be necessary to attain a market share increase. In such a situation, one might time heavy advertising to begin before most competitors start. As a result, a brand can achieve greater and quicker visibility before the normal buying season starts. Another specific goal might be to outspend competitors in some particular month. This could require withdrawing money allocated to the yearlong advertising effort for the concentrated attack.

Other marketing/media goals also affect timing. New-product introductions, for example, require a timing pattern of heavy initial advertising (first quarter of sales year) and relatively lighter weights later on.

Product Availability

In certain marketing situations, marketing demand outstrips a manufacturer's ability to supply the product. Even if a company is building a new plant to keep up with demand, the added capacity will not be ready for some time. In such a case, the timing of advertising has to be related to production availability. Most often a problem with availability occurs when new products are introduced, but it occasionally happens when there is a surge in sales of existing products.

Promotional Requirements

If the advertiser plans an aggressive sales promotion campaign for a brand preceding or during the brand's regular advertising campaign, this will affect timing. A cents-off deal, for example, might require aggressive advertising when the campaign to announce the promotion starts.

CHAPTER EIGHT

Strategy Planning II

Weighting, Reach, Frequency, and Scheduling

C hapter 7 discussed three major media-planning strategy decisions: to whom to advertise, where to advertise, and when to advertise. These decisions must be made early in the planning process because they control other strategy decisions. The additional decisions discussed in this chapter include choices about geographic weighting, reach and frequency, and scheduling.

Geographic Weighting

Geographic weighting is the practice of giving extra consideration to one or more markets that have more sales potential than other markets, due to location, demographics, or other reasons. A record of good sales or good potential for sales for the product category and the brand being advertised can make one market more important than others. If all geographic markets had an equal record of sales or sales potential, then there would be no need to add extra advertising weight. But markets are rarely equal in value, so weighting is necessary.

There is another reason for weighting markets. Advertisers who buy national media usually find that the gross impressions delivered by a media plan do not align with differences in local sales potential. Some markets might have good sales potential but receive relatively few impressions from national media, whereas others have weak sales potential but receive many more impressions than required.

Exhibit 8-1 illustrates the difference in gross rating points (GRPs) delivered by a nighttime network TV schedule in different markets. As the table shows, the delivery of GRPs by a national medium such as network television is generally distributed unevenly among markets. The delivery of cable television impressions is similarly skewed. If the delivery of these GRPs happened to closely match sales potential

EXHIBIT 8-1

An Index of How Network Television Delivery of GRPs Varies by Market

	NETWORK PRIME-TIME HOUSEHOLD GRPS: INDEXED
National average	100
New York	113
Miami	96
Lansing	89
Chicago	106
Corpus Christi	78
Minneapolis–St. Paul	103
Huntsville	90

Source: The Nielsen Company, *Network Programs by DMA Report, Volume 2,* all networks, May 2009. Used with permission.

in each market, there would be no need for adjustment. Unfortunately, this rarely happens, so advertising weights must be adjusted.

The final determination of the need for weighting is the wide variance in media costs—again, not necessarily in relation to sales potential. On one hand, a planner who allocates dollars on a proportional basis might be unable to buy as much advertising as required in the best markets because costs are too high. On the other hand, the planner might be able to buy more impressions than needed in less expensive markets.

To illustrate the variation in media costs, Exhibit 8-2 analyzes cost per thousand (CPM) for several spot TV markets. Recall that CPM numbers can reflect the relationship between target audiences delivered and the costs of media in delivering those targets. Exhibit 8-2 shows that media CPMs for reaching women ages 25–54 in various markets are inversely proportional to the size of each market. Smaller markets (e.g., Wilmington, Albany, Utica, Charlottesville) often have a higher CPM than larger markets (e.g., New York, Chicago, San Francisco) to reach a given target audience. This difference is because the fixed costs of running a television station are relatively constant, but stations in the larger markets can amortize those costs over a larger population base and so charge less per thousand impressions.

EXHIBIT 8-2

CPM Analysis

MARKET	% U.S. HOUSEHOLDS	SPOT TV CPM, WOMEN 25–54 (PRIME TIME)
New York	6.49	$74.81
Chicago	3.05	74.11
San Francisco	2.16	93.49
Wilmington, Del.	0.16	79.91
Albany, Ga.	0.14	114.47
Utica, N.Y.	0.09	110.63
Charlottesville	0.07	194.25

Source: SQAD Inc. Used with permission.

Forms of Weighting

Different weighting techniques will accomplish the same objectives. The simplest way, the *dollar allocation technique,* allocates proportionately more money to good markets. Therefore, if Market A accounts for 10 percent of total sales, it receives 10 percent of the advertising budget. This technique, however, does not consider varying media costs.

A second technique, *gross impression weighting,* does consider varying media costs. The planner calculates the total number of impressions that can be bought for the budget based on the average CPM and then allocates these impressions in proportion to sales. Low cost (low CPM) markets receive more impressions (more GRPs) while more expensive markets receive fewer.

Exhibit 8-3 illustrates the differences between the first and second weighting techniques. The table shows that when dollars are allocated proportionately, gross impressions vary. When gross impressions are allocated proportionately, dollars vary.

Why do these two techniques differ? Dollar allocation does not consider media gross impressions. Therefore, 10 percent of the available dollars buys more impressions in Market A than in Market B, because cost per thousand is lower in Market A. So the dollar allocation technique leaves Market B with fewer gross impressions per year than Market A, even though sales potential is equal. To equalize the number of gross impressions in A and B, the planner will tend to favor gross impression allocation.

EXHIBIT 8-3

Differences in Weighting Methods

	DOLLAR WEIGHTING			GROSS IMPRESSION WEIGHTING		
	TOTAL SALES	CPM	10% OF DOLLARS	NUMBER OF GROSS IMPRESSIONS 10% DOLLARS BUY	10% OF IMPRESSIONS	COST OF 10% OF IMPRESSIONS
Market A	10%	$2.50	$100,000	40.0 million	32 million	$80,000
Market B	10	3.75	100,000	26.7 million	32 million	120,000
Total			$200,000	66.7 million	64 million	$200,000

Source: Ogilvy & Mather.

Nevertheless, each technique has different values. Dollar allocation tends to generate the following results:

- More impressions in cost-efficient markets—that is, markets where the cost per thousand is relatively low
- Fewer impressions in less efficient or high-CPM markets
- The opportunity for good markets to develop their potential because more gross impressions are received in these markets, presumably generating more sales
- A slightly unbalanced advertising weight-to-sales ratio

Gross impression allocation tends to generate the following results:

- Proportional communication pressure, regardless of cost
- Balanced reach and frequency based on sales potential, meaning well-developed markets get proportionately more reach and frequency than poor markets
- The opportunity for good markets to develop their potential because more gross impressions are received in these markets, presumably generating more sales
- A slightly unbalanced advertising-to-sales ratio

When deciding which weighting techniques to use, the planner should consider which best meets the marketing objectives. In many instances, gross impression weighting is considered better because it is more directly related to communication goals. One central goal of media strategy planning is to reach large numbers of target audiences with a certain amount of repetition. Within a given budget, gross impression weighting accomplishes this goal best because it considers media costs. In the dollar allocation technique, even if costs are directly proportional to sales, audiences still might not be reached often enough or in sufficiently large numbers.

Exhibits 8-4 and 8-5 provide another picture of the relationships of both processes. Exhibit 8-4 shows again that even when dollars are matched perfectly

EXHIBIT 8-4

How U.S. Dollar Allocation Matches Sales Distribution

MARKET	SALES (%)	COST (THOUSANDS)	TOTAL COST (%)	DOLLAR ALLOCATION GROSS IMPRESSIONS THAT CAN BE BOUGHT (MILLIONS)	TOTAL GROSS IMPRESSIONS (%)
A	45%	$675	45%	343	48%
B	30	450	30	214	30
C	15	225	15	93	13
D	10	150	10	64	9
Total	100%	$1,500	100%	714	100%

Source: Ogilvy & Mather.

EXHIBIT 8-5

How Gross Impression Allocation Matches Sales Distribution

MARKET	SALES (%)	GROSS IMPRESSIONS PLANNED FOR (MILLIONS)	TOTAL GROSS IMPRESSIONS (%)	COST OF GROSS IMPRESSIONS PLANNED (THOUSANDS)	TOTAL COST (%)
A	45%	318	45%	$637	42%
B	30	212	30	444	30
C	15	106	15	251	17
D	10	71	10	168	11
Total	100%	707	100%	$1,500	100%

Source: Ogilvy & Mather.

against sales percentage, gross impressions do not match (except in Market B). Exhibit 8-5 shows that when gross impressions are matched perfectly against sales percentages, dollar costs do not match (again, except in Market B).

Share of Voice (Message Weight Distribution)

A planning concept that is sometimes used in making media decisions is called *share of voice* or more appropriately, *message weight distribution.* This concept requires a planner to determine how much advertising is being done for a brand relative to the amount being done for competitive brands. A share of voice is a percentage of total advertising weight for each brand.

The assumption underlying share of voice is that if a brand is not spending an amount equal to or exceeding the expenditures of competitors, then it might not be able to achieve its goals. This assumption is not necessarily valid, because many variables other than media spending affect the success of an advertising campaign. Success likely depends at least in part on the superiority of the brand, the uniqueness of the copy, the amount and quality of distribution, or the frequency and quality of promotions, to name a few variables. In fact, many planners do not use the share-of-voice concept at all, and others think of it as a general ideal that can help in determining allocations, budgets, or both.

If, however, one is inclined to determine share of voice, it is important to do so on other bases than comparing the percentage of dollars spent. "Dollars spent" do not buy a constant number of gross impressions or target rating points. Thus it would be better to begin by finding how many gross impressions or target rating points can be purchased for a given number of dollars, and then convert this information into percentages. Comparisons can be made, for example, on the basis of the actual number of messages (or commercials) delivered.

Exhibit 8-6 shows the share of TV messages to women 18–49 for nine brands. It is important to note that the share of voice (TV messages) does not match share of TV dollars in the example shown. Exhibit 8-6 also analyzes nine competitors and their message weight deliveries. The table shows that Brand A has 35 percent of the market but spends only 25 percent of the total TV dollars and has a relatively lower percentage of message delivery than does Brand B.

The planner should ask a number of questions to determine why Brand A has such a high ratio of market share to message share. Is Brand A inherently superior in quality to B? Does Brand A have better distribution? Better copy? Most other brands show a high degree of consistency between market share and message share.

EXHIBIT 8-6

Share of Voice (Message Weight Distribution) for Nine Competitors

BRAND	SHARE OF MARKET	SHARE OF TV DOLLARS	SHARE OF TV MESSAGE TO WOMEN 18–49
A	35%	25%	19%
B	26	25	28
C	17	16	16
D	8	8	12
E	7	4	6
F	4	3	6
G	3	2	4
H	N/A	14	8
I	N/A	3	1
Total	100%	100%	100%

Source: Paul Roth, "How to Plan Media," *Media Decisions* (1976): 26.

Additional message weight analysis should be made of individual markets to see how they, too, relate to market share.

Guidelines for Geographic Weighting

No one formula is used for determining advertising weights to apply in different geographic areas; instead, weighting decisions are usually a result of many factors. Using one or the other of the techniques described, a planner can weight advertising in geographic markets in a number of ways. The following guidelines are important considerations in weighting.

A general concept is to apply extra weight to markets where sales volume or market share is high. In a market-by-market analysis, a planner might look at the brand development index (BDI) and compare it with a category development index (CDI). At times, more weight is added to markets with high BDIs. More often, however, when a CDI is high and a BDI is low for a given market, additional weight is added to bring the market up to its potential (as shown in the CDI).

Market potential, as a basis for weighting, depends on any one, or perhaps all, of the following considerations:

- History of each market's responsiveness to advertising—If a local market has not responded well to advertising in the past, then additional weight might not help.
- History of profitability—Although additional weight in a local market can improve sales volume or market share, it might do so at an unprofitable level. There is a point of diminishing returns relative to profits as extra weight is added to a market.
- Pipeline problems—If distribution levels in a market are low or difficult to increase, or if there are other marketing channel problems, then these problems will influence the amount of extra weight to apply.
- Sales force input—Some companies use salespeople as sources of marketing intelligence at the local level. Their information can affect the manner in which weight is applied.
- Local market idiosyncrasies—Some local markets have problems in communication or selling that may not exist in other markets. For example, an advertiser might find that an equal number of GRPs applied to both large and small markets usually produces greater awareness in smaller markets, regardless of other factors. If such idiosyncrasies exist, then the weighting decision should account for them.
- Competitive noise levels—If competitors advertise heavily in a market, the net effect of the noise level will require heavier weight in that market.
- Cost-efficiency of advertising in the market—Additional weight could cost too much or result in cost-inefficiency.

After evaluating these considerations, the planner should decide on a course of action to influence the final weighting. Does the advertiser want to defend strengths in good markets? Improve weaknesses in problem markets? Develop opportunity markets? After making this decision and considering other factors, the planner can make weighting decisions for local geographic areas.

Case Studies 8-1, 8-2, and 8-3 are examples of how different advertisers have used weighting techniques. No single method is used to the exclusion of all others. Each technique meets the needs of individual advertisers.

Allocating Weights to Spot TV Markets on Pro-Rata Basis

This example shows weights by the amount of money allocated to each spot TV market in a media plan. Only five markets are shown, but this technique could be used for more than 100 markets if necessary.

For purposes of illustration, assume that a manufacturer sells a product in five geographic areas (or markets). Exhibit A shows sales percentages for each of the five areas, along with a proportional allocation of the budget to each sales area. Also shown is the percentage of network television delivery in each sales area.

EXHIBIT A

A Budget Allocated Proportionately to Sales Made by Each Area

AREA	SALES MADE BY EACH AREA	BUDGET GOAL	NETWORK DELIVERY*
A	30%	$1,500,000	25%
B	15	750,000	15
C	10	500,000	20
D	10	500,000	10
E	35	1,750,000	30
Total	100%	$5,000,000	100%

*Delivery is based on a number of selected network programs that cover targets.
Source: J. Walter Thompson Company, *Allocating Advertising Weight Geographically* (1973): 9.

The table shows that each area received a proportional amount of dollars equal to the percentage of sales made in the area. However, a close look at the relationship between sales and network delivery percentages shows some anomalies. For example, Area A delivered 30 percent of total sales but has only 25 percent of total network delivery. As a result, the advertiser might have to allocate some of the budget to local television.

The problem that arises is how to divide the television budget between network and spot so that each area receives an equitable portion of the budget. Ideally, a planner would like the percentage of network television delivery to match sales percentages in each market. Therefore, if a market provides 20 percent of total U.S. sales, then it should receive 20 percent of the budget. Unfortunately, when advertisers use network television, the delivery in some markets is more than is needed, and the delivery in other markets is less than is needed.

For example, if sales in Market A are 30 percent and the percentage of total U.S. network program delivery is 20 percent, then the advertiser needs some way to bring

---

CASE STUDY 8-1   **Allocating Weights to Spot TV Markets on Pro-Rata Basis** *(continued)*

television delivery up to the 30 percent level. One way to do this would be to add a certain amount of dollars to local spot television. However, if a market accounts for 10 percent of sales and network television delivery is 20 percent of the U.S. total, one cannot easily cut network, market by market. So a technique has been created to take dollars from network television in certain markets and add them to spot television to bring each market up to a percentage equal to its sales. The following steps in this technique apply to Exhibit B.

EXHIBIT B

Allocation of Budget to Network and Spot TV

SALES AREA	SALES MADE BY EACH AREA	BUDGET GOAL	TOTAL NETWORK DELIVERY	INDEX: NETWORK TO SALES DELIVERY	NETWORK BUDGET	SPOT TV (LOCAL)
A	30%	$1,500,000	25%	83	$ 625,000	$ 875,000
B	15	750,000	15	100	375,000	375,000
C	10	500,000	20	200	500,000	—
D	10	500,000	10	100	250,000	250,000
E	35	1,750,000	30	86	750,000	1,000,000
Total	100%	$5,000,000	100%		$2,500,000	$2,500,000

Source: J. Walter Thompson Company, *Allocating Advertising Weight Geographically* (1973): 9.

1. A national advertiser buys a regional feed of network television advertising in five markets. (It is rare to buy so few markets with network TV, but it illustrates the solution that would work for all 210 markets.)
2. The planner starts by allocating a predetermined national budget of $5,000,000 for the five markets. The pro-rata system would allot each market the same percentage as it accounted for in sales. Market A received $1,500,000 (i.e., 0.30 × $5 million); B received $750,000 (0.15 × $5 million), etc.
3. Now the marketer has to know how much network delivery went into each market. This can be obtained from Nielsen's *Network Programs by DMA Report.* All the impressions for all the markets are added, and a percentage of delivery is calculated. These percentages are the data in the column labeled "Total Network Delivery." Although this information is readily available for network TV, the delivery of cable and syndication must be estimated.

4. The planner now can see some anomalies. For example, Market A was underdelivered, because it developed 30 percent of sales but received only 25 percent of national television delivery. It should have received 30 percent. Market B was right on target with 15 percent sales and 15 percent network delivery. Theoretically, B does not need additional spot television. Market C is overdelivered. It had 10 percent sales but received 20 percent network delivery.

5. To clarify over- or underdelivery, an index is calculated for each market:

$$\text{Index of delivery} = \frac{\text{Percentage of network TV delivery in a market}}{\text{Percentage of sales in the same market}}$$

Here are indices of delivery: A = 83; B = 100; C = 200 (C is the most over-delivered market); D = 100; and E = 86.

6. At this point, the planner calculates the total for the five markets based on Market C's overdelivery (with only 10 percent of sales). The formula for this would be as follows:

$$x(0.20) = \$500{,}000$$

Solving for x, the answer is $2,500,000, which becomes the network budget. Another $2,500,000 would be used for the spot TV budget. So $2,500,000 is the budget based on Market C's TV delivery.

7. To find the amount that would go into a new network allocation, multiply each market's pro-rata budget by delivery percentage. That number has been recorded in the column labeled "Network Budget" and was obtained as follows:

$$\text{Market A: } 0.25 \times \$2{,}500{,}000 = \$625{,}000$$

$$\text{Market B: } 0.15 \times \$2{,}500{,}000 = \$375{,}000$$

$$\text{Market C: } 0.20 \times \$2{,}500{,}000 = \$500{,}000 \text{ (unchanged)}$$

8. Each market's new network budget is subtracted from its pro-rata budget, and this amount is now a first estimate of how much money to allot to spot TV to enable each market to match sales percentages with delivery. Check the math for the spot TV budget. Note that Market C received no money for spot TV. Why?

Weighting Markets on the Basis of Minimum BDIs and CDIs

The previous chapter discussed how BDIs and CDIs are generally used in selecting target markets. These two evaluative statistics can also be used to weight markets on the basis of minimum standards. This method begins with setting sales goals for each individual market. Then 5 percent of the budget is cut from each market and reallocated to problem and/or opportunity markets. A problem market might be defined as follows:

- At least 1 percent of brand sales
- CDI and BDI less than 100
- An unfavorable sales trend

In contrast, an opportunity market would meet criteria such as the following:

- At least 1 percent of brand sales
- CDI higher than 100, but BDI lower than CDI
- Client's brand showing an unfavorable sales trend within a successful product category

In general, when CDI is higher than 100, the category is doing well. A BDI lower than 100 usually indicates a brand is not doing well.

The 5 percent that was cut from each market's budget is now distributed to both problem and opportunity markets. The idea underlying this practice is that problem markets are strengthened by additional dollars, but opportunity markets need extra dollars to optimize potential. At the same time, all markets were allocated some money based on potential.

In this example, all markets will receive some advertising weight through the use of network television or national magazines. The weights discussed in this case are added to national weights.

Weighting Markets by Combining Quantitative and Qualitative Values for Each Market

Advertisers can also use the technique of weighting by combining quantitative and qualitative values for the markets. An advertiser used this technique to purchase network TV to provide national coverage and spot TV to weight the best markets. The value of each market was determined as follows:

1. Calculate the cost index. The cost index is simply the CPM for each individual market divided by the average CPM for all spot TV markets in the country. If the average CPM for the country is $2.50 and the CPM for Market A is $3.50, then the cost index would be 140:

$$\text{Cost index} = \frac{\$3.50}{\$2.50} = 140$$

2. Calculate the CDI/CPM value for each market. If Market A has a CDI of 120, then the CDI/CPM value for each market would be 86:

$$\frac{120}{140} = 86$$

   Market A now has less value than it had before, because the CDI/CPM value is so low.
3. Determine each market's responsiveness to advertising. This is primarily a qualitative judgment. If sales last year rose by more than 15 percent in a market, that market could be described as responsive. If sales rose between 3 percent and 15 percent, it might be described as somewhat responsive. If sales rose less than 3 percent, it might be described as not responsive. (An alternative method for making this decision is at the end of this section.)
4. Judgmentally assign extra weight on the basis of the following criteria. Group A markets receive 50 percent more weight than average because of these conditions:

- CDIs are high.
- CPMs are reasonable.
- Network delivery is low.
- Responsiveness to advertising was good in the past.

CASE STUDY 8-3 **Weighting Markets by Combining Quantitative and Qualitative Values for Each Market** *(continued)*

Group B markets receive 25 percent more weight than average because combinations of the considerations with Market A yield a lower number but show that the market is important. Group C markets receive no spending for spot TV.

Exhibit C shows three sample markets assigned extra weight as just described:

EXHIBIT C

Sample Markets Assigned Extra Weight

MARKETS	SHARE OF U.S. POPULATION	INDUSTRY SALES (MILLIONS)	NETWORK TV DELIVERY	CDI	CDI/SPOT CPM	SALES TREND LAST YEAR	WEIGHTING USED
Chicago	4.0%	4.7	97	117	158	+ 19%	A—add 50%
Seattle	1.2	1.8	85	150	117	+ 6	B—add 25%
Indianapolis	1.1	1.2	109	101	83	− 1	C—none

Responsiveness to advertising could be determined differently. For example, an advertising-to-sales ratio (or A/S index) could be calculated as follows: If sales in Market A were $1,450,000 and advertising in that market were $340,000, then the ratio of advertising to sales would be $340/1,450 = 0.235$. Then an index of advertising to sales could be calculated, dividing the A/S index for Market A by the A/S index for the entire country (e.g., $0.235/0.405 = 0.58$). These indices could be added to the CPM average for each market and the CDI for each market, resulting in a multiple-factor index, as shown in Exhibit D:

EXHIBIT D

Market A Multiple-Factor Index

MARKET A

CDI/CPM index	86
CDI	120
A/S index	58
Total	264

Average for Market A (264 ÷ 3)   88

$$\text{Population of Market A as \% of total U.S.} \times \text{Average index} = \frac{\text{Percent of the total}}{\text{allocation for Market A}}$$

$$0.05 \times 88 = 4.4\% \text{ of total allocation}$$

This technique could be used to allocate spot dollars proportionately throughout the country.

Reach and Frequency

Recall that reach refers to the number of people exposed to a vehicle at least once, and frequency refers to how often the average person who was reached is exposed over a given period of time (often four weeks). Almost all media plans show their reach and frequency because advertisers need to know how many people will see the ads. But some plans emphasize reach more than frequency, and others do the opposite. This section describes the different types of situations for emphasizing each.

When to Emphasize Reach

As a general rule, emphasizing reach is appropriate whenever anything new is being planned in the marketplace. The meaning of "new" can be applied to announcing a new price, for example. Consumers usually will not respond to a message until something has been changed in the marketplace in a way that benefits them. A new price can be a benefit if it is lower than it was. Old marketing practices do not need to be changed if they are judged to be successful in selling. Like a reduced price, the following examples of new marketing factors that require a reach strategy can benefit some consumers to some degree:

- New distribution (stores that now carry the brand)
- New features of a product that meet consumers' needs
- New advertising copy (new words or pictures)
- New sales promotion incentives
- New packaging
- New models of the brand being introduced
- New media being used for the first time
- New positions in the store where the brand is to be found
- New servicing opportunities
- New home-delivery patterns
- New marketing or advertising objectives for the brand

One difficult decision facing a media planner is setting the level of reach needed for a media plan. It is difficult because there is little hard evidence from research or experimentation that provides the necessary direction. What is known about how much reach to use is the product of tradition, experience, common sense, and research done for particular brands in certain market situations. But there is little evidence to indicate that a given reach level is correct for a given marketing situation. Therefore, the guidance provided here—based as it is on widely held beliefs—has to be general. Even with all these qualifiers, some planners will disagree with this approach.

New-Product Introduction/Brand Awareness It is generally held that high reach is necessary for introducing a new product, the rationale being that few people know the name of the brand or its value. As many people as possible must be informed, thus the need for high reach. But determining just how much reach is necessary is difficult.

The purpose of high reach is to generate awareness of the new brand. The reach level depends to some extent on the objectives for brand awareness level. Is the goal to make 65 percent of the targets aware of a brand name? Some people will need only one exposure to a vehicle to become aware of that brand. Others will need multiple exposures, so a certain level of frequency will be needed in addition to reach.

Some planners might opt for a reach level higher than the desired level of brand awareness, on the assumption that not everyone exposed to a vehicle will be exposed to the ad and the brand name. Others will want reach and frequency, which for planning purposes can be expressed in GRPs. Within a given number of GRPs, the reach and frequency levels can be juggled to bring either one to a required level. Some available research has attempted to relate GRP levels to brand awareness levels. For example, one study conducted by a well-known advertising agency found that about 2,400 household GRPs (about 1,500 target rating points) had a 60 percent chance of producing about 70 percent brand awareness. Although the research failed to indicate the time period over which the weight was delivered, many consider this GRP level effective for a new-product introduction and would schedule it over 13 weeks.

Advertising Support for Sales Promotion Activities Sales promotion activities also need a high degree of reach because consumers must be made aware when certain deals or promotional options are available. In planning media to advertise a cents-off deal, a high level of awareness is a requirement. As before, the precise amount of reach needed at the necessary frequency level is a judgment.

Competitors' Levels One media-planning strategy might be to set a reach level equal to or surpassing that of competitors who are deemed to be vulnerable to attack. Presumably these competitors have products that are not as good as the brand in question, or perhaps they are not advertising enough or to the right targets. Setting a reach level equal to or higher than that of certain competitors offers a potential advantage to the planner, who may use it as one way to determine how much reach ought to be attained.

Budget Another consideration in planning reach is the budget. No matter which media are chosen, a fixed budget size limits the amount of reach possible. To set a reach level, the planner simply calculates the amount of target reach that can be afforded within the available budget, plus the amount of continuity desired. (Review Exhibit 5-15 for the trade-off among reach, effective frequency level and budget.)

Another media strategy stretches media dollars and reach as well. This strategy is to cut ad unit sizes so more money will be available to buy new reach. (The same strategy can be used to buy more frequency.) If the planned ad unit is 30-second commercials or full-page ads, the advertiser can stretch media dollars by running 10-second IDs or half-page ads. But there is a penalty for cutting unit sizes. The cost of smaller unit sizes usually is not exactly proportional to larger sizes. A 15-second spot on network TV costs half as much as a 30-second unit, but in spot TV, 15-second commercials cost from 65 to 75 percent as much. Likewise, a half-page ad costs 55 to 65 percent of a full-page ad.

Previous Levels Probably the best level of reach is determined by looking at what levels were used previously. If a brand has successfully achieved certain marketing goals in the past with a given level of reach, this same level (or proportional adjustment) should probably be used again.

In essence, the amount of reach needed for a media plan is based more on judgment and experience than on research evidence. Because media plans almost always require a certain amount of frequency, the combination of reach and frequency can be calculated in terms of GRPs. But research on GRPs and communication effects is inconclusive, and what may exist is probably old and irrelevant. As before, the "How much is enough?" question of setting the GRP level is a matter of judgment and experience.

When to Emphasize Frequency

Whenever repetition, not dispersion, is the key selling strategy, the planner should emphasize frequency. This has implications for reach, too, because reach and frequency are inversely related: at a given GRP level, as frequency is increased, reach will decrease. Consider the following examples of these relationships:

- High reach: 60 reach $\times$ 2.3 frequency = 140 GRPs a month
- High frequency: 9.3 reach $\times$ 15 frequency = 140 GRPs a month

As seen in the second example, it is possible to have very high frequencies and yet reach less than 10 percent of the market. This would happen if the buyer placed the entire schedule on one, very targeted cable network or radio station. It could happen, for instance, if a radio salesman offers an attractive special promotion featuring its top on-air personality, causing the advertiser to put its entire budget on that one station. So it is possible, but not a very smart use of this mass medium. Can a planner tolerate failing to expose 90 percent of the target even once, although the remaining 10 percent will see it an average of 15 times? Deciding how much frequency is enough to do the job and the related budgetary question of how many people can be exposed at this level (effective reach) are the most challenging issues facing media planners. Despite a great deal of thinking and research on this subject, there is still no simple answer beyond the cliché, "It all depends."

The bottom line is, frequency should be emphasized over reach whenever repetition of a message is necessary. Generally, high frequency is necessary to compete in a highly competitive market or when a product is sold frequently. Most planners find that there are practical reasons for needing more than minimum amounts of frequency.

Determining the optimal frequency level is a challenge: many media planners believe that for effective communication to take place, the target audience should receive at least three exposures. Other planners disagree, saying that the frequency level must vary depending on the situation. The following paragraphs describe conditions that can affect the amount of frequency needed.

Uniqueness of Message The uniqueness of the advertising message, for example, can affect the necessary frequency. The more innovative and unusual the message is, the more likely consumers will notice it and pay attention to it. The converse is also true: a rather ordinary ad message might need many more than four exposures to be seen and remembered. (In all discussions on frequency levels, the planner must be aware that creative executions vary from brand to brand, and the creative element can argue for more or less frequency than the competition uses.)

Perceived Value of the Brand Another consideration affecting the frequency level is the perceived value of a brand as compared with the values of competitors' brands. When a brand has an important and easily perceivable benefit not shared by competitors, then less frequency is called for. In other words, the brand has an easily exploited advantage over competitors. But when a brand is very much like all other brands in a product category, more frequency is necessary for the message to be noticed or remembered.

Noise Level The noise level in a product category also plays a role in deciding how much frequency is needed. If many similar brands are being advertised simultaneously, consumers will find it difficult to recall the message for any one brand amid the confusion caused by the noise level of competitors. When few competitors advertise, less frequency is required.

Competitors' Levels Some planners think a frequency level should be based on the level of that used by a brand's most serious competitive threat. A similar tactic is to single out the competitor who is the most vulnerable to a brand's promotional attack efforts. This view calls for a frequency level that equals or surpasses that competitor's level, with the objective of gaining an advantage.

Media Values Media values can also be used in conjunction with GRP planning to determine frequency (as well as reach) levels. *Media value* is simply the judgment that a given medium has been found, through experience, to be more effective for a brand and its creative message, thus justifying more frequency in that medium. The chief problem, however, in combining media evaluations and frequency levels is that of making too subjective an evaluation of each medium. Is daytime television always less than 35 percent as effective as prime-time television? To say it is always less effective is an unreasonable assumption. For certain brands, in certain marketing situations, at certain times, the 35 percent differential is true, but generalizing is dangerous. The method is a good one, however, when research evidence can be used to back up a generalization about media values.

Frequency levels in media plans therefore range quite a bit. When planners base decisions on the threatening or vulnerable competitor technique, frequency levels average as many as 15 exposures a month. But these levels are not selected in a scientific manner in terms of a cause-and-effect relationship. Even when various frequency levels are tested in three or four local markets and one is found to be better than others, there is no guarantee this level can be projected nationally. Among many national advertisers who have used test marketing for setting frequency levels, the experience varies from a few who have had excellent results to many who have had costly failures.

Effective Frequency and Reach

The question of how to set effective-frequency (and effective-reach) levels cannot be answered very well. Although the three-plus level has been used for a number of years, planners should not automatically assume this should be the goal for every media plan. The reason, as discussed in Chapter 5, is that it is oversimplified. The three-plus concept overlooks too many variables in planning.

One way to estimate the number of exposures needed for communication to take place is to begin by reviewing the different variables that can affect it. Then starting with a frequency level needed to account for these variables, add them to what is already known about effective frequency. In other words, considering all the variables that affect normal frequency, one might arrive at a two-plus level. Adding that to the three-plus level arrived at by some research on effective frequency results in a five-plus level. However, a planner could end up with a one-plus plan just as well, depending on these variables.

Joseph Ostrow, in a talk at a 1982 Advertising Research Foundation conference, spelled out the variables that planners should first consider. Ostrow's ideas are presented in Case Study 8-4, along with some numbers that could be applied for every consideration that Ostrow recommends.

CASE STUDY 8-4

How to Set Effective-Frequency Levels

One problem facing media planners is deciding how much effective frequency a media plan should have. Although the research can be interpreted to suggest a three-plus level, there is great dispute about it.

One suggestion about how to set a frequency level was made by Joseph W. Ostrow, former executive vice president of the Foote, Cone & Belding agency, at the 1982 Effective Frequency Conference sponsored by the Advertising Research Foundation.[1] Although this concept was presented almost 30 years ago, it is still used today and has found its way into the planning philosophies of numerous top advertising agencies.

Ostrow specified a number of conditions that should influence the decision, based on considerations about marketing, media, and creative strategy. He pointed out that "the right level of frequency for a media plan is the point at which effective communication takes place." These conditions might include, for example, "getting consumers to understand the message; helping consumers become more positive about a product (or service) or influencing the purchase decisions directly."

Some additional suggestions are provided here for Ostrow's model to help solve the problem of setting the correct frequency level. The planner should add a certain amount of frequency points to a base if the marketing, media, or creative condition meets his or her needs. (These additional frequency points are only suggestions.) The planner should use these additional points by starting with a base, such as a three-plus level, then adding or subtracting points as the situation dictates.

Here is an example of how to use these suggestions. Suppose a planner is faced with the following situations for a new-product introduction:

---

1. Joseph W. Ostrow, "Setting Effective Frequency Levels," *Effective Frequency* (New York: Advertising Research Foundation, 1982): 89–102.

1. The introduction is in a highly competitive market.
2. The product has a short purchase cycle.
3. The brand will be among those that are less well known.
4. The product is not used daily.
5. The ad copy is somewhat complex.
6. The copy is more unusual than competitors'.
7. The copy will be in large ad units.
8. There is high ad clutter in category media.
9. The media environment is compatible with the product.
10. Advertising will be continuous.
11. Many media will be used.
12. There will be many opportunities for repetition.

The planner should consult Ostrow's considerations and note the suggested point levels to add for setting effective frequency levels, as shown in Exhibit E.

The next step is to determine how many additional points beyond three-plus should be added to arrive at an effective frequency level. Ostrow's criteria are the source of these considerations; we have used the criteria to suggest points. Note that not all of Ostrow's criteria apply to a given situation. However, it is conceivable that a planner's own criteria should be added to the list to make it more relevant.

EXHIBIT E

Factors That Affect Effective Frequency

FACTOR	FREQUENCY NEEDED	COMMENTS
Marketing Factors		
Established brands	Lower	Repetition helps consumers learn a message.
New brands	Higher	New brands need to be learned.
High market share	Lower	High market share assumes that brand loyalty must be high, so less frequency needed.
Low market share	Higher	
Dominant brand in market	Lower	Large brands do not benefit from more repetition if the market is saturated.
Smaller, less well-known brands	Higher	Smaller brands can benefit from more frequency.
High brand loyalty	Lower	An inverse relationship usually exists between frequency and brand loyalty.
Low brand loyalty	Higher	

CASE STUDY 8-4   How to Set Effective-Frequency Levels *(continued)*

FACTOR	FREQUENCY NEEDED	COMMENTS
Long purchase cycle	Lower	Consumers think more about products with longer purchase cycles.
Short purchase cycle (High-volume segments)	Higher	
Product used daily	Higher	Products used daily, or more than once daily, probably need higher frequency.
Product used occasionally	Lower	
Needed to beat competition	Higher	In heavy-spending categories, more frequency is needed above the level that achieves effective communication.
Advertising to older consumers or children	Higher	Special targets need higher frequency levels.
Copy Factors		
Complex copy	Higher	Copy research augmenting good copy is needed to determine how copy is perceived.
Simple copy	Lower	
Copy less unusual than competition's	Higher	Copy uniqueness translates to less frequency.
Copy more unusual	Lower	
New copy campaign	Higher	Just as a new-product introduction needs higher frequency, so does new copy.
Continuing campaign	Lower	
Image type copy	Higher	Image campaigns are deemed more complex and subtle, needing more frequency.
Product sell copy	Lower	
More different kinds of messages	Higher	This covers the question of how much message variation there is, and is tied to the number of commercials in a pool of commercials.
Single kind of message	Lower	
To avoid wear-out: New messages	Higher	Has advertising worn out? Measurements will need to be made to learn the answer.
Older messages	Lower	
Small ad units	Higher	Advertising units, in either broadcast or print, will need more or less frequency.
Larger ad units	Lower	
Media Factors		
High ad clutter	Higher	This is an oddity, because high clutter requires more frequency, which adds to the clutter.
Lower ad clutter	Lower	

FACTOR	FREQUENCY NEEDED				COMMENTS
Compatible editorial environment	Lower				An example of compatible environment would be a dog food ad appearing in a television pet show.
Noncompatible environment	Higher				
Attentiveness high	Lower				Some media vehicles have higher attentiveness levels than others.
Attentiveness low	Higher				
Continuous advertising	Lower				Interruptions in advertising, such as in pulsing or flighting, need more frequency.
Pulsed or flighted advertising	Higher				
Few media used	Lower				Each medium used requires a minimum level of frequency.
More media used	Higher				
Opportunities for media repetition	Lower				Certain media offer better and more opportunities for repetition, and these require less frequency.
Fewer opportunities for repetition	Higher				

Marketing Factors

Established brands	−0.2	−0.1	+0.1	[+0.2]	New brands
High market share	−0.2	−0.1	+0.1	+0.2	Low market share
Dominant brand in market	−0.2	−0.1	+0.1	[+0.2]	Smaller, less well-known brands
High brand loyalty	−0.2	−0.1	+0.1	+0.2	Low brand loyalty
Long purchase cycle	−0.2	−0.1	+0.1	[+0.2]	Short purchase cycle (high-volume segments)
Product used daily	−0.2	[−0.1]	+0.1	+0.2	Product used occasionally
			+0.1	[+0.2]	Needed to beat competition
			+0.1	+0.2	Advertising to older consumers or children

Copy Factors

Simple copy	−0.2	−0.1	+0.1	[+0.2]	Complex copy
Copy more unusual than competition's	[−0.2]	−0.1	+0.1	+0.2	Copy less unusual than competition's
Continuing campaign	−0.2	−0.1	+0.1	+0.2	New copy campaign
Product sell copy	−0.2	−0.1	+0.1	+0.2	Image type copy
Single kind of message	−0.2	−0.1	+0.1	+0.2	More different kinds of messages
To avoid wear-out: New messages	−0.2	−0.1	+0.1	+0.2	Older messages
Larger ad units	−0.2	[−0.1]	+0.1	+0.2	Small ad units

CASE STUDY 8-4   **How to Set Effective-Frequency Levels** *(continued)*

Media Factors

Lower ad clutter	−0.2	−0.1	+0.1	(+0.2)	High ad clutter
Compatible editorial environment	−0.2	(−0.1)	+0.1	+0.2	Noncompatible environment
Attentiveness high	−0.2	−0.1	+0.1	+0.2	Attentiveness low
Continuous advertising	(−0.2)	−0.1	+0.1	+0.2	Pulsed or flighted advertising
Few media used	−0.2	−0.1	+0.1	(+0.2)	Many media used
Opportunities for media repetition	(−0.2)	−0.1	+0.1	+0.2	Fewer opportunities

Source: Joseph W. Ostrow, "Setting Effective Frequency Levels," *Effective Frequency* (New York: Advertising Research Foundation, 1982). Reprinted by permission.

As discussed in Chapter 5 and best illustrated in Exhibit 5-15, setting the effective-frequency level is just the first step. Planners must also decide what percent of the target will be exposed at this level. For instance, the Ostrow method might suggest that a person must be exposed five times for effective communication to take place. But at this level, as Exhibit 5-15 shows, it would cost almost $20 million to expose half the target at that level—a cost that may be out of line with the brand's budget.

Final Thoughts About Reach and Frequency

Although a media planner is expected to show how many people will be reached by an ad campaign and to know the effect on reach of various strategies, the number that is produced by the computer is primarily determined by the GRP level—the more weight, the more reach. Reach can be increased by scattering the weight across more vehicles, but that may require going into those that are less efficient or less well targeted. Multimedia campaigns with more than 500 GRPs of television will be operating in the flattened part of the reach curve—additional GRPs add mainly frequency at the rate of about one exposure per 100 GRPs. In short, while it is important for a planner to understand how reach and frequency work, there is relatively little a planner can do to influence it, so reach tends to be of less interest to most advertisers than the other variables of a media plan.

Scheduling

An important part of timing advertising is scheduling it so that it appears at the most propitious selling times. A major objective of scheduling is to control when advertising appears by plotting advertising timing on a yearly flowchart. There are three major methods of scheduling advertising, each with a somewhat different pattern: continuity, flighting, and pulsing. Exhibit 8-7 shows yearly time period graphs for each pattern.

The media planner must decide, as part of the strategy, which pattern to use. The first step in selecting a pattern is to examine purchasing patterns for the product category. Because most product categories have unique purchasing patterns, it is important to learn what they are before thinking about a scheduling pattern. An unusual example of a purchasing cycle is the market for Christmas trees. They are rarely purchased at any time of the year other than November or December. This would suggest the need for a seasonal flighting, or bursting, advertising pattern. In contrast, face soap is a product purchased throughout the year, though with heavier consumption in the summer. For such a product, the best scheduling plan might be pulsing (year-round advertising with "heavy-up," or extra weight, in the summer).

EXHIBIT 8-7

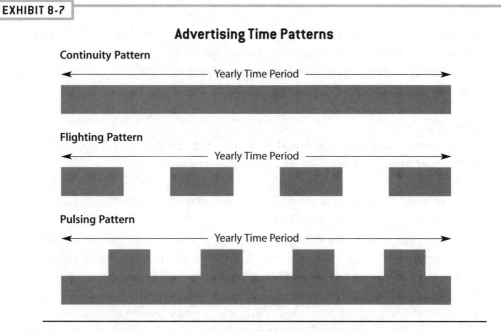

Continuity

As its name suggests, the *continuity* pattern (sometimes called *straight-through advertising*) is continuous, sometimes with short gaps at regular intervals when no advertising is done. One continuity pattern would be to run one ad every day for 365 days. Another continuity pattern would be one ad a week for 52 weeks. The time gaps show up in a pattern of dashes on a flowchart.

Continuity is necessary when an advertiser has a message that it does not want consumers to forget. Continuous advertising works as a reminder, keeping the message always before the consumer. That is a strong argument for continuity. Another advantage of continuity is that it covers the entire purchase cycle, because there will be no gaping holes in time. This assures the planner that most of the customers are reached at all times, both when they will be purchasing and during times when they might not be buying. The recency theory of advertising, as presented in Chapter 5, suggests this is the most effective strategy, and many service and packaged-goods advertisers begin their plan with continuity scheduling and then modify it as needed to account for clearly identified reasons.

Another reason for using continuity is that it permits the advertiser to take advantage of larger media discounts granted when so much advertising is purchased. Such discounts provide cost-efficiencies, because the cost per target reached will tend to be lower than in plans that do not contain such discounts. In addition, the advertiser will have an advantage in obtaining certain kinds of desirable positioning within media. Because the advertiser is buying a fairly large block of advertising, it is easier to find the broadcast programs or times that are most favorable. There can also be positioning advantages in print, where certain parts of the magazine or newspaper become more readily accessible to anyone who will buy a great deal of advertising over a long period.

Flighting

Flighting (sometimes called *bursting*) is an intermittent pattern with gaps of time when no advertising is done. Advertising done once a month might be called flighting. Most often, however, flighting patterns are more irregular, with heavy concentrations of advertising at certain times interspersed with no advertising for shorter lengths of time, called hiatus periods.

An advantage of flighting over continuity is that it allows the advertiser to meet competition better by placing advertising at the most favorable times relative to competition. Advertising can be concentrated in periods of high sales potential, either in broadcast time or print space. Advertising can be timed precisely to reach the best purchasing cycle periods with little waste when buying is slow.

Ostensibly, flighting is used when there are budgeting limitations or sharp sales fluctuations. The advertiser buys ads only when sales are growing and drops out when sales trends are declining. This tends to save money. Furthermore, flighting allows the planner to support advertising in one medium by using another medium simultaneously. If an advertiser plans to use television as the basic medium, then flighting allows concentration of radio and newspaper support at the same time.

Finally, flighting allows a series of commercials to appear as a unified campaign rather than as a series of unrelated ads. Concentrating them at certain times of the year causes the ads to appear to the consumer as part of a single communication entity. By concentrating advertising, an advertiser can sometimes catch competitors off guard and gain an advantage over them, especially if the competitors tend to use continuity rather than flighting in their strategy. The advantage is simply that the advertiser buys much heavier weight than competitors for a relatively short time.

But there are risks in flighting, too. The first is that so much advertising may be concentrated in one time period that the commercial's effectiveness wears out before the flight is over. Great amounts of flighting in concentrated periods tend to build high frequency.

A second drawback of flighting is that so much time may elapse during the hiatuses between flights that consumers might forget the essence of the advertising message. However, the effectiveness of advertising does not stop the moment advertising is stopped. The continuing effectiveness of advertising after the flight ends can be thought of as a stockpile of awareness that market mix modelers call "adstock." This stock of awareness decays over time at an average rate of about 10 percent per week. So if awareness at the end of a flight is 10 percent, after one hiatus week awareness would be 90 percent, after two weeks 81 percent, after three weeks 72.9 percent, and so on. This 10 percent weekly decay is what researchers consider the average case, but the rate of decay for a specific product or campaign can be determined only by a custom awareness tracking study.

Finally, competitors sometimes take advantage of the advertiser by placing heavy ad weights at precisely the time the advertiser is not advertising. During those times, competitors have an advantage over the advertiser.

Pulsing

Pulsing is a mixture of continuity and flighting, and represents the best of both techniques. With pulsing, all of the advantages of continuity and flighting are possible, with none of the disadvantages. Pulsing is the safest of the three because it covers different marketing situations. Not all advertisers, however, are advised to use pulsing. It best fits product categories that are sold year-round but have heavier concentrations of sales at intermittent periods.

Both continuity and flighting can develop the same reach and frequency over a long period (such as 16 weeks), as shown in Exhibit 8-8. However, there will be considerable differences of reach and frequency over the short run, as shown in Exhibit

8-9. The table shows that for a four-week on-air period the flighting pattern had a considerably larger reach than continuity had. The reason is the larger concentration of GRPs.

EXHIBIT 8-8

GRPs in Continuity Versus Flighting

WEEK NO.		1	2	3	4	5	6	7	8	9	10	11	12	13	14	15	16	
Continuity pattern	GRPs	40	40	40	40	40	40	40	40	40	40	40	40	40	40	40	40	Total 640
Flighting pattern	GRPs	80	80	80	80	*				80	80	80	80	*				Total 640

*Higher four-week reaches due to higher GRPs.
Source: Ogilvy & Mather.

EXHIBIT 8-9

Reach and Frequency of Continuity Versus Flighting

	CONTINUITY	FLIGHTING
Monthly GRPs	160	320
Reach	57	76
Frequency	2.8	4.2

	CUMULATIVE REACH	
FREQUENCY DISTRIBUTION: NUMBER OF TIMES REACHED	CONTINUITY	FLIGHTING
1	57.1	75.8
2	39.1	61.5
3	25.8	49.4
4 or more	15.7	39.0

Source: Ogilvy & Mather.

The question of flighting versus continuity is one of the age-old debates in advertising. In the end, the planner must resolve this dilemma by using judgment and experience with the advertised brand.

CHAPTER NINE

Selecting Media Classes

Intermedia Comparisons

The preceding chapters covered broad, major strategy decisions comprising a part of the activities involved in media planning. This chapter and the next deal with the selection of media, including decisions that usually follow marketing strategy decisions, such as the selection of media classes—whether to use television, magazines, newspapers, Internet display, Internet search, or some other medium. This chapter focuses on the selection of media classes, and the next chapter covers decisions about selecting specific vehicles within classes.

Comparing Media

To make decisions about media classes, a planner must make *intermedia comparisons*—that is, comparisons among different media. Comparisons among media vehicles in the same class—such as among Magazines A, B, and C—are called *intramedia comparisons*. Obviously, intermedia comparisons should precede intramedia comparisons.

The main question with intermedia comparisons is whether they can logically be made on a statistical basis. Although it is sometimes valid to compare media classes statistically, in most cases it is not. The numbers for one media class are usually not comparable to those of another class. Comparing readers, viewers, and listeners is like comparing apples, roast beef, and sushi. The definition of a reader is so different from that of a television viewer or a radio listener that comparing these numbers is misleading. For example, would it be correct to compare the cost per thousand viewers of a television program with the cost per thousand readers of a magazine? Only partially. Audience numbers tell us if one vehicle delivers more audience at a better cost-efficiency than another in a different media class.

But it is questionable whether a television commercial, which is measured in terms of the number of people who are watching during the average commercial minute of a program, can be compared to the total number of people who have read or looked into a magazine during its 30-day publication period or the time it takes to accumulate the desired number of impressions from a website. Besides, there are obvious differences in creative impact between a television commercial, with its sight, sound, and motion; the static appearance of a four-color print advertisement; or a banner displayed on a website.

Yet such comparisons must be made whenever it is necessary to choose among the many different media classes. Although the planner provides important input, the decision about which media to use is shared by all who work on a campaign: the agency account team, the creative group, the media planner, and most important, the advertiser who must give final approval before any work begins.

Consumer Media Classes

Following is a brief review of reasons for and against using major measured consumer media—newspapers, magazines, newspaper supplements, television, cable TV, radio, Internet display, Internet search, direct response (including direct mail and telemarketing), outdoor, and transit. The pros and cons of each medium are summarized in Exhibit 9-1. The pros and cons of using a medium often grow out of a planner's perceptions and impressions rather than from objective evidence. Therefore, some media experts might take exception to the reasons or limitations stated here.

EXHIBIT 9-1

Pros and Cons of Consumer Media Class

MEDIA CLASS	REASONS TO USE	LIMITATIONS
Newspapers	Sense of immediacy Local emphasis Flexibility	Lack of target audience selectivity High cost Limited coverage Higher national advertising rates Small pass-along audience Variation in ROP color quality

MEDIA CLASS	REASONS TO USE	LIMITATIONS
Magazines	Selectivity Access to light TV viewers Fine color reproduction Long life Pass-along audience Controlled circulation	Early closing dates Lack of immediacy Slow building of reach
Newspaper supplements	Local market impact with magazine format Good color fidelity Depth of presentation Broadened coverage area Less competition on Sundays High readership Flexibility	Little pass-along or secondary readership No demographic selectivity Limited readership High cost
Television	Sight, sound, and motion for dynamic selling Flexibility Reach of both selective and mass markets Cost-efficiency	High cost Low attention DVR commercial skipping Short-lived messages High commercial loads (clutter) No catalog value
Cable TV	National audience Added reach and frequency Relatively low cost Less susceptible to DVR recording Precisely defined target audiences Broader spectrum of advertisers Reduced total and average spending costs	Fragmented audiences Less than full national coverage
Product Placement TV	Less expensive than paid commercial advertising Not overtly presented as advertising	Lack of control by the advertiser Limited communication value

(CONTINUED)

EXHIBIT 9-1   (CONTINUED)

MEDIA CLASS	REASONS TO USE	LIMITATIONS
	Implied endorsement by entertainment characters using the placed product	Variable exposure time
		Obsolescence
	Ability to select program environment consistent with product's image	
Radio	Reach of narrow demographic target audiences	Many stations in one market
	High frequency	No catalog value
	Supporting medium	Low attentiveness for some formats
	Excellent for mobile populations	
	High summer exposure	
	Flexibility	
	Geographic flexibility	
	Active medium	
Internet display	Low-cost corporate legitimacy	High cost to achieve adequate reach
	Great creative flexibility	Constantly changing medium
	Precise targeting by behavior, geography, timing, or other factors	Lack of consistent research
		Conflict between Internet sales and traditional sales channels
	A great many ways to evaluate alternative sites	Low response (click-thru) rate
	Supplemental information	Limited penetration
	Easy documentation of effectiveness	
	Low-cost marketing research tool	
Sponsored search	Proven interest in product or service	Requires target interest
	Direct link to advertiser's website	Requires active management of buy due to auction-based pricing
		Requires previous knowledge of the advertiser
	Two-line sales message	Plain text only—no graphics, logo, or picture
	Complete response metrics	No exclusivity—side-by-side appearance with competition

MEDIA CLASS	REASONS TO USE	LIMITATIONS
Mobile advertising	Most personal marketing channel available Measurable for return on investment (ROI) purposes Permission-based opt-in Opportunity to reach consumers on the road prior to retail store purchase Ability to deliver coupons with a UPC code	Small screen size limits creativity Slow network speeds Lack of standards across carriers and platforms Success of the medium depends on the primary carriers Privacy
Direct mail	Easy verification of response Personal quality Flexibility Long life for certain mailings Potential savings	High cost Inaccurate and incomplete lists Variance in delivery dates Clutter and consumer resistance
Outdoor advertising	Wide coverage of local markets High frequency Low CPM Largest print ad available Geographic flexibility High summer visibility Around-the-clock exposure Simple copy theme and package identification Mass coverage of metropolitan area	Limited to simple messages No guarantee of high recall High out-of-pocket cost Limited availability in upscale neighborhoods
Transit media	Mass coverage of a metropolitan area High frequency Relative efficiency Flexibility Opportunity to position messages to consumers on the way to their points of purchase	Limited message space High competition from other media and personal activities Frequent inspection

(CONTINUED)

EXHIBIT 9-1 (CONTINUED)

MEDIA CLASS	REASONS TO USE	LIMITATIONS
Out-of-Home Video	Additional brand exposure Flexibility Sight and motion Builds reach Highly targeted Production efficiency	Lack of standardized research across all venues Availability varies market-by-market and within markets Limited reach potential Fragmentation of suppliers Proof of play and proof of performance reporting varies by supplier Complex creative production due to multiple suppliers and venues

Newspapers

In recent years, the business model of large city newspapers has been challenged by the Internet—especially websites such as Craigslist—that have cost newspapers the very profitable classified advertising. Circulation is also down as young adults turn to the Internet and mobile phone displays to get the latest news. This is having the greatest effect on the big city dailies and less of an impact on community newspapers that report on local high school sports, town council meetings, the police blotter, and so forth.

Despite these negative trends, as of the summer of 2009, the following reasons for using newspapers and their limitations are still relevant. At the same time, newspaper owners and managers are in the process of reevaluating their product to maintain their appeal in the new communications environment. In short, they are making whatever changes are necessary to continue their long-term viability as a business.

Newspapers—Reasons for Using

Sense of Immediacy Readers tend to perceive newspapers as being the most immediate local medium in the market. Every day a newspaper contains something new, and with the news come new advertisements. Newspapers are considered to have a "now" quality at all times. This quality is important when advertisers want to communicate something immediately to a mass local audience. When manufacturers introduce new products to the market, they usually include newspapers as part of the media mix.

Local Emphasis Almost all daily newspapers have a local quality that is important to advertisers. Even if advertisers use a national medium such as network or cable television, they might also want to use a medium with local impact. All selling is local, and the newspaper helps emphasize that fact by advertising local merchants' names and addresses.

Flexibility Newspapers are geographically flexible—they can be used nationally, regionally, and locally in a media plan. Even when a manufacturer's markets are widely scattered, it is possible to reach them by using local newspapers.

Production flexibility allows copy to be changed easily and quickly. For example, some national advertisers want to have different prices for the same products in different markets. Special production techniques are also available. Perhaps an advertiser wants to include preprinted inserts in newspapers in certain geographic markets. Newspapers offer these and other production alternatives.

Preprinted Color Inserts Through the use of preprinted inserts, newspapers can compete favorably with magazines in given markets. Color printing gives the advertiser brilliant, lifelike colors similar to those that enhance the brand's advertisements in magazines. Furthermore, any printing technique can be used on any quality paper to provide high-fidelity color.

Sampling Ability Many advertisers use home-delivered copies of newspapers to deliver a sample of a new product. These can include small packages of breakfast cereal, laundry detergent, skin cream, or virtually any other product that can be easily packaged and safely delivered to a mass audience. The sample is frequently contained in the brightly colored wrap that keeps the newspaper dry and is the first thing readers see when they go to pick up the newspaper from the driveway. The sample is invariably accompanied by a cents-off coupon to encourage purchase once the product has been tried.

Broad Appeal Because newspapers are read by so many individuals in each market, total reach per market can include many individuals in each family. When a product's target audience includes adults and children alike, then newspapers are an ideal medium.

Catalog Value A newspaper often serves as a catalog for consumers who are doing comparison shopping. Many consumers search their daily newspapers before they go shopping. The effect of such a search is that consumers are presold before they walk into a store to buy the product. Some readers even cut out ads and bring them along as a reminder.

Ethnic Appeal Although newspapers are considered a mass medium, they have the power to reach selective ethnic classes as well. If the local newspaper does not reach these markets, however, then an ethnic newspaper might do the job.

Newspapers—Limitations

Lack of Target Audience Selectivity Although individuals can be targeted through the use of various sections of the paper (investors in the business section, male tire buyers in the sports section), the advertiser must pay for the copies that are delivered to people who do not read these sections. This makes newspapers a relatively inefficient media buy for targeted campaigns. Newspapers are high-coverage but low-composition media vehicles.

High Cost Although newspapers are indeed a flexible medium, the cost of buying national coverage is very high and is prohibitive for national advertisers with limited budgets. National coverage can be achieved with the *Wall Street Journal, USA Today,* and the *New York Times*; however, these are upscale, targeted publications whose combined coverage is only about 3 percent.

Limited Coverage Achieving adequate coverage in major markets through newspapers can be challenging and expensive. The large-circulation daily newspapers seldom cover more than a third of major-market designated market area (DMA) households. Placing an ad in all the papers in a market may fail to cover even 50 percent. For example, the *Seattle Times/Post-Intelligencer* combination covers 19 percent of the Seattle DMA (circulation ÷ DMA HH). An ad in all 14 newspapers serving Seattle covers only 38.4 percent of the market.[1]

Higher National Advertising Rates Most daily newspapers charge more for national advertising than they do for merchants with a local address. Of course, an advertiser that must advertise in a particular local market will pay the premium rate without question.

---

1. SRDS *Circulation 2008.*

Small Pass-Along Audience Newspapers are rarely passed along to other readers as are magazines. Therefore, advertisements in yesterday's editions have a limited time value. Relatively few other people will see the newspaper after family members have finished reading it.

Variation in ROP Color Quality An advertiser buying advertisements printed in run-of-press or run-of-paper (ROP) color will find great variations in color fidelity from market to market. This variance means the message may be more effective in one market than in another, even though all markets have the same value.

Magazines—Reasons for Using

Selectivity Magazines are very successful in reaching certain kinds of selected audiences. Every year, special-interest magazines are started to meet the needs of niche groups such as tennis or chess players, cooking enthusiasts, hobby fans, those wanting to know more about investing in the stock market, and so forth. The list is endless and can be appreciated by a visit to the magazine section of local book-stores, where they sell hundreds of these special-interest publications. In addition, some magazines have demographic editions, such as a physicians' edition, a college students' edition, or one limited to chief executive officers. Finally, magazines often have geographic editions that enable the planner to reach broad or narrow markets. This versatility and flexibility enable the planner to use magazines in many different ways.

Access to Light Television Viewers Advertisers often use magazines to provide additional media weight to people in upper-income, upper-education demographics who tend to be light television viewers.

Fine Color Reproduction Many magazines are able to reproduce advertisements with excellent color fidelity. The necessity for fine color reproduction is obvious for certain kinds of product advertising such as ads for food, clothes, and cosmetics. Magazines also outdo newspapers in controlling color variations from copy to copy.

Long Life Magazines usually have a long life—at least a week and sometimes a month or even years. The effect of long life is that the advertiser can continue to build reach long after the present campaign has formally ended. Even if the product featured in the ads has been discontinued, the effect on a person who reads an ad years after it originally ran is to build brand awareness for long periods. However, long-term exposure to the advertising will not help the planner attain short-range goals, so in some situations this advantage can be a disadvantage.

Pass-Along Audience Magazines usually have pass-along audiences, which increase the reach to people in barbershops, waiting rooms, in-flight, and so on. The size of the pass-along audience varies from magazine to magazine.

Controlled Circulation Because magazines are able to locate and meet the needs of special-interest groups, many of them can offer *controlled circulation.* In this arrangement, the publisher is able to identify a special group of targets, typically by profession or occupation, and then send each of these individuals the magazine free of charge. The publisher then informs advertisers that its audience consists of people in a given industry as reported by BPA (www.bpaww.com). The audit report shows circulation by job classification, function, or title. However, since each magazine has its own definition of the various job functions, comparing magazines, even in the same field, can be a challenge. Most controlled-circulation magazines are in the business field.

Magazines—Limitations

Early Closing Dates Some magazines require advertisers to have their artwork and type for four-color ads in the printing plant as much as two months before the cover date. Consequently, the marketing, creative, and production work on the campaign must be completed so far ahead of publication date that the advertiser loses the advantage of timeliness. It is even possible for a marketing situation to have changed by the time an ad appears in print.

Lack of Immediacy With the exception of weekly newsmagazines, most magazines lack a sense of urgency and immediacy. In other words, readers might not even look at the latest issue of a given magazine until some time after it has reached their homes. Not even newsmagazines have the sense of immediacy associated with newspapers, broadcast media, and the Internet.

Slow Building of Reach Because some readers do not open their magazines quickly, reach tends to build slowly in this medium. Some readers read a small portion of a magazine immediately and then continue at later dates and times, whenever it is convenient. Active, busy people sometimes will scan through a number of issues at one time, to catch up with their reading. At other times, they just ignore a number of issues and read only the most current one.

Newspaper Supplements—Reasons for Using

Local Market Impact with a Magazine Format Newspaper supplements such as *Parade, USA Weekend*, and *American Profile* in the small C and D counties offer an advertiser the advantage of being able to reach local markets with a format that closely resembles magazines. Therefore, many of the qualities of magazines are also qualities of supplements. Most important, however, is the ability of the planner to reach many local markets with a magazine format, although there are limitations on a planner's ability to buy supplements on a market-by-market basis.

Good Color Fidelity Newspaper supplements are usually printed on gravure presses. This gives them high color fidelity. The *Wall Street Journal Magazine* is printed in large format 11.5" by 10" slick-coated stock, comparable to the finest consumer magazines—quality that is appropriate for its fashion, jewelry, and other upscale advertisers.

Depth of Penetration Whereas magazines usually have limited penetration in any given market because of their specialized natures, supplements have high penetration because they are distributed with Sunday newspapers. Thus, supplements reach large numbers of individuals for whom the editorial features are of general interest.

Broadened Coverage Area One bonus of using supplements is the ability to reach some markets normally covered by daily newspapers that do not carry the supplement. This is possible because newspapers serving large metro areas often have extensive area coverage far beyond the metropolitan area. Consumers in these bonus markets carrying the supplement usually read their local newspapers on weekdays but a large metro paper on Sunday.

Less Competition on Sundays Supplements usually have less competition for the reader's attention from other media on Sunday mornings when they are relaxed and spend more time reading than on other days.

High Readership Because supplements have large penetration in individual markets, it is not surprising that they are widely read, especially by women. Working women tend to have the time to read this format—because it is available on Sunday, it is part of a newspaper, and many features tend to cover women's interests.

Flexibility Supplements allow the planner to place advertising locally, regionally, or even nationally. But supplements also allow production flexibility such as the option of running a full-page ad in some markets while running smaller ads simultaneously in other markets. This flexibility is limited to larger markets.

Newspaper Supplements—Limitations

Little Pass-Along or Secondary Readership Because supplements come with weekend newspapers, they inherit some of the weaknesses of newspapers. One of these is that supplements are rarely passed along to others; instead, they usually are thrown away after the family has read them. In addition, one rarely finds supplements left in hair salons or doctors' or dentists' offices for secondary (pass-along) readers, as one finds magazines.

No Demographic Selectivity Newspaper supplements, like the newspapers that carry them, have virtually no demographic selectivity. The new demographically targeted supplements such as *Relish* and *Spry* target women; however the advertiser must still pay for copies delivered to those households and readers who are not interested.

Limited Readership Not everyone in a home that receives a Sunday newspaper reads the inserted supplement. A 2004 study by Mediamark Research & Intelligence, LLC (MRI) found that 75 percent of the people in homes receiving the carrier newspaper read the *Parade* supplement, and 55 percent of the homes receiving *USA Weekend* read the supplement.[2] DRAFTFCB media research recommends a 65 percent factor for *USA Weekend*.

High Cost Because of the supplement's high circulation and coverage, the cost of an ad is two to four times more than in mass-circulation women's magazines such as *Better Homes & Gardens* or *Good Housekeeping*. Advertisers can buy half the circulation for a little more than half the price, but that is still a sizable investment for a publication that is primarily a one-day read.

Television—Reasons for Using

Today video is displayed on three platforms: conventional television, the personal computer, and the mobile smart phone. While the content may be the same, the way viewers approach and access the video differs substantially. For most planners, the word *television* refers to the traditional medium—a set in the family room or

---

2. Mediamark Research & Intelligence, LLC, "Measuring Sunday Magazine Readership," 2004.

other place where viewers relax and are entertained with news, sports, and other produced programs.

Sight, Sound, and Motion for Dynamic Selling Audiovisual demonstrations are one of the best teaching methods known. The combination of sight, sound, and motion gives the advertiser the benefit of a technique that comes closest to personal selling. Television selling is very dynamic. It is also one of the best methods of demonstrating the uses or advantages of a given product.

Flexibility Network, cable, and syndicated television offer broad national coverage, while spot television allows the planner to use markets in any number of combinations. Spot cable allows geographic targeting down to the neighborhood level.

Reach of Both Selective and Mass Markets Television can be used to attract both selective and mass markets through program and cable channel selection. When professional football games are broadcast, the audience is largely male. Children's programming on Sunday morning or cable channels and daytime television tend to reach selected audiences. On the other hand, some programming such as movies, comedies, or special events will attract audiences consisting of many different kinds and ages of people.

Cost-Efficiency Television can be cost-efficient at times. Daytime television and cable, for example, usually have low costs per thousand, as does fringe time. Although the overall costs are high, the audiences are large.

Television—Limitations

High Cost The cost of commercial time is beyond the means of some advertisers. The widespread use of 15-second and even 10-second commercials reflects advertisers' need for lower total cost. TV commercial production is also expensive compared to other media.

Low Attention Only about 60 percent of the people who watch prime-time programs report paying full attention to the TV set. Attentiveness is even lower in other dayparts, especially early morning, when only about 25 percent of viewers pay full attention.[3]

---

3. Mediamark Research & Intelligence, LLC, Spring 2009.

DVR Commercial Skipping Typically, more than two-thirds of the time, viewers fast-forward through the commercials on programs they have recorded on their DVR. The effect of this is minimized by the use of the C3 ratings, which only count people viewing the commercial minutes at normal speed up to three days after telecast. It can be further minimized by concentrating weight in news, sports, and cable that viewers are more likely to watch live. DVR recording is most concentrated in the high-rated prime-time programs, late fringe, and daytime soap operas.

Short-Lived Messages Although audiovisual messages have the potential for high recall, the nature of television commercials is such that viewers either pay attention or miss the message entirely. The commercial's life tends to be fleeting.

High Commercial Loads (Clutter) There are 15.5 to 16 minutes of nonprogram material per hour in prime time on the broadcast and cable networks. Daytime television has substantially more.[4] Although there is limited research into the specific effects of clutter on commercial effectiveness, advertisers are becoming more and more concerned as commercialization increases.

No Catalog Value It is evident that viewers do not search for commercials when they are in the market for a product. Although they pay greater attention to a commercial if they are in the market for the product advertised, they usually have little idea of the exact time such commercials will be broadcast.

Cable TV—Reasons for Using
Cable television has shown dramatic growth in the past 15 years, caused in part by the 2009 conversion to all-digital television. Cable is now a national medium with a stature that complements network television. 90.3 percent of U.S. homes can now receive the national broadcast and cable networks. About 62 percent are wired for cable, and an additional 28 percent have a satellite dish or other service that allows them to receive the national cable networks.[5] Because of this high penetration, the number of advertisers who have added cable to their media plans has grown enormously. Over the past 10 years, spending in cable has more than doubled: from $12.6 billion in 1999 to $27.5 billion in 2008. Over the same period, spending on the general-market broadcast networks increased 23 percent, from $14.0 billion to $17.2 billion in 2008.[6]

---

4. Mindshare analysis of TNS data, 2008.

5. The Nielsen Company, National Media Related Universe Estimates, July 2009.

6. Universal McCann, Robert J. Coen estimates, 2009.

Cable is now a readily accepted and even expected part of any national television plan. In prime time, advertiser-supported cable accounts for 47 percent of all household television viewing.[7] Advertisers with a broad target audience, such as women ages 25–54, will typically employ more than 25 cable networks.

National Audience With over 90 percent penetration by wire or satellite, cable networks represent a truly national medium, whether used alone or in combination with more traditional media.

Added Reach and Frequency Although advertisers can use cable in lieu of network TV, it can also be added to network TV and any other media chosen for a media plan. The effect of this strategy is to add more reach and frequency. When cable is used this way, some of the weight goes to increasing reach, while impressions in cable homes already reached by other media add frequency to the plan.

Relatively Low Cost Although cable's rates are rising, it still costs less than advertising on the major television networks. National cable cost per rating point is roughly 30 percent that of broadcast TV.

Less Susceptible to DVR Recording Analysis of DVR viewing records shows that people are far less likely to record programs on the cable networks than they are the high-rated prime-time programs on the networks. Since there is less recording, there is also less commercial skipping during playback.

Precisely Defined Target Audiences Cable programmers have been better able than broadcast networks to define the kinds of audiences who watch their programs— whether for sports, music, or education. This enables advertisers to focus more accurately on targets they want to reach; however, planners face the familiar trade-off between high composition and low coverage from these highly selective cable channels.

Broader Spectrum of Advertisers When competitors are advertising on certain cable networks, it is sometimes strategically important for other competitors to be in the same medium. As more advertisers use cable, it will draw other product category advertisers, and audiences can expect to find certain kinds of products there.

---

7. The Nielsen Company, Total Viewing Sources, May 2009.

Reduced Total and Average Spending Costs National cable television, costing less than network television, can help reduce total and average spending costs for advertisers who need effective media at a lower cost. Shifting even as little as 20 percent of an advertising budget to cable can reduce costs.

Cable TV—Limitations

Fragmented Audiences As noted earlier, cable today accounts for 47 percent of all television viewing,[8] but with almost 90 advertiser-supported channels reported by Nielsen, the audience is so fragmented that the average channel receives less than a 1.0 rating, and many receive less than 0.5. So although each cable network goes to great lengths to promote its unique personality, the average cable channel is watched in only 14 percent of U.S. households over the course of a week. The most popular cable channel is watched in 39 percent of homes even though it is available on cable and satellite systems covering 86 percent of households.[9]

Less than Full National Coverage Although 90 percent of homes can receive cable channels, penetration varies by cable network. Some, such as ESPN, CNN, and USA, do reach just about all cable households. Newer channels may cover less than 5 percent of the United States. This must be taken into account when placing ads on networks that appear to be selective to the marketing target, but may offer only limited reach potential.

Product Placement—Reasons for Using

Less Expensive than Paid Commercial Advertising Advertisers get the brand mention, the package, and possibly continuing reference to the product over the entire program. Total on-screen time could be even more than a paid commercial.

Not Overtly Presented as Advertising This kind of advertising appears to be part of the entertainment content, as contrasted with conventional advertising that might be ignored.

---

8. The Nielsen Company, Total Viewing Sources, May 2009.
9. The Nielsen Company, *Television Activity Report*, 2nd Quarter 2009, Monday–Sunday 24-hour total.

Implied Endorsement by Entertainment Characters Using the Placed Product
Positive feelings toward the actors or characters can carry over to the named products they use.

Ability to Select Program Environment Consistent with Product's Image A product can be placed on comedy programs, drama, reality, and so on, as desired. Use of the product is a natural element of the program's content (Sears Craftsman tools used on ABC's "Extreme Makeover: Home Edition").

Product Placement—Limitations

Lack of Control by the Advertiser Control by the advertiser varies depending on the particular contract, but ultimately the program's producer and director determine how the product will be shown, for how many seconds, and in what context.

Limited Communication Value There are no opportunities for copy points, image, multiple messages, and so on.

Variable Exposure Time On-screen time can vary from just a few seconds to multiple exposures over the length of the program. Delivery is out of the advertiser's control.

Obsolescence Packaging and graphics may change over time, but once a program is syndicated, the placement is forever.

Radio—Reasons for Using

Reach of Special Kinds of Target Audiences Radio is able to reach narrow target audiences very well (ethnic, youth, upscale financial, etc.). Through programming specialization, a radio station becomes known for its "sound" and attracts special kinds of audiences, such as men, women, teens, farmers, ethnic populations, or the elderly. Many ethnic groups have programs dedicated to their interests. Religious groups, too, have found radio to be an excellent communication medium.

High Frequency Where a great deal of repetition is necessary, radio is the ideal medium. The total cost is relatively low, and usually many stations have time available to permit building a media plan with high frequency.

Supporting Medium Because of the low cost and good reach of special target markets, radio is often used as a supporting medium. Often, when a plan uses print predominantly, radio can be added at low cost to bring sound into the plan.

Excellent for Mobile Populations Because most Americans own and drive automobiles, radio becomes a means of reaching them while they are traveling. Many people drive long distances to and from work, and the distances are getting longer as suburbs develop farther from cities. Listening to the radio in what is known as "drive time" helps pass the long commuting time and is an excellent means of reaching commuters.

But commuters are not the only ones who travel every day. Homemakers often take their cars to shopping centers that are located far from their homes. They, too, will often turn on the radio to help pass the traveling time. In fact, radio is the last medium that homemakers are exposed to before they enter retail stores. Local retailers might very well carry on a campaign to communicate with these customers before they arrive at the stores.

High Summer Exposure Because we are a mobile population and so many people travel during the summer months, radio is an excellent medium to reach them en route. Some experts dispute this, however, claiming that radio tune-in is no higher in the summer than it is at any other time. The time when listeners tune in, however, does change during the summer, especially among teenagers, who are not in school during the day.

Flexibility Radio, like television, can be used locally, regionally, or nationally. Radio also offers a number of production advantages, because copy can be changed quickly and added to or eliminated from a program quickly. Despite these advantages, radio is not highly regarded for its great production flexibility.

Local Coverage Availability Advertisers usually purchase local radio, because it reaches a given market well. But AM radio signals can be carried far from the originating market into other geographic areas, especially at night. For a national advertiser trying to build brand awareness in many different markets, this added feature is perceived as a bonus when a planner buys local radio.

Radio—Limitations

Many Stations in One Market In many large metropolitan markets, so many radio stations are vying for attention that only a relative few are listened to by even 20 percent of a market's adult population. For example, the New York metropolitan area has 42 AM and 54 FM stations.[10] A planner who wants to build large reach via radio will have to buy more than one station—usually at least five stations.

Another consequence of the large number of stations available is the fragmentation of audiences caused by specialized programming. On the one hand, specialized programs waste few exposures because the program structure is not attractive to everyone. On the other hand, they fragment the audience too much for an advertiser who wants a mass—not class—audience.

No Catalog Value Like television but even more so, radio messages are fleeting. Listeners miss many advertisements, and they forget others that they only partially hear.

Low Attentiveness for Some Formats Listeners treat some radio formats as "background" music. They may give the messages on these stations less attention than messages on stations that feature all news or talk. Listening to the radio is rarely a person's primary activity.

Internet

As seen in Exhibit 9-2, in the first six months of 2009, Nielsen Online reported over 1.4 trillion advertising impressions. These are divided into two broad categories: sponsored search accounts for almost one-third of impressions; the balance are display ads, divided into flash, standard GIF and JPEG images, compound images/text and rich media.

EXHIBIT 9-2

Digital Advertising Impressions by Technology

TECHNOLOGY	IMPRESSIONS (BILLIONS)	PERCENT
Sponsored Search	444.8	31.3%
Display		
Flash (Generic)	383.3	26.8
Standard GIF/JPEG	327.1	23.0
Compound Image/Text Ad	225.7	15.9
Rich Media Vendors	42.3	3.0
Total Display	978.3	68.7%
Grand Total	1,423.0	100.0%

Source: The Nielsen Company, Nielsen Online, AdRelevance, Jan.–June 2009. Used with permission.

10. SRDS Radio Advertising Source, August 2009.

Internet Display—Reasons for Using

Active Medium Unlike television or radio, which are relatively passive media used primarily for entertainment, the Internet requires active participation. The user enters the address of the website he or she wants to visit, and the Internet delivers the page to the user's computer. Nothing happens until the user again takes action by clicking on a link or entering a response. But once a request has been made to a website, it can search through virtually unlimited files to return data, pictures, audio, and video. This ability makes the Internet ideally suited to the transactional communications that are part of most businesses.

Great Creative Flexibility As of summer 2009, 81.7 percent[11] of active Internet users go online via high-speed Internet, opening the medium to a broad range of rich media creative options in addition to the conventional banners. While these creative units account only for 3 percent of the digital advertising impressions, they allow for a broad range of creative options, including full motion video in the banner, peel-back ads that open to reveal a video message, a video player that runs when the user's mouse rolls over the ad, and even the opportunity to have a lead generation form that is revealed by the mouse. To see the latest examples of creative digital advertising, go to www.pointroll.com/showcase.html.

Low-Cost Corporate Legitimacy Today, virtually every company has a website that introduces its product or service to potential customers, suppliers, employees, and anyone else wishing to do business with them. A website is the first place to go for information. Lack of an Internet presence sends a strong message that a company either doesn't exist or is so far behind the times that any dealings with it would be suspect.

Supplemental Information The Internet is heavily used as a medium for publishing information. Virtually all major consumer magazines, newspapers, television stations, and cable networks have a website that supplements their traditional media product. In addition to reinforcing the medium's brand image, these sites bring in revenue from advertising placed by companies that want to deliver a message to the site's visitors. Although some sites have attempted to charge a subscription fee in exchange for a password that grants access, the great majority offer their editorial content for free.

---

11. Mediamark Research & Intelligence, LLC, Spring 2009.

Websites also can be used to provide detailed information about a manufacturer's entire product line. Because there are no size constraints, sites can provide product information, technical specifications, operating instructions, dealer locations, answers to frequently asked questions (FAQs), and telephone numbers and addresses of company offices. Websites can also provide customers with an opportunity to give feedback, ask questions, and make comments. In this way, a website becomes a strong additional element in the advertiser's marketing plan.

Easy Documentation of Effectiveness Because the Internet is a transactional medium, the advertiser knows exactly how many prospects were delivered by each website where an ad is placed. There are also reports showing the time of day when a site is visited, how much time a visitor spends, how deeply the visitor goes into the site, and many other characteristics of the visitor's contact.

Low-Cost Marketing Research Tool The Internet is an inexpensive, fast-turnaround medium for conducting marketing research. This methodology has become so attractive that even the large research companies like Nielsen and MRI are employing it, though not for their primary services because of concerns about the representativeness of the sample (non-Internet users are excluded) and because of a high percentage of "professional respondents" who participate in many surveys for the enjoyment or incentives.

Internet Display—Limitations

High Cost Having a website is similar to having a toll-free telephone number: it is open to anyone, but advertising is needed to create awareness that the site exists. This requires a possibly expensive conventional advertising campaign in traditional media, as well as digital advertising in the form of buttons and banners that will lead prospects directly to the advertiser's website.

Conflict Between Internet Sales and Traditional Sales Channels Advertisers must be careful not to undercut conventional sales from their own stores or distributors. Yet if the price offered online is the same as local retail, there is no incentive to buy from the Internet, especially if the company charges additional fees for shipping and handling.

Variable Value The Internet is most valuable for products that are information based—travel, financial services, hotel reservations, online auctions, and the like. When the dot-com bubble burst in late 2000, companies offering information-based products were more likely to survive than companies that merely took a retail sales model online.

Limited Penetration Although 86 percent of adults have access to the Internet, only 73 percent go online in the average month.[12] Their lack of exposure is a drawback when they are prospects for the advertiser's products.

Sponsored Search (Search Engine Marketing [SEM])

In the past 10 years, Internet search has become a medium in its own right, offered by Google, Microsoft Bing, and the search option in many conventional websites. While advertisers cannot control where their product will appear in the natural (sometimes called "organic") list of URLs that comes up in response to a search term, they can buy a two-line text ad that appears in the sponsored-search box adjacent to the natural search listing. More about planning and buying search advertising will be in Chapter 10.

Sponsored Search—Reasons for Using

Reaches People with Proven Interest in Product or Service People who enter a keyword are, by definition, looking for information about a product or service. They are in the market and are looking for the best way to meet their needs. It's also the lowest cost per lead of any medium.

Direct Link to Advertiser's Website People who are introduced to the advertiser can get additional information with the click of a mouse.

Ability to Deliver a Short Brand Message for Little or No Cost Since the advertiser pays only for clicks, it is possible to have virtually free brand exposure by purchasing keywords that have little likelihood of being clicked on.

Complete Response Metrics Advertisers know exactly how many impressions were served and what percent of those resulted in a click-through to the advertiser's website. This is comparable to the response rate metrics provided by direct mail and other direct response media.

---

12. Mediamark Research & Intelligence, LLC, Spring 2009.

Sponsored Search—Limitations

Requires Target Interest in the Product or Service Sponsored-search advertising assumes the user is in the market for the product *now*. While that person may be the best prospect, his or her short-term need is not appropriate for building a long-term relationship or establishing a base of awareness and trust that may not be needed for months or years.

Auction-Based Pricing, Requiring Active Management of the Buy As will be discussed later, sponsored-search advertising is sold as an auction, with the order of placement on the list depending on how much a buyer is willing to pay. This can change from day to day and even hour to hour, requiring much more attention than is necessary for a conventional media buy. Also, because of this auction pricing, there is no way for the competitive monitoring services to show sponsored-search spending—only impressions.

Requires Previous Knowledge of the Advertiser Although the ad may be displayed to someone interested in the product, since it will appear in a list with its many competitors, the user will be more likely to click on the link of a product that he or she is already familiar with.

Plain Text Only—No Graphics, Logo, or Picture This may change as time goes by, but as of the summer of 2009, there is no opportunity to show the brand's logo, sales tag line, or other brand identification beyond its name.

Side-by-Side Appearance with Competition In a world where every advertiser wants their ad to appear alone, sponsored-search advertising appears in a list side-by-side with its competitors, many of whom the user may be equally familiar with. Being present is better than not, but this is something to consider in using the medium.

Mobile Advertising—Reasons for Using

Most Personal Marketing Channel Available People consider their cell phone to be a necessary part of their daily dress. Advertising on mobile devices can be more impactful than other mass media, but the advertiser must be sensitive not to intrude on the user's "space."

Measurable for Return on Investment (ROI) Purposes Just as on a personal computer, every keystroke is recorded and can be used as a measure of response for advertising media that are paid on a cost-per-click basis.

Permission-Based Opt-In For SMS (simple media/message system) text advertising, the opt-in requirement ensures the ads go to people who want them. While a strength, it could also be a limitation by cutting down the number of people who can be exposed.

Opportunity to Reach Consumers on the Road Prior to Retail Store Purchase Smart phones that are equipped with mapping capability can direct customers straight to the store or can show where the nearest location of a given retailer is.

Ability to Deliver Coupons with a UPC Code The high resolution of today's mobile phones allows the advertiser to send a coupon with a UPC code on the mobile display screen, which can be scanned at the checkout counter.

Mobile Advertising—Limitations

Small Screen Size Limiting Creativity Advertising is limited to a simple banner or brand identification unless the user clicks through to the advertiser's website that fills the whole screen.

Slow Network Speeds In some areas, wireless technology is expensive. At this writing, a few cities are served with fourth generation (4G) technology and many more have 3G, but large parts of the country are not even that fast. Slower speeds and spotty coverage reduce the value of the medium, though with the near-universal use of smart phones and the users' demand for speedier access, this limitation will become less of a factor over the life of this book.

Lack of Standards Across Carriers and Platforms This complicates the buying process across multiple hardware platforms and carriers. With any new technology, different companies will find different ways to accomplish the same tasks. Although the result looks the same to the user, the differences under the hood add complexity for the media planner and advertiser.

Success of the Medium Depends on the Primary Carriers The business model of the primary carriers does not yet value mobile advertising. Their revenue comes primarily from selling long-term, highly profitable service contracts.

This reduces their incentive to develop systems and support services that will aid advertisers.

Privacy Potential privacy legislation regarding security, unsolicited messages, location-based ads, advertising to children, and so on may limit the medium's ability to reach its potential.

Direct Mail—Reasons for Using

Direct response is a marketing strategy that often uses direct mail or telemarketing. This discussion of direct mail and telemarketing refers only to *outbound advertising*, whereby the marketer contacts the consumer. A direct-response strategy may also include *inbound advertising*, in which the consumer seeks out the marketer (e.g., calling the toll-free number on a package).

Direct mail can be the most selective of all media, provided that the advertiser knows the names and addresses of a target audience and has a list that is up-to-date and complete. When such a list is available, there is minimal waste, so the advertiser pays only for targets that are reached. Another list source can be a marketer's own database of names. Lists of names and addresses can also be purchased from brokers. *The SRDS Direct Marketing List Source* provides direct-mail lists for virtually any target.

Easy Verification of Response It is relatively easy to learn whether a direct-mail piece was effective: one simply counts the number of responses to an offer. The number of inquiries from direct mail might or might not be related to sales, but inquiries from direct mailings do constitute one form of measurement. Often the advertiser sends alternative copy treatments by direct mail, and the most effective one is easily verified. It is relatively simple to measure response functions in direct mail compared to traditional media.

Personal Quality Most advertising is impersonal because it is impossible to address anyone by name. Direct mail, using specific names and addresses, comes closest to overcoming this problem. Of course, not all recipients of direct-mail pieces appreciate advertisers calling them familiarly by name. But many people do appreciate seeing their names in print and often pay more attention to the offer as a result.

Flexibility Direct mail is probably the easiest of all media to tailor precisely to the geographic marketing needs of an advertiser. The beauty of this flexibility is that direct mail can be adjusted to small markets (by block or even by household) and also can be adjusted to as large an area as needed.

The medium is also flexible in terms of production. Almost any size and kind of paper and any kind of ink or special printing technique is possible. Advertisers with special creative problems turn to direct mail because it is so versatile. Samples of a product can be mailed with ads, special die cuts can be made, and special kinds of foldings and packaging are available only in this medium.

Long Life for Certain Mailings Consumers tend to keep direct-mail catalogs for a long time and share them with friends. If the advertising material has value, it will be kept. Some educational materials also share this quality. If the educational matter has value, such as a chart showing how to administer first aid or a booklet on how to eliminate stains on clothing, consumers might retain it for a long time.

Potential Savings No special envelope, special addressing, or extra postage is necessary when direct-mail advertising is sent along with bills or other packages. The bills must be sent anyway, so the addition of a direct advertisement might not even cost extra postage. There are creative limitations, however, due to weight restrictions and size of the contents of an envelope or package. Printing costs must be borne as well, but even when the total weight of advertising enclosed with a bill is greater than the bill alone, there will still be substantial savings because there are no extra costs for the envelope and addressing. The addition of the advertising usually increases the total cost only slightly.

Direct Mail—Limitations

High Cost Unless it is being piggybacked with another mailing, direct mail can be expensive. The main factor is, of course, the cost of postage. Beyond this, there are at least two additional situations where direct mail can be more expensive than any other medium. The first is when a production technique requires the use of heavy embossed or other expensive papers, or some unusual method of engraving, artwork, or printing. The second is when large mailings are made that cannot take advantage of bulk mailing privileges. There is no reason to think that postage rates will decline in the future, and these high costs will continue to affect direct-mail usage.

Inaccurate and Incomplete Lists Without an accurate and complete mailing list, direct mail cannot do its best. So many Americans move frequently that it is difficult and expensive to keep lists up-to-date or develop new ones. In the past, it was possible to buy large mass mailings at low cost and not be concerned about the accuracy of the list. But today's high postage and production costs require the use of accurate and complete lists.

Variance in Delivery Dates Even if a large mailing is taken to the post office at one time, the pieces will be delivered at widely different times. If time is not essential to the marketing objectives, then the lag does not matter. But timing of an advertising message is often critical, and the direct-mail user cannot control it very well. Compared with other media, direct mail comes off second-best in respect to timing. When ads are placed in newspapers, they are printed on the day requested. When broadcast commercials are purchased, they are delivered not only on the day, but at the hour requested. In comparison, direct-mail delivery dates are unpredictable.

Clutter and Consumer Resistance With the increasing popularity of direct-mail advertising, special techniques and more costly packaging are needed to entice consumers to even open the envelope.

Outdoor Advertising—Reasons for Using

Wide Coverage of Local Markets Outdoor advertising is able to build large local coverage of the mobile population in many markets in a 30-day period. However, this coverage does not represent reading of the messages, only potential exposure to them.

High Frequency Billboards also have high frequency in reaching the mobile population of a market. It is in this area that billboards are strongest. Although the differences in reach of a 100 versus a 50 showing are not great, the frequency levels are quite different.

Largest Print Ad Available Size is a powerful attraction. Outdoor advertising allows the advertiser to buy the largest print ad available. The use of attractive color printing plus dramatic lighting and at times, moving portions and even live models, offer the advertiser great attention-getting power.

Geographic Flexibility Outdoor advertising can be used locally, regionally, and nationally. Even within any given market, it is possible to add emphasis wherever desired. Movable billboards enable an advertiser to concentrate messages in places where there are no fixed positions, such as a city's financial district or areas that are not zoned for outdoor advertising.

High Summer Visibility Media plans often include billboards in the summer because they increase the visibility of a brand name at a time when people are traveling. Warmer weather encourages people to take to their cars, and it is possible to reach them through billboards and other outdoor signs.

Around-the-Clock Exposure Because many billboards on main thoroughfares are lighted, anyone passing at any time of day or night can see the message. As long as there is a mobile population, this is an opportunity for exposures.

Simple Copy Theme and Package Identification When the message is relatively short and simple and the package is distinctive, outdoor advertising can be an excellent way to attract attention and build frequency for the message. Building brand awareness is a strength of the medium.

Outdoor Advertising—Limitations

Simple Messages The best use of outdoor advertising is for a simple message with a simple typeface; complex or long messages, especially with the small printing necessary to accommodate a lot of words, do not work well and are a waste of the advertiser's dollars. The best way to ensure readability is to use the copy testing services of the outdoor companies.

No Guarantee of High Recall Outdoor provides high reach and sometimes good recall of ad messages, but it is not necessarily true that high reach means high recall. The creativity of the message is an important criterion in assessing people's ability to remember the message. Because of the nature of this medium, people often look at billboards but are unable to recall what they saw.

High Cost Although the cost per thousand (CPM) is low, outdoor advertising has a high out-of-pocket cost when compared to some other media, according to the Institute of Outdoor Advertising. For a 100 showing nationally (top 50 markets), the cost is more than $5 million for a month.[13] Considering that outdoor advertising is a medium often in the background, that it requires very short messages, and that drivers' interests are focused primarily on the road ahead, this cost is prohibitive for many advertisers.

---

13. OAAA/SRDS Out-of-Home Advertising Source, reported in *2009 Marketer's Guide to Media.*

Limited Availability of Best Locations Prime outdoor-advertising locations on freeways or high-traffic roads often are held by long-term advertisers who are given the right of first refusal when their contracts expire. Key positions are available to occasional advertisers who allow their boards to rotate to a different location every month—some are excellent, some are not as good, but they eventually give the advertiser total market coverage. Also, zoning restrictions limit the availability of billboards in upscale neighborhoods.

Transit Media—Reasons for Using

Transit media involve interior and exterior displays on mass-transit vehicles and terminal and station platform displays.

Mass Coverage of a Metropolitan Area When an advertiser wants to reach individuals in the heart of a market, then mass-transit advertising is desirable. It is primarily a vehicle for reaching adults either on their way to or returning from work. But its reach is extensive.

High Frequency Transit media take advantage of normal travel patterns that are duplicated many days throughout the year. As a result, it presents an opportunity for a great deal of repetition of message delivery.

Relative Efficiency Based on potential exposures, transit can deliver large numbers of individuals at low unit costs.

Flexibility An advertiser can select transportation vehicles in which to place ads that reach certain kinds of demographically defined groups. The advertiser does not have to select all mass-transit systems, only those that are known to have large numbers of the target audience.

Opportunity to Position Messages to Consumers on the Way to Their Points of Purchase Local advertisers can buy messages that reach consumers on their way to their retail stores. Therefore, it is possible that for some consumers the transit ads will be the last medium they are exposed to before making a purchase.

Transit Media—Limitations

Limited Message Space Most often, large or complex messages cannot be disseminated in this medium. Transit advertisements rarely have enough space available to carry such messages.

Heavy Competition from Other Media and Personal Activities Transit is not an intrusive medium. Instead, it largely competes for attention with other things such as the attractiveness of scenery, the nature of the transit vehicle, or other people. The person who travels to and from work on the same transportation vehicle is often tired, bored, reading, doing e-mail, or browsing the Internet on a smart phone. Exterior displays often require extra creative pulling power to attract attention.

Frequent Inspection Because transit advertising is exposed to the natural elements as well as graffiti, care must be taken to replace posters that become dirty, defaced, or otherwise unacceptable. This requires frequent inspection, a cost that must be included in budgets for outdoor media.

Out-of-Home Video—Reasons for Using

Additional Brand Exposure Video display near product purchase at grocery stores and other retail outlets can reinforce other advertising immediately before the shopper is ready to buy.

Flexibility Video allows for flexibility in terms of creative message, time of delivery, geographic location, and creative format. Creative can be changed quickly and often as needed. For instance, the board could advertise winter clothing immediately after a snowstorm.

Sight and Motion A moving video display, with sound in some venues, is far more impactful than a fixed board. The medium attracts attention in a way that a conventional board cannot.

Builds Reach Video builds reach beyond what is possible with in-home media. This is especially valuable for reaching young adults who are light television viewers. Video units can be place in restaurants, bars, health clubs, and other locations frequented by young adults.

Highly Targeted Geographic, demographic, and product usage targeting is an easily accomplished and an obvious strength of the medium.

Production Efficiency The ability to use creative that was produced for other video media provides for efficiency. Standard video formats allow using existing creative, saving the cost of custom production.

Sophisticated Research In some venues, research can be customized to the individual venue, showing how long the viewer is in the area of the display, how many people pass it, and then how many people are exposed to the ad.

Out-of-Home Video—Limitations

Lack of Standardized Consistent Research Across All Venues Because there are so many different forms of out-of-home video, from gas station pump tops to restroom walls to movie theater lobbies, there is no consistent way to evaluate the medium. The Digital Place-based Advertising Association (DPAA) at www.ovab.org is working to create guidelines for audience measurement.

Availability Varies Market-by-Market and Within Markets Out-of-home video depends on custom hardware that must be manufactured and installed in each location. This is costly and leads to strong but spotty coverage of a market. Planners considering video in grocery stores should ask, "What percent of a market's All Commodity Volume (ACV) is accounted for by the stores that are installed with this video display?" ACV is the annual dollar volume of all sales in a market's retail stores.

Limited Reach Potential Traffic past any one unit is low compared to traditional mass media or even traditional out-of-home venues. Substantial reach requires the costly installation of units across a market, as hardware must be installed in each location.

Fragmentation of Suppliers Each medium is a different company, requiring a separate contract. Companies such as SeeSaw Networks (www.seesawnetworks.com) have been formed to facilitate planning out-of-home video campaigns across multiple venues and out-of-home video suppliers.

Proof of Play and Proof of Performance Reporting Varies by Supplier This is another consequence of the fragmentation of the medium. It is being addressed by DPAA and companies such as SeeSaw Networks.

Other Media

Numerous other media options give planners additional ways to reach target audiences that may be more selective and have even more impact than traditional media. Another quality of the new media is that they often provide a means for making media planning more creative. Some of these techniques are innovative and more interesting than the techniques available for traditional media. They can help make media more effective in delivering an advertiser's messages to a particular target.

This section explains details of some of the major new media. However, this text will not evaluate all such media in detail. The media options discussed here are some of the best known or most widely discussed.

Place-Based Media

A large number of new media are distinguished by the fact that they are located out-of-home in a particular place. Exhibit 9-3 lists a small sample of some of the best-known categories of place-based media and a brief explanation of each. A complete listing is available in the *SRDS Out-of-Home Advertising Source* (www.srds.com).

Each of these specialized media has its own advantages and limitations, but the general advantage of place-based media is that advertising can be seen in areas relevant to the products or services offered. Therefore, these media have more meaning for audiences than ads seen out of context. Often consumers are already motivated to buy, but these ads provide added impetus.

In general, a disadvantage of place-based media is that they are not available whenever wanted, as traditional media are. Timeliness of the message suffers. Furthermore, when consumers are tired, the message is not always seen or heard as when audiences are rested. Also, sometimes the advertisements are seen as intrusions rather than as helpful product information. Some consumers simply do not want to see these media and ignore them whenever they can, no matter what kind of information and entertainment are offered.

Another problem with place-based media is nonstandard measurement. The new Digital Place-based Advertising Association (DPAA) at www.ovab.org has been created to help marketers and agencies evaluate, plan, and buy out-of-home video. The organization has the support of many industry organizations and is expected to bring more discipline and accountability to this new medium.

Database Media Planning

Database media planning (sometimes called *data mining*) is a technique of building a list of individuals who are known to be purchasers of a given brand. Each person on this list is known by name, address, phone number, and sales potential, as a minimum. Then the data are placed in a computer to form the database. In essence, advertisers can theoretically eliminate waste in advertising because they know who the targets are and how to reach them. Limitations are privacy concerns and the high cost of direct response advertising.

EXHIBIT 9-3

Categories of Place-Based Media

Aerial	Banner-towing airplanes
Airport/airplane	Displays inside airports
	In-flight video programming
	Bar news network located in airport bars
	Video monitors located throughout airports carrying entertainment and commercials
	Laser billboards (rear-screen projection billboards)
Convenience stores	Ads attached to waste containers in stores
	Convenience store media (from ceilings, above coolers, etc.)
Golf courses	Colored posters framed behind Plexiglas, featuring golf subjects in clubhouses
	Colored ads on redwood tee-markers
	Ads on front and side of golf carts
Grocery stores	Ads on grocery carts inside stores
	Checkout channel: commercials on TV sets mounted above checkout aisles
	Pop radio: commercials interspersed with music and information heard throughout store
	Aisle ads: posters in aisles or ads on shelf (shelf talkers)
Health clubs	Full-color ads displayed on wallboards in general traffic areas and/or locker rooms
Movie theaters	Colored ads displayed in lobbies of movie theaters
	On-screen entertainment during intermission
Physicians' waiting rooms	Integrated multimedia system consisting of TV, magazines, wall-boards, and take-home booklets
Schools	Newspaper dispensers with ads on them
	Campus media boards: posters framed and displayed in cafeterias, residence halls, etc.
Shopping malls	TV advertising shown between feature clips in malls and stores
Stadia/arenas	Use of giant, color-TV-quality matrix with instant replay of sports plays and commercials
Advertising in motion	Full-color decals and signs applied to sides and rear of trucks
	Mobile ad units

Cross-Media (or Multimedia Integration)

Cross-media (also called *multimedia integration*) partnerships have received a great deal of coverage in the trade press. The basic idea of cross-media planning is the assembly of a select number of different media for the purpose of reaching specific target audiences for clients. The media are put together as a package that can include network television, cable, magazines, the Internet, and other media, tailored to meet diverse target audience needs.

The package, therefore, is an alternative to the more typical practice of dealing exclusively with one medium, like network television, or a group of media that tend not to be selective. The goal is to do a better job of communicating with hard-to-reach audiences and to take advantage of multimedia opportunities that combine promotions with advertising. But there are other appeals, too. For example, cross-media is a way to implement the principle of integrated marketing communications, plus value added and synergy.

Value added is closely aligned with cross-media planning. These terms are used to describe any element of a cross-media deal beyond the actual media buy, including special events. These are offered at a discount rate or no charge at all. Examples include premium positioning and bleed ads at no extra cost; tie-ins with other media such as direct mail and cable; in-store promotions or product sampling; bonus pages, custom publishing, and exposure on the vehicle's website. Media, for example, will often add to a cross-media deal by printing booklets or providing trips to tennis or golf tournaments. Clients have come to expect value-added programs, and media companies are quite willing to give them.

Determining the cost–value relationship of cross-media deals is tricky. The reason is that they are supposed to have synergy beyond values offered by traditional media. In other words, the totality of media values is supposed to be greater than the sum of each medium's contribution alone. But as some experts have commented, nobody yet knows how to calculate how much greater.

Cross-media deals are typically offered by large multimedia companies that hope to bring more revenue to the entire corporation than would be possible by negotiating one medium at a time. Since these packages sometimes mix very attractive properties with other venues that are struggling for business or may even be off target, planners must ensure that each piece meets the advertiser's marketing objectives. When done correctly, packages of highly targeted, desirable venues can be very beneficial for an advertiser. Review Exhibit 1-1 for an example of a successful cross-media campaign using the ESPN properties for Coors Light beer.

Advantages of Cross-Media In a survey, 31 percent of respondents cited lower CPMs on cross-media deals as the primary advantage, and 27 percent cited the ability to deliver a single message in a variety of media as a secondary advantage. Low CPMs represent media cost-efficiency. In effect, those who choose cross-media for efficiency are looking for better media buys for the money.

Disadvantages of Cross-Media The value of cross-media deals varies case-by-case. However, cross-media plans certainly are more interesting communication vehicles to both consumers and advertisers, especially when the deal is designed for a particular client's needs.

Intermedia Comparisons for Nonmeasured Media

Almost every medium in existence has some qualities that are useful for one or another advertiser. As such, there are times when nonmeasured media are useful. A *nonmeasured medium* is one that lacks a periodic measure of who is exposed to it by a recognized research firm. The word *periodic* here is key. Often a nontraditional medium will hire a reputable firm like Nielsen to conduct a one-time-only study that provides its demographics and exposure metrics. Unfortunately, even reputable firms are suspected of being biased in favor of the company that pays for the research, because the company has a vested interest in the outcome. The way the sample is chosen, the way the questions are asked, the particular location chosen, and the time of year can all be selected to paint the most optimistic picture. An important part of DPAA's mission is to provide standards for the conduct of these studies. Whether they are accepted depends on whether the industry is willing to pay the higher cost for this higher-quality research.

One way to approach the dilemma of noncomparable measuring techniques for intermedia comparisons is to use response to advertising as a criterion of effectiveness. If it could be shown that an ad in one medium generates more recall than an ad in another medium, then a planner might assume that the medium with the higher recall is better. However, the ad or ads used for comparative purposes cannot be indiscriminately chosen. Nor can recall of one medium versus another be measured as the average recall of many ads, because some products or brands are inherently more interesting than others and therefore generate higher recall scores.

To prevent such bias, researchers usually measure the same ad in two different media. As a result, researchers hope, any variation in the recall scores is the effect of the medium rather than the ad. For example, if a cola product is being tested on television and a similar ad is tested in a print medium, it would be difficult, if not impossible, to keep the copy and creative elements constant. A commercial for a cola drink usually features an announcer's voice, whether on or off camera. Most of the time, the message features action and music rather than still scenes. Then, too, the audience sees the message on many different-sized television screens, some in large screen HD, others on a small set on a desktop.

If a similar cola ad were placed in print, the size of the ad would probably be constant from magazine to magazine, and there would be no sound of a well-known personality's voice and no music. Furthermore, if the print ad were placed in a magazine, there would be competition for attention from other ads, whereas the television program in which the commercial was placed would have no competition for attention at the same time (unless the viewer zapped a commercial while playing back the program on a DVR).

Therefore, any results of recall measurements could not be considered unbiased. Any one of the variables exclusive to the ad in a given medium could account for the greater or lesser recall scores. Although such techniques are helpful for other purposes, they are not entirely valid for use in intermedia comparisons. In addition, by the time the ad agency has gone to the expense of developing creative executions, it is a foregone conclusion that the medium will be used. Since any research would cost time and money (possibly even more than the cost of the media itself), and since planners would ignore any research that suggests a medium is ineffective, it is doubtful that such a study would be conducted in the first place. The concept is presented here to illustrate the practical difficulties inherent in the common but simplistic belief that copy testing research will help an advertiser decide which medium is most effective.

Often a medium in one class, such as magazines, will spend a great deal of money to prove that it is better than a medium in another class. Although the results are interesting, they cannot be considered valid for intermedia comparisons because of the problem of vested interests. As they say, "Don't ask your barber if you need a haircut."

Finally, the overall subject of recall scores is controversial within the research community. The question is whether a high recall score indicates that product sales will increase. Does high recall necessarily relate to changing the consumer's attitude in a positive way toward the product? Does recall relate to persuasion? Many research professionals believe that recall does not relate to sales effectiveness.

Media Mix

In planning strategy, the planner must decide whether to use a single medium or a number of media. When more than one medium is used, the result is called a *media mix,* meaning that the plan mixes a number of media classes to reach certain target audiences.

Most media plans employ a mix of media because a single medium, such as television, cannot reach the target market in sufficient numbers or with sufficient impact to attain a media objective. When a planner does not define the target market narrowly, the targets represent such a broad spectrum of consumers that the only way to reach them is through multiple vehicles. Most planners narrow the definition of targets to reach only those with the best potential. Another situation that might call for a media mix strategy occurs when a planner has segmented targets into two key groups, each of which is about equal in importance.

During the process of deciding which media to use, a media planner ought to ask, "What part of the market cannot be reached with a single medium?" Generally, vehicles within one media class can reach a substantial part of a market, perhaps 90 percent. The percentage of the market not covered might not be worth the extra cost of employing an additional medium. If 20 percent of the population accounts for 80 percent of product consumption, and this 20 percent is within the reach of a single medium, it is inefficient to try to reach more with additional but different media. Inefficiency means that the additional media have substantially higher CPMs than the original medium. See Chapter 5 for how to calculate multi-media reach and frequency using random duplication.

When to Use a Media Mix

The following objectives are some important reasons for using a media mix:

- To extend the reach of a media plan (adding prospects not exposed by using a single medium)
- To flatten the distribution of frequency so there is a more equal number of people who are exposed to a medium for varying numbers of times
- To add gross impressions, assuming, of course, that the second or third medium is cost-efficient
- To reinforce the message or help audience members remember it by using different kinds of stimuli (a process called "creative synergy")
- To reach different kinds of audiences, perhaps differentiated by lifestyle as well as demographics
- To provide unique advantages in stressing different benefits based on the different characteristics of each medium
- To allow different creative executions to be implemented

EXHIBIT 9-4

An Evaluation of Traditional Media for Different Uses*

KIND OF USE	LEAST VALUE	LITTLE VALUE	SOME VALUE	MORE VALUE	BEST VALUE
Authority	Outdoor	Radio	TV	Newspapers	Magazines
Beauty	Radio	Newspapers	Outdoor	TV	Magazines
Bigger than life	Radio	Magazines	Newspapers	TV	Outdoor
Demonstration	Outdoor	Radio	Newspapers	Magazines	TV
Elegance	Newspapers	Radio	TV/outdoor	TV/outdoor	Magazines
Entertainment	Outdoor	Magazines	Newspapers	Radio	TV
Events	Outdoor	Magazines	Radio	Newspapers	TV
Excitement	Newspapers	Outdoor	Radio	Magazines	TV
Features	Radio	Newspapers	TV	Magazines	Outdoor
Humor	Outdoor	Magazines	Newspapers	Radio	TV
Imagination	Outdoor	Newspapers	Magazines	TV	Radio
Information	Outdoor	Radio	TV	Magazines	Newspapers
Intimacy	Newspapers	Outdoor	TV	Magazines	Radio
Intrusion	Radio	Newspapers	Magazines	Outdoor	TV
Leadership	Newspapers	Outdoor	Radio	Magazines	TV
News	Outdoor	Magazines	Radio	TV	Newspapers
One-on-one	Outdoor	Newspapers	Magazines	Radio	TV
Package identification	Radio	Newspapers	TV	Magazines	Outdoor
Personal	Outdoor	Newspapers	TV	Magazines	Radio
Prestige	Outdoor	Radio	TV	Newspapers	Magazines
Price	Outdoor	Magazines	TV	Radio	Newspapers
Product in use	Radio	Outdoor	Newspapers	Magazines	TV
Quality	Newspapers	Radio	Outdoor	TV	Magazines
Recipes	Outdoor	Radio	TV	Newspapers	Magazines
Sex appeal	Newspapers	Radio	Outdoor	TV	Magazines
Snob appeal	Outdoor	Radio	TV	Newspapers	Magazines
Tradition	Outdoor	Newspapers	TV	Radio	Magazines

*Evaluations are subjective.
Source: DDB Needham Worldwide, *Which Media Do It Best?* (promotional brochure).

Criteria for Media Selection Beyond the Numbers

Media usually are selected on the basis of quantified data showing the abilities of alternative media to reach select target audiences.[14] In many cases, however, media planners make comparisons on an objective and subjective basis, covering materials cited in this chapter. The latter two criteria deal with the strengths of media to do certain things better than others. Unfortunately, these latter criteria are subject to debate and sometimes are simply the idiosyncratic perceptions of either a planner or the client.

DDB Needham Worldwide, Inc., presents the criteria in Exhibit 9-4 as a means of promoting the message and the medium in making selection decisions. If a planner disagrees with these decisions, at least the chart will encourage more thought about just what makes one medium more useful than another for achieving a client's objectives.

---

14. This section is adapted from DDB Needham Worldwide, *Which Media Do It Best?* (promotional brochure).

CHAPTER TEN

Principles of Planning Media Strategy

This chapter explains important principles that affect the creation and implementation of media plans. Some advertising practitioners consider media planning to be a few notes on the back of an envelope. Our approach is to have enough detail in the plan to implement the marketing strategy, so that the advertiser has as complete control as possible of a desirable outcome. In fact, our goal is to have the media plan implemented so that media and marketing objectives are fulfilled as planned. If this takes place, part of a desirable solution to the problem should be attained. The other part is control of the advertising message.

Media Strategy Concepts

Earlier, this book defined *media strategy* as a series of actions that planners take to attain media objectives. In addition, media strategies should achieve an advantage over competitors. If media objectives are achieved, it is because optimum strategies were employed. Thus, it is necessary to first state the objectives and follow with correct media strategies.

Will media strategies that have advantages over competitors always succeed? Not necessarily. Other factors—lower prices, good distribution, or better quality—also play a role in determining success. However, media strategies that have more weight, spend more money, and have better coordination across media classes are examples of gaining an advantage over competitors. This idea assumes that most other factors in the media plan are equal between competitors and the advertiser. It is hard to see how a plan with less reach, less frequency, and so on can make much difference in a competitive battle. Several prevailing media strategies are discussed in the following paragraphs.

Dominant Brand Presence in Media

A common practice in planning is to buy small amounts of media, presumably to save money. The result is that audiences do not notice the advertisements. In other words, small bits of media rarely accomplish much. Although setting the exact number is a matter of judgment, most planners agree there is a certain minimal amount of weight needed to cross the threshold and have an effect. It is better to combine media units into a few large media units to achieve presence.

Usually, being "big" in media is better. However, being dominant, or spending more money than a competitor, does not always guarantee success. The idea is to be visible and have a noticeable presence. This gives advertising a chance to be seen.

Advertise When People Are Buying

The uninitiated think advertising can make people buy a given product or brand. This belief is not supported by experienced advertisers. For seasonal products like tire chains, lawn mowers, or Christmas trees, it is almost impossible to sell out of season. Occasionally, fur coats are sold in the summer when drastic price reductions are made. However, when large numbers of consumers are buying the competition's brand at a certain time of the year, that is usually a good time for you to sell your brand. The combined effect of all the advertisers will boost awareness of the product category, to the benefit of all advertisers.

Most advertisers have track records of sales by month, and these will show the optimum times for advertising. The strategy is to find these times and "heavy up" (increase) media weight to take advantage of the natural selling opportunity. On the other hand, for the many products that are sold at a steady rate throughout the year, the recency theory would suggest it is best to schedule media continuously, without heavy-ups.

Creative Strategy's Impact on Media Strategy

Creative strategy is a significant consideration in planning strategy. In fact, it is often the starting place for all media planning. *Creative* indicates that some media are much more appropriate to the message than others. For example, when full color is needed, then print media are best because there is little variation in an ad's appearance from one carrier to another. (In contrast, consider the differences in color from one television set to another.) Sometimes creative can be written so that it will be effective in all media. At other times, creative is restricted to a small market segment or is designed to be run in nontraditional media.

Alternative Media Strategies

Media planners should always assume that when they are choosing a suitable strategy, usually more than one is available. Some alternative courses of action are equally viable, and a few are usually better than others. Exhibit 10-1 lists alternative media strategies that might be used to achieve a given media objective.

One problem with planning strategies, however, is finding the best from among the alternatives. Sometimes it is necessary to justify that the best one was chosen, by writing a rationale in the media plan that explains why one was chosen over others. If it is not written, someone in the client's organization might ask for an oral explanation of the choice.

What Media Planners Should Know Before Starting to Plan

Although planners might want to start writing a media strategy from the moment they are assigned to a product and brand, they should first fully understand the other elements of the overall marketing strategy. These other considerations are discussed in the following paragraphs.

EXHIBIT 10-1

Alternative Media Strategies

National coverage (buying all stations in a network television lineup)

Large national reach

Buying different dayparts to reach women at home and women who work out of the home

Buying national magazines or national newspapers

Buying local advertising in top 100 markets

Buying network radio

Buying national cable (e.g., ESPN)

Marketing Problems

Almost all marketers have one or more marketing problems that require relatively quick solutions. These problems could be national, regional, or local in scope and might deal with many different aspects of business, such as advertising, sales, manufacturing, and sales promotion. However, marketing or advertising problems usually include the advertising message (or creative), sales volume, market share, and profits.

The marketer is responsible for devising solutions to these problems. Solutions are usually marketing mix elements (product, price, place, and promotion, which includes advertising, sales promotion, public relations, and direct marketing). When a solution calls for advertising, then media automatically become an important ingredient in the solution.

A careful and complete analysis of the problem often helps make a proposed solution obvious. On the other hand, a loose or careless definition provides a bare minimum of direction. The media planner should know precisely what the marketing problem is, including a history of the brand that is relevant to the present problem and the solutions that have been proposed.

Once the marketing problem is understood and the role of advertising has been identified, planners can determine the role of media in solving the problem. The next step is the development of media objectives and the strategies that will be used to achieve them.

Recommended Actions

The marketer who uses advertising recommends courses of action (strategies) to solve the problems. Exhibit 10-2 shows alternative solutions to a marketing problem of declining sales. Each solution requires a different media strategy. If, for example, one solution is reducing prices, then the media planner could recommend large target reach and high frequency as two strategies. Reach will provide broad dissemination of advertising messages—the marketing strategy cannot work well if few consumers know that prices are lower. With greater reach, more consumers are more likely to take advantage of the offer. Furthermore, high frequency is necessary to help the message overcome the clutter of commercials that appear on television and radio.

Complexities of a Strategy

Strategy decisions are rarely simple, and their effects occur in many different ways. Neither of the two media strategies previously mentioned would always be feasible. The planner would need a different strategy if these require more money than the client is willing to spend, for instance. In that case, the planner must create a strategy to fit the budget. One way to do this is to limit the high reach and frequency to

---

| EXHIBIT 10-2 |

Declining Sales: Possible Marketing Solutions

Reduce prices

Get wider, larger, or better product distribution

Reduce price and use advertising to publicize

Use advertising to announce

Use innovative advertising messages to attract attention and communicate offer

Use sales promotion incentives

Use integrated marketing communications

Improve product quality

Use more attractive packaging

Choose new target segments (with different demographics or lifestyles)

---

the three or four months when sales responses for the product have traditionally been high. Beer advertising, for example, could require a strategy that limits advertising to summer months or that uses a flighting strategy.

If the situation is more complex (e.g., consumers who regularly bought a certain brand have switched brands), the solution would require an explanation of just how these consumers are supposed to respond to advertising communication. In this example, the marketer should try to motivate the consumer to switch back to the original brand.

Marketing situations requiring the use of different media for public relations, sales promotion, and advertising have a unique problem: all of the communications objectives must appear seamless to consumers. The media strategist should remind creative personnel that multiple communications objectives can be confusing to consumers, because each was produced with a different communication technique. The goal should be to help the advertising speak with one voice in its use of various media.

How the Product Will Be Sold

A media planner should know how the product will be sold and which marketing mix elements will be used. The term *how* refers to the creative department's perception of the proposed advertising: will it communicate with consumers? Generally, this is part of creative strategy. Specifically, it applies consumer behavior principles and research to explain how consumers might react to advertising.

How Advertising Sells a Product to One Customer

Gus Priemer, former marketing and media manager of S. C. Johnson & Son, Inc., urged media planners to first understand how to sell a product to *one customer* before planning large-scale media. Priemer also noted that planners should be able to describe how advertising communication is expected to work to influence the consumers' behavior toward a brand. The failure to do both is often the cause of unsuccessful strategies, because no one is sure how the consumers will respond to marketing efforts. If a planner cannot perceive how one person buys, how can he or she know what will happen when the advertiser is dealing with millions of consumers?

When a product's price is reduced, three elements can affect the consumer: price, communication method, and media choice. Simply telling consumers that a product's price is reduced often has little or no effect. Sometimes this is because the price is obtuse, such as when advertising features only the percentage discounts given. This type of information makes the consumer work to figure out the dollar value of the discount and can create doubt that the offer is genuine. Sometimes the price reduction is so insignificant that it has no motivational impact on the consumer.

The second factor in determining the success of the communication is the way the offer is announced. If the ad is dull and unnoticeable among more interesting ads or lacks audience appeal, then the communication will fail. Even the personality of a presenter can make a difference in getting communication through.

The third element of a successful communication is media choice. Television probably has the best chance of getting a message to consumers, because it provides emotional and factual presentation techniques to help it sell. Media work best when combined with a motivating force—like price reduction—and an attractive message placed in a strong medium.

Sometimes the solutions are so obvious that no written rationale is needed. If, for example, the selling technique is to lower prices, the consumer motivation will be that because prices are lower (perhaps lower than all competitors' prices), the consumer will buy the product to save money and get a good or superior product value at the same time. In this case, the motivation does not really require that someone write every strategy statement about selling.

How to Neutralize the Competition's Strategy

Media strategies take place in a dynamic marketing environment in which competitors try to outsell each other and gain a larger market share. Planners of a media strategy cannot ignore these competing approaches, especially when any one of them is directly attacking their brand. How can a media planner neutralize the competition's strategy? In the area of media planning, certain successful strategies can be devised. Here are some examples:

- Reach more members of a target market than competitors do
- Reach a different demographic target market
- Use higher average frequency
- Reach targets in new and different media formats
- Run a special promotion in conjunction with a medium
- Use media creatively

Cost of Strategies

Once general strategies have been determined, the planner will provide a rough estimate of the cost to implement them and compare that to the amount of money in the media budget. If the advertiser has already given the planner a number that represents the most the client will spend, then the planner has to devise the solution with strategies that do not go higher than the budgeted amount.

At times, a planner might devise two different strategies. One strategy will cost about the amount the client wanted. Another strategy, called an *investment spending strategy*, will cost more because the planner believes more money will return more in sales than the smaller budget.

Other Elements of Media Strategy

The media strategy section must reveal the decisions about the way the objectives will be accomplished. These decisions reflect the demographic characteristics of the people the advertising is supposed to reach (target audience), the way the choice of media complements the creative strategy, the balance between reach and frequency, the need for continuity, and the need to implement the plan within the budget.

Media Targets

To whom will advertisements be directed—users, persons who influence users, or both? The typical plan states the target in two ways: as a planning target and as a buying target.

The *planning target* is usually stated in terms of users or purchasers of the product as reported in Mediamark Research and Intelligence, LLC (MRI) or other research. Here are some examples:

- Female homemakers in households that use frozen pizza
- Regular golfers who play at least once a month
- Working women
- Heavy users of low-calorie domestic beer

The planning target can be used to select print vehicles because MRI will tell the planner how many "regular golfers," for example, read various magazines. But broadcast media are bought only on the basis of age and sex demographics. Therefore a *buying target*—that is, a target categorized by age and sex demographics—must also be defined. Exhibit 10-3 shows suitable broadcast buying targets to match the planning targets in the previous list.

The more specifically a planner identifies targets by demographic or other means, the easier it will be to find media that will reach those targets. Occasionally, planners use some other descriptor, such as psychographics. The goal, however, is to be as specific as possible. Too broad a target, such as adults 18–64, means the plan will waste exposures on individuals who never buy a given product or brand under any circumstances.

Once the media target has been specified, all subsequent decisions are based on how well the media being considered will reach this target. Media objectives often include a statement indicating where targets are located geographically, when that is a strategic consideration. Sometimes this information is stated in the strategy portion, rather than the objectives portion, of the plan.

Creative Strategy

The creative strategy and creative executions are the heart of an advertising campaign, whether one is planning a national campaign for an automobile manufacturer or a local campaign for a retail store. The reason should be obvious: copy

EXHIBIT 10-3

Broadcast Buying Targets That Match Planning Targets

PLANNING TARGET	BROADCAST BUYING TARGET
Principal shoppers in households that use frozen pizza	Women 25–54
Regular golfers who play at least once a month	Men 35–64
Working women	Women 25–49
Heavy users of low-calorie domestic beer	Men 21–34

and art are the communication that drives advertising. They sell! Media might or might not sell, depending on the marketing situation, but unless the copy has been well planned and written, the product is unlikely to sell. Copy (including words, pictures, sound, color, white space) is a motivating force; copy is what gets into the minds of consumers and affects sales in many ways.

Because of creative's importance, planners should not proceed until they know what the creative is and which media the creative people think would best suit the message. In fact, creative personnel should discuss their strategies before planning begins with media personnel. If they do not, then it is up to media planners to seek out creatives and learn which media are preferred. In fact, media planners can have worthwhile suggestions for creatives.

The creative strategy affects the choice of media classes and individual media. It also affects the degree of creative media planning that can result (discussed later in this chapter). It is inconceivable that a planner would ignore the creative plan.

Reach and Frequency

When planners select media they are, in effect, choosing those that will deliver a given number of target audience impressions. Delivery, however, is nothing more than exposures. Because all research data represent measurements taken in the past, the data therefore represent only estimates of exposures. The future will be somewhat different. But the number of estimated exposures contracted for in a media plan can be patterned in such a way as to maximize either reach or frequency, or to attain a given level of effective reach and frequency.

More explicitly, media objectives should state the frequency goal and the percent of the target that will be reached this number of times. Here, too, an explanation is needed to justify, logically, why any given level is desired.

Continuity

It should be apparent that media objectives will affect the kinds of strategies that later evolve. One important goal that will affect the timing of advertising during weeks and months of a year is continuity—the consistency of advertising placement. The various scheduling options were discussed in Chapter 8. Like reach and frequency, continuity results in many contradictory patterns of placement if not controlled.

One placement pattern, for example, consists of advertising that appears every day of the year; another is limited to placing ads once a week. Which is better? The answer depends on a number of factors. What is the brand's marketing goals and strategy? Do they require a given pattern? Does the creative strategy require a different pattern? For example, if the creative strategy includes a very complex message in television commercials, will audiences be able to grasp the meaning if the commercials are shown once a week, or will a pattern of frequent showings be required? If the latter, then the media goals will have to be based, to some extent, on flighting and exposure concentration.

Budget Constraints

Even though the relationship of marketing objectives to media objectives is clear, a number of constraints often temper the planner's decision. The size of the budget, if known ahead of time, is one such constraint. Many times, the marketing budget is set before any media planning takes place. In such a situation, the media objectives will have to be written with the budget in mind.

If no budget is available, then media objectives can guide the setting of a budget, at least as far as the cost of time or space is concerned. Once planners have a general idea of their goals, they are in a position to estimate what it will cost to achieve them. Sometimes a budget cannot be set at the stage of developing media objectives, but must wait until the strategy has been worked out.

In such cases, media objectives will have to be rewritten later to accommodate the size of the budget. A series of marketing/media priorities should be set so that the planner achieves the most pressing goals, while secondary goals wait for another day. The client might reduce the size of a budget recommended by a media planner after examining marketing/media objectives and strategy.

Creative Media Strategy

In Chapter 1, we discussed the creative media plan as a problem to be solved. In this chapter, we will suggest ways to implement a creative media strategy that will help solve this problem to a great extent. First, the media planner should understand what is meant by the term *creative media strategy.* There is no universally agreed-upon definition of this term, but in general, such a strategy is innovative enough to secure for an advertised brand some advantage over competitors' brands. The strategy might accomplish this by helping the advertising stand out against competitors' advertising, giving the messages a better chance of being absorbed.

Guidelines for a Creative Media Strategy

Many advertised brands in a product category tend to use similar media strategies. If all brands in a category are also similar, then consumers will have difficulty distinguishing one brand from another. Perhaps a creative media strategy will help solve the problem. More specifically, we offer four guidelines for implementing a creative media strategy.

Make Your Media Strategy Different from and More Innovative than Competitors' A creative strategy is easily distinguished from competitors' strategies. However, simply being different is not enough. There is no evidence that a plan that is different from competitors' plans will accomplish anything. But media and marketing planners will testify that truly innovative plans can accomplish key goals and attain competitive advantages. The key elements of innovation are ideas that make a brand's advertising stand out from the competitors' advertising. The most effective plans are based on insights into the day-to-day lives of consumers as people and the ways they relate to the product being advertised. This assumes advertising messages have something to say that is meaningful to consumers. This also means the creative media dollars should return more than a typical brand's media strategy.

The Ability to Be Creative Does Not Depend on Additional Dollars Innovative strategies that cost more than what is considered normal are not valuable unless there is evidence that the increased spending will result in superior returns. Fortunately, it is possible to be creative without spending more.

Media Strategy Should Start with Quantitative Proof . . . Then Go Beyond Numbers A creative media strategy is not a substitute for quantitative proof that the best media have been selected and used. Without measures of reach, frequency, effective frequency, and other kinds of useful numerical data, a planner would have to rely on instinct. It is difficult to convince clients who are spending large amounts of money for media to rely on instincts as proof. A solid media plan is built on good quantitative proof *and* a good creative strategy.

Creative Media Strategy Should Be Relevant to the Problems of the Brand Being creative is sometimes interpreted as being "offbeat" or "new." It is important to make a creative media plan relevant to the marketing situation, not just "different." A media planner should contribute to the overall marketing plan with creative media strategies. Planners typically are thought of as "number crunchers," or people with only quantitative skills. Both stereotypes ought to be dismissed. When given an opportunity to be creative, a media planner should be able to think of innovative ways to solve problems.

Examples of Creative Media Strategies

The following examples summarize creative strategies that various advertisers used to achieve special attention for their messages.

Problem: Kodak's headquarters is in Rochester, New York. Its competitor in the copier field, Xerox, was about to sponsor the U.S. Open golf tournament in Rochester. The planner's challenge was to offset this competitive (and embarrassing) local Xerox exposure.

Solution: On the first day of the tournament, Kodak's agency published an ad in *USA Today* that looked just like the newspaper's real front page, except that all the stories were about Kodak's copiers. The single-page ad appeared in a special section on the U.S. Open and wrapped around the front page so that the first thing readers saw was the Kodak copier line; the real front page was underneath. The Kodak page appeared only in the Rochester area but was circulated at the tournament site, airports, and hotels. Kodak's planners were creative because they saw an opportunity that had not been apparent before.

Problem: Kodak needed a big media event without taxing the advertising budget.

Solution: Kodak's advertising agency suggested it buy and be the sole sponsor of a special issue of *Time* magazine. The issue had a theme that fit with the client and the medium: "150 Years of Photojournalism." This special issue went to subscribers free, as a bonus. It was also supported with a special ad campaign that appeared in key markets—a traveling photo exhibit that worked as a public relations event and received extra publicity from the local press.

Problem: An advertising agency had difficulty finding enough money to communicate with consumers in 10 of the client's key markets. The budget was only $250,000. Among those markets were Cincinnati, Cleveland, and Detroit.

Solution: The agency found an hour-long TV program on art in ancient China, produced by a station in Seattle. It bought the rights to that program and scheduled it in the 10 key markets. The agency localized the program to fit each market separately. It then got most stations in the markets to broadcast the show for free, arguing that it had a strong cultural-affairs type of appeal.

Media Strategy Is Not Science

In practice, planners have to remember that media strategy is not a science in the same manner as physics or medicine. Its outcomes cannot always be predicted with great accuracy. One significant reason for this is that the marketplace is constantly changing as competitors use many different tactics to gain an advantage over each other. In addition, the original marketing problem might not be solved after strategies have been implemented.

The outcomes of some media strategies, such as reaching 70 percent of a target market by placing ads in a certain group of vehicles, can be achieved quite well. However, it would be incorrect to assume that everyone reached saw an advertisement in the selected medium or that all those who saw an ad will respond as intended. Therefore, planning strategy includes knowing precisely what each strategy means and implies.

For the most part, planners learn what each individual strategy will accomplish from personal experience. When planners have worked with a given product category or a brand for many years, they learn what a strategy will accomplish under certain marketing conditions. As time goes by, they modify their findings to develop a body of knowledge that enables them to make better predictions of the results. Exhibit 10-4 lists questions that cover basic media strategies. They should be included in a typical media plan. For complex strategies, they should be accompanied by a rationale.

Relationships Among Reach, Frequency, Continuity, Number of Markets, and Ad Size

In planning strategy, usually five elements are closely related: reach, frequency, continuity, the number of markets to be used, and ad size. Because of their close relationship, a person cannot plan for one of these elements without simultaneously considering the others. The relationship grows out of a fixed budget size, which means, in effect, that the planner must balance trade-offs: when one of these elements is emphasized, the others will have to suffer.

The size of the ad affects media planning because it is directly related to the cost of advertising. A magazine spread costs more than a page, which in turn costs more than a half page. A 15-second commercial on network or cable TV is typically half the cost of a 30-second commercial, while in spot TV a 15-second commercial is about two-thirds the cost. So although the shorter commercials would have less impact, if the goal of a campaign was simple brand awareness, a mixture of :15s and :30s would allow longer flights, more markets, and more reach and frequency. Typically the ad size or ratio of ad sizes has been determined by the account team and the creative department, leaving the media planner to work with the four other elements.

Each of these elements costs a considerable amount of money to maximize. Emphasizing reach, for example, usually requires dispersing advertising messages

EXHIBIT 10-4

Questions for Planning Media Strategies

Marketing
1. What are the marketing problems that require media?
2. What marketing objectives and strategies have been planned?

Media
1. What are the creative strategy and recommendations for best use of creative?
2. What are the media objectives?

Strategy
1. Who should targets be (demographic, product usage, and lifestyle description of prospects)?
2. Which media classes are recommended? What percentage of the budget should go to each media class (e.g., 60 percent network TV, 20 percent spot TV, 10 percent cable, and 10 percent magazines)?
3. How much reach and frequency do we need? Effective reach and/or frequency? Why? How much reach, frequency, and GRPs are needed per quarter?
4. How large is the media budget? What percentage spending per month and quarter is required? Why?
5. What is the best timing and scheduling for this year?
   a. What pattern of continuity is recommended?
   b. Is there an introductory period? For how many weeks? Why?
   c. How heavy should introductory weight be compared to sustaining parts of the plan?
   d. Is there a heavy-up period? When? Why?
6. Geographic concentration:
   a. In which media should it occur? Why?
   b. What are the criteria for selecting markets?
   c. What is the importance of BDIs and CDIs?
   d. How many markets should we be in?
   e. What are the names of individual markets?
   f. How much weight should we plan for in each market?
   g. What are the seasonal variations in weighting?
7. Which daypart should be selected for broadcast media?
8. Media units:
   a. Sizes needed? 30 seconds or 15 seconds? Page or partial-page units?
   b. Use of special color or treatments (gatefold, etc.)?

widely so that many different persons in the target audience will have an opportunity to see the messages. Generally, one single media vehicle, such as one television program or one magazine, will not deliver a high reach. This emphasis requires multiple vehicles, greater message dispersion, and additional media weight. As the cost for reach goes up, the amount of money available for the other three elements becomes more limited.

The same holds true for continuity. If an advertiser wants to plan continuous advertising over 52 weeks, the cost will be high, leaving minimal amounts of money for the other three elements. Often as much as six or more months of advertising must be sacrificed for the reach to attain a high enough level in the remaining six months. The trade-off between flighting and continuity was discussed in Chapter 5.

Likewise, the number and size of individual markets in a plan, where national media are used in conjunction with local media, clearly affect overall costs. Even if only local media are used, the same concept prevails. The more markets used, the higher the cost, and the less money available for the other elements.

Exhibit 10-5 shows to some extent what happens when a planner manipulates the four elements within the constraints of a fixed budget. The figure shows some ways to vary the weights of reach, frequency, continuity, and number of markets. One part of a planner's job is to weigh each of the four alternatives and decide which needs more emphasis (usually at the expense of the others). Of course, if the budget size can be increased (unfortunately, it usually cannot), then different emphases can be achieved. As a consequence of this dilemma, the planner needs some criteria for weighing the alternatives.

Weighing Alternatives

The two most important elements of a media plan are reach and frequency. Because they occupy such an important position in a plan, they are usually considered before continuity or number of markets. When a media budget is larger, it is possible to achieve both high reach and high frequency levels. But most often, the cost is too high to do both.

If high reach is planned, it will probably cause the frequency level to decline somewhat, because reach and frequency are inversely related. If, however, reach is very high (more than 90 percent), then frequency can be increased by extra dollar expenditures, because most of the money will go into building frequency and a very small increment will go to building reach. This is the natural consequence of trying to reach new people who have not already been reached by some other mass vehicle.

Higher reach will be necessary when the media objectives call for anything new. Reach is also needed for building brand awareness. If a brand awareness level is now at 25 percent and an objective is to raise it to 50 percent, then higher reach will be required and frequency will be sacrificed. Another objective calling for higher

EXHIBIT 10-5

Alternative Strategies Within a Fixed Budget

Reach	Frequency
Continuity	Number of Markets

You cannot plan for equal strategies on a fixed budget.

Reach	Number of Markets
Frequency	Continuity

To buy heavy amounts of continuity or markets, you must sacrifice reach and frequency.

Reach	Frequency
Number of Markets	Continuity

Other combination strategies must sacrifice one or another of the goals.

Reach	Frequency
Continuity	Number of Markets

Most media plans do not have enough money to reach all goals.

reach is the announcement of various kinds of promotions, such as cents-off deals, special coupon promotions, or refund offers. Such promotions must build a great deal of awareness so that consumers will take advantage of the offer. Still another high-reach situation occurs when changes in the brand or changes in the creative strategy are important. Finally, more reach is needed when it becomes necessary to meet or exceed competitive reach levels. One goal could be to steal customers from a competitor by showing them that the advertised brand better meets their needs, in which case enough reach is needed to equal or better the competitor's reach.

More frequency is needed, at the expense of reach, when the brand awareness levels are already high due to the cumulative effect of past advertising. At that point, more frequency is needed to meet or surpass frequency levels of competitors.

When the advertising noise level of all competitors is already high, then more frequency is needed to meet or surpass frequency levels of competitors. There are certain marketing situations in which a minimum judgmentally determined frequency threshold must be passed before consumers start paying attention to the message. The effectiveness of the media plan is then directly related to high frequency, but the planner must also consider what percent of the target will be exposed at that level for a given budget.

Even if brand awareness is a campaign or creative objective, the campaign might require advertising in a pattern that matches the purchasing cycle of a product class. Some products are not sold to any great extent at certain times of the year. Computers, for example, require heavy media usage in spring, early fall, and at Christmastime. Reach levels also will probably be high at those times. In contrast, beer is sold all through the year, with summer peaks. For this product, reach levels might have to be sacrificed at some times of the year to have enough money to cover the year and at the same time spend heavily during the summer. When high reach is necessary, continuity sometimes needs to be sacrificed. In some situations, advertisers drop out of advertising for as long as six months, allowing the product to keep selling at lower volume levels, to have sufficient money to advertise at high levels during peak-volume seasons.

The final variable affecting the budget allocation is the number of markets to be used. Planners arrive at a number by using either of two methods. The older method consisted of creating national media plans in which the number of markets would not be considered until after other strategies were decided. Another technique starts with a market-by-market analysis and sets strategies for each market. To simplify planning, markets are then grouped into tiers that reflect different reach/frequency goals. For example, Group A markets would receive high-level support, Group B markets would get intermediate-level weight, and Group C markets would receive minimum-level sustaining support via what spills in from the national media.

Setting Priorities

An important step in weighing the strategy trade-offs is that of setting priorities. A planner should do this early so that it will be easier to decide which element is most or least important. Priorities come from media objectives, and some objectives are obviously more important than others. If there is any doubt, then a planner must not only state the priorities but also explain why one objective is more important than another and how much more important. Once the priorities are clear, the allocation of a budget to the five variables should be relatively clear.

Choosing Media Strategies

The discussion in this chapter to this point has been on elements that affect the planning of media strategies. Now the question arises, Which strategy from among the alternatives is the most appropriate? Many strategies could be used in one media plan, so planners need guidelines for studying alternatives. This section discusses a select group of strategies that media planners often confront.

Prevailing Wisdom

Remember that media strategy is not a science. There is little evidence one can refer to in trying to make the best decision. Many of what are called "best strategies" have not been proven to be best objectively, but are judged to be best by a planner based on the facts available. Many times, however, strategists speak with so much conviction that it is assumed they must be correct. On the other hand, many strategists have learned by experience what works best, and they use this learning in future decision making. In these cases, they are using their experience as a different form of research.

One must realize that the effects of some strategies cannot be measured. As an example, it is almost impossible for most marketing and media planners to prove how many sales were actually delivered as a result of a media strategy's contribution, because the strategy cannot be parsed out separately. What seems to be working might instead be the product of other variables that are difficult to measure. Furthermore, media responses are mostly affected by advertising's creative efforts.

Media's effectiveness is probably the most difficult of all advertising variables to measure. Ads are responded to, but mostly as a result of creative efforts. We can find out how many magazines were subscribed to, how many were sold on newsstands, how many readers there were, and even whether audiences saw a given ad in certain magazines. But how many sales did the magazine produce? That is not known, and it is probable that we will never know precisely this kind of information. The exception to this is direct-response advertising. With the use of toll-free and 900 telephone numbers or business reply cards, it is possible to directly attribute sales to a distinct media vehicle. The effect of digital advertising can also be precisely measured in terms of click-through from the banner to the advertiser's website, and from there to product inquiry or actual online sales.

Typical Media Strategies and Alternatives

The following discussion covers selected marketing or media problem situations and the prevailing strategy opinions about them. It examines some of the major strategies that planners have to deal with, shows how and why these strategies are used, and discusses alternatives.

Scheduling When the market for a brand seems flat during the entire year (i.e., sales are approximately even during all 12 months), the scheduling strategy and the recency theory suggest that advertising should be done every month. This implies that because consumers buy a product category evenly, the scheduling should reflect this evenness. This kind of scheduling therefore would call for even continuity during all 12 months at a minimum 50 target GRPs per week when on air.

What is missing from a high-continuity strategy is the effects of all competitors' advertising. *Even continuity* means that spending is approximately the same during each month. But this strategy ignores the competition, unless the competition is also supporting its brand throughout the year. The net effect of even spending is to have lower reaches and frequencies (communication opportunities) each month unless a huge amount of money is spent. On the other hand, the strategy is certain to deliver advertising to buyers who would be missed during hiatuses if media weight was flighted. See the shelf-space model of media planning presented in Chapter 5.

Flighting If the competition concentrates its advertising support during certain times of the year, a better scheduling strategy can be to sacrifice even continuity to concentrate money at certain periods during the year. The advertiser would choose periods when its own brand can be prominent compared to competitors' brands. This strategy is called *flighting* and is based on the assumption that advertising will be more effective with additional frequency over a short period of time. A schedule might concentrate advertising into bursts of four to six weeks at a time at about 100–125 target GRPs per week, with a two- to three-week hiatus between each burst. The effect of this strategy is that (assuming the budget is a fixed amount) more money is available to be spent during the bursts. The planner assumes that the accompanying positive effect on sales from greater reach and frequency when the bursts occur will exceed the loss of sales during hiatus periods.

Heavy Introductory Effort If a brand is just being introduced, it has the problem of breaking through consumers' mental sets that have endured without this new brand. Competitive brands might have a strong hold on the market, making it difficult for the new brand to establish a foothold. A strategy here would require heavy spending at the beginning of a campaign, sacrificing advertising during the latter part of the year to ensure that enough money is available to properly launch the brand. The introduction could run from one to three months and would deliver 1,200–1,500 target GRPs over the period.

The Information Resources, Inc., research mentioned earlier confirmed that "the concentration of higher TV weight into fewer weeks is related to an increase in sales."[1] The study concentrated only on television advertising, but the same concepts would apply for other advertising media, with the exception that television is more dynamic.

In most new-product introductions, the client is willing to spend more money to get the product launched in the marketplace. But this additional money might not be enough. Beginning media planners are often surprised to learn that as much as 70 percent of an advertising budget is recommended to be spent in this introductory period. You might ask, "What happens to advertising during the rest of the year, when so little money is left?" The experienced planner will usually respond by saying, "If sales are not strong with an introductory heavy-up, the client is likely to cut the budget planned for sustaining support." One of the principles of strategy planning is to make advertising appear as large as possible for maximum effect. So the up-front strategy for a new-product introduction is the best alternative.

Heavy-Up Scheduling Most planners spend more on advertising when consumer buying is heaviest and spend less at other times. This is known as *heavy-up scheduling*. Many brands have two to four months a year of heavy buying activity. The opportunity to get competitors' customers to switch brands during these heavy-buying seasons is greater at this time if advertisements say something worthwhile.

Advertising should show a brand's superiority over others. These heavy buying seasons are usually the best times to advertise because consumers are more responsive to advertising for the product category than at other times. It cannot be assumed that heavying up for two or three months will automatically cause sales to increase proportionately. Most consumers are looking for good values to meet their needs and wants.

However, a planner can have an advantage over competitors who also recognize that the buying season is the time to advertise. If all competitors are spending more at the same time, they might nullify each other. This could require a strategy for one competitor to start a month or two before all the others start heavy spending, and thereby get a jump on the market.

---

1. Information Resources, Inc., 1991; summary from FCB/Chicago Media Matters, February 1992.

Geographic Market Weighting *Geographic market weighting* means adding either dollars, GRPs, or a larger number of advertisements in a geographic market because that market has greater sales potential than others. Each of these dollars, GRPs, or ads represents the same idea to some extent. When any of them is added, it is assumed, advertising has a better chance of being more effective than the same market with lesser weights.

The need for extra weighting in certain markets is based on market potential, which is usually uneven nationally. A brand might be selling well in some markets and poorly in others. The assumption is that adding weight to low-volume sales markets represents a bigger risk than adding weight to markets that have already been producing good sales.

One principle of weighting, then, is to add extra weight to a market equal to its relative sales contribution. This is called *pro-rata budgeting,* which suggests that a market that produces 6 percent of a company's sales should receive at least 6 percent of the advertising budget. Under this principle, the weighting of markets can be based on the relative sales volume each market has already produced. Pro-rata budgeting has established a positive track record that serves as a guideline for weighting.

When some markets have done poorly and there is reason to believe that one of the reasons for the poor sales is the lack of advertising weight, then the pro-rata technique might not be adequate. A planner could experiment with added weight to see what will happen. Without evidence that sales would increase with more advertising weight, the pro-rata technique is a low-risk alternative.

Combining Media or Vehicles Another strategy deals with how many different vehicles or media are optimum for achieving a media goal. In answering this question, the nature of the goal is a consideration. However, if the goal is building reach (e.g., 70 percent of a target market), then the media and dayparts or vehicles should be selected with consideration for the diversified audiences they reach. There are many ways to achieve the desired 70 percent reach, both within an individual medium and across media. For example, the use of multiple media means there is less duplication within each individual medium. This is one way to build reach.

Planners also use multiple media to build concentrated reach of a demographically defined target market. Each medium will bring new audience members to a plan. But as each additional vehicle is added to a list, more weight goes into building frequency than reach, because the target audiences of the latest-added medium have already been reached by the media selected first.

Conversely, if the media goal is to build frequency, then it is appropriate to concentrate weight on a small number of vehicles. As weight is added to the same vehicles, frequency increases as the same people see the ad over and over again.

One consequence of the inverse relationship between reach and frequency is that it is possible to buy high frequency and have reaches that are so small as to be of questionable value. A media mix that produces an average frequency of 20 might have a reach of only 12 percent. The value of high frequency would be lost on such a small market reach. This is something a planner has to avoid.

Going beyond the numbers, multimedia campaigns can be used to increase the impact of the advertising by presenting the product's story with many different voices. Exhibit 10-6 presents one example: in 2006, the S. C. Johnson company introduced a new kind of shower cleaner with an integrated multimedia campaign that surrounded the target with the brand's message.

EXHIBIT 10-6

S. C. Johnson Scrubbing Bubbles Automatic Shower Cleaner Introduction

Scrubbing Bubbles Automatic Shower Cleaner was a new kind of product that cleaned showers with an automatic spray. The target was older than for most consumer package goods, the message more complex, and the product more expensive than traditional shower cleaners. The marketing objective was to introduce the brand, create excitement among the consumers, and, given the price commitment, provide an incentive that would spark trial.

The solution was to use a combination of media that would surround the consumer, providing the needed reach and depth of communication with the theme "MAID for your shower."

National Television—Prime Time, Daytime, News, Cable
- Three creative executions strongly increased brand awareness.
- Tags were used to promote freestanding insert (FSI) and Web coupons and Refreshing Spa Refill.

Direct Response Television
- "Mommy's Secret" :60 drove consumers to the product website.
- Various incentive offers included starter kits, coupons, and free caddies.

Spot Radio
- Three creative executions used tags to promote FSI and Web coupons.
- Partnering with radio stations for local radio promotion "Singing in the Shower" generated thousands of promotional mentions.

Print—Consumer Magazines
- "Maid Arms" and "Touch Your Shower Clean" ran in various weekly and monthly magazines during summer 2006.
- Overall ad awareness for print increased dramatically.

Online Promotion
- The website www.DirtyShower.com generated excitement by redirecting consumers to the brand's website during prelaunch period.
- The website attracted many thousands of visitors in four months.

Skymall Placement
- This included cover placement and full-page content.
- In-flight magazines resonate with older and more affluent consumers.
- It was the third-greatest Skymall success story ever!

Source: S. C. Johnson, Inc. Illustration: James Shepard. Photo: Glen Gysler. Used with permission.

Share of Voice In developing a competitive media strategy, the most common, if most simplistic, measure is *share of voice (SOV)*, expressed as percent of dollars spent. Knowing that our brand spent $30 million last year out of total category spending of $150 million (SOV = 20 percent) tells us a great deal about the brand's relative position in the marketplace and in the minds of our consumers. Our brand accounts for only 20 percent of total category advertising. Put another way, the consumer sees four competing commercials for every one of ours.

Dollars are a crude measure because they do not tell us how they affect the many important marketing variables. It would be more precise to describe share of voice in terms of national GRPs. But that hides geographic differences in media weight, as well as possible creative differences in the commercial message. Yet a market-by-market competitive analysis by commercial length will hide possible differences in impact across different dayparts and program venues.

From this it should be clear that as the competitive analysis becomes more detailed, the planner runs the risk of getting lost in the numbers. These factors should be examined when they are directly relevant to the media strategy of the brand. Otherwise, the more general share-of-voice statistic is going to give the truest picture of the forces that drive the marketing situation.

Channel Planning Software

The process of balancing trade-offs and determining which media are the best for a given product and set of marketing objectives has been characterized as "channel planning." Pointlogic, a Netherlands company,[2] has developed software that allows a planner to quantify the many variables that go into media planning and produce a relative ranking of media based on that input. The Pointlogic tools are used in more than 65 countries. In the United States, Pointlogic's Compose process and computer software begins with consumer research into the characteristics that drive the purchase decision of 58 products and services. Those drivers include price, convenience, customer service, high quality, and so on, and the ability of each of 35 media (channels) to communicate those drivers.

A survey of media experts then identifies how well each channel satisfies various marketing objectives: reach people in the home, provide high frequency, allow market selectivity, deliver a consumer coupon, create immediate awareness, and so on. To use the system, the planner enters the target audience, the product, the

---

2. www.pointlogic.com.

marketing objectives (create awareness, encourage trial, stimulate conversation, etc.), and the channels that might be considered. Using a graphic interface, planners input the relative importance of the various drivers and the characteristics that are needed from the candidate channels. Exhibit 10-7 shows the result: a graphic display that ranks each of the candidate channels based on all the various inputs. The statistical engine at the heart of the generic Compose system is called Chorus, which can be modified to reflect an agency's custom research, unique planning style, and graphic treatment. Like any computer system, its results should be viewed

EXHIBIT 10-7

Sample Channel Ranking Output from Compose System

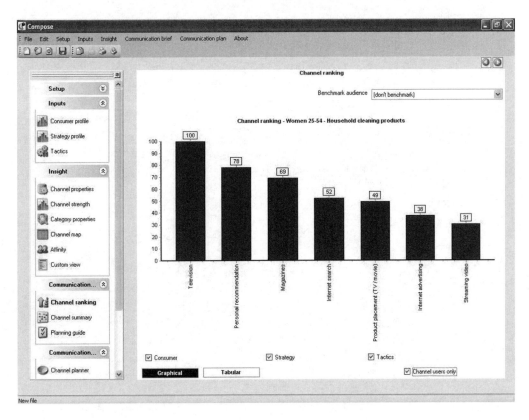

Source: Pointlogic USA. Used with permission.

as one of many inputs to the media planning process. Typically the results confirm the planner's expectations. However, agencies find it useful as additional, independent support for the recommendation.

The channel planning program is best run in a meeting with all the stakeholders, possibly even including the client. It serves as a focal point of (often controversial) discussions on the relative importance of the many factors that go into selecting the best media. In the author's opinion, this meeting is the most valuable aspect of using channel planning software.

CHAPTER ELEVEN

Evaluating and Selecting Media Vehicles

After devising strategies, the next step in media planning is to evaluate and select media vehicles. In this step, media buyers come into the picture. The planner provides criteria for buying, and the buyers follow the criteria as closely as possible. This kind of activity helps keep a number of different people working on the account closely orchestrated toward common goals and efforts.

With the exception of print and online, vehicle selection is determined primarily by professional buyers. Although the primary factor is cost, there are other considerations, which vary depending on the medium. For television, for example, the media plan specifies which dayparts are to be used, but buyers select stations and programs within those dayparts on the basis of cost (cost per thousand [CPM]), rating size (coverage), and audience composition for the age/sex target audience. For radio, buyers choose stations on the basis of cost, format, average quarter-hour rating, and cumulative audience. The buyer's goal for both TV and radio is to purchase a schedule of vehicles (programs, stations, time periods, etc.) that deliver the planned gross rating points (GRPs) within the authorized budget. Newspapers are selected primarily according to their geographic coverage of the market under consideration. Outdoor billboard locations are selected on the basis of visibility, traffic flow, and market coverage. Online websites are selected on the basis of their composition for the target audience, the appropriateness of the website for the product, engagement (time spent) with the site, CPM cost efficiency, and technical ability to target advertising to specific audiences.

Unlike broadcast and outdoor advertising, magazine vehicles are usually selected by the planner on the basis of a variety of considerations in addition to media cost-efficiency. These considerations will be discussed in detail in the following section.

Determining Media Values for Magazines

An elementary principle for selecting media is to select vehicles that reach as much of the target audience as possible at a cost-efficient price. Although this principle seems to suggest that this is all there is to the selection process, nothing could be further from the truth. A more advanced principle is to determine each vehicle's value in terms of the desired criteria and then select those that best meet these criteria. Some of them can be measured quantitatively, and the numerical values of various criteria can be combined into a single number. Others are qualitative, and it is more difficult to assign numerical weights to these. But the selection should consider both. Exhibit 11-1 lists the most important objective and subjective criteria usually considered in magazine selection.

Target Reach, Composition, and Cost-Efficiency

The most important criterion in determining media values is a combination of three principles: (1) finding vehicles that reach a large number of targets with (2) a high enough composition to avoid waste and (3) at a low CPM. The logic of using these three principles in combination should be obvious. Advertising and marketing today are directed to certain demographic targets. Assuming these targets can be identified precisely, it follows that media vehicles should be selected to reach the largest number of targets efficiently with minimum waste. There is no reason to think that these principles will change as new media forms are developed.

Magazine Planning Process

How do magazines get selected for a media plan? Most planners follow a six-step process that leads to the final magazine schedule. Note that several of these steps require the use of proprietary computer systems that are available only by subscription from the data suppliers or third-party software vendors such as IMS or Telmar. Their use is shown here to illustrate these real-world processes.

1. Determine the List of Candidate Magazines. This is the time to cast a broad net to include any magazine that might be appropriate for the plan. Candidates can be

EXHIBIT 11-1

Criteria for Determining Media Values of Magazines

Primary Objective Criteria
1. Composition and coverage
2. Delivery of demographic targets
3. Cost-efficiency of delivered targets
4. Delivery of product-class user targets
5. Delivery of strategic targets
6. Delivery of psychographic targets

Secondary Objective Criteria
1. Primary versus pass-along readers
2. Editorial features or other content related to brand's image
3. Special editions, issues, or sections in print
4. Media imperatives
5. Color reproduction
6. Circulation trends in print vehicles
7. Geographic flexibility
8. Production flexibility
9. Positioning opportunities within print vehicles

Subjective (or Qualitative) Criteria
1. Writing tone
2. Reader respect
3. Leadership in media class
4. Believability

identified by looking at the advertiser's experience in prior years, magazines used by competitors, and industry sources such as SRDS. Media planners also become aware of candidates through their frequent contacts with sales representatives from magazines that might be appropriate. Planners see sales presentations that give reasons why a particular magazine should be considered. As part of their efforts to maintain goodwill, sales representatives treat planners to luncheons, after-work parties, and other social events that are designed to make them aware of the sponsoring magazines and encourage planners to include them in the preliminary analyses. Through these contacts, planners learn of magazines that should be included on the candidate list.

2. Identify the Most Efficient Magazines with the CPM Ranker. In this step, the planner ranks all candidate magazines according to their CPM efficiency against the target audience. Typically, costs are based on the open rate of a four-color bleed ad without any consideration for negotiation. This puts all of the candidates on an equal footing at this early stage in the process.

Exhibit 11-2 shows a sample CPM ranker for a magazine plan directed to female principal shoppers in households that are heavy users of frozen pizza. Recall that *composition* is the percent of the magazine's total audience who are heavy users of frozen pizza. *Coverage* is the percent of heavy users who read the magazine. The key to this ranker is the CPM. Magazines are ranked from most to least efficient, but be aware that differences of a few pennies are generally not significant. In this case, the planner made the judgment to continue considering all the magazines with a CPM of less than $100. *Working Mother* has a high 139 composition index, but its high CPM against this target makes it far less efficient than the other books. So it is out of the running for this campaign.

Although a subscription to the research is needed to get the product user readership and CPM, total adult CPM can be calculated from information that is available at no registration cost on the Internet at www.mriplus.com.

3. Create a Plan That Delivers the Most Reach for the Given Budget. All proprietary planning software has an optimizer function. Planners enter the budget, the target audience, and the list of candidate publications (with costs). The optimizer looks at thousands of alternatives and arrives at the plan that offers the most reach for the budget. Be aware that this is only a numerical solution based on the rate-card price; it doesn't account for any qualitative measures such as special positioning, additional exposure on the magazine's website, promotional opportunities, or a variety of other factors that need to be considered. But it does establish a benchmark that shows how much reach can be achieved.

Exhibit 11-3 shows the results of an optimization run—the theoretical highest-reaching plan for a $3 million budget. Notice that the planner drew the cutoff line at *Good Housekeeping*. All the magazines above that line are included in the optimization, while those below the line are out of consideration for this campaign. This plan costs $2,956,909. It will reach 74.1 percent of target heavy frozen-pizza users and deliver that target at an average $58.95 CPM impressions. Other statistics such as the net reach in thousands and the CPM net reach are presented, but they are seldom used and can be suppressed in the display if desired.

EXHIBIT 11-2

CPM Analysis of Female Principal Shoppers Who Are Heavy Users of Frozen Pizza

Base: Female principal shoppers
Population: 98,276 (000)
Target: Heavy users of frozen pizza, 4+ packages in the last 30 days
Population: 16,481 (000)
Percent of base: 16.77%

	AUDIENCE (000)	COMP (%)	COVERAGE (%)	INDEX	4-COLOR BLEED COST	4-COLOR BLEED CPM
Total heavy users of frozen pizza	16,481	16.8%	100%	100	—	—
Magazines Included in Optimizer						
1. People	4,910	19.9	29.8	119	$241,975	$49.28
2. Parents	2,902	25.8	17.6	154	162,900	56.13
3. Woman's World	1,354	21.6	8.2	129	95,565	70.58
4. Family Circle	3,300	20.7	20.0	123	247,200	74.91
5. O, The Oprah Magazine	1,983	16.9	12.0	101	150,730	76.01
6. Woman's Day	3,295	18.5	20.0	110	252,390	76.60
7. In Touch Weekly	1,158	23.4	7.0	139	100,496	86.78
8. Redbook	1,589	22.5	9.6	134	148,200	93.27
9. Good Housekeeping	3,626	19.1	22.0	114	344,475	95.00
Magazines Excluded from Optimizer						
10. Everyday with Rachael Ray	1,162	22.1	7.1	132	127,500	109.72
11. In Style	1,219	17.5	7.4	104	138,600	113.70
12. Real Simple	1,051	15.4	6.4	92	160,000	152.24
13. Working Mother	393	23.3	2.4	139	67,935	172.86

Source: Mediamark Research & Intelligence, LLC, Spring 2009. Used with permission.

4. Refine the Optimal Schedule to Reflect Marketing Judgment. The planner now adjusts the optimal plan to reflect any marketing factors that would suggest emphasizing one magazine over another. For instance, one might decide that it is important to have both of the "store" magazines in the plan (i.e., both *Family Circle* and *Woman's Day*). The planner notes that the six pages in *People* will add more

EXHIBIT 11-3

Magazine Optimization Model

Target: Female Principal Shoppers/Frozen Pizza: Heavy Users
(4+ Packages/Last 30 Days)
Population (000): 16,481

MAGAZINE	OPTIMAL
People	6
Parents	1
Woman's World	4
Family Circle	—
O, The Oprah Magazine	1
Woman's Day	1
In Touch Weekly	3
Redbook	—
Good Housekeeping	1
Total insertions	17
Total cost	$2,956,909
Gross impressions (000)	50,158
GRPs	304
CPM gross impressions	$58.95
Reach percent	74.1%
Average frequency	4.10
Net reach (000)	12,209
CPM net reach	$241.98

Source: Mediamark Research & Intelligence, LLC, Spring 2009. Used with permission.

frequency than reach and can be cut back. With this in mind, the planner drops one insertion in *People* and replaces it with an insertion in *Family Circle*.

The planner makes these changes and reflects them as an alternate schedule (Exhibit 11-4). Notice that the alternate plan is slightly less efficient ($61.01 CPM versus $58.95 CPM), but it does a better job of meeting the marketing objectives, while marginally reducing the reach. At $2,962,134, the alternate plan is still under

EXHIBIT 11-4

Magazine Optimization with Marketing Adjustments

Target: Female Homemakers/Frozen Pizza: Heavy Users
(4+ Packages/Last 30 Days)
Population (000): 16,481

MAGAZINE	OPTIMAL	ALTERNATE
People	6	5
Parents	1	1
Woman's World	4	4
Family Circle	—	1
O, The Oprah Magazine	1	1
Woman's Day	1	1
In Touch Weekly	3	3
Redbook	—	—
Good Housekeeping	1	1
Total insertions	17	17
Total cost	$2,956,909	$2,962,134
Gross impressions	50,158	48,548
GRPs	304	295
CPM gross impressions	$58.95	$61.01
Reach percent	74.14	73.74
Average frequency	4.1	3.99
Net reach	12,219	12,153
CPM net reach	$241.98	$243.74

Source: Mediamark Research & Intelligence, LLC, Spring 2009. Used with permission.

budget. Note that all these rates are "open rates" and do not reflect substantial additional savings that are possible with negotiation.

5. Negotiate Position, Cost, and Merchandising with the Magazine Sales Representative. Media planners are responsible for recommendations that involve millions of their clients' advertising dollars. But their decisions also represent success or failure to the representatives of the magazines whose job it is to sell advertising pages. In step 4, the decision to drop an insertion in *People* represents the loss of almost $242,000 for that magazine's sales representative. On the other hand, it meant an additional $247,200 order for the representative from *Family Circle.* The planner uses these competitive forces to obtain the best media placement and lowest cost for the advertiser.

Note that for broadcast media, planners develop the goals in terms of GRPs, reach, frequency, scheduling, and market selection. But decisions regarding particular programs, TV stations, and broadcast networks are handled by professional buyers and negotiators who often live in another city and may belong to another company that has "agency of record" responsibility for all of the advertiser's products. An advertiser with many products may split media planning responsibilities among many agencies, but consolidate the buying to maximize clout with the broadcasters. For magazines, on the other hand, the planner and buyer are typically the same person.

Starting with the revised "optimal" schedule, the planner now talks to the sales reps to see which magazine will give the best price. Although advertisers who buy only a few pages typically pay the open rate, steep discounts are offered for heavy, continuing schedules. These negotiated rates are highly confidential and specific to each advertiser. Even planners in the same agency working on different accounts would never compare notes on what they actually paid.

The other area open to negotiation is position. Traditionally, advertisers request in their insertion order for their ads to appear "far forward, right-hand page." Research indicates that ads in the front of the book are slightly more likely to be remembered than those in the middle or back, but despite the small advantage, those words have become a standard by which magazine negotiations are measured. There will be more about position effects later in this chapter. Magazines also compete for the business by offering merchandising such as contests, proprietary research, new-product sampling opportunities, tickets to sports events, luncheons with key reporters, and other inducements.

6. Present the Recommended Schedule to the Client and Adjust as Necessary. Although magazine sales representatives deal primarily with the media planner, they also make sales calls on the advertiser. Most clients accept the planner's recommendation as presented, but it is not uncommon for the planner to be told to add an insertion in a different magazine because the advertiser has made a side deal with the representative. This is no reflection on the ability of the planner; it just serves as a reminder that, in the end, it is the advertiser's money, and advertisers are free to spend their money as they see fit.

Other Media Values

Many other factors besides CPM should be considered when evaluating and selecting media vehicles, especially at steps 3 and 4 in the process. Some of these factors are discussed in the following paragraphs.

Secondary Audiences

The total audience reported by research services such as Mediamark Research & Intelligence, LLC (MRI) includes two kinds of readers. Primary readers are those who purchased the magazine themselves or who live in a household where somebody subscribes. Secondary, or pass-along, readers come upon the magazine in a public place such as their doctor's office or read a friend's copy. Early studies reported less ad recall among secondary readers, suggesting that they are less valuable to the advertiser. A few planners reflect this in their analysis by scaling down (discounting) the secondary readership. If secondary audiences are deemed less valuable, then it seems reasonable to discount them in some way.

One method for discounting the pass-along or secondary audience is simply to cut their numbers in half. For example, suppose Magazine A has a total audience of 37 million, of which 75 percent is primary and 25 percent is pass-along readers. The latter group (25 percent of 37 million) is discounted 50 percent.

Exhibit 11-5 shows an example that treats the pass-along audience first at full value and then at a 50 percent discounted value. The example is based on the total audience. Typically, media planners discount only the demographic group that comprises the target audience, such as men ages 18–34 or women who graduated from college.

Not everyone agrees that the pass-along audience should be discounted. In a classic paper on the subject, Seymour Marshak, formerly manager of advertising

---

EXHIBIT 11-5   **Two Bases for Analyzing the Audiences of Magazine A**

FULL-VALUE BASIS	NUMBER (MILLIONS)	OUT-OF-HOME AUDIENCE DISCOUNTED 50% BASIS	NUMBER (MILLIONS)
Primary audience	27.75	Primary audience	27.75
Pass-along audience	9.25	Pass-along audience	4.63
Total audience	37.00	Total audience	32.38

and distribution research for the Ford Motor Company, said it would be better to determine the value of a pass-along reader on the basis of how important that individual was in the target audience and then determine what opportunities he or she had to see a given advertisement in a given medium.[1] For example, pass-along readers might be even more important than primary readers when they receive only 1 or 2 exposure opportunities compared to primary readers who might receive more than 20 opportunities. This assumes that high frequencies (or many exposure opportunities) are not automatically good media strategy. Each marketing/media situation is different. Foremost in this kind of evaluation is the assumption that pass-along readers are the most important target audiences and have to be reached if the advertising message is to have the proper effect. In conclusion, although there are good reasons for and against discounting the pass-along audience, most advertisers give them full value. Where possible, the decision should be based on logic and clearly identified marketing reasons, rather than subjective judgment alone.

Editorial Environment

Occasionally vehicles that reach targets efficiently are not suited to an advertiser's message, because the editorial environments of the vehicles under consideration are incompatible with the ad message or with the advertiser's content restrictions (no sexually explicit, violent, or other undesirable editorial content). This concept is related to the need for psychographic data to fit demographic data. Two college graduates of the same age and in the same income class could lead radically different lives. Similarly, two media vehicles can reach the same demographic targets with about the same cost-efficiency, but each will feature editorial material of interest to different kinds of readers. This difference is important in determining a media vehicle's advertising value.

For example, suppose an advertiser for women's shampoo is considering nine potential vehicles, each of which reaches the demographic targets fairly well. But the editorial environments differ widely, as Exhibit 11-6 shows. A magazine's editorial environment can be evaluated in detail with Hall's Reports (www.hallsreports.com). Hall's categorizes the editorial content of more than 170 publications using a classification system that incorporates more than 250 editorial categories. These include Apparel, Beauty, Business, Health, Travel, World Affairs, and many more. This system is updated every year to reflect current trends. Data is updated monthly and is delivered via a Web-based data retrieval system.

---

1. Seymour Marshak, "Forum Question: Generally Speaking, What Value Do You Place on the Secondary or Pass-Along Reader?" *Media/Scope* (February 1970): 26.

EXHIBIT 11-6

Hall's Reports of Consumer Magazine Editorial Content

January 2009–July 2009
Report Criteria: Cross-tab report, One-time category list, Women beauty magazines

MAGAZINE	WOMEN'S HAIR CARE TOTAL		WOMEN'S SHAMPOOS/ CONDITIONERS/COLOR		WOMEN'S STYLES/ ACCESSORIES		WOMEN'S STYLING PRODUCTS	
	PAGES	PERCENT	PAGES	PERCENT	PAGES	PERCENT	PAGES	PERCENT
Allure	52.2	8.4%	11.3	1.8%	30.5	4.9%	10.4	1.7%
Cosmopolitan	40.7	4.4%	9.9	1.1%	20.3	2.2%	10.5	1.1%
Elle	13.3	1.6%	4.1	0.5%	5.8	0.7%	3.4	0.4%
Glamour	43.4	5.1%	3.3	0.4%	26.3	3.1%	13.8	1.6%
Marie Claire	30.5	3.6%	6	0.7%	17.4	2.1%	7.1	0.8%
More	7.4	1.3%	3.2	0.6%	2.6	0.5%	1.6	0.3%
Seventeen	59.2	10.2%	3.6	0.6%	36.3	6.3%	19.3	3.3%
Vogue	17.9	2.1%	4.5	0.5%	11.6	1.4%	1.8	0.2%
W	4.6	0.6%	0.8	0.1%	2.9	0.4%	0.9	0.1%

Source: Hall's Reports, LLC, January–July 2009. Used with permission.

As this example shows, *Seventeen* magazine devoted almost 60 pages, 10.2 percent of all editorial, to women's hair care in the six months from January to June 2009, but the pages were concentrated in women's styles and accessories. On the other hand, *Allure* had more editorial pages related to shampoos, conditioners, and color than *Seventeen*, and so might be a better match for that specific product.

By including these qualitative measures in the analysis, the planner can account for more subtle influences on advertising effectiveness than just the relatively simplistic measures of reach and cost-efficiency.

Special Opportunities in Magazines
Media planners who want to reach special or limited markets will find that magazines can be adapted to meet their needs. This is because some media have devised special demographic or geographic editions for just that purpose. Exhibit 11-7 lists some of the demographic breaks that are available in major consumer magazines.

EXHIBIT 11-7

Some Demographic Editions of Magazines

PUBLICATION	NAME OF EDITION	TARGET
Better Homes & Gardens	Better by Design	Upper-income homes
AARP	Age 59 & Under	Preretirement adults
AARP	60+	Retirement age adults
Parenting	Early Years	Parents of toddlers
Parenting	School Years	Parents of school-age children
Reader's Digest	Family	Adults under age 55 with children
Reader's Digest	Mature	Adults over 55
Prevention	Family	Adults under age 55
Prevention	Masters	Adults over age 55

In addition to offering special demographic and geographic breakouts, most of the larger-circulation magazines offer two-way (and in some cases even four-way) copy splits. *Reader's Digest*, for example, can distribute special copy to one out of every four subscribers across the nation through the use of zip coding and block coding. Other magazines use sophisticated printing and binding techniques that allow advertisers (for an extra charge) to print directly on the bound-in page the name and address of neighborhood stores where a product can be purchased.

These capabilities vary by magazine and in many cases are known only to the sales representatives. Maintain a positive relationship with the sales reps and inform them of your marketing objectives so they will best be able to match their magazine's capabilities to your needs.

Media Comparatives

Although some vehicles reach target audiences very well, the data on reach sometimes hide important facts. For example, a planner may find that television best reaches a given target audience, but those reached are light television viewers and heavy magazine readers. In other words, reach figures do not indicate the degree of exposure to a given medium. *Media comparatives* is the name given to an analysis by MRI that provides information on the degree of exposure to television and magazines.

Television comparatives show the percent of the target and selectivity index for people who are heavy television viewers and light magazine readers. *Magazine comparatives* show the same statistics for persons who are heavy magazine readers and light television viewers.

Thus media comparatives are a means of comparing magazines and television based on the degree of exposure to each medium. They also show how many users of various product categories are accounted for by the four groups measured. Exhibit 11-8 provides an MRI media comparative analysis for heavy users of frozen pizza.

This analysis shows that heavy users are 13 percent more likely to be heavy consumers of both magazines and television than the average female homemaker. It suggests that a media plan directed to this target group should use both media, rather than concentrating all weight in one or the other. The data do not answer all questions, but rather add another quantitative dimension to help solve the selection problem, as well as the problem of allocating money.

Position Alternatives

During negotiation, some print vehicles offer advertisers selected positions such as front-of-book or next to compatible editorial material, which if accepted can help the advertiser reach the target with more impact. Sometimes the vehicle charges premium rates for a preferred position, but the buyer's goal should be to get it

---

EXHIBIT 11-8

Media Comparatives for Female Principal Shoppers Who Are Heavy Users of Frozen Pizza

FROZEN PIZZA: HEAVY USERS (4+ PACKAGES/LAST 30 DAYS)

	POPULATION	TARGET (000)	HORZ%	VERT%	INDEX
Media comparatives: heavy magazines, heavy TV	24,218	4,584	18.92%	27.81%	113
Media comparatives: heavy magazines, light TV	24,662	4,698	19.05	28.51	114
Media comparatives: light magazines, heavy TV	24,766	3,306	13.35	20.06	80
Media comparatives: light magazines, light TV	24,630	3,892	15.80	23.62	94
Total	98,276	16,481	16.77%	100.00%	100

Source: Mediamark Research & Intelligence, LLC, Spring 2009. Used with permission.

without paying extra. The planner should consider the availability of favored positions as a factor in weighing one vehicle against another. Vehicles that offer selected positions can be a better buy than those that do not. The value of certain positions will be discussed later in this chapter.

Advertising Clutter and Product Protection

In both television and print media, it is possible to measure the amount of clutter that occurs. Presumably, the medium that reaches the maximum number of targets at the best cost-efficiency and with the least clutter would be the most desirable. There are, however, exceptions to this assumption. For example, in certain magazine classes (e.g., fashion and shelter), readers buy the magazine specifically to shop through the advertising.

But if all competitors are in the same magazine and many other ads are also in the magazine, it is questionable whether that vehicle is the most desirable for a specific advertiser. Brands with a clear-cut competitive advantage over other brands should prosper when placed near competitors. Other brands, perceived as less desirable, suffer from such competition. Generally, clutter is undesirable, and product protection is something to seek. This means keeping competitive ads within the vehicle at a reasonable distance from the advertised brand.

In evaluating clutter in a print medium, one should consider the Starch studies, which show that the readership of the average advertisement in a magazine declines as the number of ads in the vehicle increases. In television and radio, product protection, although desirable, is usually available only to advertisers who buy enough minutes in a program to qualify as a sponsor.

Circulation Trends

An objective measurement of a magazine's value is its trend in circulation. Because advertising is sometimes planned more than a year ahead of time, media planners might want to study the latest Audit Bureau of Circulations (ABC) figures for the last five years to see what has been happening. If a magazine under consideration has shown a decline, it may be dropped from the list. On the other hand, magazines with increasing circulation trends are considered more valuable, although they can be expected to charge more in anticipation of increased readership.

Advertising Copy Checking and Product Restrictions

Some media have a reputation for examining the veracity of all advertising copy and claims and annually reject many pages of advertising. They publicize this fact regularly. The assumption here is that readers, knowing of this practice, will prefer to read ads in such a vehicle rather than other vehicles that do not have this policy. *Good Housekeeping*, many newspapers, and network television organizations are among those that check copy carefully. Planners should allow time for this review, especially for new products or new creative.

As part of their effort to maintain a quality reputation, some magazines refuse all advertising from potentially controversial product categories such as tobacco, alcohol, and direct-mail personal products. These policies are spelled out in the magazine's sales material and in SRDS. Planners working for these types of products must be aware of these policies and avoid recommending magazines that will ultimately refuse to carry the ads.

Response to Coupons, Information, or Recipes

Measurements of the number of readers who ask for information or clipped recipes is available in MRI and can provide a planner with the type of qualitative data that help him or her differentiate one magazine from another. On the other hand, reader response to a particular advertiser's coupons is not public and can be difficult, if not impossible, to obtain. Some advertisers will share the general direction of coupon response, but they typically hold detailed response rates by magazine confidential, even from their own advertising agency and media planners.

Available Discounts

Sometimes the value of a medium is directly affected by the nature of the discounts that it offers. If a number of ads are planned for a calendar year in several vehicles that are otherwise about equal, the best value is the vehicle offering a substantial discount. Although target coverage and composition are important criteria, if all else is equal, the magazine with the greatest discount (hence the lowest CPM) will get the order.

The pressure of cost negotiations caused most magazines to provide unpublished discounts to high-volume advertisers. Those buying only one or two pages can expect to pay rate card, but for larger schedules, the published prices are just the starting point for negotiations. Large companies will use their clout by adding up the pages from all of their divisions to negotiate a single, extremely favorable (and highly confidential) corporate rate that can be used by all planners working on the account. The advertiser assigns a print "agency of record" the task of keeping track of all corporate pages, conducting these rate negotiations, and keeping planners informed of the negotiated price of each magazine.

Geographic Flexibility

This reflects the degree to which a medium can be used to precisely reach geographically superior markets while at the same time avoiding relatively weak markets. Generally, local media such as newspapers, spot radio, spot television, outdoor, and to some extent online are considered flexible media in the geographic sense. Magazines have some flexibility with their regional editions, but advertisers wanting to limit coverage to individual markets use an independent company, Media Networks, Inc. (www.mni.com), whose business is placing national advertising in local markets.

Issue-to-Issue Volatility

MRI's new Issue Specific Readership Study provides a factor that adjusts the audience of each issue to the average. The readership to some issues was above the average, others were below. Using three years of this data for 176 magazines, Baron, Klein, and Jacobs calculated the standard deviation of these scores and so identified magazines whose readership was relatively stable versus those that were highly volatile.[2] Exhibit 11-9 shows the scores for the business category. The authors suggest this gives planners the margin of error in the number of people who will see a given issue of a magazine.

As with any standard deviation, the Volatility Score quantifies the amount of variation. In this example, the readership of 68 percent (1 standard deviation) of the issues of *Kiplinger's Personal Finance* magazine fluctuates plus or minus 7.5 percent from the average. This contrasts with a more volatile magazine like *Inc.* that has a volatility score of 15.7. The readership of a given issue of *Inc.* could be as much as 32 percent above or below the average. In seeking to explain the differences in volatility from one magazine to another, the researchers found a strong negative correlation between volatility and MRI's Reader Quality measures that will be discussed later in this chapter. The less volatile (more stable) magazines tended to have higher reader quality scores. The volatility score is useful as a tiebreaker when CPM and other factors are roughly equal. In addition to the higher qualitative measures, the less volatile magazines are preferable because the audience for future issues will be closer to the average-issue audience that was used for the CPM and reach/frequency calculations.

---

2. Roger Baron, Caryn Klein, and Lori Jacobs, "The Volatility Score: A New Measure of the Issue-to-Issue Stability of a Magazine's Audience." Worldwide Readership Research Symposium, Valencia, Spain, October 2009, www.readershipsymposium .com.

EXHIBIT 11-9

Volatility Score of Business Magazines

EDITORIAL CLASS	MAGAZINE	VOLATILITY SCORE
Business	Kiplinger's Personal Finance	7.47
Business	Money	7.71
Business	Smart Money	10.79
Business	Wired	11.08
Business	Forbes	14.40
Business	The Economist	15.16
Business	U.S. News & World Report	15.26
Business	Inc.	15.74
Business	BusinessWeek	15.97
Business	Entrepreneur	15.97
Business	Newsweek	16.09
Business	Time	16.22
Business	Fortune	17.72
Business Average Volatility Score		13.81

Source: Baron, Klein, and Jacobs, "The Volatility Score: A New Measure of the Issue-to-Issue Stability of a Magazine's Audience," Worldwide Readership Research Symposium (Valencia, Spain: October 2009), www .readershipsymposium.com.

Qualitative Values of Media

As stated earlier, media selection is based mostly on the ability of specific media vehicles to reach precise target audiences with high cost-efficiency and little waste. Other considerations in planning include the total cost of the medium plus the reach and frequency to be generated. Before making a final decision for or against any medium, however, the planner should also consider the qualitative values of each medium and decide how important these values are for the plan.

A *qualitative value* is some characteristic of a medium that enhances the chances that an advertising message carried within it will be effective. Comparing the qualitative merits of one medium versus another (e.g., TV versus magazines) is a highly subjective exercise. The relative characteristics are obvious, but the decision that one is more appropriate than the other for a given campaign is the kind of judgment planners avoid, since it cannot be supported with research. Furthermore, the choice of which media to use has such far-reaching consequences that it is typically a joint decision of the account group, the creative team, the client, and the media planner.

Qualitative distinctions are based on the assumption that media are not simply passive carriers of advertisements; they also play an active role. These distinctions assume that a magazine offers a unique environment, with a personality that can rub off on its advertisements and make them more effective in communicating their messages.

The problem with studies of magazine environment is deciding what to do with the results. Knowing that one magazine has a different and presumably better image than another does not tell the planner anything about the magazine's advertising effectiveness—if its image is even related to effectiveness. In addition, qualitative studies conducted by one magazine seldom mention its competition, making side-by-side comparisons impossible. They were conducted to support the magazine's sales effort. Therefore, image studies conducted by the magazine's research department, though a form of determining a qualitative value, have little importance in media planning.

Types of Qualitative Values

Notwithstanding early research on general qualitative values, there is still little consensus about the matter. When planners do use such values, they are apt to prepare the following kind of statement for their plans: "We feel that Magazine A reflects greater authority and prestige than other magazines, so we recommend purchasing x number of ads in it." Other terms that are used in the same manner as *authority* and *prestige* are *impact, mood, believability, atmosphere, excitement,* and *leadership.*

The expression "we feel" and the absence of numerical support are the tip-off that a planner has no data or solid research to back up the statement. However, qualitative measures still have a place in media planning. MRI and other research companies ask their respondents several questions that can suggest qualitative differences among magazines. These are discussed in the following paragraphs.

Reading Days How many days in total are alternative magazines read? If a magazine is opened at any time on a given day, this constitutes a reading day. If, for example, there is evidence that Magazine A is read more total days than magazines B, C, D, and E (all under consideration), then the planner has one more qualitative reason to select A. More reading days represent more opportunities to see ads.

Time Spent Reading In a similar manner, MRI respondents estimate how much time they spend reading each magazine that they say they read or looked into in the last publication period. These measurements indicate that the magazine with the largest number of reading hours is more attractive than others. This conclusion assumes that audience members have more opportunities to see ads if they spend more time reading.

MRI provides a number of qualitative measures that are all plausibly related to the likelihood that an ad will be noticed, but planners have needed a single measure that will represent all of them. In their study of the Volatility Score described earlier, Roger Baron, Caryn Klein, and Lori Jacobs found a significant inverse correlation between the qualitative measures and volatility. So the more a magazine is read at home, the less volatile. The more days that a magazine is picked up, the less volatile. The more time spent reading an issue, the less volatile, and so on. This significant correlation allows planners to use volatility as a single metric surrogate for the many reader quality measures. In short, the less volatile the issue-to-issue readership, the higher the reader quality. This is summarized in Exhibit 11-10.

Subjective Qualitative Values

Planners and magazine sales representatives sometimes use subjective (generally unquantifiable) qualitative terms to characterize the value of a media vehicle. Probably the most misused of all media qualitative value terms is *impact*. Print media executives often claim that their magazine has more impact than other magazines. If they mean that an ad in their magazine will sell more of the product than an ad in any other magazine, this cannot be proved and is therefore conjecture on the part of the executives. It is generally impossible to determine the effect of a media vehicle and a single ad on sales.

Conceivably, a careful testing program could be conducted for one advertiser, with strict controls, to prove that more people recalled a given ad in one magazine than in any other. But recall and sales are quite different. How can one prove that what sold the product was not the price, the packaging, the distribution, or the sales promotion? Some vehicles are better than others, but not on the basis of impact, which is too vague a concept to be used in media planning. Only when a clear-cut cause-and-effect relationship can be established for the brand and the vehicle on sales can the concept of impact be used.

EXHIBIT 11-10

Correlation Between Reader Quality Measures and Readership Volatility

VARIABLES	PEARSON CORRELATION WITH VOLATILITY	TWO-TAILED SIGNIFICANCE (BOX = < 0.05 PROBABILITY CORRELATION IS DUE TO CHANCE)
% Read in home	−0.362	0.000
Median reading days	−0.327	0.000
Average reading days	−0.323	0.000
Average issues read out of four	−0.312	0.000
Median issues read out of four	−0.310	0.000
Median reading time	−0.277	0.000
Average reading time	−0.266	0.000
Three-year average circulation	−0.253	0.001
Average magazine quality rating	−0.213	0.005
Median magazine quality rating	−0.208	0.006
Median age	−0.207	0.006
Any of nine actions taken	−0.181	0.016
Ad page exposure (APX)	−0.170	0.024
Number on cover ("5 Best Ways to …")	−0.164	0.030
Total readers	−0.161	0.033
Percent primary readers	−0.140	0.063
Average interest in advertising	−0.132	0.081
Median interest in advertising	−0.123	0.104
Celebrity on the cover	0.106	0.161
Percent single-copy sales	0.078	0.303
Readers per copy	0.072	0.344
Percent women	0.012	0.872
Unnamed person on the cover	0.129	0.088
Advertising percent of pages	0.189	0.047
Publication frequency (issues/year)	0.193	0.010

Source: Baron, Klein, and Jacobs, ibid.

The *core reader* is another measure that is sometimes used, although researchers disagree on exactly what is meant by the term. According to one definition, a core reader is anyone who says he or she read at least three out of four issues. This seems logical enough until we realize that the definition helps magazines that derive a large percent of their circulation from subscriptions, as compared to those that are distributed primarily through newsstand sales.

Using Qualitative Values

Qualitative rationales for selecting media have a place in planning procedures. But users of such measures should keep in mind some reasonable guidelines:

- Qualitative, or subjective, rationales should never totally replace quantitative CPM and reach substantiation.
- Qualitative consideration should be used after quantitative analysis has been made.
- If possible, more than one person should contribute to making the subjective analysis, to reduce the possibility of individual bias.
- Planners should be suspicious of media-sponsored research concerning qualitative values such as "high impact," "liked most," and so forth. Much of this kind of research is highly promotional, rather than objective. It is very difficult to transfer the findings from one medium to another or from one media vehicle to another.

A 2005 study by Roger Baron, Britta Ware, and Justin Edge attempted to identify which of more than 30 qualitative and quantitative measures of magazine circulation and audience were most highly associated with ad recall. These variables accounted for 27 percent of the variance in ad recall. Put another way, almost three-quarters of the difference in recall from one magazine to another were due to factors that were not measured. Furthermore, ad quality accounted for the largest (11 percent) share of the variance that was explained. A group of variables, characterized as "Involvement," accounted for 7.9 percent of the variance, but no single variable accounted for more than 1 percent.[3]

Conversely, data from the VISTA Print Effectiveness Rating Service shows a consistent relationship between qualitative measures and ad recall. The typical ad generates 63 percent recall among readers who rate the publication "one of my favorites" compared to just 29 percent of those rating a magazine as "poor." A similar relationship was observed for time spent reading, number of issues read out of

---

3. Roger Baron, Britta Ware, and Justin Edge, "Identifying Key Metrics for Magazine Planning," Worldwide Readership Research Symposium, Prague, 2005, www.readership symposium.org/papers/736.pdf.

the last four, number of times an issue was read or looked into, and copies obtained by subscription versus in a public place.[4]

In conclusion, qualitative values of media do exist, but their relationship to ad effectiveness is inconclusive. They are simply not objective enough to be used alone for decision making. Perhaps ways will be found to prove that one medium indeed has more impact than others, but at present it cannot be proved. Experts can only agree that media are not passive carriers of ads. They do have qualitative values, but their use in planning is highly judgmental.

Ad Positions Within Media

Assuming that media vehicles have been selected, the budget allocated, and a schedule worked out, media planning could, in theory, end at this point. In practice, however, planners and others interested in media still have questions: Is there nothing else that can be done to help in the advertising communication process? Are reach, frequency, and cost-efficiency all there are? The problem is to find ways for the media planner to go beyond delivery and not only get vehicles exposed, but also get ads within those vehicles exposed, and finally, get the ads read.

To a great extent, this last responsibility belongs to the creative people—account planners, writers, and art directors who have special talents for getting advertising communication through to the reader. The copy people, for example, can write scintillating headlines and meaningful words. The art director can devise fascinating layouts. The creative people can ask for four-color ads, bleed pages, reverse printing, gatefold-size ads, two-page spreads. They can print ads on unusual stock such as acetate or aluminum foil. They can use unusual inks such as DayGlo or perfumed inks. These are but a few of the many options open to the creative personnel in getting ads noticed and read.

What, then, can media planners do to help the situation? As part of the buying negotiations, they can ask for certain positions within media that are thought to be better than other positions. This, however, leaves them open to questions about positioning research and strategy.

Problems of Positioning Research

A number of media positions are thought to be better than others. For example, the fourth cover (the outside back cover) of a magazine is generally conceded to be

---

4. Affinity, LLC, VISTA Print Effectiveness Rating Service Database, January 2007–June 2009, as reported in *Magazine Dimensions*, 2009.

the best place in a magazine for an ad. In fact, research confirms that the fourth cover is indeed one of the best positions. One study found that ads on the fourth cover have 30 percent higher recall.[5] But since the back cover is sold for a premium price, there is a question whether the additional impact is worth the additional cost. Nonetheless, there is some logic, even without research, to suggest that a fourth-cover position is valuable. There is not much agreement among experts about other media positions. The research tends to be inconclusive.

Perhaps the foremost problem of position research is that it is difficult to separate measurements of position from copy effects. Most research techniques used to establish the effects of position are really a mixture of copy and position. In some research studies, another dimension, that of size, is added. Then, too, averaging data for position effects that contain widely varying degrees of copy effectiveness do not truly represent the effects of position. Averaging tends to be unduly affected by extreme copy-effect scores. Some media experts question whether there is any totally valid copy-measuring device. Even assuming that most are valid, there is still no way, through present-day measurements, to know the effect of position alone.

A solution would be to design experiments involving ad copy that is held constant with the only variable being position. Because the same ads would be measured in different positions in different media vehicles, the effects of position alone could be found. However, there still is dissatisfaction with much research devised to measure position, because it is not carefully controlled to eliminate bias. Because the advertiser's primary concern is selling product, there is little incentive to test alternative position options. Samples are often nonrandom and selected haphazardly. Questionnaire design and interviewing controls are not always the best. As a result, much position research is suspect.

A major consideration in deciding whether to use a special position in a vehicle is the premium cost. Some positions are not worth the extra cost. And even if a position seems to be worth the cost, the questionable nature of the existing research can make it difficult to support a decision one way or the other.

Some Position Effects

Following is a brief summary of position effects that some media planners accept. The reader is cautioned about accepting them as valid evidence. They are presented to show a sample of the kinds of positions that could affect the communication power of advertisements placed in vehicles.

---

5. Undated Gallup & Robinson report in *Magazine Dimensions*, 2009.

Position in Magazines Using Starch Adnorm data as a guide, fourth-cover positions are usually considered better than any inside positions. Early studies suggest that second-cover and page-one positions are about equal and are the next best after fourth-cover positions. Front-of-the-magazine positions (from page 3 to about page 20) are the next best positions, and right-hand pages are somewhat better than left-hand pages, with some exceptions. These studies conflict with some planners' belief that ads are more effective if they appear near compatible editorial (e.g., a food ad placed near a recipe) that is usually farther back in the magazine. More detailed information on the effects of position and ad size are available on the website of the Magazine Publishers of America (MPA) at www.magazine.org.

Although there is virtually no research to substantiate the value of these positions for a given campaign, advertisers have come to expect that their agencies will have sufficient "clout" with the magazines that *they* will be given the choice spots. Because, obviously, only one advertiser can run on the back cover or page one or opposite the table of contents, planners compete fiercely to secure those premier positions—if not page one, then at least somewhere near the front. Planners keep track of the positions they are given by each magazine, and they use this information in subsequent negotiations. At a minimum, planners should expect an even rotation of their ads throughout the magazine.

Position in Newspapers Ads near the front of newspapers are considered better than those near the back, but the differences are small. There is no significant difference between right-hand and left-hand pages. Inside a newspaper section is better than the last page of the section. There is little difference between ads above or below the fold. Editorial environment affects the readership of ads—obviously, ads for male products do better on sports pages, and ads for female products do better on women's pages.

Position in Television Attention to TV programs is greatest during prime time and late fringe and poorest in early morning when the family is getting ready for work and school.[6] Research suggests that a 30-second commercial has about 60–75 percent the recall of a 60-second commercial, and a 15-second commercial has about 60–75 percent as much recall as a 30-second commercial.

Second-by-second analysis of television commercial pods shows that the first position retains the largest share of the audience from the preceding entertainment, while seconds later in a pod show sharp declines as people tune to other channels

6. Mediamark Research & Intelligence, LLC, "Percent of Viewers Paying Full Attention," Spring 2009.

or fast-forward their DVR through the break. This was apparent in Exhibit 4-13, which shows the declining audience during each minute of a commercial break. Since the first pod position is acknowledged as most desirable, some broadcasters hold out that position for their program promotion spots. Broadcast buyers should check the pod position of every spot in their schedule to ensure, at a minimum, that they are given a fair rotation.

In the past, it was thought that people paid more attention to high-rated than to low-rated programs, and more attention to commercials that were inside the show compared to those in breaks between shows. Recent studies have cast doubt on these generalizations regarding position effects, most likely due to changes in television formatting that place many local commercials within the program.

To sum up, research on position effects, with a few exceptions, is inconclusive, and in any case, is largely beyond the control of the media planner or buyer. As good stewards of the advertiser's dollar, at a minimum planners should keep track of the positions where their advertising runs. In print, record the page number of the ad and the total number of pages in the issue. In broadcast, record the minute of the program where the ad appears and the position in the pod. These data are readily available from the competitive research services. They just need to be recorded and acted upon at the next negotiation.

Internet Media Vehicles

Many of the processes and considerations discussed in this chapter are germane to evaluating, selecting, and buying Internet media. However, the processes are different enough to bear separate consideration.

Evaluating and Selecting Internet Media

As with any media plan, the first step is to identify the campaign objectives as they relate to the Internet. In short, the planner must clearly identify the value of the Internet for this advertiser. For hotels, financial services, automobiles, consumer electronics, and advertisers of high-ticket considered purchases, the value of the Internet is obvious. The Internet's role is to drive consumers to the advertiser's website, where they will find detailed product information and an opportunity for direct sales via a secure online order.

The task of finding appropriate sites for digital advertising is directly comparable to the task of vehicle selection in traditional media. The planner must answer the question, "Where on the Internet can I find people who would be interested in the advertiser's product?"

This can include maximizing direct-response sales and return on investment, building brand awareness, referring visitors to the advertiser's website, obtaining research from online questionnaires, or giving visitors additional sales information.

A key element in this process is determining the "metrics of success." That is, how will the effectiveness of the Internet campaign be measured? Some options include dollar volume of sales from the advertiser's website, sales profitability, number of visitors clicking through to the site, and change in brand awareness or attitude toward the advertiser before and after the campaign. There must be agreement on this point before the campaign begins. This agreement avoids the all-too-common situation where the advertiser starts with one objective, perhaps to build brand awareness, but then considers the campaign a failure if sales or website visitation are below expectations despite strong awareness growth.

Once there is agreement on the target audience, campaign objectives, and success metrics, the next step is to identify websites that are selective to the target. There are three general approaches to online targeting: contextual, behavioral, and demographic.

Contextual Targeting This approach places ads on websites that are likely to be visited by the same people whom the advertiser is targeting. So a luggage advertiser would buy impressions on travel-oriented websites and on sites appealing to businesspersons who are likely to be the heaviest travelers. Contextual targeting relies on judgment and insight into the lifestyle of the product users. Geographic targeting is a form of contextual targeting—advertisers wanting to reach customers in Chicago might place ads on the website of Chicago newspapers, TV and radio stations, and Chicago weather or traffic reports.

Behavioral Targeting (BT) This approach takes conceptual targeting a step further and physically places a cookie on the computer of people who have visited, say in this example, travel-related websites, and in turn, other sites these people have visited that may not be as obvious (international weather, international vaccination recommendations, exchange rate sites, etc.). This data is used by the publishers or is sold to online networks that will serve, for example, a luggage ad to computers that have this cookie. Behavioral targeting is much more precise, but it also raises privacy issues that may limit its usefulness. It is further limited by the widespread practice of cookie deletion (computer owners who routinely delete all the cookies). Finally, the cookie identifies a computer, but not the person using it. The family member who browsed the travel website, so earning the cookie, may not be the same person who is served the ad on that computer at another time. Nevertheless, BT is an important tool for online advertisers.

Demographic Targeting This approach helps the user select websites based on the demographics of their visitors. Many sites ask visitors to register before allowing entry to their advanced services, recording key demographics such as age, gender, family size, and other characteristics. These registered sites can then assure advertisers that all the impressions are going to the desired demographics. Unregistered sites serve ads to any browser that visits.

Two syndicated research services, Nielsen Online (www.nielsennetratings.com) and comScore (www.comscore.com), provide the demographics of visitors to all sites whether registered or not. Their software allows comparison and ranking of sites by coverage and composition, and is used by online planners in the same way as magazine planners use MRI. These services provide detailed demographics and product usage of website visitors, using survey research similar to MRI. The Nielsen service is called NetView; the comScore service is called Media Metrics. Each has recruited a panel of Internet users who agree to put tracking software on their computer. When recruited, panel members report their basic demographics followed by a long questionnaire on their usage of various products and services—the same kind of questions asked by MRI and Simmons. When panel members sit down at the computer, they log in and identify themselves. Then the software records every keystroke, allowing the researchers to know when the visits occurred, what sites were visited, how long the person stayed at the site, what pages within the site were explored, how long the person stayed on each page ("stickiness"), and other data, including campaign reach/frequency, that are useful to planners. Because the services gather data automatically, they are able to report on thousands of websites.

Exhibit 11-11 shows the top websites for adults ages 18–34 as reported by Nielsen's NetView.

Exhibit 11-12 shows comScore's list of websites that have the highest composition of adults ages 18–34 who are heavy users of quick-serve restaurants (QSR).

Note that the site's audience is expressed with the same coverage and composition concepts that were used for magazines. And as with magazines, the ideal plan uses a mixture of both high-coverage and high-composition sites.

Exhibit 11-13 shows comScore's reach/frequency analysis of an online campaign in various sports websites directed to adults 18–34.

While the narrower A18–34 heavy QSR user target was available, the sample size was too small to accurately report the reach/frequency of individual sports websites. So we broadened the target to total adults 18–34. This need to expand the

EXHIBIT 11-11

Top Websites for Adults 18–34 According to Nielsen NetView, Ranked by Composition

Site	Level	Unique Audience (000)	Unique Audience Composition (%)	Composition Index for Unique Audience	Coverage (%)
Google	Brand	36,166	24.71	107	80.53
Google Search	Channel	33,773	25.44	111	75.20
Yahoo!	Brand	31,862	24.87	106	70.28
Facebook	Brand	28,987	26.42	115	64.53
YouTube	Brand	24,094	26.42	115	53.65
MSN/Windows Live/Bing	Brand	23,735	23.69	103	52.85
Yahoo! Homepage	Channel	22,181	27.86	121	49.39
Fox Interactive Media	Brand	20,936	34.40	149	46.62
AOL Media Network	Brand	20,428	25.02	109	45.49
Yahoo! Mail	Channel	18,838	26.16	114	41.95
Myspace.com	Channel	17,625	35.93	156	39.25
Yahoo! Search	Channel	15,866	24.78	108	35.33
Amazon	Brand	15,079	24.78	108	33.58
Google Image Search	Channel	14,948	33.94	147	33.28
Google Maps	Channel	14,128	26.88	117	31.46
eBay	Brand	13,422	26.35	114	29.89
Ask Search Network	Brand	12,855	24.05	104	28.63
Yahoo! Answers	Channel	12,503	33.96	148	27.84
Blogger	Brand	12,358	28.53	124	27.07
About.com	Brand	11,404	28.18	122	25.35
MSN Homepage	Channel	11,151	23.16	101	24.83

Source: The Nielsen Company, Nielsen Online, NetView, July 2009. Used with permission.

EXHIBIT 11-12

Top Websites for Adults 18–34 Who Are Heavy Quick-Serve Restaurant Users According to comScore, Ranked by Composition

comSCORE. | MyMetrix

Marketer ▾ | Media Metrix ▾ | Segment Metrix ▾ | Reach Frequency ▾ | Plan Metrix ▾ | Ad Metrix ▾ | MediaBuilder ▾ | gSearch ▾ | Video Metrix ▾ | Mobile ▾

Search

Help | Save | Print | Download | Edit | Run Report

Plan Metric Key Measures

	Media	Target Audience (000)	% Reach	% Composition Unique Visitors	Composition Index	Target Lift Index	Average Daily Visitors (000)	Average Minutes per Page	Average Usage Days per Visitor	Average Minutes per Visitor	Average Pages per Visitor
	Total Internet	16,277	100.0	10.1	100	100	11,324	0.6	20.9	1,841.5	2,909
	Top 100 Properties [Undup.]	N/A	N/A	N/A	N/A	N/A					
1	Google Sites	14,870	90.1	10.9	108	117	6,746	0.8	13.8	250.7	313
2	Yahoo! Sites	14,590	89.6	11.2	110	98	5,135	0.9	10.6	239.8	254
3	Microsoft Sites	12,008	73.8	10.7	106	78	3,187	1.0	8.0	126.4	130
4	FACEBOOK.COM	9,878	60.7	11.6	115	91	3,265	0.6	9.9	167.4	291
5	AOL LLC	8,617	52.9	10.4	103	67	1,866	1.1	6.5	104.4	98
6	Fox Interactive Media	8,476	52.1	13.4	132	137	1,680	0.5	5.9	126.6	231
7	Ask Network	8,075	49.6	10.9	108	93	899	0.3	3.3	10.1	19
8	Amazon Sites	7,125	43.8	11.0	108	89	707	0.6	3.0	18.4	31
9	eBay	6,710	41.2	11.3	111	119	1,245	0.6	5.6	75.1	127
10	Wikimedia Foundation Sites	6,425	39.5	11.0	108	118	686	0.9	3.2	16.1	17
11	CBS Interactive	5,953	36.6	11.5	113	74	603	1.2	3.0	18.0	15
12	Viacom Digital	5,784	35.5	15.3	151	91	567	2.2	2.9	51.1	23
13	Turner Network	5,401	33.2	10.2	101	68	961	1.1	5.3	23.2	22
14	Glam Media	4,896	30.1	9.8	97	64	376	0.9	2.3	11.4	13
15	craigslist, Inc.	4,831	29.7	12.5	123	212	983	0.3	6.1	158.2	518
16	Answers.com Sites	4,739	29.1	12.3	122	122	270	0.7	1.7	2.9	4
17	Demand Media	4,637	28.1	11.4	112	57	288	1.0	1.7	3.4	4
18	Apple Inc.	4,267	26.2	8.8	87	93	637	0.7	4.5	12.0	16
19	Wal-Mart	4,186	25.7	9.9	98	123	335	0.6	2.4	23.4	37
20	New York Times Digital	3,781	23.2	8.8	87	47	239	0.7	1.9	4.9	7
21	Comcast Corporation	3,300	20.3	9.8	97	29	256	0.9	2.3	12.0	14
22	Adobe Sites	3,267	20.1	10.9	107	79	197	0.8	1.8	5.2	7
23	Target Corporation	3,166	19.5	9.6	95	118	209	0.6	2.0	13.4	23
24	Weather Channel, The	3,160	19.4	10.2	101	122	675	1.0	6.3	13.5	14
25	Best Buy Sites	3,065	16.9	13.2	130	106	225	0.6	2.2	12.6	20
26	NetShelter Technology Media	2,966	18.2	12.5	123	95	197	0.6	2.0	5.6	9
27	Verizon Communications Corp.	2,933	18.0	10.4	103	70	282	0.6	2.9	17.9	31
28	WordPress	2,927	18.0	11.7	115	98	211	0.6	2.2	2.8	5
29	The Mozilla Organization	2,839	17.4	11.5	114	52	285	1.0	2.8	4.3	4

Legend

Displaying 1–30 of 102

Summary | Help (?)

Geography
US–Plan Metrix
Location
All Locations
Time Period
Months
November 2009
Target
18–34 yrs old AND Heavy
(fast food visitise 7 days)
Media
Top 100 Properties
[Undup.]
Measures
Target Audience (000)
% Reach
% Composition Unique
Visitors
Composition Index
Target Lift Index
Average Daily Visitors
(000)
Average Minutes per Page
Average Usage Days per
Visitor
Average Minutes per
Visitor
Average Pages per Visitor

Media Metrix 2.0 Legend

Source: comScore, Inc. Used with permission.

EXHIBIT 11-13

Reach/Frequency Analysis of an Online Sports Campaign Directed to Adults 18–34 According to comScore

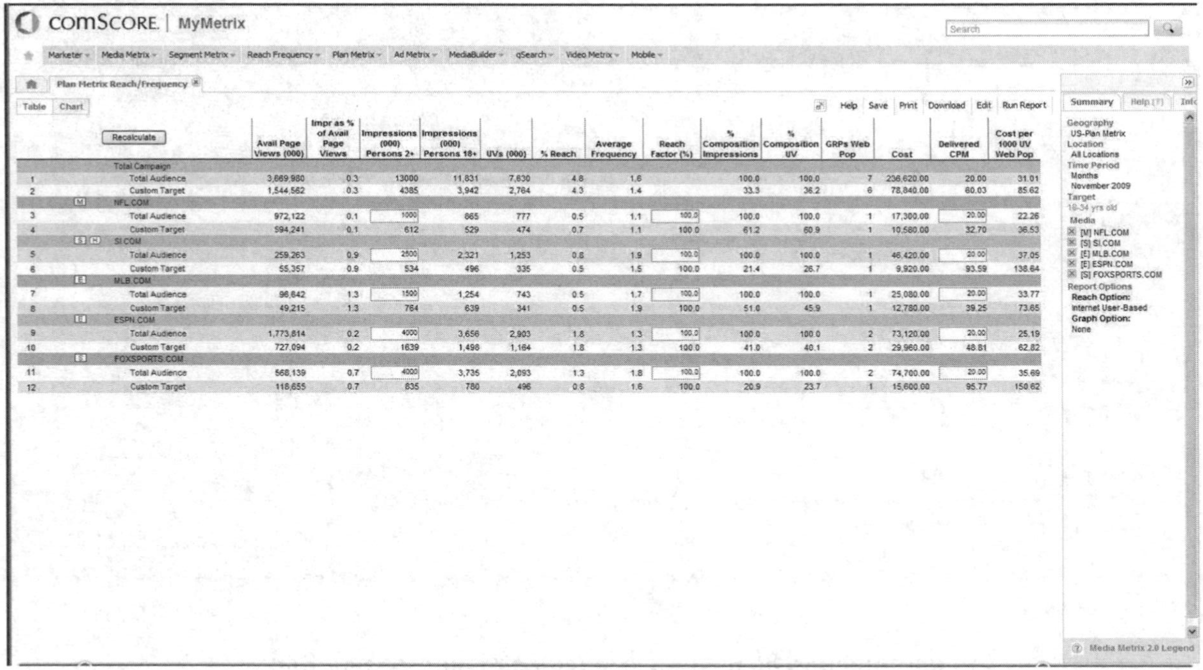

		Avail Page Views (000)	Impr as % of Avail Page Views	Impressions (000) Persons 2+	Impressions (000) Persons 18+	UVs (000)	% Reach	Average Frequency	Reach Factor (%)	% Composition Impressions	% Composition UV	GRPs Web Pop	Cost	Delivered CPM	Cost per 1000 UV Web Pop
	Total Campaign														
1	Total Audience	3,669,980	0.3	13000	11,831	7,630	4.8	1.6		100.0	100.0	7	236,620.00	20.00	31.01
2	Custom Target	1,544,562	0.3	4385	3,942	2,764	4.3	1.4		33.3	36.2	6	78,840.00	60.03	85.62
	[M] NFL.COM														
3	Total Audience	972,122	0.1	1000	865	777	0.5	1.1	100.0	100.0	100.0	1	17,300.00	20.00	22.26
4	Custom Target	594,241	0.1	612	529	474	0.7	1.1	100.0	61.2	60.9	1	10,580.00	32.70	36.53
	[S] [H] SI.COM														
5	Total Audience	259,263	0.9	2500	2,321	1,253	0.8	1.9	100.0	100.0	100.0	1	46,420.00	20.00	37.05
6	Custom Target	55,357	0.9	534	496	335	0.5	1.5	100.0	21.4	26.7	1	9,920.00	93.59	138.64
	[E] MLB.COM														
7	Total Audience	96,642	1.3	1500	1,254	743	0.5	1.7	100.0	100.0	100.0	1	25,080.00	20.00	33.77
8	Custom Target	49,215	1.3	764	639	341	0.5	1.9	100.0	51.0	45.9	1	12,780.00	39.25	73.65
	[E] ESPN.COM														
9	Total Audience	1,773,814	0.2	4000	3,656	2,903	1.8	1.3	100.0	100.0	100.0	2	73,120.00	20.00	25.19
10	Custom Target	727,094	0.2	1639	1,498	1,164	1.8	1.3	100.0	41.0	40.1	2	29,960.00	48.81	62.82
	[S] FOXSPORTS.COM														
11	Total Audience	568,139	0.7	4000	3,735	2,093	1.3	1.8	100.0	100.0	100.0	2	74,700.00	20.00	35.69
12	Custom Target	118,655	0.7	835	780	496	0.8	1.6	100.0	20.9	23.7	1	15,600.00	95.77	150.62

Source: comScore, Inc. Used with permission.

target audience definition to obtain an adequate sample size happens frequently in media planning. While perhaps not as precisely targeted as we would like, it is close enough for marketing purposes.

Note also that delivery is expressed in GRPs, reach, and frequency, the same concepts we used for traditional media. It is also important to note the base for the GRPs. For online GRPs to be comparable with traditional media, the base should be total U.S. population. Online suppliers, and even this research source, use the smaller "Web population" as the base, inflating the GRPs (impressions divided by the smaller Web population base).

As noted, both Nielsen NetView and comScore require a subscription for a person to access the data. Google's Ad Planner (www.google.com/adplanner) is a free service that offers the same basic demographic information, but lacks reach/frequency analysis and many of the more detailed metrics such as product usage, time spent on a website, number of pages visited, and so on. Nevertheless, it can go a long way to helping create an online media plan for students and advertisers with a limited research budget.

Ad Planner is based on Google's vast search engine technology. It allows users to select websites defined by geography (state and metro area), language spoken, demographics, sites visited, keywords searched, or a range of almost 50 lifestyle interests. For the selected sites, it displays coverage, composition, unique users, page views, advertising specifications, and other data. If the scope is limited to the United States, Ad Planner also shows the demographic composition of websites in terms of age, gender, household income, education, and presence of children. Ad Planner provides basic website metrics for almost 60 countries. Information includes unique visitors (estimated cookies), reach, page views, total visits, average visits per visitor, and average time on site.

Exhibit 11-14 shows the top websites visited by adults ages 18–34, according to Ad Planner. The sites can be sorted by coverage, composition, or any of the other reported metrics. As we have seen before, the most demographically selective sites have the least coverage, while the larger sites, such as www.yahoo.com, give much greater coverage but also have much more waste. A good media plan will place ads on both types of sites.

Quantcast (www.quantcast.com) is another free resource that provides information on virtually every website (up to one million), but like Google's Ad Planner, the information is only at the top domain level. Quantcast offers detail by age, sex, presence of children, household income, and education. It shows the trend of impressions over user-selected time periods, other websites visited by people who visited the target site, and traffic frequency by "site addicts," "regulars," and "passers-by." It also provides impressions by designated market area (DMA), a capability not

EXHIBIT 11-14

Top Websites for Adults 18–34 According to Google Ad Planner, Ranked by Coverage

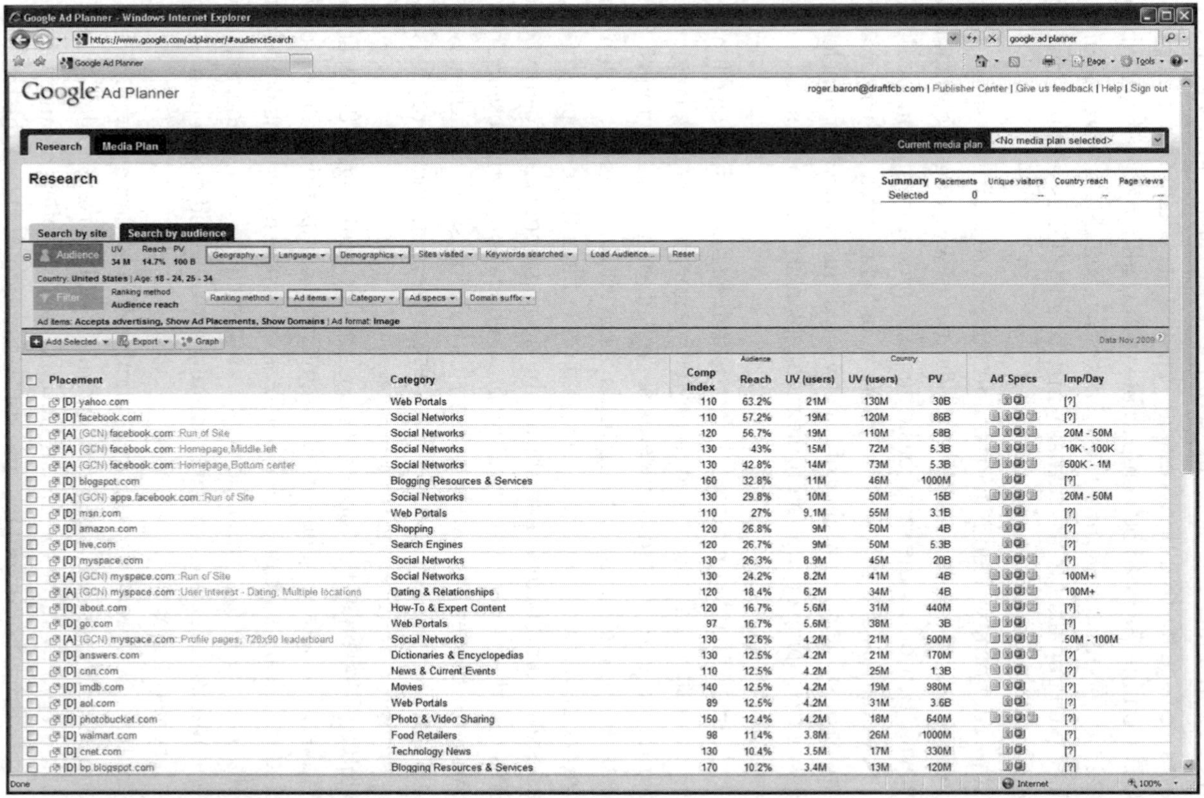

Placement	Category	Comp Index	Audience Reach	Audience UV (users)	Country UV (users)	PV	Ad Specs	Imp/Day
[D] yahoo.com	Web Portals	110	63.2%	21M	130M	30B		[?]
[D] facebook.com	Social Networks	110	57.2%	19M	120M	86B		[?]
[A] (GCN) facebook.com::Run of Site	Social Networks	120	56.7%	19M	110M	58B		20M - 50M
[A] (GCN) facebook.com::Homepage,Middle left	Social Networks	130	43%	15M	72M	5.3B		10K - 100K
[A] (GCN) facebook.com::Homepage,Bottom center	Social Networks	130	42.8%	14M	73M	5.3B		500K - 1M
[D] blogspot.com	Blogging Resources & Services	160	32.8%	11M	46M	1000M		[?]
[A] (GCN) apps.facebook.com::Run of Site	Social Networks	130	29.8%	10M	50M	15B		20M - 50M
[D] msn.com	Web Portals	110	27%	9.1M	55M	3.1B		[?]
[D] amazon.com	Shopping	120	26.8%	9M	50M	4B		[?]
[D] live.com	Search Engines	120	26.7%	9M	50M	5.3B		[?]
[D] myspace.com	Social Networks	130	26.3%	8.9M	45M	20B		[?]
[A] (GCN) myspace.com::Run of Site	Social Networks	130	24.2%	8.2M	41M	4B		100M+
[A] (GCN) myspace.com::User interest - Dating, Multiple locations	Dating & Relationships	120	18.4%	6.2M	34M	4B		100M+
[D] about.com	How-To & Expert Content	120	16.7%	5.6M	31M	440M		[?]
[D] go.com	Web Portals	97	16.7%	5.6M	38M	3B		[?]
[A] (GCN) myspace.com::Profile pages, 728x90 leaderboard	Social Networks	130	12.6%	4.2M	21M	500M		50M - 100M
[D] answers.com	Dictionaries & Encyclopedias	130	12.5%	4.2M	21M	170M		[?]
[D] cnn.com	News & Current Events	110	12.5%	4.2M	25M	1.3B		[?]
[D] imdb.com	Movies	140	12.5%	4.2M	19M	980M		[?]
[D] aol.com	Web Portals	89	12.5%	4.2M	31M	3.6B		[?]
[D] photobucket.com	Photo & Video Sharing	150	12.4%	4.2M	18M	640M		[?]
[D] walmart.com	Food Retailers	98	11.4%	3.8M	26M	1000M		[?]
[D] cnet.com	Technology News	130	10.4%	3.5M	17M	330M		[?]
[D] bp.blogspot.com	Blogging Resources & Services	170	10.2%	3.4M	13M	120M		[?]

Source: Google. Used with permission.

available in Ad Planner. Additional information is available for websites that place a beacon on every page served, allowing them to be "Quantified."

Taken together, Ad Planner and Quantcast are free services that give planners a wealth of data about Internet websites that might be used for a campaign. However, as free services, they lack the depth of information available from the subscription comScore and Nielsen online services.

Planners can also use competitive reporting services such as Nielsen's AdRelevance service (www.nielsennetratings.com) and Kantar Media (www.kantar mediana.com) to show which sites are used by an advertiser's competitors. It is important to note that due to their sampling methodology, reported competitive data for the Internet is not as accurate as it is for traditional media, where every ad is counted.

Ad Networks While most online campaigns focus on a select group of websites, the extreme fragmentation makes it difficult to achieve adequate reach going one site at a time. To help resolve this, ad networks were created to distribute an advertiser's message over hundreds or even thousands of websites that have agreed to receive these ads, often at a significantly reduced price. Ad networks can be selected that focus on specific interests such as food, kids, entertaining, social commentary blogs, and so on. While the advertiser gives up a measure of control over where its ads appear, it gains from the greatly increased reach and lower CPM offered by ad networks.

Another tool for buying online media is the ad exchange, an impression-by-impression auction marketplace that connects website publishers and buyers in real time. It gives buyers immediate access to inventory that meets campaign goals through behavioral targeting, defined bids, and frequency caps on inventory purchases. These systems, operating as an auction, sell inventory to the buyer that pays the highest price. As of this writing, ad exchanges are a relatively new business model that may or may not succeed as more advertisers and publishers get involved. We can expect other models to emerge as the industry evolves.

Finally, online measurement is a moving target. Nielsen, comScore, and Google are constantly updating their software and adding to their capabilities. New services such as Quantcast, Hitwise, BlueKai, and others not even on the radar today can further inform the planning process. To stay informed about the latest developments, planners are encouraged to attend the Internet Advertising Bureau (www.iab.net) webcasts and other activities. Finally, talk to the respective sales representatives to get the most up-to-date understanding of the services that are available.

Buying Internet Display Advertising

After selecting a number of appropriate sites, the planner sends each a request for proposal. This request identifies the advertiser; campaign objectives and strategies; the planner's name, address, phone number, and e-mail address; the dates of the campaign; ad unit size; target audience; and the expected budget. The website's advertising department confirms the site's ability to accept the advertising and gives the number of impressions that can be bought for this budget. From this the planner can calculate the site's CPM and compare it with other submissions. For sites that compute CPM from total persons 2+ impressions, like magazines, it can be useful to use composition data from Nielsen or comScore to help understand the target audience CPM. This step is not necessary for sites that can guarantee the target audience CPM from registered visitors.

The computer that serves the ad ("third-party ad server") makes a record each time a banner or other ad unit is sent to a visitor's browser. This documented exposure is the natural unit of value that allows digital advertising to be priced in terms of CPM impressions. After negotiation, a planner might say, "I agree to buy 2,000,000 impressions on ESPN.com at $20.00 CPM, for a total cost of $40,000." The insertion order is sent or the contract is signed, and creative materials and rotation instructions are provided to the third-party ad server, which begins sending the advertiser's banners, pop-up ads, or other creative messages to the designated target visitors whenever they visit the ordered (ESPN.com) website. Each impression is counted. When the ordered two million impressions have been delivered, the campaign ends, and the advertiser is billed.

The decision to order, in this case two million impressions, is a critical difference between the Internet and traditional media. When an advertiser places an ad on a television program that is watched by two million people, two million impressions have been delivered at that moment—that is, two million people have seen the commercial. On the Internet, an advertiser must wait until two million people have browsed to that website and been served an ad. Since many advertisers are using a website, those impressions don't go to the first two million people to come along. On smaller sites, it may take several days or even weeks to accumulate that many impressions.

While the website's promotional material may claim hundreds of millions of visits, the only thing that matters from an advertiser's standpoint is the two million impressions that are purchased. Exhibit 11-13 shows FOXSports.com received 568.1 million impressions (also called "page views") in July, but the advertiser bought only four million impressions. Also, for some sites the impressions reflect delivery to browsers, without any indication who is viewing them. Others ask visitors to register and provide basic demographic information, allowing these sites to sell demographically targeted impressions. So it is important for the buyer to know if a website is selling persons 2+ impressions or registered (A18–34) impressions.

In addition to CPM impressions, advertisers may agree to pay only for site visitors who click through the banner and are then redirected to the advertiser's site. Because the click-through rate is typically less than 1 percent of the people exposed, the CPM click-throughs will be much higher than CPM banner impressions. On the other hand, these people are far more valuable because they have demonstrated interest in the advertiser's product. In addition to CPM impressions, advertisers may agree to pay only for site visitors who click through the banner and are then redirected to the advertiser's site or those who view the ad and go to the site later (view-throughs or postimpressions).

Advertisers can also buy site sponsorships, ad placement only in selected cities or zip codes, or placement on selected pages of a larger website (similar to placing an ad in a particular section of a newspaper). Some sites allow planners to deliver impressions only when the local temperature, pollen count, or rainfall meets some criterion. For example, a soft-drink company might want to deliver impressions only when the local temperature exceeds 90 degrees. Advertising can be delivered only at certain times of day (daypart scheduling). The possibilities for customized pricing models and modes of advertising exposure are virtually unlimited.

Many websites keep track of visitors by placing a small record called a *cookie* on the hard disk of the visitor's computer. This enables the site to identify repeat visits. One creative execution will be served at the first visit; then on subsequent visits, the existence of a cookie will alert the server to send a different ad. This keeps the creative fresh and improves the chances that the visitor will click through to the advertiser's website. This also allows the site to keep track of the number of impressions served a given visitor (browsing computer), enabling the advertiser to place a frequency cap on exposures, which is the maximum number of times a given ad will be served to a visitor. This method also enables "retargeting," which allows advertisers to deliver additional messages to people who have shown an interest in the product.

Some companies use cookies to develop a profile of the visitor's browsing behavior. Through arrangements with hundreds of websites, a record is made whenever a given computer, identified by the cookie on the hard disk, appears at any one of them. This allows the profiling company to identify a person who, for instance, visits a sports website, a financial site, a golf pro site, an auto racing site, and a business news site. When that person (cookie) shows up again, the profiler knows to serve a banner for a financial service advertiser, for instance. Another user, whose cookie indicates an interest in child-oriented sites, would be served a banner for products targeting parents. This "behavioral targeting" is a widely used way of targeting digital advertising.

Buying Internet Search Advertising

In September 2009, according to Nielsen Online, 30 percent of all Internet advertising impressions were from sponsored search, making it the fastest-growing form of online advertising. Planning and buying search advertising is totally different from that of traditional media or even online display banners. Accordingly, the following section was written by David L. Smith, CEO and founder of Mediasmith, San Francisco, and Bob Heyman, managing director of The Digital Engagement Group.

Search is typically viewed as a lead-generating medium that, as of this writing, is largely dominated by Google. It has been called the most efficient lead-generating medium ever, and it probably is. Search can also be used for branding and research.

The two dominant types of search are paid keywords, also referred to as pay-per-click (PPC) and search engine marketing (SEM), and search engine optimization (SEO), also referred to as natural or organic search. SEM, or paid keywords, is much like a direct-response media buy. SEO is more like PR, and there is an art to getting on the front page and at the top of the listings.

SEM has to do with buying keywords and phrases that trigger a sponsored link. Payment is on a per-click basis: if nobody clicks, there is no payment. Google and other search engines have many tools to assist you in the search buy. SEM is typically purchased online, directly from the Google website. Keep in mind that the 80/20 rule applies here: 20 percent of the keywords generate 80 percent of the traffic. Thus it is important to expand the list of top-performing words. You should know the keywords your competitors are using. And you must also carefully plan what words to put into the meta tags, which are lines in the HTML code of a website that describe and classify its contents for search engines.

To maximize value for paid and primarily organic search, the keyword buyer must work closely with the website developer to ensure that the same words that are being bought are programmed into the content of the site and the meta tags. For instance, if a pharmaceutical advertiser buys the words "high cholesterol," those same words must appear in the meta tag line of code as:

```
<meta name="keywords" content="high cholesterol"\>
```

Keywords and phrases are bought through an auction on a competitive basis. The higher-traffic keywords have a significant amount of competition that bids up the price. So the keywords "high cholesterol" would be more expensive than "toenail fungus." The highest bidder generally gets the top listing, but variables such as the click-through rate and the appropriateness of the search to the content on the site also come into play. It is best to be in the top position, or at least in the top three positions. Click rates decline quickly after the first listing. Google sends the top three to other sites, giving them broader reach and distribution.

In Google the paid listings are generally on the right-hand column and identified as "sponsored links." The free listings are the main or left-hand listings. Some paid listings can be at the top of the free listings. These are usually obvious, as they are shaded a different color.

Some best practices for paid search include:

- Consider whether to use just Google or to include other first- and second-tier search engines such as Yahoo! and Microsoft's Bing (which as of fall 2009 are potentially combining their efforts).
- Since you are paying for each click, keep a close—even daily—watch over your campaign to ensure staying within budget. If costly clicks are coming in faster than expected, an SEM buy can be adjusted hour-by-hour as needed. Most advertisers have an "allowable" that they can afford to spend on an acquisition to make it profitable.
- Optimize your bid management to ensure the best balance between buying so many keywords that you are unable to handle the rush of business and so few that there is no effect. A number of tools can help you, including Marin Software (www.marinsoftware.com), DoubleClick (www.doubleclick.com), Eyeblaster (www.eyeblaster.com), Clickable (www.clickable.com), and Kenshoo (www.kenshoo.com). These applications include controls for managing entire SEM campaigns, in addition to the bid management tools. However, these costly tools of the trade must be accounted for when setting up a search buying unit.
- Be on the lookout for click fraud, the criminal use of automated systems that generate a flurry of robotic clicks to increase revenue to the website's publisher and the middlemen. The search engines can help detect click fraud, but outside tools such as Click Facts (www.clickfacts.com) and Click Forensics (www.clickforensics.com) can also be useful.
- Discovering the best keywords is an ongoing process. Tools such as WordTracker (www.wordtracker.com), KeywordSpy (www.keywordspy.com), and Keyword Tracker (www.keywordtracker.com) can help.
- Unlike traditional media or even conventional online display advertising, SEM optimization is a 24/7 proposition. Be prepared to watch the campaign carefully to ensure it is meeting your marketing objectives.

- Brand protection is important. Watch for competitors bidding on your brand name or strategic keywords such as your advertising campaign tagline. You can fight this by insisting on your trademark rights (if the rival user is violating search engine rules) and by preemptively buying top placement for your most important brand-associated keywords.

While SEM is a paid auction, SEO represents the free listings. Like public relations, SEO is an art unto itself and there are many specialists, often outside of the media department.

SEO is defined as the process of editing and organizing the content on a Web page or website in such a way that it is more likely to be given a high position when specific keywords are entered. At the same time, it is important that external links to the site are correctly titled and in abundance. This is done with the aim of achieving a higher organic search listing and thus increasing the volume of traffic from search engines. Although it is technically free, there is a cost associated with paying the IT department or the content developers who build websites to be SEO compliant. Because this is extremely important to be successful in search, SEO is not free and can be a costly and time-consuming process.

It is a good idea for the media planner who is doing paid search to work in conjunction with the SEO specialist to coordinate best practices. These include the following:

- Organize aspects of a site's construction to raise its ranking according to a search engine's algorithm. This changes often, and SEO must be an ongoing process, not just one time.
- Recognize that SEO is a long-term proposition that can take months to show positive results.
- On-page factors still count: site structure, meta tags, and so on.
- Off-page factors are huge: number and quality of inbound links, paid link strategies, generating inbound links with press releases and blogs.
- Take advantage of Universal Search, a Google system that blends listings from its news, video, images, local, and book search engines with those it gathers from crawling Web pages. Make sure all video and audio assets are optimized for search.

It is important for SEO and SEM to work together. Many studies show that they both improve when there is a coordinated effort.

As mentioned earlier, search can work from a branding standpoint. After all, if you find a term that is beneficial to you, has high traffic, and has few competitive bidders, you can deliver a lot of impressions that are virtually free, since you pay for only the ones that are clicked. A number of companies have done this successfully.

Video search (included in Universal Search, which can handle many formats in addition to keywords) is a rapidly growing practice. Other fast-growing areas of search at the time of this writing include mobile search, real-time search (Twitter and other microblogs), and social search using Facebook and other social networks that can reveal what people like and dislike.

A final note: the capabilities and techniques of SEM and SEO change so quickly that the particulars of planning and buying are likely to be very different over the life of this text. They have a permanent place in marketing communications, but it is important for planners to stay current with the latest ways of using these new and rapidly evolving media forms.

The Continuously Evolving Online World

Updated in the spring of 2010, this book cannot possibly cover all the many technologies and business practices in use even today. Any attempt to do so would be useless, given the complexity of the Internet and the rapid pace of change. No doubt many of the media opportunities presented here will be out-of-date even when the book is published. As technology advances, a constant stream of improvements and new services will make digital advertising even more effective, but at the same time will require greater understanding of how to get the most out of the medium.

For all the changes, there is truth in the old saw, "There is nothing new under the sun." Regardless what form the new creative units take—banner, rich media, pre-roll advertising before streaming video, SEM and SEO search, online capability merged with HDTV, 3-D television, social media, mobile, Twitter, and others not yet in existence today—whatever comes must still be primarily evaluated in terms of the fundamental concepts of cost efficiency, coverage, and composition of the vehicles, and response to the advertiser's message, however that is measured. It is incumbent on the planner to keep informed as the medium changes and as new opportunities and challenges present themselves.

CHAPTER TWELVE

Media Costs and Buying Problems

Every media alternative considered for the media strategy has a different cost. The final media plan emerging from the marketing strategy should effectively maximize the delivery of the designated marketing target in the most cost-efficient manner. Therefore, the media planner must be familiar with market definition and be fully versed in how people use various media. In some instances, as is the case with television time, the cost of media varies with supply and demand. Other media, such as magazines and newspapers, remain fairly constant in cost, thereby providing more predictability as planners develop costs for the media plan. But even for these media, the cost per insertion for advertisers running a heavy schedule is highly negotiable. The cost of search varies greatly depending on the many factors that affect an auction.

The costs that go into the final media plan are always in a state of flux. Estimating such costs is as much an art as a science; it depends heavily on the experience and professionalism of the media planner and the media buyer. If a plan is based on costs that are out of line with marketplace realities, it can result in delivery of a faulty media plan. For example, if a planner estimates that 100 gross rating points (GRPs) of prime-time television can be purchased for $200,000, and the actual cost of that time is $300,000, the deliverability of the plan is seriously impaired. The client can then justifiably question the value of that media plan, as well as the competence of the planner.

Estimating media costs is a complex task. In addition, different media have different problems connected with the buying process. This chapter will identify the importance of the planner's involvement in the media-buying process and explain why this involvement requires familiarity with both the cost of media and the problems associated with purchasing different media types.

Some Considerations in Planning and Buying Media

The value of a media plan is related to how well it delivers the designated marketing targets at the lowest cost with the least amount of waste. The criteria for determining how well the plan accomplishes its mission are related to such concepts as reach, frequency, and target market impressions delivered. The gross number of target market impressions, coupled with the reach and frequency associated with those impressions within the designated budget, form the nucleus of an effective media plan. The media planner must go through a calculated process of matching the cost of various media alternatives with the delivery of the plan to arrive at the optimal relationship between cost and delivery.

For example, in June 2009, Nielsen tells us the cost per rating point (CPP) for women 18 years of age and older for daytime network television is $5,434 (:30 basis), and the CPP for the same audience segment in nighttime network is $28,884. A set budget placing all dollars in daytime network will deliver five times more GRPs to women 18+ than will nighttime network based on these costs. For a $15 million budget over a one-year period allocated to 30-second commercials, the planning computer estimates that the average four-week reach and frequency for nighttime would be lower (25 percent) than the same budget in daytime (43 percent), as illustrated in Exhibit 12-1. However, the reach of nighttime will be higher than the daytime reach over the total 52-week period. Conversely, the frequency in daytime will be higher than the frequency in nighttime over the total year. This is for illustration only since a planner would rarely recommend placing the entire budget in a single television daypart.

From this discussion, it is clear that a key part of the broadcast planner's work is determining the best daypart mixture—that is, deciding how many rating points should be placed in each daypart. In the past, this was only possible as a trial-and-error process with a computerized reach/frequency analysis system that analyzed one schedule at a time.

For at least the past 20 years, sophisticated broadcast optimizers have become available that will estimate the reach of thousands of combinations and then report the plan that offers the most reach for a given budget. Although the daypart optimizer caused great excitement in the industry when first released, it has since taken its place as one of many tools used routinely by planners and buyers.

Planners have also become aware of the optimizer's limitations. First, the results are largely determined by the CPP given for each daypart. But since these are only estimates of future prices, the resulting "optimal" plan may not reflect market conditions when the buy is made. Second, and equally important, optimizers can work

EXHIBIT 12-1

Women 18+ TV Delivery by Daypart for $15 Million Budget

	NIGHT NETWORK	DAY NETWORK
Commercial unit	:30	:30
Population women 18+ (000)	116,090	116,090
W18+ average audience (000)	2,891	2,156
Cost/30-second commercial	$71,930	$10,091
Average rating	2.5%	1.9%
CPM	$24.88	$4.68
CPP	$28,884	$5,434
Total affordable GRPs ($15 MM divided by CPP)	519	2,760
Average four-week GRPs (total GRPs/52 × 4)	40	212
Average four-week reach/frequency	25%/1.6	43%/5.0
Total 52-week reach/frequency	73%/7.1	67%/41.1

Source: The Nielsen Company, "Household and Persons Cost Per Thousand," June 2009; DRAFTFCB Reach, 2007. Used with permission.

only with past audience data, but their results must apply to the next season's programs, which may not even exist at the time of the analysis. Finally, many plans have virtually identical reach. 74.3 percent is not statistically different from 74.2 percent, yet it may result from very different GRP levels (and hence, different total plan cost per thousand [CPM]). The best optimizers show the top 10 plans, allowing planners to select the one that best meets the advertiser's marketing needs. These factors limit the usefulness of optimizers and reinforce the need for judgment in developing a broadcast plan.

Although broadcast is planned with CPP, comparisons among media are usually based on costs per thousand gross impressions or on net reach. Whichever method is used, the cost-efficiency of media delivery is important. The medium with the largest reach may not necessarily be the best buy, because it might provide less cost-efficiency. Exhibit 12-2 shows a rough comparison of alternative media deliveries and cost-efficiencies.

EXHIBIT 12-2

Alternative Media: Cost and Delivery

	ADVERTISING UNIT	NATIONAL EQUIVALENT COST ($000)	WOMEN 18+ (000)	WOMEN 18+ CPM	MEN 18+ (000)	MEN 18+ CPM
Network TV—prime time (7 net—reg.)	:30	$108.8	3,296	$33.02	2,259	$48.19
Network TV—daytime (5 net)	:30	27.1	1,577	17.17	899	30.11
Cable TV—avg. net-work—prime time	:30	2.8	236	11.78	216	12.85
Network TV—early news (M–F 3 nets)	:30	74.2	1,804	41.13	2,175	34.11
Syndication (avg.)	:30	16.6	1,303	12.71	816	20.32
General magazine (5-mag. avg.)	Pg 4/C Bl	171.8	13,695	12.55	9,951	17.27
Women's magazines (5-mag. avg.)	Pg 4/C Bl	257.5	17,672	14.57	3,254	79.14
Network radio (:30)	:30	$2.29	1,161	1.97	1,084	2.11
Outdoor (top 50 markets, 4-week)	50 showing	5,080	2,662	1.91	2,447	2.08

Source: The Nielsen Company, Monitor-Plus, Average June 2008–June 2009. Used with permission. Mediaweek, *Marketer's Guide to Media,* 2009.

An examination of the table shows that different coverage levels are achieved by different media vehicles, with certain implications for CPP. The media planner's task is to combine familiarity with media costs and delivery dynamics with the goals of the marketing plan to reach designated audiences. The planner must be careful to employ correct media cost assumptions in the development of the plan.

Tables like these should be used with caution because the definition of an impression is different for each medium. For national broadcast, it is the number of people exposed to the average minute of the program or the average commercial minute at the time it airs. For magazines, it is the total number of people who have read or looked into the average issue over the many months when it is available. Newspaper impressions are also readership of the average issue. Outdoor is based on vehicles passing the boards over a 30-day period. Note that neither online display nor search media are shown here, because of the totally different way they are bought and priced. In short, while it is a common practice, planners who compare the efficiency and even the combined reach and frequency of multiple media should recognize they are comparing apples and oranges—or perhaps more accurately, apples and sushi.

To ensure they are using the most accurate and up-to-date costs, planners must maintain close contact with cost mechanisms in the media marketplace. Costs reflect not only the supply-and-demand conditions of each medium, but also the strong influence of the nation's economy. Exhibit 12-3 shows the year-to-year changes in media unit costs over the past 10 years as estimated in September of the preceding year. It projects 2010 network TV costs down 11 percent versus 2009, while spot TV costs will be up 4 percent as the economy improves after the recession.

We cannot overstate the need to include media buyers in the development of media cost estimates. Media agencies employ buying specialists whose sole responsibility is the purchase of media. Such media buyers are in regular contact with the media suppliers with whom they do business on behalf of the agency and client. During the course of the numerous media buyer–seller transactions, the buyer acquires a familiarity with what is occurring in the marketplace. Such familiarity can assist the media planner in forecasting media price changes. Media buyers are expected to maintain good relations with media suppliers to facilitate this flow of information. Media planners should make it a point to maintain close communications with the media buyers so as to tap this source of media cost information.

Media agencies develop expertise in estimating media costs based on the agency's total experience. Over a period of time, the agency can compile media cost information in various markets or nationally by generalizing from various specific buying experiences. To develop this information, it is not necessary to breach security within an agency, although they rarely buy for competitive advertisers in the same product category. Generalized experience is one reason why many agencies organized their buyers as market specialists who purchase media in their assigned market for every brand that the agency handles. The specialists become intimately acquainted with their markets and can usually negotiate more favorable rates than buyers who are active in a market only from time to time.

In addition to input from the buyers, planners can use the subscription-based service SQAD (www.sqad.com), which provides up-to-date cost estimates for spot TV and radio and network television. This is useful for planning markets where there is little current buyer experience, but even there, actual costs may vary depending on the stations selected, the amount of lead time before the schedule goes on air, and the buyer's negotiating skill.

Once the media plan has been implemented and the schedules completed, the media planner should examine how closely the media cost estimates match actual costs. This is called a *postbuy analysis.* By conducting a postbuy analysis, the

EXHIBIT 12-3

Media Cost per Thousand Percent Increase/Decrease Over Prior Year

	2000 (OVER 1999)	2001 (OVER 2000)	2002 (OVER 2001)	2003 (OVER 2002)	2004 (OVER 2003)	2005 (OVER 2004)	2006 (OVER 2005)	2007 (OVER 2006)	2008 (OVER 2007)	2009 (OVER 2008)	EST 2010 (OVER 2009)
Consumer Price Index	3.4	2.8	1.6	2.3	2.7	3.4	3.2	2.8	3.8	-0.4	na
Network TV	11.0	-6.5	2.1	2.6	5.0	-1.5	0.0	-3.0	2.0	-2.0	-11.0
Spot TV	10.0	-8.5	7.0	-2.0	10.0	-8.0	5.0	-10	6.0	-12.0	4.0
Cable TV	9.5	-1.0	-1.5	7.5	12	7.0	0.0	0.0	0.0	2.0	0.0
Network Radio	14.0	-6.0	2.5	3.0	3.0	2.5	0.5	1.0	2.0	1.0	2.0
Spot Radio	12.0	-9.0	1.5	2.5	0.0	3.0	-1.0	-3.0	1.0	-10.0	3.0
Magazines	3.0	2.0	4.6	4.0	3.6	3.5	2.0	4.0	3.0	-2.0	1.0
Newspapers	3.5	-3.5	3.0	2.0	2.5	3.5	3.5	2.0	1.0	-2.0	-2.0
Out-of-Home	na	na	na	na	na	na	na	na	5.0	4.8	3.9
Internet	na	na	na	na	na	na	na	na	na	-1.9	0.0
Total media	8.0%	-4.5%	3.6%	2.1%	5.5%	-0.4%	1.9%	-1.9%	1.0%	-2.2%	-2.0%

Source: Consumer Price Index, annual average, all items; American Association of Advertising Agencies (4As), *Media Matters,* October 5, 2009.

planner can sharpen the capability to forecast costs by reviewing what went into the original estimates. Such trial-and-error devices assist the media professional in developing the personal art of media cost forecasting. Major variations between cost estimates and actual plan delivery cost might reflect flaws in understanding or thinking or might be the consequence of significant cost changes in the media marketplace that could not have been anticipated. In any event, the media planner, in checking back over the implemented plan, should consider the exercise an important learning experience.

Media Costs

As shown in Exhibit 12-4, national advertisers spent almost $70 billion in national television, radio, and magazines in 2009.

Within these broad media types are numerous alternatives with which the media planner must be acquainted. In addition to understanding general media cost relationships between television and magazines, for example, the professional planner must be familiar with costs of network versus spot and the different availabilities within the general broadcast medium, as well as the changes over time. This assignment is complex and difficult, but necessary.

Television

Combined television expenditures, the first four categories in Exhibit 12-4, accounted for 58 percent of total advertising dollars spent in 2009. Note that spending in national cable is now on a par with national broadcast television. Most of the television investment was for consumer goods and services. However, there has been a growing use of the medium by industrial and business-related advertisers. In view of the magnitude of the investment in television, a media-planning professional must be fully conversant with all phases of the medium.

The major characteristic of television, insofar as media costs are concerned, relates to the "perishability" of the inventory. Generally speaking, there is a fixed amount of television time available for sale (called *inventory*. Unlike a magazine or newspaper, which can expand or contract the number of advertising pages available for sale in any given issue) a commercial minute that is unsold can never be recovered. The sellers of television time must contend with this perishability concept in selling the medium.

Although marketplace pricing conditions prevail at any given time, these prices are subject to change as advertisers' demand for that time increases or decreases. The stronger the demand and the earlier the sale in relationship to the program air

EXHIBIT 12-4

National Advertising Media Expenditures (Jan.–Dec. 2009)

	DOLLARS SPENT	
MEDIA	MILLIONS	PERCENT
Network TV	$24,138	18.6%
Cable TV	24,404	18.8
Syndicated TV	2,198	1.7
Spot TV (All 210 DMAs)	24,235	18.6
Spanish-Language Network TV	6,824	5.3
Spanish-Language Cable TV	652	0.5
National Magazine	15,505	11.9
Local Magazine	436	0.3
National Sunday Supplement	1,068	0.8
Local Sunday Supplement	54	0.0
National Newspaper	1,357	1.0
Local Newspaper	10,762	8.3
Network Radio	991	0.8
Spot Radio	5,063	3.9
Outdoor	3,241	2.5
FSI Coupon	446	0.3
Internet	8,574	6.6
Grand Total	$129,948	100.0%

Source: The Nielsen Company, Monitor-Plus, 2009. Used with permission.

date, the more likely that pricing will be higher. Less advertising demand close to air date can create lower pricing, assuming inventory availability. These interrelated conditions of perishability, demand, and inventory create a dynamic marketplace.

Because these market conditions are constantly changing, broadcast planners must ensure that they have the most recent costs before they begin the planning process. These costs are expressed in terms of CPP and are obtained either from the buyer who is responsible for executing the plan or (with the buyer's approval) from published sources such as SQAD. This contact with the buyer is critical because the planner is, in essence, saying, "I want you to buy this many GRPs, and I'm giving you that much money to do it." If planners give the buyers more money than they need, the returned excess becomes an embarrassment because it could have been spent in other places. Conversely, if the buyers are given too little money, then they will be unable to buy as many GRPs as the plan calls for—an equally embarrassing situation. Buyers typically have 5–10 percent leeway, but anything more than that will require a letter to the client explaining what happened.

Buyers need *all* of the following information to provide planning costs:

- Geographic area (total United States or list of markets)
- Buying target audience (women 25–54)
- Commercial length (30-second)
- Dayparts to be used in the plan (daytime, prime, news, late fringe, kid)
- Schedule dates (typically there is a different CPP for each quarter)
- Special buying instructions, such as the need to purchase high-rated (high-cost) programs, sports sponsorships, promotional requirements, program content restrictions, and so on

Based on this information, buyers will estimate the planning CPPs to be used. These costs are based on the buyers' recent experience in the market, contacts with station sales representatives, and their sense of future market demand. Typically, one group of people is responsible for buying national broadcast (network, cable, and syndication), while another group buys local market spot TV and radio.

Large companies that employ the services of several advertising agencies maximize their buying clout by giving all buying responsibility to a single organization (ad agency, buying service, or media specialty company). This *agency of record* is responsible for providing cost-per-point estimates to all planners who work on the business.

Planning costs are highly confidential because they are the basis for price negotiation. Obviously, if a station finds out that the buyer expects to spend $500 per point, there is little incentive to offer a package that comes in at $450.

Under the broad heading of television, there are basically four subcategories: national network, local spot, syndication, and cable. Let's start this section with a short discussion of a television-wide concept: dayparts.

Dayparts For both planning and buying purposes, the day is broken into a series of time periods that reflect different program types and audiences, called dayparts. Typical dayparts and time periods are listed in Exhibit 12-5.

These dayparts are the basis for planning television campaigns. The planner's task is to determine how many GRPs should be purchased in each daypart to achieve the plan's media objectives. Dayparts will be discussed in more detail in the following section.

EXHIBIT 12-5

Television Dayparts

DAYPART	DAY/TIME	KEY DEMOGRAPHICS
Early morning (EM)	M–Su/7–9 A.M.	Business/professional
Morning kids (EM)	M–Su/7–9 A.M.	Kids
Daytime (DAY)	M–F/10 A.M.–4 P.M.	Women; adults 50+
Early fringe (spot only) (EF)	M–F/4–6 P.M.	Women; kids
Early news (EN)	M–Sa/6–7:30 P.M.	Adults 50+
Prime access (spot only) (PA)	M–Sa/7:30–8 P.M.	Total persons
Prime time (PR)	M–Sa/8–11 P.M., Su/7–11 P.M.	Total persons
Late news (spot only) (LN)	M–Su/11–11:30 P.M.	Adults 25–54
Late fringe (LF)	M–F/11:30 P.M.–1 A.M.	Adults 25–54
Weekend sports (WS)	Sa–Su/10 A.M.–6 P.M.	Men 18+; professional
Saturday late fringe (LF)	Sa/11:30 P.M.–1 A.M.	Teens; adults 18–34

Network TV Certain parts of the broadcast day are programmed by the national networks: the American Broadcasting Company (ABC), the Columbia Broadcasting System (CBS), the National Broadcasting Company (NBC), the Fox network (FOX), the CW, and ION. In addition, Nielsen reports the audience to the Hispanic television networks, Univision, Telemundo, and Telefutura. Exhibit 12-6 illustrates the dayparts when network programming is usually made available to affiliates (the individual stations that constitute a network lineup).

The number of stations serviced by a given network can vary from 150 to 210, depending on the strength of the network programming available. The networks sell time to advertisers, who run commercials within specific programs. These programs can appear throughout the entire country in various parts of the day (e.g., daytime network, prime-time network, or late night).

Prime time (Monday-Saturday from 8:00 P.M. to 11:00 P.M. and Sunday from 7:00 P.M. to 11:00 P.M. eastern standard time [EST]) generally provides the highest ratings because of the large number of homes using television (HUT). This time period tends to deliver a family audience with high reach levels of most viewing segments. Prime time also reaches the most light viewers, although this group makes up only a small proportion of the audience at any one time. Media costs for prime time are generally the highest of all network time segments available for sale. The

EXHIBIT 12-6

Daypart Programming Available for Network Use

6 A.M.	7	8	9	10	11	12 P.M.	1	2	3	4	5	6	7	8	9	10	11	12 A.M.	1	2

LOCAL	Network	LOCAL	Network daytime programs	LOCAL	NETWORK	LOCAL	LOCAL ACCESS	Network prime-time programs	LOCAL NEWS	Network late-night programs	LOCAL

cost for 30 seconds in prime time, as indicated in Exhibit 12-2, averages $108,800. Individual program costs will vary, depending on rating level (substantially more for the higher-rated shows) and the amount of inventory available for sale. As discussed earlier, the less inventory, generally, the higher the cost.

Daytime network (10:00 A.M. to 4:00 P.M. EST) is normally the least costly of the network dayparts. This results in an extremely efficient cost-per-thousand delivery of homes and homemakers, although the audience composition tends to skew to older adults. Typically, daytime network is supplemented with cable and syndication programs such as "The Oprah Winfrey Show."

Late-night network programming (11:30 P.M. to conclusion EST) varies from network to network and over time. This time period is generally programmed with talk or news programs such as the "The Tonight Show with Jay Leno," "The Late Show with David Letterman," and "ABC Nightline" during the week, and variety entertainment shows such as "Saturday Night Live" on the weekend. Because fewer sets are in use than during prime time, pricing for the late night shows tends to be about $21,600 for 30 seconds, with an average household rating of 1.5.[1] Although the rating levels for late night are comparable to daytime, late night includes a dual audience (both men and women), which is not generally the case in daytime. Thus pricing for that dual audience tends to be somewhat higher than daytime.

Most network programming on weekends is in the sports and children's areas. Sports programming, for the most part, is the domain of the male-oriented advertiser. Such products as beer, male grooming aids, investment counseling, and

---

1. The Nielsen Company, *Household and Persons Cost Per Thousand Report*, June 2009.

automobiles are heavily represented on weekend sports programming. In general, there is a limited amount of broad-scale sports programming compared with other network program time. Therefore, pricing tends to be comparable to prime time on a CPP basis. However, many advertisers believe the value of identifying with a major high-interest sports event rubs off on brands associated with such programming.

Children's programs, often referred to as "kid TV," are the primary fare on Saturday mornings. Nearly all of this programming is cartoons, but there are some live-action shows, especially in the action/adventure and sports areas. The predominant audience is children, and the advertising, therefore, is highly child oriented. Advertisers of cereal, toys and games, fast food, and candy concentrate a significant portion of their advertising budget in kid TV. The growth of cable networks such as Nickelodeon and the Cartoon Network have made kid programming available throughout the day and have reduced advertisers' dependence on Saturday morning as the sole national kids' daypart.

The diversity of programming provided by the networks ranges from the all-family interest generated in prime time to highly selective shows of interest to relatively few households. Such diversity provides the media planner with rich opportunities for reaching broad national markets with programming aimed specifically to the interests of target markets. Costs for such programming will change as marketplace demand changes, so the media planner must be ever alert to the buying implications of the programming selected for inclusion in the media plan.

Local Stations Announcements can be purchased on local television stations in each DMA, which are either affiliated with a network or are independent. Affiliated stations carry network programming at certain times of the day. Independent stations do not have any network affiliation and so must program the entire day on their own. They can choose to produce programs in their own studios (such as local news), or they can purchase syndicated programs.

Costs for local announcements vary from market to market based on the size, the audience delivered, and advertiser demand for the available commercial time. Generally, the costs for scheduling announcements in markets like New York, Los Angeles, and Chicago are higher than those for smaller markets because of the large number of people reached by the big-city stations. Although the out-of-pocket cost is higher, the proportionally larger audience tends to lower the CPM.

Costs are highly negotiable and depend on the expected size of the audience. For the dayparts where there is not enough advertiser demand, or in soft economic times, stations will sell units at a negotiated cost per inquiry (PI). These commercials are characterized by requests for direct response to an 800 number and the cry, "Operators are standing by." This is the least desirable way for a station to sell time, because their revenue is controlled by the quality and appeal of the PI advertiser. Unusually large amounts of PI advertising, especially in prime time, is an indication of a slow economy.

Time is made available for sale, whether the station is network-affiliated or independent, across almost the entire day. Even within dayparts programmed by the networks, such as in prime time, certain segments of time are set aside for local sale. This means that it is possible for a local advertiser to purchase a 30-second announcement (if available) in a network-originated program or between programs at the station break. There are also availabilities on cable networks from the local cable operators. With the growing audience to cable programs, this has become an important venue for local advertisers, although as of this writing, the competitive research services do not report spending on cable in local markets.

In addition to availabilities adjacent to, and on occasion, within network programming, commercials can be placed in what is termed *fringe time*. In general, the fringe dayparts and the programming contained in them might look something like Exhibit 12-7.

EXHIBIT 12-7

Sample Fringe Schedule (New York)

STATION	LOCAL TIME (EST)	PROGRAM
WCBS (CBS affiliate)	6:00 P.M.–6:30 P.M.	Local news
	6:30 P.M.–7:00 P.M.	Network news
	7:00 P.M.–7:30 P.M.	"The Insider"
	7:30 P.M.–8:00 P.M.	"Entertainment Tonight"
	11:00 P.M.–11:30 P.M.	Local news
	11:30 P.M.–12:30 A.M.	"Late Show with David Letterman"
WPIX (CW affiliate)	5:00 P.M.–5:30 P.M.	"My Wife and Kids"*
	5:30 P.M.–6:00 P.M.	"George Lopez"*
	6:00 P.M.–6:30 P.M.	"Family Guy"*
	6:30 P.M.–7:00 P.M.	"Friends"*
	7:00 P.M.–7:30 P.M.	"Two and a Half Men"*
	7:30 P.M.–8:00 P.M.	"Family Guy"*
	10:00 P.M.–11:00 P.M.	Local news
	11:00 P.M.–11:30 P.M.	"Two and a Half Men"*
	11:30 P.M.–12:00 midnight	"Friends"*

*Syndicated reruns of programs formerly on the networks.

Pricing for dayparts and specific programs within dayparts varies based on audience delivery and availability of commercial time. Costs are provided by the buyers who will be purchasing the time. Their estimates are based on their experience with the market, but if this is a new market for them or one that has not had recent activity, both planners and buyers will use SQAD, the most commonly accepted source of spot television costs. This service offers low, average, and high planning CPP estimates for all 210 designated market areas (DMAs) and a variety of commonly used demographics. Exhibit 12-8 shows an example of the SQAD computer report of costs for four major markets. Note the difference in costs by daypart.

Costs are updated monthly and are accessed through SQAD's proprietary computer software. More general household data are available through the *Marketer's Guide to Media*. For more information about SQAD, see their website at www.sqad.com.

Estimating the cost of a television campaign is simply a matter of multiplying the cost per rating point (CPP) by the number of GRPs to be bought. In Exhibit 12-8, the average cost to buy one women 25–54 rating point in the listed markets totaled $9,740 for prime time and $2,304 in early morning. So for example, it would cost $1,948,000 to buy 200 GRPs of prime time in each of the four markets (200 ×

EXHIBIT 12-8

SQAD DATAVue

Spot TV CPP
Target: Women 25–54
Quarter/Year: 3rd quarter
Level: Average

MARKET	RANK	POPULATION	EARLY MORNING	DAY	EARLY FRINGE	EARLY NEWS	PRIME ACCESS	PRIME	LATE NEWS	LATE FRINGE
New York	1	4,409,584	898	931	1,252	1,074	1,930	2,832	1,864	1,073
Los Angeles	2	3,734,035	827	992	1,558	1,102	2,312	4,497	1,537	1,330
Chicago	3	2,058,991	331	357	449	658	1,016	1,426	933	321
Philadelphia	4	1,623,366	248	267	354	385	547	985	519	268
Total		11,825,976	2,304	2,547	3,613	3,219	5,805	9,740	4,853	2,992

Source: SQAD Inc., July. Used with permission.

$9,740). The same weight in early morning would cost $460,800 (200 × $2,304). The same arithmetic applies to national television, only with the national CPP.

Syndication *Syndication* is the development or packaging of programming that is sold directly to the advertiser or cleared on a market-by-market basis by the company that produces the program, the syndicator. Clearances for a syndicated property can range from a program run one time in a few markets to a weekly series clearing in 70–90 percent of the United States for extended periods. Each station makes its own decision about which syndicated programs to buy and when to put them on the air. The stations in a market compete intensely for the best programs. Although it happens rarely, stations have been known to buy a program and then not put it on the air, just to keep it away from a competitor. Syndicated properties include first-run talk shows, specials, sports events, entertainment, information, and game shows, as well as off-network reruns of sitcoms and serials. Exhibit 12-9 lists the top 10 syndicated properties in second quarter 2009. Nationalized household ratings, impressions, and the syndication distributor are listed.

Syndicators and local TV stations make four types of deals: straight barter, part barter/part cash, all cash, and scatter. In *straight-barter syndication* the local station receives the program and a percentage of the commercial time within the program for local sale in return for airing the show. *Part-barter/part-cash syndication* requires the local station to pay a license fee to broadcast the program. This arrangement gives the local station control of most of the commercial time, with the syndicator selling a smaller percentage of the commercial minutes to national advertisers. In an *all-cash syndication* deal, the local station pays cash for the syndicated property and can sell all the commercial time to both local and national advertisers. *Scatter syndication* is a unique situation in which the stations are obligated to run national commercial spots for a specific syndicator. The local station can drop or retain the syndicated show, but if the station elects to run the show, it must run the program in a predetermined time. The time period restriction gives the syndicator the means to guarantee national coverage by daypart for its national advertisers.

The costs and efficiencies of the top-rated syndicated properties are comparable to network program costs and efficiencies. However, overall syndicated cost-efficiencies generally run up to 25 percent better than network cost-efficiencies.

Cable TV

Cable TV can be purchased on either a national or spot basis. Although each cable network schedules programming differently, general dayparts mimic traditional network TV: early morning, daytime, prime time, and late night. However, many

EXHIBIT 12-9

Top 10 Syndicated Programs—Second Quarter 2009

PROGRAM NAME	LIVE HOUSEHOLD RATING	AVERAGE AUDIENCE (000)	PROGRAM ORIGINATOR
"Wheel of Fortune"	6.19	7,085	CBS TV Distribution
"Jeopardy"	5.21	5,961	CBS TV Distribution
"The Oprah Winfrey Show"	4.38	5,017	CBS TV Distribution
"Two-Half Men"—Synd.	4.33	4,962	Warner Bros. TV
"Entertainment Tonight"	3.91	4,473	CBS TV Distribution
"Judge Judy"	3.88	4,440	CBS TV Distribution
"Family Guy"—M–F, Synd.	3.63	4,155	20th Television
"CSI New York"—Synd.	3.24	3,705	CBS TV Distribution
"Seinfeld"	3.17	3,628	Sony Pictures TV
"Law & Order: SVU"—Synd.	2.87	3,290	NBC Universal

Source: The Nielsen Company, Nielsen Television Index. Used with permission.

advertisers buy a "run-of-station" (ROS) schedule that rotates the commercials throughout the broadcast day. This ensures the advertiser will get the maximum possible reach of the network, as well as taking advantage of the lower CPM that networks will give ROS advertisers.

Until recently, cable was considered a new medium, one that played only a minor, if any, role in most media plans. Today, cable plus "alternate delivery services" (ADS) such as direct broadcast satellite can reach 90 percent of U.S. TV households, with 89 measured cable networks currently on air.[2] In May, when the broadcast networks still feature first-run programming, advertiser-supported cable accounts for 60 percent share of household prime-time viewing. In July, when the broadcast nets are in reruns, cable's share goes up to 65 percent.[3]

With this large a share of viewing, cable is an essential part of any television buy. In addition, it allows better targeting of selective audience groups. For example, Arts & Entertainment targets upscale, educated individuals; ESPN primarily reaches men; and Nickelodeon attracts children ages 2–17. This type of selectivity,

2. The Nielsen Company, *Nielsen Television Activity Report*, July 2009.
3. The Nielsen Company, Total Viewing Sources, May and July 2009.

referred to as *narrowcasting*, allows advertisers to be extremely focused in their targeting efforts, although planners must keep in mind the coverage/composition trade-off seen in other media. Advertisers with a broad target audience, such as women ages 25–54, typically buy more than 20 cable networks to ensure reaching a large percentage of the target audience.

Cable also tends to be more cost-efficient than other TV options. Exhibit 12-2 shows cable's CPM women 18+ is roughly a third that of broadcast-network prime time. So by including cable in its plan, an advertiser can add reach to the broadcast schedule and at the same time lower the CPM exposures to a national network TV plan.

Magazines

The two major print advertising categories are magazines and newspapers. Pricing for print space tends to be slightly more stable than for broadcast media because magazines and newspapers can adjust up or down the number of pages they print on an issue-to-issue basis. Thus the cost of printing is somewhat variable, in contrast to the fixed commitment of television and its resultant perishability of commercial time.

Newspapers and magazines generally issue *rate cards* that cover future costs, although published magazine rates are no longer reliable, due to negotiated rates and package deals. A media planner constructing a plan for a year in advance must be careful in projecting magazine rate increases during the course of the year, particularly if the magazines the buyer plans to use are among those negotiating their rates. In those cases, the buyer must make judgment calls about the rates to be used in the future media plan.

There is considerable diversity within the broad category of magazines. Some of the categories include general-interest, women's service, and home magazines.

General-Interest (Dual-Audience) Magazines Publications such as *Reader's Digest, National Geographic,* and to some degree *People, Time,* and *Newsweek* are viewed as general-interest magazines in view of the diverse audiences they reach. Their editorial content by nature does not exclude any potential reading group. Along with the large circulation delivered by these publications goes a commensurately high cost per page. Exhibit 12-10 shows sample costs and circulation numbers for these magazines.

Women's Service Magazines More editorially selective publications, such as *Ladies' Home Journal, Good Housekeeping, Family Circle, Woman's Day,* and *Redbook,* gear their interest primarily to women. The editorial content of these publications is designed to be informative and entertaining. Male readership, as a percentage of total readership, is not very high compared with general-interest magazines. Exhibit 12-11 shows the rate card costs for these selected magazines.

General-Interest Magazines: Sample Costs and Circulation

MAGAZINE	COST PG 4/C	CIRCULATION (000)	TOTAL ADULT READERS, AGED 18+ (000)
National Geographic	$204,495	4,699	32,069
New Yorker	131,974	1,004	4,611
Time	314,812	3,518	20,749
Newsweek	215,800	2,728	17,679
People	241,975	3,720	43,603

Source: Mediamark Research & Intelligence, LLC (www.mriplus.com), July 2009. Used with permission.

Women's Service Magazines: Sample Costs and Circulation

MAGAZINE	COST PG 4/C	CIRCULATION (000)	TOTAL ADULT READERS, AGE 18+ (000)
Ladies' Home Journal	$246,600	3,831	12,195
Good Housekeeping	344,475	4,630	23,936
Family Circle	247,200	3,835	19,792
Woman's Day	252,390	3,894	20,481
Redbook	148,200	2,207	8,660

Source: Mediamark Research & Intelligence, LLC (www.mriplus.com), July 2009. Used with permission.

Home (Shelter) Magazines Other magazines segment their editorial target in a different way, namely by environmental considerations such as sports, children, or the home. Magazines such as *Better Homes & Gardens,* for example, speak to the interests and concerns of homeowners. By their editorial nature, these magazines tend to be adult and dual-audience oriented. Here again, selectivity of editorial content as well as audience gives the advertiser an opportunity to position a commercial message in a highly compatible environment. The open rate costs for some of these magazines are listed in Exhibit 12-12.

Categorization of these magazines is somewhat arbitrary. One could argue, for example, that *Better Homes & Gardens* is really a general-interest publication based on the duality of the readership. In the final analysis, categorization is not nearly as important as the quantity and quality of the readership, compatibility of editorial with the sales message, and the cost of running the insertion—all of which must be taken into account by the media planner. A cost delivery relationship, however, is a good starting point in categorizing magazines from which to select those to qualify based on editorial content.

Other Magazine Editorial Categories The previous three categories are the largest, but consumer magazines fall into dozens of other editorial categories. Some of these are listed in Exhibit 12-13, along with the number of magazines in each.

EXHIBIT 12-12

Home Magazines: Sample Costs and Circulation

MAGAZINE	COST PG 4/C	CIRCULATION (000)	TOTAL ADULT READERS, AGED 18+ (000)
Better Homes & Gardens	$454,600	7,658	39,018
Martha Stewart Living	154,600	1,954	11,172
House Beautiful	135,251	846	6,307
Traditional Home	172,040	977	4,624
Sunset	108,867	1,236	4,953
This Old House	85,250	976	5,685

Source: Mediamark Research & Intelligence, LLC (www.mriplus.com), July 2009. Used with permission.

EXHIBIT 12-13

Magazine Editorial Categories

EDITORIAL CATEGORY	NUMBER OF MAGAZINES
Adventure and Outdoor Recreation	2
Automotive	11
Babies	3
Boating and Yachting	3
Bridal	3
Business and Finance	9
Computers	3
Entertainment and Performing Arts	7
Epicurean	5
Fashion, Beauty, and Grooming	4
Fishing and Hunting	7
General Editorial	7
Health	5
Home Service and Home	20
Mature Market	2
Men's	14
Motorcycle	3
Music	4
News—Weeklies	7
Parenthood	4
Photography	2
Science and Technology	2
Sports	10
Teen	2
Travel	4
Video and Computer Gaming	2
Women's	19

Source: SRDS, June 2009.

Newspapers

In 2008, there were 1,408 dailies and 905 Sunday newspapers in the United States,[4] in addition to thousands more nondaily newspapers (weekly, biweekly, etc.). While this is down only slightly from 1,483 dailies and 905 Sunday papers 10 years ago, further losses are expected due to the loss of automobile, real estate, help wanted, and other advertising that has moved from newspaper's highly profitable classified sections to the Internet. Readership has also declined with the advent of 24/7 news availability online and younger adults' failure to get into the habit of reading newspapers. Only 27 percent of 18–34 year olds read a daily newspaper compared to 56 percent of adults 55+.[5]

Although this trend is primarily affecting the big-city dailies, their Sunday editions continue to survive. And outside the big city, small-town papers remain profitable by meeting the need to cover high school sports, the police blotter, town council meetings, and all the other local activities that are below the radar of the big city papers.

While the medium is changing, newspapers continue to provide advertisers the distinct benefits of flexibility in adjusting efforts from market to market, quick closing dates, strong local market coverage, and individual market identification. As with other media, newspapers are also highly diverse in the ways they can be bought and the advertising units available for sale. The major categories include run of paper (ROP), supplements, and custom inserts.

Run of Paper ROP advertising can be purchased in virtually any size, from a full page down to just a few inches, in both black-and-white and color. If one color is added to black and white, the premium runs about 10–15 percent. Where available, four-color cost premiums run 20–40 percent. However, it is possible to package certain groups of newspapers to reduce the cost premium or to eliminate it entirely. ROP space is sold by the column inch for a set of standard advertising units (SAU) that ranges from a few inches to a full page. In recent years, specific dimensions have varied by paper.

Supplements Newspaper-distributed Sunday magazines offer the advantages of color reproduction, regional geographic flexibility, and in-home readership during the more relaxed Sunday environment. These publications are preprinted and inserted into the Sunday newspapers. The largest, *Parade* and *USA Weekend*, are

---

4. Newspaper Association of America, "Number of U.S. Daily Newspapers," reprint of *Editor & Publisher* estimate, www.naa.org.
5. Mediamark Research & Intelligence, LLC, Spring 2009.

edited for a general national audience and offer the largest circulation of any publication in the United States. Their costs and circulation levels are shown in Exhibit 12-14. Locally edited Sunday magazines, with the exception of the *New York Times Magazine*, have largely disappeared since the last edition of this book.

The large, general-interest publications are supplemented by more targeted Sunday magazines from the Publishing Group of America. *American Profile* is edited for rural communities. *Relish* is a Sunday food and recipe-oriented magazine. And *Spry* is a lifestyle Sunday magazine that targets women.

EXHIBIT 12-14

Major General-Interest Syndicated Supplements:
Sample Costs and Circulation

MAGAZINE	COST PG 4/C	CIRCULATION (000)	TOTAL ADULT READERS, AGED 18+ (000)
Parade	$960,200	33,000	72,706
USA Weekend	619,445	23,400	48,231

Source: Mediamark Research & Intelligence, LLC (www.mriplus.com), July 2009.

Used with permission.

Custom Inserts In addition to ROP and magazine supplements, newspapers can carry advertising inserts that are printed by outside firms and stuffed into the paper along with the other sections. These inserts can be used in many different forms. They can be printed on fine-quality or inexpensive papers, in many different sizes, used as single sheets or booklets, and printed in many different ways. All of these alternative production techniques allow advertisers to create unique advertising that will communicate whatever they want and can afford. Costs for custom-tailored inserts vary, depending on how elegant they are. Each newspaper charges a different price for stuffing and carrying the inserts. Note that inserts are normally bought by the advertiser as part of its consumer promotion plan, rather than by the ad agency's media planner.

Radio

Radio is offered on a national network basis and on an individual local-market spot basis.

Network Radio Network radio programming available for advertiser sale includes primarily news, music, sports, and politically oriented talk shows. Costs for network radio announcements are comparatively low, averaging about $2,500 for a 30-second announcement, and deliver an average rating of 1.2 to men and 1.0 to women. Note that the standard commercial length for network radio is 30 seconds, while spot radio is based on 60-second units.

Spot Radio Formats of local radio stations vary widely from market to market. In major markets, such as New York, Los Angeles, and Chicago, numerous radio formats appeal to a wide variety of listener interests. Programming ranges from talk shows to various kinds of music formats to total news. In smaller markets, stations concentrate on local news, country music, and music with more general appeal.

As is the case with spot television, the diversity of the medium makes it extremely difficult to generalize about costs. In overall terms, however, spot radio selectively purchased against designated target audiences can be an exceptionally cost-efficient medium for reaching these audiences. Spot radio costs are available from SQAD Radio, using the same computer system that delivers television costs.

Internet

Digital advertising prices are stated as the cost per thousand impressions delivered to the user's browser. As with all media, the price varies substantially, depending on the size of the ad.

Banners By far the most commonly used and least expensive creative unit is the banner ad. Banners are measured in terms of *pixels*—the small, discrete elements that together constitute an image. Exhibit 12-15 shows the most commonly used ad sizes. Typical cost for banners is $20.00 per thousand impressions (persons 2+); however, there is a wide range around this average.

For an additional charge, advertisers can take advantage of a variety of targeting options to deliver banners customized to the person visiting the site. For example, visitors in a given zip code could be shown ads for travel to featured vacation spots. Business travelers (more precisely, visitors whose cookie indicates that this computer was used to book airline tickets for business) could be shown a banner with promotional rates to business centers.

EXHIBIT 12-15

Commonly Used Digital Advertising Units

Banners and Buttons

    468 × 60—Full Banner
    234 × 60—Half Banner
    88 × 31—Micro Bar
    120 × 90—Button 1
    120 × 60—Button 2
    120 × 240—Vertical Banner
    125 × 125—Square Button
    728 × 90—Leaderboard

Rectangles and Pop-Ups

    300 × 250—Medium Rectangle
    250 × 250—Square Pop-Up
    240 × 400—Vertical Rectangle
    336 × 280—Large Rectangle
    180 × 150—Rectangle
    300 × 100—3:1 Rectangle
    720 × 300—Pop-Under

Skyscrapers

    160 × 600—Wide Skyscraper
    120 × 600—Skyscraper
    300 × 600—Half-Page Ad

Source: Internet Advertising Board (www.iab.com).

Rich Media With the maturing of the Internet, the effectiveness of banners has fallen off sharply. Typically, far less than 1 percent of people exposed to a banner will click through to the advertiser's website. As indicated in the sample rate card, websites are offering larger and more creative units (wide banners, skyscrapers, wraparounds, and others) in hopes of improving response. But the most effective technique employs sound, motion, and intrusiveness to get the user's attention. These so-called *rich media* employ a variety of visual elements:

- Animated banners, moving cartoons, flashing words, alternating colors, and other effects
- Streaming banners that display a continuous stream of text such as a newswire or video
- Streaming audio banners that play a commercial or audio track when the banner is presented
- Pop-up ads that appear when a page is requested but before it has completely loaded (sometimes called *interstitial ads* because they are delivered between the pages of requested content)

Rich media ads experience higher click-through rates than banners. However, they are considerably more expensive, and they are not accepted by all websites. Furthermore, as the use of rich media increases, there is the possibility of user backlash against interruptions to Internet browsing. Also, many browsers employ pop-up filters that prevent banners and rich media ads from appearing, increasing the time it takes to deliver the planned impressions.

Other Digital Advertising There are many other ways of using the Internet. These include site sponsorships and targeted e-mail. To address concerns about user backlash, some advertisers use "opt-in" advertising, delivered only if the user requests to see certain kinds of advertising. Another option is to use direct links to the advertiser's website from words in the site's content or from a logo display.

Out-of-Home Media

Out-of-home media come in a wide range of availabilities that differ dramatically in size and location. Out-of-home media are the most local of all media forms, inasmuch as one advertising unit can be purchased in one very specific location geographically. The most popular varieties of out-of-home media are poster panels, painted bulletins, and transit advertising.

Poster Panels A *poster panel* is an outdoor advertising structure on which a pre-printed advertisement is displayed. The most widely used poster sizes are standard, junior, and 3-sheet. The standard poster, or 30-sheet poster, measures approximately 12 feet high by 25 feet long. The junior panel, or 8-sheet poster, is about one-fourth the size of a standard poster. The 3-sheet poster is used extensively at transit or train stops. It is 60 inches by 46 inches.

Poster panels are generally sold in packages of daily GRPs, called *showings*. For example, a 50-GRP package, or "50 showing," will deliver in one day exposure opportunities equal to 50 percent of the population of the market. The cost for posters varies tremendously from one market to another, and often from one location to another in a given market. The cost to purchase a 50 showing for one month in standard 30-sheet posters in the top 10 markets of the United States is approximately $1.5 million. The same purchase encompassing the top 50 markets is about $3.8 million.[6]

As noted in Chapter 11, the outdoor industry is developing a new metric that will be used as the basis for outdoor sales using impressions and GRPs. The objective is to measure the medium with the same language as television. Given the long tradition of measuring outdoor media in terms of showings, it remains to be seen if the conversion to demographic GRPs will be successful.

Painted Bulletins A *painted bulletin* is an outdoor advertising structure that is painted with the advertising copy. "Paints" are generally larger than posters and measure, on average, 14 feet high by 48 feet wide. Paints are sold both individually and in packages. The cost for one painted bulletin can range from as low as $3,000 in smaller markets to more than $20,000 in high-traffic areas of larger markets for an average month.

There are basically two types of paint availabilities: permanent and rotary. In the case of a permanent paint, the advertiser buys the specific location for one or more years, and the units vary in size. Permanent paints are usually in the most desirable locations, along the most heavily traveled highways, and are priced accordingly. Because existing advertisers have the right of first refusal when their contracts come up for renewal, the best locations are rarely available to new advertisers. The rotary bulletin is moved from location to location within a market on a set schedule (30-, 60-, or 90-day cycles, depending on the market). Rotary locations are typically in high-traffic areas along expressways and major arteries, giving advertisers broad exposure to the market over the purchased cycle. They are sold individually or in packages.

Transit Advertising Transit advertising is available on buses, taxi cabs, trains, and in carrier terminals (train stations, airline terminals, etc.) in selected cities. Numerous sizes and shapes can be purchased, including spectaculars that cover the entire bus. Advertising costs vary depending on the market, the medium, the size of the advertisement, the length of the purchase, and the scope of the purchase.

Out-of-Home Video Display In the past few years a new form of outdoor advertising has been made possible by the size and flexibility of out-of-home video display

6. BPI Communications, *Marketer's Guide to Media*, 2009.

units. These are placed in public spaces where constant traffic presents an opportunity to extend the reach of a conventional advertising campaign. These places include shopping malls, gas stations, grocery stores, movie theater lobbies, elevators in office buildings, restaurant restrooms, bookstores, cafeterias, and so on. The SeeSaw Networks (www.seesawnetworks.com) offers more than 30 different venues. The Digital Place-based Advertising Association (DPAA, www.ovab.org) was created to help marketers and their agency partners more easily evaluate, plan, and buy this media as part of their overall communications strategies. Their guidelines bring consistency to the measurement of this highly diversified new medium.

Media-Buying Problems

The television media planner works with dayparts, GRPs, reach, frequency, scheduling, and geographic weight to accomplish the brand's marketing objectives. But the plan only says that *this* many GRPs will be purchased for *that* much money. It is the job of the professional buyer to decide which programs will carry the advertising. The buyer is responsible for placing the commercials on programs that will deliver the desired GRPs within the allotted budget. Knowledge of how media sell their product is vital both for the development of the plan and for its ultimate implementation. This section discusses some of the timing and buying implications associated with various media. Here again, as in the case of cost estimating, the major distinction rests between broadcast and print.

Network TV

Network television is a negotiated medium; it is bought and sold somewhat like a commodity on the commodities exchange. The market for network television is a supply-and-demand market whose goods are highly perishable. A minute not sold is a minute wasted, resulting in lost revenue for the network. Consequently, the first problem the network television buyer must consider is timing. Other factors include packaging and costs.

Timing Incorrect timing and mistakes in assessing when to buy can lead to severe implementation problems. For example, if the network buyer waits too long before committing the designated budget, all of the availabilities could be exhausted, thus leaving nothing to buy. Generally, the earlier the network buy is initiated, the more likely the buyer will obtain desired programming in terms of audience delivery and stability. The longer the buyer waits before committing to a buy for a specified period, the less likely it is that the most desirable programming will be available.

Waiting does, however, increase the possibility of lower pricing for the inventory that remains if demand is low.

The ideal time to buy is when sellers are anxious to sell, just before others enter the market. In general, in a seller's year, an advertiser should buy early, before prices rise and quality inventory is gone. In a buyer's year, an advertiser should buy as late as inventory is available and prices are likely to be favorable.

Packaging Network television time can be purchased in packages of shows or by the individual program. Scatter packages—multiple programs with a few commercials per program during the course of the advertising schedule—provide maximum programming dispersion. Therefore, they tend to generate broader reach for the available budget. In addition, scatter packages reduce the risk of not delivering the specified weight levels, because the outcome of the buy is not based on one or two programs achieving their audience levels. In preparing packages, networks typically include a mixture of high-rated prestige programs and new, unproven shows that reduce the overall CPM while still delivering the target audience.

Most network time is purchased as scatter packages, but networks also make individual programs available for sale on a continuity basis. Commercials regularly appearing on one or two shows can be highly effective when the planner can identify the specific audience values in those shows that achieve the objectives of the media plan.

Cost Considerations Determining network costs depends on three factors: (1) demand by advertisers, (2) estimates by both buyer and seller of audience delivery and CPM, and (3) network overhead and expenses in doing business. By far, advertiser demand is the most important determinant of network costs. Seasonal demand and the strength of the network and its programming best illustrate the effect of supply and demand on the network television marketplace. During the time of the year when an advertiser's sales are expected to be greatest, advertising time is in great demand, so network prices are high.

For example, for toy makers, the pre-Christmas season, the fourth quarter of the year, is a time of great seasonal demand. In addition, advertisers generally prefer high-rated, popular programming in any given daypart. Such programming enables them to reach a large audience in a good commercial environment. This preference increases the price for that particular programming. In many cases, it increases pricing for an entire daypart on a network if that particular program dominates the daypart. To deliver the planned rating points within the budget, buyers will accept units in lower-rated, less desirable programs that lack the marquee value but deliver the target audience efficiently.

Another set of key determinants of network pricing consists of the buyer's and seller's estimates of audience delivery and the resulting CPM. In most major agencies, network TV buyers estimate delivery for all network programming before negotiations begin. They base their estimates on consistent tracking of audience shares from week to week to determine audience trends. Network buyers are also aware of any network scheduling changes, new programs, and program cancellations. In addition, the networks project audience delivery. Network projections are usually higher than agency projections.

For example, assume a buy in fall prime time when 45 percent of women are using television (PUT). The dialog between the network salesperson and the agency buyer might run something like this:

> **Network salesperson:** This is a great new show by the same people who developed "Survivor." It's sure to do at least a 12 share and a 5.4 rating.

> **Agency buyer:** Oh, give me a break. Everybody and his brother is doing a "Survivor" knockoff. It'll be lucky to do a 9 share.

Keep in mind that the average woman age 18+ cost per point of network prime time is about $33,585. When the network salesperson says the show will do a 12 share, the rep is saying that a :30 spot will cost $181,359 (.12 $\times$ 45 $\times$ $33,585). The buyer thinks it's worth only $136,019.

When a substantial long-term network buy is made using mutually agreed-upon audience projections, the network normally guarantees delivery. If the network does not meet its guaranteed projections, it must offer compensatory units.

Finally, the network's expenses also affect network pricing. The network will try to cover the cost of programming and business overhead. An expensive production is priced at a premium to offset its costs. In addition, there are mechanical charges for national and regional advertisers. In the past, networks charged an "integration" fee to splice the commercial into its proper place in the tape containing the program. Modern computerized traffic management systems have eliminated this manual operation, but networks continued to impose the charge until 2008, when advertiser pressure forced some networks to drop it. Additional fees are also charged to regional advertisers for the labor of setting up regional feeds, program cut-ins, and regional blackouts.

Buying Network TV

Once the media plan has been approved, the action shifts to the professional media buyers, who must translate into specific programs the television activity that is presented on the flowchart in the general terms of target audience groups, dayparts, and campaign dates. Before a buyer starts to negotiate, planners prepare a set of deal points that have been reviewed by the client. These may include the budget, CPM within a certain price range, guaranteed audience delivery, positioning within a commercial pod or publication, added-value merchandising, limitations on objectionable content, cancellation privileges, and anything else the buyer needs. These become part of the advertiser's formal approval to begin the negotiations.

Advertisers purchase network television in three primary ways: up-front (or long-term), scatter (or short-term), and opportunistic (or last-minute) buys.

Up-Front (Long-Term) Buys An *up-front*, or *long-term*, *buy* is the purchase of inventory for all four quarters of the coming broadcast year. Advertisers' dollars are committed up front in the spring or summer for the following television season, which begins in September. Up-front buying usually involves a guaranteed audience delivery, expressed as a guaranteed cost-efficiency and consisting of premium inventory. If the purchased programs fail to deliver the expected rating points, the networks will honor the contract by offering additional "audience deficiency" commercial units at no charge. Committing dollars in the up-front market gives the advertiser insurance against sellouts but little flexibility with regard to possible cancellation. At best, networks will generally grant cancellation options on a portion of the last half of a long-term buy.

Scatter (Short-Term) Buys A *scatter*, or *short-term*, *buy* is the purchase of inventory within a specific quarter, made before the start of that quarter. Scatter buys are negotiated on a quarterly basis and give the buyer a better fix on the marketplace. That is, the buyer knows pricing from the up-front market as well as pricing from the previous quarter. Scatter buys offer the advertiser more financial flexibility, with dollar commitment required only one to two months before the air date. Buying scatter does, however, involve inventory and efficiency risks, because the best inventory might already be sold. Also, scatter has historically tended to be less efficient (priced higher) than the up-front market. Finally, networks rarely guarantee scatter buys.

Opportunistic Buys *Opportunistic buys* involve the purchase of inventory on a last-minute basis if the networks have any remaining inventory to sell. Opportunistic buys depend on the availability of inventory. So they carry the risk of being shut out of the market when the exposure is needed. On the positive side, these buys can sometimes be very efficient, because the networks are trying to get rid of last-minute inventory just prior to air date.

Other Types of Network Buys Occasionally, advertisers purchase network television programs on a full or partial *sponsorship* basis. A full sponsorship involves purchase of all of the commercial time available in one or more telecasts of a program. Partial sponsorship requires purchase of at least three or four 30-second units of commercial time in one or more telecasts of a program.

In the early days of television, sponsorship was common. Today, although very few hours of network television are fully sponsored, partial sponsorship is common. Sponsorships have several advantages. Audiences identify the sponsor with the program. The advertiser gains additional exposure in the form of opening and closing billboards. Sponsors may be able to use cast members in commercials. Sponsorship also can enable participation in high-quality programming. Sponsorship is especially valuable for advertisers with multiple divisions and product lines where brands with minimal advertising budgets can get high-visibility exposure.

However, sponsorships are generally expensive. Also, the advertiser takes a chance that the program will not do well. An additional drawback is that audience reach is limited with a single program, compared to spreading the buy over a variety of programs.

Special-event network programming can be purchased unit by unit or as program sponsorship. Specials such as holiday parades, election night coverage, and award presentations provide a good environment for new-product introductions and for seasonal advertisers because they frequently have mass audience appeal and high visibility. In general, special-event programming carries a premium price.

Network regional time also is available. In a regional network buy, an advertiser buys only a portion of the country, and another advertiser or advertisers buy the rest. Regional network availabilities can benefit advertisers who seek certain types of programming identification, have products with less than national distribution, or are introducing new products to specific regions. Regional network time purchases are generally difficult to execute and involve considerable planning and discussions with the network sales departments. An alternative for national advertisers with multiple product lines is to purchase a unit that covers the entire country, then use regional feed patterns to deliver different commercial messages to different parts of the country.

Finally, once the buyer and network salesperson come to an agreement on exactly what programs will be purchased, the expected rating of each telecast, the associated cost, and all the other details of the buy, the order is put "On Hold." The network reserves this inventory for the advertiser with the expectation that a legally binding commitment will follow within 24–48 hours. This gives the advertiser a final opportunity to review the buy, ensure the money to pay for it is available, and that it meets the advertiser's marketing needs. While it is technically possible for an advertiser to drop the hold, doing so is akin to not showing up for a wedding, with the resulting bad reputation for future orders.

Spot TV

The United States has 210 spot television markets (DMAs) with more than 1,200 commercial television stations. The number of stations per market, which directly influences spot inventory, ranges from a high of 11 in Los Angeles to 3 or 4 stations in many small markets.

Major markets with multiple stations offer a considerable spot inventory from which to select. The multiplicity of spot commercial availabilities in such markets allows the buyer to be somewhat selective about programming and timing. Spot schedules are generally purchased two weeks to two months in advance of the start date of the schedule. Spot time can be bought for specified flight periods or on a continuing basis until canceled. Most station contracts call for cancellation notice to be given four weeks before the end of a schedule.

Syndicated TV

Syndication is bought much like network television: the advertiser makes one national buy. However, unlike buys for network television, syndication buys can include either packages of time on several shows or time purchased on one program. Here again, the percentage of national coverage varies by syndicated property, and pricing varies according to coverage, projected performance, and demand. Audience delivery guarantees are often available.

Cable TV

Cable TV is negotiated the same way as network TV—the buy is negotiated on a CPM efficiency basis with a guaranteed audience delivery. Like network TV, the cable networks are pitted against each other during negotiations to provide the best possible pricing. The cable marketplace is unique because each network has limited mass appeal. Except for the cable networks that program like network TV (e.g., USA), most target specific demographic groups. Nevertheless, it is possible to pit these niche networks against each other in negotiations, as long as the buyer is not particular about program environment. As noted earlier, most advertisers spread their cable buy across multiple networks—often more than 20 nets to ensure adequate reach of the national buy.

Cable can also be purchased market by market in the same manner as spot TV, but the process is far more complicated. Orders must be placed, one at a time, on each cable system that serves an area. Although this allows very precise geographic targeting, managing the price negotiation, purchase, stewardship, and payment for potentially thousands of low-cost commercial units is highly inefficient. In addition, because the ratings are generally less than 1.0, and because of the small Nielsen sample in spot markets, no local ratings are available for most cable programs. This makes local cable a valuable medium for retail advertisers, which can measure its effectiveness by store traffic. Local cable is less useful for national advertisers that do not need spot cable's geographic targeting capabilities.

Magazines

Although magazines publish a rate card in SRDS, the medium has become extremely negotiable, especially for high-volume advertisers. Most national publications accept space reservations guaranteeing that advertising space will be available in the desired issues. Space reservations can be made almost any time in advance of the issue. The final date for contracting to appear in a given issue is called the closing date. This date varies by publication. Closing dates for monthly magazines will generally be 45 to 60 days in advance of the issue date. Closing dates for weekly publications normally fall about three to seven weeks prior to issue.

National magazines provide regional and test-market circulation breakouts for achieving coverage in specified geographic areas. The regional availability can include multiple states or just a limited area, such as New York City. The rest of the circulation carries either another advertiser or editorial material. Magazines also make available test-market circulation breakouts that conform closely to television market coverage patterns, thus permitting test translations of national plans into local test areas. Normally, advertisers must secure costs and availabilities of such special breakouts from the magazines before placing an order, because the numbers are subject to change. Media Networks, Inc. (www.mni.com), allows advertisers to place an ad in the copies of national magazines that are distributed to individual DMAs.

Many magazines also make available what are called *A and B copy splits.* This means two different blocks of copy can appear in alternate copies of the magazine in the same issue. These copy splits provide opportunities to test alternative copy approaches, or different brands can use splits when national coverage is desired and half of the circulation is considered adequate for each brand. Some magazines also make available demographic breakouts. Such demographic editions allow advertisers to place ads only in copies going to physicians, businesspeople, or some other breakout provided by the publication.

As media planners continue their education, they should keep abreast of the flexibilities provided by the ever-changing publishing industry.

Newspapers

Unlike magazines, newspapers are not generally considered a negotiable medium for national advertisers. The rate card sets the price, and that is what advertisers pay. Large local advertisers (supermarket chains, major retail stores, shopping centers, and others with a specific local street address) negotiate prices at the (unpublished) local rate. Those prices are significantly lower than what is paid by national advertisers. This can lead to intricate negotiations when national advertisers such as fast-food chains buy newspaper space on behalf of their local franchisees.

Space closing for ROP space is only a few days before the actual issue. If a special unit is desired, such as a two- or four-color half-page, then additional time in ordering such space is generally required. However, the advance notice to the newspapers is still relatively short, compared with the longer closing dates of national magazines.

Newspapers have been very aggressive in developing special sections geared to various audiences and issues. For example, many food advertisers look for what is called the "Best Food Day." Best Food Day in most markets is Wednesday or Thursday, the days that major food chains schedule their advertising. The advertising is positioned adjacent to the special editorial sections that the consumer is likely to read before going to market. Positions within these sections are generally available at no extra cost.

Other sections that can be advantageous in reaching selected audiences include sports, business, and special features on fashion, grooming, and home care. In addition to such regular opportunities for positioning, newspapers offer availabilities for special preprints, such as card stock inserts. In most cases, the advertiser provides the particular preprint to the newspaper. Such advertising units have to be ordered well in advance to ensure space availability.

Radio

Network radio programming tends to offer relatively few format types, such as news and sports, some special events, and personality commentators. Network radio is purchased in the same way as network television: that is, with a contractual obligation for a specified number of commercials over a designated period.

Spot radio provides different buying opportunities in view of the tremendous selectivity and diversity of programming and stations in many major markets. Arbitron rating information is available in most markets but does not provide the total picture in buying radio. The number of men, women, and teenagers listening at various times to specific radio stations can be identified. However, the format—whether contemporary music, country-western, stock market reports, weather, or sports—can be an important factor influencing station selection. The planner must rely heavily on the buyer's experience in executing a local-market radio buy and ensuring a close match among the commercial copy, audience, and station format.

Arbitron is the primary source of local radio ratings; however, Eastlan measures the audience in more than 100 markets from the smallest to midsize markets such as Green Bay, WI. Additional information is available from their website, www.east lan.com.

In a recent development, The Nielsen Company has begun measuring spot radio audiences in 51 small to midsize markets using a modified diary technique. The service has picked up large radio station groups, including Clear Channel and Cumulus. This service can be seen as expanding to challenge Arbitron.

Internet

An Internet ad campaign can involve dozens of websites and potentially millions of ad impressions rotated among numerous creative executions to multiple target audiences. This daunting task has led to the emergence of *third-party ad servers* such as DoubleClick Inc. (www.doubleclick.com) and Atlas Solutions (www.atlas solutions.com). These services automate the execution of digital advertising programs. For an additional 40–50 cents per thousand, they assist in planning, budgeting, insertion order generation, creative trafficking, and post-buy analysis. Planners tell the ad server which sites they have bought, the number of impressions to be delivered on each, the creative executions and rotation instructions, and the target audience. Then when called on, the server delivers an ad to the user's Web browser. When the contracted number of impressions have been delivered, the server bills the advertiser.

Although the medium has matured, there remain numerous issues and shortcomings to the audience measurement. One relates to the simple act of counting impressions. The ad server maintains a count of the ads that it delivers, and the website maintains its own count. The two invariably disagree because there is no standard way of counting exposures. For example, one may count ads when they are sent out (even if the user clicks away while it is still downloading), while the other counts an ad only when it has been successfully displayed. The magnitude of the discrepancy can range from just a few hundred impressions up to a significant proportion of the campaign.

The Internet is a continually evolving medium. It is beyond the scope of this book to go into greater detail regarding Internet buying and planning. The basic tools were covered in Chapter 11. The fundamentals of audience size, coverage, composition, reach, cost efficiency, and frequency are timeless. Beyond that, unlike traditional media, the capabilities of the Internet change so quickly and so often that a hardcover textbook, with a gap of almost a year between writing these words and their appearance in print, cannot hope to be an authoritative guide. Social networking, Twitter, mobile Internet, YouTube, Hulu, pre-roll video advertising, and a host of other services and tools have become available just in the past few years— each have their own value and procedures for use as advertising vehicles. Others will surely emerge between this writing and when it is published, not to mention during the edition's several years of life.

There is not even consensus in the industry about where the online planning function should reside. Some agencies see online as just another medium, to be planned along with radio, TV magazines, and the other traditional media. Others see it as an online group within a planning department—people responsible for the online portion of a media plan, but working side-by-side with the traditional planners. Still others see online as such a specialty that it can be handled only by a company whose sole expertise is planning and buying online media. Wherever Internet planning is handled, it is clear that anyone involved with online media should stay current with the industry, participate in seminars held by the Interactive Advertising Bureau (www.iab.net), and maintain contact with the representatives of the online publishers.

CHAPTER THIRTEEN

Setting and Allocating the Budget

Despite the time and thought that have been given to it, one of the most difficult tasks facing advertising and agency planners is that of determining the optimum amount of money to spend for advertising. The main difficulty in determining the budget size is that no one knows precisely how a given amount of money spent for advertising will affect sales or other marketing goals. In a timeless explanation, media expert Herbert D. Maneloveg summarized the problem as follows:

> Our major problem, I believe, is that we really don't know how much advertising is enough. And we haven't done much about trying to find out. Not until lately. When someone asks about the amount of advertising pressure needed to make a potential consumer aware of the merits of a brand, we fumble and grope. When asked to justify an increase or decrease in advertising budget, we are lost because of an inability to articulate what would happen with the increase or decrease: if sales go up, we credit advertising; if sales go down, we blame pricing, distribution, and competition.[1]

In other words, there is no simple cause-and-effect relationship between the amount of money spent and the sales results that are supposed to occur because of the expenditure. Some manufacturers have learned from experience how much money they should spend to obtain a desired share or sales volume at a given time. But even these manufacturers do not assume the relationship will remain constant

---

1. Herbert D. Maneloveg, "How Much Advertising Is Enough?" *Advertising Age* (June 6, 1966): 30.

at all times. At some time or other, they and most other advertisers are in the same quandary about how much to spend on advertising.

What further complicates the matter is that each brand usually has a number of competitors whose changing activities make it difficult to anticipate correctly what they will do. The dynamic marketplace situation makes the task of budget setting—including having to estimate probable competitors' activities and allow a portion of money for contingencies—difficult for most advertisers.

Finally, advertising is not the only factor that contributes to the sale of a product. Other elements of the marketing mix, such as pricing, sales promotion, personal selling, and packaging, also play a role. But who can separate the precise contribution of advertising from the effects of the other marketing mix elements?

Despite these problems, advertising budgets must be established, and the task is performed based on as much knowledge as is available at the moment. This chapter outlines some of the major methods and problems of setting budgets, along with their advantages and disadvantages.

Setting the Budget

Before they begin, planners must be absolutely clear about what the advertising budget is expected to cover. Many marketing executives consider promotional brochures, sales meetings, coupon redemption, and even coffee cups or T-shirts to be part of advertising. This is in addition to the obvious advertising-related expenses of commercial production, talent charges, print production, and so on. Regardless of how the budget is determined, in the end planners need to know how much money is available for "working media," that is, the cost of advertising time and space.

They must also know if this figure is "gross" or "net." Gross means that the cost includes agency commission. The agency bills the advertiser the gross amount, but pays the media 85 percent, the net charge—this is a privilege granted to formally recognized advertising and media agencies. If the advertiser bought directly from the media, they would pay the gross price. Virtually all traditional media prices are gross.

Sometimes, especially for online media, the costs are expressed as net and do not build in a 15 percent commission for the ad agency. Planners might be asked to go the other way and calculate what the gross cost would have been. The formula is simple:

$$\text{Gross cost} = \text{Net cost} \times 1.1765$$

Planners also need to know the dates of the advertiser's budget or "fiscal" year. For some, this is a standard calendar year beginning on January 1, but for others, the year may begin on July 1, or on September 1 with the start of the school year, or it may be tied to governmental years, which begin on October 1. Whatever the dates, the media plan and flowchart must reflect these budgeting realities.

In most media flowcharts, weeks are expressed in terms of the broadcast calendar. Weeks begin on Monday, and months end with the final Sunday, even if a few days after that fall in the next nomth. This decades-old convention greatly simplifies media billing. In this section we will discuss the various methods of determining budget size—both traditional and nontraditional—as well as several of the factors that must be considered in the budgeting process.

Traditional Methods of Budget Setting

A number of methods are widely used to determine the budget: percent of sales, competitive spending, objective and task, expenditure per unit, and the subjective judgment of what is affordable. Those used most often tend to be simple to understand and quick and easy to compute. In the ideal situation, these different methods will yield roughly similar budget levels.

Exhibit 13-1 reports on an international study of budgeting methods used by the top 100 advertisers in Canada, the United Kingdom, and the United States. About half of these advertisers used several methods, but the most commonly used was "objective and task," either on its own or in combination with other methods (most often the affordable and percent-of-sales methods). These will be discussed in detail in the following sections.

Percent of Sales   To arrive at budget amounts, the *percent-of-sales method* multiplies projected sales revenue for the year by a given percentage to be spent on advertising. The amount of money available for advertising purposes, therefore, is based directly on the sales achievement of the brand. As sales increase, so does the advertising budget. If sales decline, the budget also declines. The heart of this method is the *multiplier,* the percentage by which the sales base is multiplied. In determining which percentage to use, one must consider the cost of goods and the pricing policy of each industry. If a brand costs 15 cents to manufacture and distribute and sells for $1.25, a considerable margin is available for advertising, promotion, and profit.

The first step in setting a budget based on percent of sales is to determine the expenses incurred in manufacturing and distribution. The difference between this cost and the selling price helps determine the margin available for advertising,

EXHIBIT 13-1

Methods Used by Top 100 Advertisers to Set Advertising Budgets

BUDGETING METHOD	NUMBER OF COMPANIES USING METHOD*	PERCENT OF TOTAL USAGE
Objective and task	61	32%
Affordable	41	21
Percent of anticipated sales	32	17
Percent of last year's sales	10	5
Unit sales	9	5
Competitive relative	25	13
Competitive absolute	13	7
Total usage	191	100%

Sample base: 100 completed questionnaires (Canada, 36; United States, 36; United Kingdom, 28).

*Amounts add to more than 100 because 52 companies gave multiple responses.

Source: C. L. Hung and Douglas C. West, "Advertising Budgeting Methods in Canada, the UK, and the US," *International Journal of Advertising*, vol. 10, no. 3 (1991).

promotion, and profit. (There are, of course, other costs to be factored in, such as overhead.) Smaller margins mean a smaller percentage available for advertising.

The key to this method of setting budgets is finding the best multiplier. This multiplier is often set arbitrarily. At other times, industry standards are used as a base. Advertising Age Data Center publishes advertising/sales ratios every year for data center subscribers at www.adage.com/datacenter.

The percent-of-sales method of budgeting might appear to be totally inflexible. This is not true. Often the percent of sales is only the starting point. After the percentage is multiplied by gross sales, the total can be adjusted to compensate for special marketing situations. When there are special marketing needs, extra dollars are added. Some companies, instead of adding to the total, will raise the multiplier when they are introducing a new product or when they are faced with very heavy competition. In some instances, however, the percentage multiplier remains constant year after year, no matter how much sales vary. When this happens, the multiplier tends to become a historical figure that is rarely questioned.

The multiplier is also affected by product pricing. Sales of low-ticket products such as drugs or supermarket items depend heavily on advertising, while high-ticket items such as appliances, cars, and home furnishings are less dependent on advertising. A guideline for determining whether the multiplier should be large or small is that the more advertising is used as a substitute for personal selling, the higher the multiplier (or the higher the margin to advertising).

The percent-of-sales budgeting method is easy to manage and understand. It is self-correcting as sales volume changes, and it can maintain a consistent profit margin. It also is suitable for both financial and marketing group needs.

However, there are many criticisms of the percent-of-sales method. For one, it seems illogical, because advertising is based on sales, rather than the other way around. When sales decline, the company will spend less for advertising, when perhaps it should spend more. Also, unless the advertising-to-sales ratios are analyzed by area, better sales areas will tend to get better and weaker sales areas will get little relief. This technique also assumes there is a direct linear relationship between advertising and sales, which is seldom true despite its intuitive appeal.

Another criticism of this method is that it does not encourage companies to provide the research money needed to find the relationship between advertising and sales. The advice offered by marketing expert Alfred A. Kuehn holds true:

> Perhaps the best of these rules [methods of setting budgets] for an established brand is "budget a percentage of expected sales equal to the industry average." This rule is of particular interest since it is self-adjusting over time, and appears to be a low-risk policy for a firm that does not have a better understanding of the effects of advertising than do its competitors.[2]

On the other hand, if all competitive brands used this method and employed about the same multiplier, advertising budget sizes would be approximately proportional to market share, thus limiting investment spending for advertising warfare among competitors.

Competitive Spending The *competitive spending method* depends on setting the budget in relation to the amount of spending by competing brands. The amount to be spent need not be precisely the same as that of competitors, though at times it is. Sometimes, a brand that has a smaller market share than its competitor receives

---

2. Alfred A. Kuehn, "A Model for Budgeting Advertising," *Mathematical Models and Methods in Marketing* (Homewood, IL: Richard D. Irwin, 1961): 315–16.

a budget that is equal to or greater than the competitor, as a means of improving its share position.

A major criticism of this approach is that it assumes competitors know what they are doing or competitors' goals are the same as one's own. It also assumes, incorrectly, that a simple increase in advertising expenditures will automatically increase sales, market share, or both. The products of competitors might be different, or at least consumers might perceive them as different, so a company's advertising must work much harder to make sales than competitors' advertising. Certainly, the marketing goals of one company are not the same as another, and the ability of advertising to create sales also is not the same.

Another competitive approach relates a brand's share of spending to its share of market. Because a given brand always loses some customers to competitors, this technique would suggest spending at a level that puts its share of spending a few points above its share of market. For new products or to meet a goal of aggressive growth, the target share of spending could be as much as double the expected share of market. This method hinges on the advertiser's ability to predict the brand's future market share and its competitors' spending levels. It also depends, to some extent, on how the competitive set is defined.

The relationship between share of advertising and share of market is best expressed by James Peckham in his classic analysis of consumer package goods sales, *The Wheel of Marketing*:

> Almost eight out of ten, or 78%, of the successful brand leaders maintained a fifteen year share of advertising expenditures consistent with the brand's share of consumer purchases, thus continually reminding consumers of the brand, its improvements and its usage.[3]

In this book, Peckham presents an easy-to-use process for graphing the relationship between share of voice and share of market. It is called the marketing advertising pattern (MAP). Assuming a stable relationship over the past five years, the MAP can estimate the spending needed to maintain or grow the share of market.

Objective and Task The *objective-and-task method* starts with someone setting specific marketing or advertising objectives. These are costed out, and the total cost represents the budget. Objectives can be sales, share volume levels, revenues expected, income, or profit.

---

3. James O. Peckham, *The Wheel of Marketing*, published by A. C. Nielsen, 1981.

This method has two main criticisms. First, this method finesses the core problem: marketers usually do not know how much money it takes to attain any given objective. Second, the method does not consider the value of each objective and the relationship to the cost of obtaining it. Will the brand still be profitable after spending the money judged necessary to achieve any given objective?

Expenditure per Unit (Case Rate) The *expenditure-per-unit (case rate) method* is a variant of the percent-of-sales method. In this method, the budget is generated as a result of sales, but the base is units sold, not dollar sales. Many of the advantages and disadvantages of the percent-of-sales method apply also to this method. However, there are two additional disadvantages, which follow.

First, unless the method is properly handled, the company might lose control of profits. This is particularly true if the product or brand has a wide range of sizes or prices. Shell Oil Company, for example, has four types of gasoline, ranging from super regular (premium price) to regular (lowest price). Profitability varies for each. Spending on a cents-per-gallon basis must take into consideration the mix of the line.

The second disadvantage is that working with units and fixed rates of expenditures will not take inflation into account. To overcome this, the case rate must be adjusted from year to year.

Subjective Budgeting *Subjective budgeting* systems involve making decisions on the basis of experience and judgment. The person setting the budget will also consider some objective factors, such as the minimum job that advertising will be required to do or available profit margins. But after such consideration, the final figure is decided on rather subjectively.

One subjective budgeting method is known as "all we can afford." Although at first glance this approach seems illogical or crude, it can be quite realistic if the subjective decision is accurate. This method generally starts by setting a profit percentage or dollar figure and then systematically analyzing the costs of doing business. The remaining figure, after all other costs are accounted for, is spent in marketing, a portion of which is advertising. A budget made on such a basis is difficult to defend, especially when there is reason to believe that if more money had been appropriated, the result would have been higher sales and higher profits.

A boss of mine once remarked that there were two kinds of marketers: those who consider advertising an expense, and those who think of it as an investment. If an expense, the goal is to spend as little as possible, with the same mind-set as one would approach buying gas and electric utilities, supplies, and office equipment. As an investment, however, the money spent on advertising is expected to return many times that amount in sales. The approach taken will color all thinking and can set the tone for the entire advertiser–media planner relationship.

Experimental Methods of Budget Setting

Some marketing and advertising professionals believe that the best way to determine the size of an advertising budget is by testing various levels of expenditures to see which will produce the most sales at the lowest total cost. The experimental designs for this purpose range from a simple before-and-after test in one market to elaborate designs in which many markets are tested and compared with control markets. Although the details of such experiments are usually kept secret, occasionally some are publicized.[4]

Essentially, experimental tests involve trying different advertising expenditure levels in different markets. In some experimental situations, advertisers discover that they can reduce advertising expenditures without any effect on sales. In other situations, increases in advertising produce varying degrees of sales increases.

In one example, Anheuser-Busch used three sets of markets (each set consisting of nine individual markets) to test alternative expenditure levels and measure the sales effects. In one set of markets, advertising expenditures were reduced from 50 percent to 100 percent below the level that ordinarily would have been used in those markets. In another group of markets, the budget was increased at rates ranging from 50 percent to as much as 300 percent. A third group was control markets, meaning there was no increase or decrease in normal advertising expenditures.

If the experimental method is indeed as effective as some individuals assume it to be, why is it not used more often to determine budget size? There are a number of reasons. George H. Brown, former director of the U.S. Census Bureau and a marketing expert, cited two problems involved with this method. The first is the relatively high cost of conducting the experiment, which involves finding and measuring a fairly large sample. The second problem is the long time span required, perhaps a year or more. By the time the experiment is completed, the marketing situation might have changed, making the final figures irrelevant. Brown also pointed out that although the cost might not be considered too high if the payoff is accurate and valuable, the payoff might not be worth the cost.

---

4. Malcolm A. McNiven, "Choosing the Most Profitable Level of Advertising" (case study), in *How Much to Spend for Advertising* (New York: Association of National Advertisers Inc., 1969); Thomas M. Newell, "What Is the Right Amount to Spend for Advertising?" in *Papers from the 1968 American Association of Advertising Agencies Regional Convention*, Palm Springs, Calif., October 6–9, 1968.

While this may be true for traditional media and products sold through traditional channels, different sales approaches can be readily tested for those sold on the Internet. Copy can be changed almost instantly to reflect the creative approach and online venues that deliver the greatest number of sales, leads, click-throughs, or whatever else is used as a success metric. Successful techniques can be used as long as they work and be replaced when their effectiveness inevitably declines.

Chapter 14 covers the subject of experiments and testing in detail.

Factors in Determining the Size of an Advertising Budget

Although it is not possible to determine a budget size scientifically, it is advisable to approach the task by weighting a number of factors that might affect the budget size. Setting a budget in this manner can be called *atomistic* in that one could think about each factor separately and then assemble these factors into a final budget figure.

In weighting each factor, planners will find some are more important than others, suggesting that priorities for marketing the brand must be determined first. Furthermore, each factor must be judged on the basis of whether one should spend more than, the same as, or less than the previous year. Again, this is a subjective decision, but it might help the executive arrive at a final figure more easily. A brief discussion of these factors follows.

Assessing the Task of Advertising Before deciding on any figure, it is reasonable to determine what role advertising is to play. Must it do the selling job alone, or will it be added to other marketing mix elements such as reduced prices and sales promotion? If advertising must do the selling job alone, the size of the budget will have to be substantial. If it works with other marketing mix elements, the size of the budget will be less.

Important in this consideration is an understanding of the power of advertising to sell the brand. Some brands simply are not sensitive to advertising. They may be too much like other brands on the market or may lack a unique selling proposition. Or perhaps it is difficult to be creative in presenting the message through print or broadcast media.

Long- and Short-Term Goals To some extent, long- and short-term goals are set for advertising. However, when the objective is to build an image, then the budget should be treated as an investment rather than as an expense (as one would treat the budget for short-term goals). If both goals are required at the same time, then more money is required, because the advertising has a dual function. The advertising copy for immediate sales differs markedly from the copy whose goal is to build an image.

In a sense, however, the concept of dividing an advertising budget into an expense for immediate sales and an investment for long-term image building is invalid. Image-building advertising might not consist of special ads that are designed for that purpose. If the brand image is thought of as a "long-term investment in the reputation of a brand," then every ad that is run, no matter whether it opts for immediate sales or future image, contributes to that long-range goal.

The goals of the company and advertising's relationship with them affect to some degree the amount of money to be spent. Companies perceive this relationship somewhat differently, so no general principle can be extracted.

Profit Margins   People in the industry assume that where there are larger profit margins, there will be larger advertising budgets. The converse is also assumed to be true. Profit margins are a limiting factor in setting marketing and advertising goals: what one would like to do cannot be done, simply because there is not enough money available to do it. It is ironic that when profit margins must be increased, advertising expenditures also should be increased, but there is little or no money available to do the job.

Degree of Product Usage   Products that are used nationally require more money for advertising than those whose usage is limited to a relatively small geographic area. However, some local and regional advertisers find it necessary to invest heavily in their marketing area to keep up with heavy competitive spending. This is often the case for fast-food firms and automobile dealers. Spending should be evaluated in terms of ad dollars per thousand population, not total dollars, to eliminate the effect of market size.

Difficulty in Reaching Target Markets   Some markets are unique, so no single medium reaches them well. The market for yachts is a good example. Reaching these consumers requires a number of different media in addition to the obvious use of yachting-oriented magazines. Likewise, targets may be so spread out geographically that mass media must be purchased, resulting in enormous message waste. When this occurs, more money is needed to do a reasonable job. And once again we are faced with the coverage/composition trade off.

Frequency of Purchase   Most planners assume that brands or products purchased frequently will require more money for advertising than those that are purchased infrequently. An exception occurs when the advertising goals of infrequently purchased brands call for spending more money for reasons other than frequency of purchase.

Effect of Increased Sales Volume on Production Costs If there is a danger of demand exceeding supply because of advertising's power, the consequence could be that the advertiser will have to build a new plant. In that situation, the amount of money spent for advertising should be limited until the factory is built or another decision is made. The advertiser might want to reduce advertising expenditures until it is possible to supply the demand.

New-Product Introductions It is widely held that new-product introductions take a great deal of additional money to break into the market. How much more depends on the size of the market, the degree of competition, and the desirable qualities of the new brand. A guideline is that introducing a new brand takes at least one and a half times as much as is spent on established brands. Another guideline suggests that the share of spending behind a new product should be about twice the anticipated share of market.

Competitive Activity In markets where competitors are active in advertising and sales promotion, it is necessary to match or even exceed their expenditures, depending on the marketing goals of the brand in question. While the preceding factors do not indicate exactly how much to spend on advertising, they do serve as decision-making guidelines.

Allocating the Advertising Budget

Once the size of the advertising budget has been determined, then it must be allocated, or apportioned, in some reasonable way. When relating advertising to source of sales, advertising budgets are allocated to geographic areas. Many advertisers, however, particularly on a national level, allocate their budgets on the basis of national media selection, with relatively little concern for geographic business skews.

Geographic Allocations
Perhaps the most often used budget allocation technique is to allot at least equal portions to the amount of sales produced by a geographic area. The reasoning behind this method is that one takes a minimal risk in allocating the most dollars to areas where sales are known to have been good. If previous budgets succeeded in

producing or at least contributing to sales, why would not more money (or an equal amount relative to sales) be equally effective? The concept is used not only to keep the risk low, but also to optimize whatever monies are available.

If a geographic area contributed 15 percent of total sales, then this technique assumes that it would get 15 percent of the budget. Of course, there could be a problem here: it is possible that much more than 15 percent of the previous year's allocation was necessary to produce 15 percent sales. In such a case, the budget could be based on a different method of allocation, one based on the amount of profit produced by the area in proportion to total profit nationwide. Allocating on the basis of profit is simply another method of distributing effort.

Other methods could be based on the market share contributed by each area or the anticipated sales produced by each area. The numbers could also be composites of a number of marketing variables, such as population, income, retail sales of the product class, and other related variables.

In practice, formula methods of allocating budgets tend to be only the starting point, rather than the endpoint, of the allocation procedure. The numbers usually must be adjusted to take into consideration special marketing problems. One such problem could be that the media in a particular area cost much more, proportionally, than in any other part of the country. More money would have to be added to the initial allocation figure to compensate for this problem. Another problem could be that competitors have started to promote more heavily in areas that have been most profitable for the brand in question. This situation, too, requires special adjustments to the original allocation.

To illustrate how a computer formula can solve the problem of allocating an advertising media budget among 210 geographic markets, Exhibit 13-2 shows the geographic allocation model from Interactive Marketing Systems (IMS). It is called the PAL system. Although it has been used for more than 15 years, PAL remains the basic program for determining how much spot weight should go into a market after taking into account the local delivery of network, cable, and syndicated GRPs. The program also includes an estimate of consumer magazine delivery based on each market's percent of national circulation.

In Exhibit 13-2, a national advertiser wants to allocate a budget of $650,000 to both network and spot television in 210 markets. (The author admits the example is old, as the dollar amounts in a more contemporary plan would be many times larger. However, the math and procedures are exactly the same as what is used today.) The total budget was determined by one of the alternatives discussed at the beginning of this chapter.

Is this the end of the allocation process? No. Adjustments now have to be made again, perhaps on a subjective basis such as whether each local market receives an adequate amount of dollars for spot advertising. (See Chapter 8 for a further discussion of weighting techniques.)

Payout Planning

Another kind of budgeting operation that media planners use is called payout planning. A *payout plan* is a budget used in new-product introductions requiring more money than usual to launch a brand. The extra dollars come not only from sales of the brand, but also from allocating the brand's profits to advertising for a limited time.

The following data provide background to the sample payout plan. A new brand could have the following costs and pricing:

	Per Case
Selling price of brand by factory	$12.00
Costs of manufacturing, overhead, and selling the brand	−7.00
Amount available for promotion and profit	$5.00
Normal amount available for promotion	$2.50
Normal amount available for profit	2.50
Full amount available for introducing the new brand: promotion + profit	$5.00

So in new-product introductions, the manufacturer might be willing to forgo profits for a limited time and invest them in advertising, in addition to the usual advertising investment. This practice of investing both promotion and profit funds is called *full available.* In the first months, the brand does not earn enough to pay for its heavy advertising. Therefore, the company in a sense invests in the brand during the early periods of selling. But as the brand begins to sell more, it begins to be in a position to start paying back the investment that the company made. Finally, if everything goes well, the brand will be selling enough of the product to pay back the entire investment and stand on its own as a profit center. When that happens, the full available is divided so that part goes for profits and a portion for advertising.

Following is an explanation of the payout plan shown in Exhibit 13-3. Each paragraph is keyed to the number at the beginning of each row on the plan. Although payout plans are not generally calculated by media-planning personnel, the media planner should be aware of the mechanics insofar as they bear on the final advertising budget.

EXHIBIT 13-2

Television Allocation Analysis: The PAL System

Over four weeks

RANK	MARKET	(1) TV HOMES (%)	(2) BDI	(3) IDEAL DOLLARS (000)	(4) NETWORK DOLLARS (000)	(5) SPOT DOLLARS (UNADJ.)	(6) SPOT DOLLARS (000)	(7) TOTAL DOLLARS (NETWK. + SPOT) (000)
1	New York	8.44%	80	$ 43.9	$ 46.4	$ −2.5	$ 0.0	$ 46.4
2	Los Angeles	5.34	107	37.2	29.4	7.8	5.9	35.3
3	Chicago	3.76	105	25.7	20.7	5.0	3.8	24.5
4	Philadelphia	3.17	126	25.9	17.4	8.5	6.5	23.9
5	San Francisco	2.49	106	17.1	13.7	3.5	2.6	16.3
6	Boston	2.38	118	18.3	13.1	5.2	3.9	17.0
7	Detroit	2.11	103	14.1	11.6	2.5	1.9	13.5
8	Washington, D.C.	1.84	113	13.5	10.1	3.4	2.6	12.7
9	Cleveland	1.78	125	14.5	9.8	4.7	3.5	13.3
10	Dallas–Ft. Worth	1.55	100	10.1	8.5	1.6	1.2	9.7
10- market total		32.87%	103	$220.3	$180.8	$ 39.5	$ 32.0	$212.7
210- market total		100%	100	$650.0	$550.0	$100.0	$100.0	$650.0

Ranked on: Homes (000)

Cost pro rata: TVHH

Column 1. The basis for allocating dollars is the number of households in the market. Presumably, the product being advertised has adult/family appeal. The number of TV households in each market is recorded in this column as a percentage of the total United States.

Column 2. The BDIs of each market come from the client's own records.

Column 3. "Ideal dollars" represents the following formula:

$$\text{Number of TV households} \times \text{BDI} \times \text{Total U.S. budget}$$

$$0.0844 \times 0.80 \times \$650,000 = \$43,900 \text{ for the New York market}$$

Column 4. The cost of network programs in each market is derived by adding the gross impressions of all TV programs that a client intends to buy for each market and converting the sum into a percentage. For the New York market, the network dollars would be $46,400. The sum for the top 10 markets is shown as $180,800; for the entire United States, it is $550,000.

Column 5. In the New York market, the amount of network dollars is greater than the ideal dollars, so the amount is shown as a negative number (-2.5). But in Los Angeles, the differences between network and ideal dollars is positive and is the amount (unadjusted) to spend for spot TV in that market.

Column 6. Only the New York market has no dollars to spend for spot television among the top 10 (because of the negative dollars). (Data for the remaining 209 markets are not shown.) The sum of all negative numbers—like those of New York—is 31.3. (Other negative numbers in markets beyond the first 10 are not shown.) This represents overspending and must be deducted proportionately from all other markets. The formula used to adjust for the 31.3 is the following:

$$\frac{\text{Total spot dollars}}{\text{Total spot overspending}} = 100/131.3 = 76.2\%$$

Therefore, each unadjusted spot dollar is multiplied by 0.762 to arrive at the final amount of dollars to be allocated in each market. In Los Angeles, 7.8 unadjusted spot dollars $\times$ 0.762 = 5.9 dollars. This multiplication is done for every market until the 31.3 overspending is totally reduced. Some markets like New York received only network advertising messages, while most others received both network and spot.

Source: Reprinted with permission of Interactive Marketing Systems (IMS).

| EXHIBIT 13-3 |

A Three-Period Payout Plan

		PERIOD 1	PERIOD 2	PERIOD 3	TOTAL
1.	Time periods				
2.	Size of total market in millions of cases	10	11	12	
3.	Average share for the brand	12%	18%	25%	
4.	Year-end total share for the brand	15%	25%	25%	
5.	Cases (millions) purchased by pipeline	0.4	0.2	0.1	
6.	Cases (millions) purchased at consumer level	1.2	2.0	3.0	
7.	Total shipments from factory (millions of cases)	1.6	2.2	3.1	
8.	Factory income @ $12 a case*	$19.2	$26.4	$37.2	
9.	Less cost @ $7 a case	$11.2	$15.4	$21.7	
10.	Budget (dollars available for promotion and profit)	$ 8.0	$11.0	$15.5	$34.5
11.	Reallocation of budget to place heavier weight in first period	$14.9	$11.7	$ 7.9	$34.5
12.	Percentage of reallocated budget	43%	34%	23%	100%
13.	Allocation of budget to advertising and sales promotion				
	To advertising (85%)	$12.7	$ 9.9	$ 6.7	$29.3
	To sales promotion (15%)	$ 2.2	$ 1.8	$ 1.2	$ 5.2
Total		$14.9	$11.7	$ 7.9	$34.5
14.	Profit (or loss)	($ 6.9)	($ 0.7)	$ 7.6	—
15.	Cumulative investment	($ 6.9)	($ 7.6)	0.6	—

*All dollar figures are in millions. Thus 19.2 = $19,200,000.

1. **Time Periods.** Although the payout plan shows three periods, more or fewer could have been used. Furthermore, these periods could have varied from one to three years in length, or they could have been one to three six-month periods. The timing is a matter of judgment and experience on the part of the planner, who must estimate how long it will take to pay back the money necessary to get the brand launched in the marketplace.

2. **Size of Total Market.** A market can be described in any way suitable to the advertiser. Some advertisers prefer to use cases. Others use pounds of the product, packages, or dollars. The data for the number of cases that will be sold is an estimate, based on trend analysis, modified by the judgment and experience of the advertising executive. If these estimates are wrong, then the payout plan will have to be adjusted accordingly.

3. **Average Share for the Brand.** As a new product is introduced and begins to be purchased by wholesalers, retailers, and consumers, the share of market could vary considerably from month to month. So this percentage represents the average for the year, rather than the total. Either could have been used, but the more modest percentage is probably safer. Again, this is a crucial estimate. If it is incorrect, the plan has to be adjusted immediately.

4. **Year-End Total Share for the Brand.** This figure is shown only as a guide to what the executive hopes to achieve at year-end. It is not used in the calculations, though it could be substituted for average share, as previously mentioned.

5. **Cases Purchased by Pipeline.** The first factory sales could be to pipeline companies such as wholesalers and distributors (depending on how the product is distributed). This group of companies represents a portion of total sales. The amount in the pipeline at any time can be estimated from experience with similar types of products.

6. **Cases Purchased at Consumer Level.** This figure is calculated as the product of the average share expected times the number of cases expected to be sold in the total market: $10,000,000 \times 12\% = 1,200,000$ cases.

7. **Total Shipments from Factory.** Pipeline and consumer purchases are added to find total shipments: $400,000 + 1,200,000 = 1,600,000$ cases for period 1.

8. **Factory Income @ $12 a Case.** The decision was to price a case at $12. To find factory income for each period, this figure is multiplied by the number of cases expected to be sold for the period: $1,600,000$ cases $\times$ $12 per case $= $19,200,000.

9. **Less Cost @ $7 a Case.** To find the total cost, the manufacturing cost per case (set at $7) was multiplied by the estimated number of cases that will be sold: $1,600,000 \times \$7 = \$11,200,000$.

10. **The Budget.** Because the budget is composed of dollars allocated both for promotion and for profit (or full available), the amount of money available for promotion is simply the factory income minus the cost of cases sold per period: $\$19,200,000 - \$11,200,000 = \$8,000,000$. The term *promotion* as used here does not mean sales promotion, but more broadly, advertising and sales promotion. As a result of the subtraction in each period, a given amount of money is available in each. These amounts, when added together, equal $34,500,000.

11. **Reallocation of Budget.** Although $34,500,000 would be available for advertising and sales promotion, the budget as it is shown in row 10 is allocated in a strict mathematical fashion, rather than with an understanding of advertising investment needs. The budget is largest in the third period, but most of

the money is needed in the first period, where extra expenditures usually are needed to launch a brand.

12. **Percentage Budget.** The executive has reallocated the budget total ($34,500,000) in the manner believed necessary. As a result, the executive allocated 43 percent of the $34,500,000 to the first period instead of the 23.2 percent that would have been available if the budget were accepted as shown in row 10: $8,000,000 ÷ $34,500,000 = 23.2%.

13. **Allocation of Budget to Advertising and Sales Promotion.** The allocation is arbitrary, based on what the executive thinks is needed for each. Other executives with a different marketing situation and product might think the proportions should be different. Note that the $29,300,000 for advertising must be further split between commercial production and working media.

14. **Profit (or Loss).** At this point, the company must make an investment in the brand. Since the amount of money available for promotion in period 1 is only $8,000,000 (row 10) and dollars needed for the same period are $14,900,000 (row 11), the company will have to invest an additional $6,900,000. That amount represents a loss for the brand for period 1. The brand now owes the company $6,900,000 for period 1.

    In period 2, the reallocated budget is again more than the brand would earn for that period, $11,700,000 versus $11,000,000. Again the brand loses money, but not as much. If this amount is added to the amount already owed to the company from period 1, the cumulative total for period 2 is now $7,600,000. This means that the company has to give the brand $7,600,000 for the extra amount needed above sales dollars up to the end of period 2.

    However, in period 3, the brand earns enough money ($7,600,000) to pay back the amount the company has given to it. At this point, it has made a profit, paid back the money given to it by the company, and presumably will make a profit to keep it going in period 4. When the brand makes a profit, it pays out money to the company.

Not shown in this example, but what obviously should be included in real situations, is the inflation factor. Money "loaned" to a brand in year 1 is worth more than its face value will be in succeeding years.

Testing, Experimenting, and Media Planning

This final chapter addresses custom-designed research that can help a media planner find answers that are not in syndicated research volumes such as MRI, Simmons, or other services. Essentially, a media planner needs answers to questions such as these:

- In which geographic markets should we place extra money to achieve our marketing objectives?
- Will extra media weight generate enough additional sales to justify the cost?
- Which advertising timing schedule is best for this brand?
- How much money is optimum to achieve the brand's goals?

Tests and Experiments

Most of the research used to evaluate alternative media strategies falls under the general heading of tests and experiments. Briefly defined, a test is a simple field study of some advertising variable. An experiment is a carefully designed study in which the researcher controls and manipulates conditions to see how an experimental variable affects audience behavior.

Why Test or Experiment?

Testing or experimenting is necessary for a number of reasons. The most important reason was stated earlier: to help the planner make decisions. Often the planner is faced with alternatives that are seemingly equal, but there might be differences of opinion between the planner and others (such as account executives or clients) about whether to use a given alternative. A way to resolve these differences is through custom-made research.

Another reason for testing or experimenting is to avoid making costly errors. The rising cost of media time and space and the proliferation of new media alternatives make this more necessary than ever. Furthermore, clients want more and better proof that they are getting their money's worth in media and that optimum media strategies are being used.

Finally, although media planners use numerical data in making decisions, they often modify the data with their own judgment, based on personal experience. But often such personal experience is not broad enough, or the current situation is vastly different from what it was in the past. Planners need research to support their judgment and answer the question of which strategy will work best.

How They Differ

Because both tests and experiments usually involve field studies, they seem to be alike. But tests are quite different from experiments. In advertising or marketing, a *test* is a simple piece of research in which one measures a variable (or treatment) introduced into the market to see what effect it has. Although advertising can be tested in one market, most often it is tested in at least two; each market is given a different treatment. For example, in one market $500,000 could be spent for advertising, while in the other $1 million could be spent, using the same medium in both markets. Results could be measured on the basis of which amount of advertising produced the greatest sales.

At the end of the test, the $1 million might have produced 10 percent more sales than did the smaller figure. Which treatment was better? The answer depends on the decision maker, who on the basis of experience, judgment, or a payout calculation says one expenditure is better than another. In this example, twice as much money yielded only 10 percent more sales, suggesting that the incremental spending was not justified.

The most important characteristic of the test is its simplicity and its minimal controls. Although some attempts are made to see that the two test markets are alike, the nature of testing is simplicity. Not too much trouble is exerted to control extraneous factors that could affect the test's outcome. Testing provides guidelines for decision making, rather than yielding definitive and projectable results.

An *experiment* resembles a test in that similar markets are selected for treatments, but great care is exerted to make sure that the markets are equivalent. Usually the same treatments are assigned to two or more test markets, and usually two or more treatments are used. Finally, the treatments must be assigned at random by using a table of random numbers or, in simple cases, by tossing a coin. Furthermore, for measuring the results of the different treatments, a random sample must be drawn from each test-marketing unit, and two or more replications are made of each advertising treatment.

Using the random sample drawn from each of the test markets, the samples are measured through normal survey techniques to determine the effects of the various treatments. Results from experiments are analyzed much differently from test results. In tests, the percentage of change from one market to the other is probably the most sophisticated analysis. In experiments, data are cast in the form of analysis of variance or some other statistical technique that helps tell the experimenter whether there is a cause-and-effect relationship between the treatment and the result.

Which Is Better?

Testing and experimenting each have advantages and limitations. The experiment provides the highest degree of objectivity. It is better controlled, it excludes the effects of extraneous variables, and it allows statistical inference that is usually more valid than personal judgment.

On the other hand, a test is less expensive than an experiment. Many companies that cannot afford the cost of an experiment still can find answers to their problems by conducting tests. Furthermore, tests usually take less time to conduct than experiments. Often there simply is not enough time for an experiment, but something needs to be learned. A test could provide this information. Then, too, although the test design promises less than an experiment, often what it promises is enough. For example, a planner might simply want some clues, rather than a complete rationale for a decision. Finally, a test is analyzed on the basis of relatively simple logic and reasoning that everyone can understand. Those who use experiments often err by substituting the elegance of their statistics for good, common-sense reasoning. The formulas of statistics are means to an end—not the end. For these reasons, advertisers use tests almost exclusively to obtain guidance and support for their marketing decisions.

Market Mix Modeling

In the late 1990s, with the advent of powerful desktop computers and the availability of detailed grocery store scanner data, some large packaged-goods advertisers began using *market mix modeling*. This technique uses regression analysis to model the effect of a broad range of marketing variables on sales (the dependent variable). Manufacturers assemble vast amounts of information about their products, city by city, and give it to outside consultants such as Marketing Management Analytics (MMA, www.mma.com), which conduct the actual analysis. The data elements (independent variables) include, among others, the following measures:

- Weekly gross rating points (GRPs) by daypart by commercial length
- Product distribution
- Number of grocery store facings
- Price of their own and competitors' products
- Weekly GRPs of the primary competitors
- Dates and values of consumer promotions (coupons, contests, etc.)
- Weather (average weekly temperature) where relevant
- Seasonal influences

With this information, the modeler can generalize from the past to predict what will happen to sales when media weight is increased or decreased. This analysis avoids the need to conduct lengthy and expensive test marketing.

J. P. Beauchamp, senior vice president of Consumer and Shopper Insights at SymphonyIRI (formerly Information Resources, Inc.), passes on the following points regarding market mix modeling and testing:

1. Mix modeling allows a marketer to evaluate each of the discrete marketing elements to scorecard return on investment (ROI) on the same playing field (TV versus print versus trade versus consumer promotion and so on).
2. Test marketing, on the other hand, is very good at isolating the element you want to test (much better than mix), but cannot scorecard the tested element versus other marketing elements unless you add cells to do it.
3. We (our clients and us) will use mix results to help qualify other elements in a test or give additional context to other components of the marketing mix as well as to the element tested.
4. Some clients will use mix to examine small adjustments in spending. The rule of thumb is that you don't want to project outside more than 20 percent of the observed data.

Market mix modeling is expensive, both in fees to the modeler and in the time necessary to assemble the required information. Furthermore, the results are affected by errors or misinterpretation of the input data. Nevertheless, because of the technique's speed and ability to provide definitive answers to the age-old questions, market mix modeling has become an attractive alternative to test markets for some advertisers.

Test Marketing

Test marketing is the use of controlled tests or experiments (depending on how they are done) in one or more geographic areas to gather certain kinds of information or to gain experience in marketing a brand. Although any product or service can be test-marketed, marketers most often apply the process to *consumer packaged goods (CPG)*—products that consumers buy in grocery stores, discount warehouses, drugstores, and mass merchandisers.

In practice, test marketing means different things to different people. For some research-oriented people, test marketing means a precise method for gaining information or experience. At the other extreme, to some entrepreneurs, test marketing means "trying something out in the marketplace." Many other possibilities exist between these two extremes.

Test marketing is most common for new brands in existing product categories or for extensions of a product line. Even in new-product testing, the media portion of the test is usually not the first consideration, because the brand first has to be developed, packaged, and priced; selling strategies must be determined; and starting dates must be chosen. In a sense, then, media planning assumes the same relationship in test marketing that it does in an existing brand strategy: marketing considerations must be decided first.

It is important for a media planner to have a good basic understanding of test marketing, because the planner is often involved with it when translating national media plans to a local level. Although it is beyond the scope of this book to provide all the details of test marketing, the following discussion covers the essential facts for planners.

Purposes of Test Marketing

Test marketing has two major purposes: (1) to examine the viability and potential profitability of new products, and (2) to test alternative media, creative, and marketing strategies for existing brands.

New Products Before a company spends any money on a new product, managers want to know the likelihood of success for the product's concept and proposed marketing plan. Most packaged-goods companies hire outside research firms to make this assessment. One of the most widely used is The Nielsen Company's BASES, which estimates how many cases of a new product will be sold. The company uses three measures:

- Product distribution as a percent of *all commodity volume (ACV)*—the percent of grocery stores where the product is sold, weighted by store size (i.e., larger stores "count more")
- The estimated awareness of the new brand, based on the proposed media plan
- A survey of consumers' intent to buy after seeing a description of the product's concept

From this volume estimate, marketers can predict whether the brand will have enough sales to be profitable. BASES claims that for 970 validations worldwide, its average estimates are within 9 percent of actual sales, with 9 out of 10 estimates falling within 20 percent of actual sales.[1]

Once a new product's concept and proposed marketing plan appear promising, the next step is to determine whether real shoppers, in a real market situation, will try the product when it is introduced. More important, marketers need to know whether consumers will make the repeat purchases that are necessary for a brand's long-term success. A wrong decision in introducing a new product is costly, and despite all these efforts, many new products fail each year. Essentially, test marketing is conducted to reduce the risk of failure by providing top management with knowledge gained from advertising in a limited geographic area. Management then can project test findings to a large geographic area. The major objectives of test marketing are to estimate the brand's market share and volume that are likely once the brand is introduced nationally and to evaluate alternative marketing and advertising strategies that also might be effective on a national basis.

Specifically, the purpose of new-product test marketing is to help planners work out the mechanics of a market introduction while learning the local market share and effects of various strategies. If problems exist, it is better to learn about them ahead of time and solve them before national introduction. Spending a relatively small amount of money in a local market is less risky than a national introduction. Once top management learns the local brand shares, it will try to project those findings to the national market. At that point, if there is not enough profit in the brand, management will decide not to go ahead. In such a case, the investment in

---

1. The Nielsen Company, BASES website: http://en-us.nielsen.com/tab/product_families/ nielsen_bases), Global Validations, October 3, 2001.

the failed product is considerably less than it would have been had the brand been introduced nationally without test marketing.

Existing Brands Although marketers can structure their own test markets for new products, most large packaged-goods companies use either The Nielsen Company or SymphonyIRI (formerly Information Resources, Inc.). Both services have extensive experience in conducting tests and interpreting the results.

Nielsen's Scantrack service provides detailed product movement and merchandising information for food stores as well as food and drug combinations. The service obtains its information weekly from an international sample of more than 350,000 stores across 30 countries.[2] This product sales information is supplemented by Nielsen's Homescan panel, which reports demographic and other information about the people who made the purchase. Panelists use a special "wand" device to scan the UPC (bar code) of all products that come into the home, so Nielsen can track sales in all types of stores. Nielsen specialists analyze the data and provide periodic reports to their clients. These reports provide the basis for evaluating the success of test-marketing efforts for new and existing products.

The other widely used service providing packaged-goods marketing data is SymphonyIRI. Its InfoScan service obtains checkout scanner data from a sample of more than 34,000 supermarkets, drugstores, and mass-merchandiser outlets.[3] This service, supplemented by a wand-based household panel, provides data similar to Nielsen's and, like the Nielsen service, helps marketers measure the success of new products, as well as sales of existing brands.

Behavior Scan Test Market Service Although Scantrack and InfoScan can be used to measure the effects of alternative marketing strategies for existing brands, many advertisers use the Behavior Scan service of IRI (popularly referred to as B-Scan). B-Scan provides marketers and their agencies with a measurable method for evaluating the impact of different marketing strategies on consumer sales for both new and established brands. Currently, B-Scan operates four test markets, three with targetable TV capability. These three markets are Pittsfield, Massachusetts; Eau Claire, Wisconsin; and Cedar Rapids, Iowa. The market without TV testing is Grand Junction, Colorado. IRI selected these markets to ensure geographic dispersion throughout the United States, as well as typical consumer demographics and retail conditions.

---

2. http://en-us.nielsen.com/tab/product_families/nielsen_scantrack.
3. http://symphonyiri.com/ProductsSolutions/AllProducts/AllProductsDetail/tabid/159/productid/84/Default.aspx.

Television media influences are measured and controlled through local network affiliates, independent stations, and cable TV services. In addition, B-Scan tracks circulation and coupon redemption from local newspapers and women's service magazines. The service measures competitive activity, providing a clear picture of pricing, displays, and features. Coupon redemptions are also collected from every panelist.

A panel of more than 3,000 households is maintained in each of the B-Scan markets. Panel members shop with an ID card presented at the checkout counter in scanner-equipped grocery stores and drugstores, allowing the tracking of specific consumer purchase behavior, item by item, over a continuous period of time.

B-Scan's targetable TV capability exists through a special device attached to the panelist's TV set that allows the marketer to broadcast alternative commercials to households in demographically balanced cells. In this way, the test can expose one group of homes to a test commercial or media plan while another group in the same market serves as a control.

B-Scan can test consumer promotions such as coupons, sampling, or refund offers through its balanced panel subsamples. This arrangement provides a laboratory environment for tests. Through direct mail or split newspaper-route targeting, a different treatment is delivered to each group. The sales and profits from each group can then be analyzed.

In addition to the household panel data, B-Scan continuously collects sales data from a pool of 45,000 grocery, drug, and mass-merchandise stores. Sales data from other outlets, such as convenience stores or hardware stores, can also be collected on a custom basis to ensure coverage of all appropriate outlets for testing.

Despite IRI's expertise, biases of many kinds can creep into test-marketing operations. For example, test markets may experience higher distribution levels than could be expected on a national scale. Or the local markets may enjoy extra sales efforts that could not be expected nationally. Sometimes the expenditure of dollars for advertising is excessive at the local level and could not be duplicated nationally. Because residents of the B-Scan markets have historically been exposed to so many marketing tests, they may not react in the same way as people in other parts of the United States. Finally, markets change, people's attitudes change, and the economy changes. Therefore, by the end of a test-marketing operation, the national universe, as well as the local universe, might be far different from what they were during the initial test.

Advertiser-Run Market Tests

Although B-Scan and Nielsen tests are widely used, they are expensive compared to a test conducted by the advertiser using in-house resources. Following are some of the considerations and decisions that are necessary to ensure a successful test-marketing program.

Number of Markets to Use No simple rules exist for deciding on a number of markets, but necessary considerations include cost and degree of accuracy. Using fewer than three markets could be considered inadequate for predicting national share, but some kinds of information can be learned from two markets or even one market. Although most marketing experts would agree that test marketing should use three or more markets, many tests use fewer than that because the cost is prohibitive. Even if managers think that using more markets will considerably enhance the results of an experiment, they still feel great reluctance to spend the extra money.

Kinds of Markets to Include A number of criteria are used in selecting test markets. The primary factor is that a market should be representative of the universe. The markets selected are really samples from the universe. Therefore, the more they are like the larger area, the better. This would mean that the markets selected should have the same demographic distribution of population as the country (if the universe is the entire country).

As shown in Exhibit 14-1, Peoria, Illinois, has a population distribution that closely matches the population distribution of the total United States. Because of this similarity, marketers often use Peoria as a single test market. At times, it is used in combination with others. Yet despite the demographic similarity, researchers should question whether the lifestyle of Peoria inhabitants is comparable to lifestyles in other areas of the country.

Market Sizes There is a difference of opinion about the optimum market size for test markets. One expert believes that the range should be a population of 100,000–1,000,000. Another expert employs a rule that the size should be about 2–3 percent of the national population. Yet another believes that the total population involved in test marketing should not be less than 20 percent of the United States, because anything less would cause too much statistical sampling variance. Probably the size of each market is less important than the kinds or numbers of markets used. However, size is an important consideration for controlling the cost of the test. In large markets, marketers could expect to pay relatively higher media costs.

What to Test In addition to sales volume or share at a profitable level, a number of marketing variables can be tested. These include tests of advertising media weights, price levels, store promotion plans, trial and repeat buying rates, creative

EXHIBIT 14-1

Peoria Compared with the National Population (2009)

DEMOGRAPHIC	PEORIA DMA	TOTAL U.S.	INDEX
Men 18+	48.2%	48.7%	99
Persons 18–49/household	1.07	1.15	94
Persons 50+/household	0.79	0.82	96
Children 2–11/household	0.33	0.36	92
Effective buying income/household	$50,534	$48,800	104
Education (% DMA)			
Non-high-school graduates	14.5%	19.3%	75
High school graduates	32.1	28.3	113
Attended college	29.6	27.7	107
College graduates	23.7	24.7	96
Total	100%	100%	100
Occupation (% DMA)			
Professional and white collar	59.0%	60.2%	98
Blue collar	23.6	23.8	99
Service and farm	17.4	16.0	109
Total	100%	100%	100

Source: The Nielsen Company, DMA Test Market Profiles, 2009. Used with permission.

approaches, package sizes and assortments, brand names, brand awareness and/or attitude changes, and alternative media strategies. Although this list suggests that many marketing elements can be tested, an advertiser should test only one at a time to ensure that any effects, positive or negative, can be attributed to the changes in that one element.

When to Read the Test Before any test starts, there needs to be general agreement about when it is appropriate to examine the results and determine success or failure. Experienced marketers suggest running a test for at least six months, but there is often pressure to make the decision sooner, sometimes after only three months or even before that. Early results, however, can be highly misleading. Strong initial sales can indicate a successful launch with many people trying the product, but if these early buyers do not make repeat purchases, the brand cannot survive.

Conversely, brands with a long purchase cycle may need many months for consumers to run out of their current product and be in the market for a replacement. Product seasonality also can influence the timing for reading a test.

Research Designs Used in Test Marketing

Research design refers to a plan of actions to be taken in the testing. This plan, or design, is carefully worked out to obtain certain kinds of information. Most often research design refers to experimental situations where the test data will be statistically manipulated. Research design can be very simple—for example, observing a market, introducing an experimental variable, and then observing it again to learn what effects the variable had on the market. Or the design can be simple to the extent that two or more markets, presumably similar in demographic characteristics, are tested at the same time, with each one getting a different treatment.

Control Markets Before conducting test marketing, the planner must design the test in such a way as to guarantee its validity. *Validity* means that the test measures what it is supposed to measure. For example, if advertising is introduced into a test market as an experimental treatment, the planner will want to know the extent to which advertising had any effect on the outcome.

One method of ensuring the internal validity of the test is to use a control market along with a test market. A *control market* is one that does not receive any special treatment. The control market, therefore, must be selected carefully so that it shares all the demographic and economic characteristics of the test market. If the research objective is to measure advertising's effect on sales, then advertising will be used in the test market only. Sales then are measured in both kinds of markets. If sales rise higher in the test market than in the control market, one can conclude that advertising had a significant effect on sales. But if sales rise to about the same degree in both markets, then advertising had little or no effect.

The design of a test and control market for a new brand is shown in Exhibit 14-2. This kind of test can involve more than a single variable. For example, different spending levels can be tested in different test markets and compared with the control group. In addition, market shares of all groups can be tested simultaneously for the total of all test groups and compared with the control group.

Randomized Block Designs A *randomized block design* is one in which subjects to be measured are first grouped together into blocks. Each subject is carefully chosen so that he or she will be much like every other subject in that block. The selection process, however, is done on a random basis so that every person with the same characteristic has an equal chance of being chosen. Randomized blocks are

EXHIBIT 14-2

How Test and Control Markets Are Used

	TIME PERIOD 1 →	TIME PERIOD 2 →	TIME PERIOD 3 →	
TEST MARKET	Sales of new brand measured (no advertising)	Advertising introduced	Sales of new brand measured	Sales of markets compared on basis of percentage change
CONTROL MARKET	Sales of new brand measured (no advertising)	No advertising	Sales of new brand measured (no advertising)	

designed to prevent situations in which the outcome results from differences with the sample, rather than differences in the treatments.

The matching or grouping of subjects can be on the basis of age (e.g., people ages 18–34), or income (annual income of $75,000 or more), or store volume (grocery stores with less than $500,000 income). Once subjects are placed into blocks, the experimenter can compare the results of treatments among the blocks. If subjects are not combined into blocks, then the experimenter might not be able to find significant results, because the differences might be too small to be measured. The experiment can overcome this problem by using a very large number of subjects, but randomized blocks aid the experimenter in reducing the number of subjects to be used in an experiment.

Latin Square Designs A *Latin square* is a block divided into a number of cells containing coded letters and so arranged that a letter appears only once in each row and column. This design technique is more precise than the randomized block because it helps control the problem of two rather than one source of variation within markets that could not be controlled by careful selection. Exhibit 14-3 shows an example of a Latin square used in a marketing experiment. This experiment controls two variables (geographic variation and competitive expenditures) and applies three different treatments. This design assumes that each control or treatment is independent of the others and therefore will not affect the others in any way.

The problem illustrated in Exhibit 14-3 is this: if Brand X spends three varying amounts of money for advertising, which would produce the most sales, brand awareness, or other marketing variable? To make the experiment projectable to the entire country, the experiment tries different expenditure levels in different parts

EXHIBIT 14-3

A Latin Square Design Applied to a Test-Marketing Situation

DEGREE OF COMPETITIVE SPENDING	REGIONS OF THE UNITED STATES		
	EAST	CENTRAL	WEST
Low spending levels	A	C	B
Medium spending levels	C	B	A
High spending levels	B	A	C

Treatments: A = high spending level for Brand X; B = medium spending level for Brand X; C = low spending level for Brand X.

Source: Benjamin Lipstein, "The Design of Test Market Experiments," *Journal of Advertising Research* (December 1965): 6.

of the country and also in areas where different competitive spending levels took place. By controlling for both variables, the experiment eliminated them as possible reasons for variations in sales that were found through the experiment.

The method of eliminating the effects of both variables is to add the rows and average out the effect of regions. By adding the columns, it is possible to average out the effects of competitive spending levels. By adding the expenditure levels for Brand X (or treatments), it is possible to average out the effects of both regions and competitive activity to determine which Brand X spending level was best.

Factorial Design With a *factorial design,* based on a factor as an independent variable, it is possible to measure the effects of different kinds of treatments. An added advantage of this design is the ability to determine whether the factors interact or are independent. In conceptual terms, this design can create experiments to determine the influence of two or more independent variables on a dependent variable. Independent variables are those that the experimenter controls, manipulates, or varies. Dependent variables are the yield, or the effect variables; they vary depending on the independent variable.

An example of differing treatments in an experiment could be the effects of old versus new packaging, or an old package price versus a new price. The goal is to determine whether price and package changes are related to each other or are independent.

Other Designs Alvin Achenbaum suggested a *checkerboard design* as a valid means of obtaining data in test marketing. He described this design as requiring three basic elements:[4]

1. Divide a universe into groups of markets. These markets should be randomly selected and about equal in size (e.g., three television market groups from each of Nielsen's 10 geographic areas).
2. Use alternative strategies in groups of three. Perhaps one group would receive 80 percent of a current spending level, the second group 100 percent, and the third group 120 percent. Achenbaum would also use local media such as newspapers, spot television, and local magazines as the testing media. Three complete media plans at each spending level would then be produced.
3. Through syndicated retail auditing services, measure results over a year. The key to the success of this plan is representativeness, good control, and ease of measurement (because it uses Nielsen areas).

Media Testing

Media play an important role in most test-marketing operations. Although the objective of a market test is to learn whether certain marketing actions will result in a given level of sales or profits, usually other parts of a test are directly related to the selection and use of media. These other parts have different objectives, such as learning which spending levels or which media mixes to use.

Types of Media Testing

A media planner's initial responsibility in test marketing is to create a national media plan, then reduce the size of this plan to fit the individual markets to be tested. (The reduction process is called *media translation* and will be explained in detail later.) The planner might have a number of different objectives to test, but any given test should be limited to a single objective, to avoid confounding the results. (If a test market is exposed to both additional media weight and different creative executions, there would be no way to know which produced the incremental sales.) The following paragraphs describe possible objectives to test.

---

4. Alvin A. Achenbaum, "Market Testing: Using the Marketplace as a Laboratory," in *Handbook of Marketing Research*, ed. Robert Ferber (New York: McGraw-Hill, 1974): 4, 47, 48.

Complete Media Plan A national media plan might be developed for a new product that has not been marketed before. The typical objective of the marketing part of a test for such a product is to learn a brand's sales or the market share that could be developed on a national scale. In addition, alternative forms of the national media plan can be tested to see which will best fulfill the brand's media needs.

Alternative Spending Levels Testing can be used to help determine how much money should be spent on media. The following kinds of spending plans could be tested:

1. High spending versus current spending levels
2. Low spending versus current spending levels
3. High spending versus low spending levels
4. How much to allocate, either by dollars or GRPs, to various geographic markets or media

In testing allocation weights, the tester might use various kinds of weighted BDIs and CDIs to help arrive at spending levels.

Planners should ensure that the difference between the test and control cells is large enough that the effect of the incremental weight will be noticeable. Experts believe the high-spending test cell should receive at least 50 percent more weight than the control. Some may even advocate a spending level far above anything that could be sustained to find out, "How high is up?" What is the biggest increase that could be expected, regardless of cost?

Alternative Schedules It is important to know whether a media plan should use flighting, continuity, or pulsing. Although experience provides planners with some basis for judgment, a test can sometimes provide more objective information.

Alternative Media Mixes One could test the results obtained from any single medium or any combination—TV versus magazines, TV versus newspapers, national versus local media, etc. Testing of the media mix could also include comparing various dayparts in broadcast media—an exclusive daypart, such as prime time, or a combination of dayparts, such as daytime and early or late fringe. These are only a few of the possible combinations that could be tested.

Alternative Commercial Lengths or Ad Sizes The media plan can also use many different combinations of commercial lengths and ad sizes. Any of these could be varied in test markets. For example, the research could test 60-second versus

30-second commercials, or 30-second versus 15-second (or 10-second) commercials, or half-page versus full-page print ads.

Requirements for Selecting Media Test Markets

A number of criteria for selecting test markets apply specifically to media. For example, enough media options should be available in the test markets to replicate the national media that will be used later. As a result, certain small markets are unsuitable for testing purposes. The following paragraphs address additional considerations.

Media Availability A test market must have a balance of media alternatives available. For example, if television is to be part of a national media plan, then there should be at least four TV stations in the test market, because there probably will be at least four TV stations in major markets when the plan is implemented nationally. In the same manner, if radio is to be used in the national plan, then one radio station in the test market should not dominate the market. In a national marketing effort, few if any markets will be dominated by a single radio station.

Spill-in and Spill-out One quality of a test-market medium is the degree to which it is isolated from other markets. Media from markets outside the test area often *spill into* the test market. That is, people in the test market are exposed to media originating from another market. Sometimes it works the other way; media from the test market *spill out* into adjacent markets.

The degree to which media in a test market spill out messages to markets outside the test area can be a serious problem. Spill-out is generally undesirable for a number of reasons. Consumers who live outside the test market might hear or see advertising for a product but be unable to buy it because it does not yet have national distribution. These consumers could become irritated at their inability to buy the advertised brand and might not respond to later advertising, due to their annoyance at being unable to find the brand on store shelves during the testing period.

A marketer can attempt to avoid the problem by distributing the brand in the broader spill-out area, but this in turn could cause another problem: will the supply of the brand be adequate? At times, only a limited amount of a brand is available for testing purposes, perhaps just enough for the test, but not for spill-out.

There is another way to get around the problem of poor distribution in spill-out areas: print and broadcast advertisements can specifically tell consumers where to purchase the brand. This approach averts the animosity that could occur when there is no distribution in a spill-out area.

The reverse problem of spill-out is spill-in, which occurs when media originating in another market spill into the test market. The more people in the test market are exposed to media from another market, the greater the variation in the reach and frequency pattern from the pattern ordinarily expected.

Although spill-in and spill-out should still be considered, the growth of cable TV and satellite penetration to 90 percent has reduced this problem. Viewers no longer need to tune to stations in adjacent markets to see popular programs that may not be available from local stations. Also, a test can minimize the effects of spill-in and spill-out by concentrating on local news programs that typically draw few viewers in neighboring markets. However, the need to minimize spill-out must be balanced against the need to faithfully duplicate a multi-daypart test. Spill-in and spill-out are reported in Nielsen's annual "DMA Audience Allocation Report," which shows how many GRPs are delivered in a neighboring DMA for every 100 GRPs in the home market.

Both IRI and Nielsen are able to smooth out behavioral differences since they have point-of-sale data that provides truth and allows them to identify those skews and in some cases adjust for them. Similarly, they are able to make adjustments that account for differences in distribution and quality of merchandising .

Media Costs When a market becomes known as a good test area, the local media sometimes raise their advertising rates to take advantage of their popularity. Some experts think that persons responsible for the media portion of testing should not worry about higher media costs in certain markets, because other considerations (spill-in, spill-out, quality, availability, etc.) are more important. In translating a national media plan to a test market, the objective should not be to translate costs downward from a national plan, but to translate the delivery (e.g., reach and frequency) into the test market, regardless of the cost. If a test market cannot generate the necessary levels of reach and frequency, then some other market should be selected.

Test Area Coverage When test markets are being selected for media planning, enough DMAs should be used to cover at least 95 percent of the sales district, territory, etc., that is being used for the test. This assumes that the test is being made to correspond to a specific company's sales area. At times, this correspondence is not necessary, depending on what the client wants to learn from the test.

Planners must be careful in identifying the DMAs needed to cover Nielsen's Scantrack or IRI's InfoScan markets, since these areas do not clearly match DMA boundaries. Also, since DMAs are based on viewing patterns, they do not conform to political boundaries such as state lines. The St. Louis DMA, for example, straddles Illinois and Indiana.

Network Delivery   Another consideration for test market selection, especially when the test is supposed to represent the entire United States, is that the daypart usage in the test market should closely match the planned national daypart usage of television or radio.

Cable Penetration   Penetration of cable and alternate delivery systems (e.g., satellites) should be comparable to the total United States, that is, 90 percent.

Number of Markets   As discussed previously, the number of markets used in testing should be more than two or three. Despite consensus that as many as five, six, or more are desirable, often only one is used. When testing uses a single market, that one is assumed to be a Little U.S.A. market (to be discussed in the next section). Dangers of projecting from one market are well recognized.

Types of Markets   Some advertisers find it advantageous to test in large markets such as New York, Los Angeles, or Chicago. This preference assumes that these markets are more representative of the United States than smaller markets. A marketer might also try a test in an entire geographic region, such as the West Coast, where a number of various-sized population centers exist. The regional approach could be much easier to use than a single isolated market, because the planner can more easily simulate the national media plan in the area. Regional editions of national magazines may be available, saving the cost of using Media Networks, Inc., local placement in every DMA. The regional test would be less likely to be affected by local strikes, bad weather, or high competitive reactions to the test. Sometimes network buys in a region such as the West Coast are relatively inexpensive and flexible, but regional network buys are difficult to execute, if available at all, especially with the advent of satellite-delivered network programs to affiliates.

Another reason why regional test markets are preferred to individual and isolated markets is that it is easier to obtain distribution in a region. It is also easier to compare market data with media coverage. Finally, in auditing sales, it is easier and less costly to audit sales in large regions than in isolated markets.

On the other hand, there are three good reasons for not using regional tests. First, the cost might be prohibitive. Second, there could be a large amount of wasted media impressions, because not everyone in the region is being tested. Finally, a regional test is not really a laboratory or sample test, but a small-scale introduction. The testing procedure does not eliminate the risks of large-scale failure if the product is not well accepted.

Sometimes media considerations are not an important part of test marketing. As one media planner noted, "Our client was interested only in finding out if he could sell the product to the trade. In this instance, the actual media schedules were not important."[5]

Media Translations

As defined earlier, media translation is a process of simulating the effects of expensive national media plans in relatively inexpensive local test markets. This is an adjustment technique, and there are several ways to make such adjustments. Each technique is based on a different philosophy of operations.

"Little U.S.A." Versus "As It Falls" Philosophy

There are at least two philosophies regarding media translations in test marketing: the Little U.S.A. concept and the As It Falls concept. The most commonly used is the Little U.S.A. concept, which is based on the idea that some test markets are so much like the country as a whole that these markets can easily be projected to the national market. Suppose a media plan calls for one prime-time network :30 per week with a 4 national rating. The test-market translation would be a 4 rating on some local program or a number of spot commercials with 4 GRPs in that market, regardless of the local rating for that network vehicle in the test market. Another way to use the Little U.S.A. concept would be to translate it in direct proportion to the weight that would be delivered on a national basis. The measurement could be the average number of impressions to be delivered per household nationally, translated to a proportion the local market should have received.

In the As It Falls concept, the local market receives the exact media weight it would get from the national plan. Using the same example as before, with a prime-time network program rated 4, the planner might find that this program delivers a higher or lower rating in the test market, because national media deliver varying levels of advertising weight from market to market. If the prime-time program happens to deliver a 3 rating in the chosen test market, then 3 GRPs should be purchased in the test market.

---

5. B. G. Yavovich, "Quality of Local Markets Can Be a Determining Factor," *Advertising Age* (February 4, 1980): S-2.

The choice between Little U.S.A. and As It Falls generally depends on how representative the test area is relative to the national plan. If the As It Falls translation method would result in delivering an abnormally high (or low) level of media weight, some adjustment toward the Little U.S.A. is desirable. IRI tends to use As It Falls for Behavior Scan tests and established products. They use Little America for new products in new categories. Little America is also used by most agencies for matched market tests, which indicates its popularity and the fact that it is easy to do. Exhibit 14-4 shows how a Little U.S.A. media translation would be made.

The example is based on a national media plan in which network and spot television and national magazines would be the only media. The spot television plan covers markets that include 60 percent of U.S. households. To make a Little U.S.A. translation, average delivery is scheduled in local test markets as shown in Exhibit 14-4. Using the same data, the As It Falls translation first requires the planner to determine how many GRPs would go into individual markets. Whereas the Little U.S.A. technique used the average delivery, this technique requires much more detailed planning and estimation of local delivery. In making this translation, it might not be possible to buy GRPs precisely as planned, so some media get more and others less than the national plan, as shown in Exhibit 14-5.

EXHIBIT 14-4

National Media Plan: Little U.S.A. Method

MEDIA USED	SPOT MARKETS (WOMEN GRPS)	TOTAL U.S. (WOMEN GRPS)	TEST-MARKET TRANSLATION (WOMEN GRPS)
Network TV		400	400
Magazines		100	100
Spot TV (60% of U.S. covered)			
Average spot*	100	60[†]	60 (national average)
Total		560	560

*A markets received 150 GRPs, B markets 100 GRPs, and C markets 50 GRPs, but the average for all markets is 100.

[†]Average calculations are as follows: 100 GRPs in 60% of U.S. = 60

0 GRPs in 40% of U.S. = 0

Weighted average = 60

EXHIBIT 14-5

National Media Plan: As It Falls Method

MEDIA USED	SPOT MARKETS (WOMEN GRPS)	TOTAL U.S. (WOMEN GRPS)	TEST-MARKET TRANSLATION (WOMEN GRPS)
Network TV		400	380
Magazines		100	120
Spot TV (60% of U.S. covered)			
Average spot*	100	100	
A markets	150		
B markets	100		
C markets*	50		50
Total	400	600	550

*The GRPs of C markets were used because test markets were C markets in character.

Under the As It Falls approach, only 380 GRPs were purchased in network TV while 120 GRPs were purchased in magazines in the test market. The reason is that this combination of national media delivers the desired levels of GRPs in the test market. Although the difference between the two translation techniques might seem insignificant, it is the difference between average and actual plan delivery in the test market.

Translations in Radio and Television

There are a number of ways to execute the translation of a national media plan into local radio and television. One way is the *cut-in*, in which the broadcaster inserts a local commercial in a network or syndicated program in place of some other commercial originally scheduled in a market for the same advertiser. This is possible when the client already has purchased a commercial on a network and simply replaces it with the test-market commercial by cutting in only in the test market. The rest of the country would see the national commercial. A cut-in is considered an excellent way to translate for broadcast media because it keeps the program environments the same as in the national plan, and it provides the exact national weight in a local market.

Cut-ins do have drawbacks, however. Local stations charge high fees for mechanically inserting substitute commercials. Also, national advertising for some other product might suffer if it is replaced with the cut-in. Finally, cutting over cable telecasts is problematic because many systems serve a given market. Each system would have to execute the cut-in. With close to half of all viewing scattered among dozens of cable networks, the cut-in process today is seldom used outside of the IRI or Nielsen test markets.

If a cut-in is not feasible, then the planner will have to substitute local announcements for the network commercials. This could be a problem, because the spot announcement times chosen must provide the same kind of target audience and the same audience sizes that the network program in that market would provide. With spot television, the only times available at a reasonable cost might be fringe times. Although fringe time spots produce lower ratings than prime-time network programs, planners might add GRPs to those of the theoretical plan level as a form of compensation. When a prime-time spot is used (instead of a prime-time network program), the additional GRP compensation might be less than the amount of compensation used with fringe spot. Each advertiser relies on research experience to determine the degree of additional spot weight over the theoretical plan level. There is no single set of industry standards that applies to such translation methods. However, any decisions about compensation should consider two factors: compensation for loss of reach and compensation for loss of program environment. Presumably, any spots used will aim for a selected target audience.

Compensations will vary among markets, depending on the relationship of audience sizes between prime time and fringe times. In fact, daytime spots can be used in lieu of daytime network programs without any compensation, because they can be purchased either within or next to the kinds of network programs used in the national media plan.

When a national media plan calls for spot television, no compensation is necessary. Spots are simply scheduled in the same number of GRPs, length, placement, reach, and frequency called for in the national plan.

In translating network radio, the method is identical to that used for translating daytime network television. For spot radio, the translation method would be identical to spot television.

Translations in Print

Translation of newspapers is direct and simple, because the national media plan spells out all details for local markets. There are a number of options for translating national print into the test markets, which in order of desirability are as follows:

1. Local (test market) editions of national magazines. There are often restrictions, including lack of availability in the desired test market or in the desired

week, poor positioning within the magazine, and higher cost per thousand (CPM) necessitated by the additional labor.

2. Media Networks, Inc. (www.mni.com), which specializes in placing local advertising in national magazines. The service offers 10 lifestyle-defined advertising packages (Business, Family, Health & Beauty, Hispanic, etc.) available in more than 400 target markets. As with the local test-market editions, there are restrictions and limitations, but the service is able to accommodate most advertisers.

3. *Parade* and *USA Weekend* Sunday supplements. These can be purchased market by market, again with a CPM premium over a full national run, but meeting the needs of test-market advertisers.

4. Color insertion in the local newspaper.

What Successful Media Tests Have in Common

In 1991, IRI published a classic study that is still relevant today. It identified the common media and creative elements of 389 successful advertising and media weight tests conducted between 1982 and 1988. *Successful* was defined as an increase in sales that IRI was 80 percent sure did not occur by chance. The results of this and a follow-on study, referred to in the industry as AdWorks 1 and AdWorks 2, respectively, have led to guidelines that can help media planners as they structure their tests. Here are the key findings from AdWorks 1:[6]

- There is no simple relationship between the size of the weight increase and the increase in sales.
- Additional weight was more likely to increase sales when there was a change in brand or copy strategy.
- Successful media plans tended to expand the audience or shift the target emphasis. Also, they used less daytime.
- Growing and frequently purchased product categories were more likely to benefit from increased weight.
- Successful tests continued to increase volume for up to two years after resumption of traditional spending levels.
- Advertising works by getting current users to buy more of a product, rather than expanding penetration to new users.
- Heavy trade promotion (price reductions) hinders the effect of advertising; consumer promotion (coupons, sweepstakes, etc.) enhances it.

---

6. Information Resources, Inc., 1991; summary from FCB/Chicago Media Matters, February 1992.

- New brands and line extensions tend to be more responsive to media weight tests than are established products.
- For new products, the more prime time that was used, the greater the increase in sales. Front-loaded heavy-up plans also were more likely to increase sales.

AdWorks 2, conducted from 1995 to 1996 by IRI and Media Marketing Assessment (MMA)/Carat, expanded on AdWorks 1 to study more than 800 packaged-goods brands representing more than 200 product categories. Key findings from AdWorks 2 are as follows:[7]

- All the brands showed incremental sales over base equity in response to television advertising. In general, the more GRPs a brand received, the higher the percentage of total incremental sales volume due to television advertising.
- Continuity counts. Television advertising effectiveness increased as the average annual number of consecutive weeks on air increased.
- Consistent with several recall studies that indicate that :30 spots are more effective than :15s, as the percentage of :30 commercial units in a plan increased (compared to :15s), television advertising effectiveness also increased.
- Plans using multiple network dayparts and other television venues are more effective than those concentrated in one daypart or venue.

7. Media Marketing Assessment (MMA) at www.mma.com; link to "Products & Services"; "Publicly Released Highlights of AdWorks 2," October 5, 1999.

Media-Planning Resources on the Internet

The explosive growth of the Internet has made available a variety of media-planning tools and information. Virtually every medium, research supplier, and advertising-related company is represented on the Internet. The following paragraphs describe the most commonly used websites for media planners. Although some sites limit information by password to only their customers, a great deal of information is available at little or no charge. The sites contain detailed information about available services, research methodology, and top-line demographic and media data. In some cases, they offer fully functional media-planning tools that can be obtained at no charge in exchange for registering the user's name and e-mail address. The following sites were verified as of February 2010.

General Media-Planning Sites

Advertising Media Internet Center (www.amic.com) The Advertising Media Internet Center website serves as an excellent starting point for media planners. It provides links to the major media research sources, media terminology, advice from a "media guru," and other planning services.

MediaPost (www.mediapost.com) At MediaPost, media buyers and planners will find a broad range of resources, including a daily newsletter, research support, blogs, and the latest from all areas of the media world. Full access is provided in exchange for no-cost registration.

Advertising Research Foundation (www.thearf.org) The Advertising Research Foundation (ARF) is a nonprofit organization whose mission is "to improve the practice of advertising, marketing, and media research in pursuit of more effective marketing and advertising communications." It publishes the bimonthly *Journal of Advertising Research* and conducts numerous conferences and workshops devoted to the advertising profession. The ARF's website has a link to the *Journal of Advertising Research's* website (www.jar .warc.com), which allows visitors to search past issues of the journal for topics of interest. A synopsis is displayed, and article reprints and entire issues can be ordered online. Its annual Audience Measurement Conference features the latest developments in the area of media research. In addition, the ARF equips members with an array of self-service tools for research, knowledge sharing, and learning. ARF PowerSearch provides searchable access to roughly 40,000 references on advertising, marketing, and media effectiveness drawn from its own library and third-party sources. Knowledge@Hand, a listing of frequently asked questions, authoritatively summarizes topics. Morning Coffee organizes hundreds of RSS feeds, blogs, websites, and videos that are relevant to practitioners. The ARF's video library furnishes access to their conferences and forums. Last, the ARF offers assisted research and analytic services to members and nonmembers.

World Advertising Research Center (www.warc.com) The World Advertising Research Center (WARC) provides online information for the world's advertisers, advertising agencies, media buyers, media corporations, and market research organizations. A search engine allows users to locate studies in virtually any field of advertising or marketing communications that have been published anywhere in the world. Access to the complete study or article requires a full (but costly) subscription.

Kidon Media-Link (www.kidon.com/media-link) Kidon Media-Link provides Internet links to the websites of more than 2,000 U.S. and international media venues. The listing is organized by region of the world (Europe, United States, Americas, Asia, Africa/ Middle East, and Oceania) and shows the name, medium (TV, newspaper, magazine, radio, etc.), and language of the site. In addition to editorial content, most sites provide information on advertising and sales representatives.

AllNewspapers.com (www.allnewspapers.com) AllNewspapers.com is another site that provides links to international media services. This listing is organized by region, country, and media type (despite its name, the service includes all media in each country).

IMS and Telmar Computer Services (www.ims-usa.com and www.telmar.com) Although each research service has its own proprietary software, IMS and Telmar both provide access to research databases such as MRI, Experian Simmons, and others through a unified set of computer programs that offers the same look and feel for all applications.

Products of these "third-party software providers" include cross tabulations, cost per thousand (CPM) rankers, reach/frequency analysis, geographic allocation, media mix analysis, optimization, and a variety of other tools. Users must first subscribe to the basic research service and then pay an additional fee for the convenience of these third-party tools.

Media Life (www.medialifemagazine.com) This no-cost online service provides daily information about the media industry, organized by medium and by market, as well as numerous links to Internet media services. The "Medialands" tab provides detailed demographic and media information about the top 50 markets.

Ephron on Media (www.ephrononmedia.com) Erwin Ephron is a widely known and respected consultant to the advertising industry. His Ephron on Media website is a compendium of the essays he has written over the years.

Single-Source Media/Marketing Research Sites

The following services provide demographics, media behavior, and product usage from a single research sample.

Mediamark Research and Intelligence, LLC (www.mediamark.com) MRI's website describes the company's service and provides top-line audience information for magazines, cable networks, and Internet usage. It also provides reports of consumer behavior for more than 6,000 products and services in 550 categories. The website has a link to the MRI+ (www.mriplus.com) service that provides extensive information about their 200+ measured magazines as well as a wealth of other media information. Full access is provided in exchange for no-charge registration.

Experian Simmons (www.smrb.com) Formerly called the Simmons Market Research Bureau (SMRB), its primary service is the "National Consumer Survey" of product usage, demographics, and media behavior. It is similar to MRI. In addition to its coverage of general market population, Simmons conducts studies that focus on a single demographic segment, including kids, teens, gay/lesbian, Hispanics, and business leaders.

Scarborough Research (www.scarborough.com) Scarborough surveys 81 markets to provide information similar to the national MRI and SMRB research. Categories include local-market consumer shopping patterns, demographics, media usage, and lifestyle activities. Scarborough uses a mail questionnaire, allowing it to provide detailed information about each market surveyed.

The Media Audit (www.themediaaudit.com) The Media Audit is a multimedia audience survey that is similar to (and competitive with) Scarborough. The Media Audit covers 86 local markets and more than 2,000 product categories. These qualitative and quantitative data include socioeconomic characteristics, lifestyles, retail shopping habits, and other selected consumer characteristics important to local media and advertisers. The Media Audit uses a telephone interview with a random sample of persons in the markets surveyed. Limited top-line information about each market is available from their website, www.weknowthelocals.com.

Both MRI and Simmons provide, at additional cost, estimates of DMA-level usage of nationally measured products based on regional and county size selectivity. So while they cannot give the demographics of local retail outlets or tell the demographic differences between Chicago Cubs and White Sox fans, they can provide an estimate of usage and a selectivity index for all the measured product in each of the 210 DMAs.

Broadcast-Planning Sites

The Nielsen Company (www.nielsen.com) Although most Nielsen data are protected, the Nielsen website offers an overview of the TV rating service, a description of how television audiences are measured, and occasional free reports on current topics. A massive amount of data is now available online in PDF file format to subscribers at www.nielsenanswers.com. These reports were formerly released only in hard copy.

Arbitron (www.arbitron.com) Arbitron is the primary source of audience ratings for local radio stations and radio networks throughout the United States. The Arbitron website provides information about the company's reports, market populations, and the latest information about its rating service. The free "Radio Today" report offers an overview of the radio industry and listening habits.

SQAD (www.sqad.com) SQAD is the primary source of planning cost per rating point (CPP) for national television, local market spot TV, and spot radio in all DMAs and radio metros. SQAD's WebCosts service provides planning costs for image-based digital advertising. The SQAD website gives an overview of SQAD's methodology, tips on how to use the data, and the current household CPP by daypart for each market. Although almost all television buys are planned on demographic target GRPs, such as women ages 25–54, the household CPPs are available for a nominal charge from Mediaweek's *Marketer's Guide to Media*. See an example of a SQAD report in Chapter 12.

Cabletelevision Advertising Bureau (www.thecab.tv) The Cabletelevision Advertising Bureau (CAB) is a trade association that exists to promote cable television as an advertising medium. Its website presents the strengths of cable TV in comparison to broadcast network and syndication. For a nominal cost, planners can order detailed audience information, program schedules, and other material about advertiser-supported cable television networks.

Television Bureau of Advertising (www.tvb.org) The Television Bureau of Advertising (TVB) is the not-for-profit trade association of America's broadcast television industry. TVB provides a diverse variety of tools and resources, including this website, to support its members and help advertisers make the best use of local television. The website provides a broad range of information about the television industry, viewing trends, cable and satellite penetration by DMA, advertising expenditures in all media (not just TV), and useful facts about the television market. Some of the reports are available only to TVB members. Because the TVB is supported by local stations, there is only limited information about cable and network television.

Direct Marketing Association (www.the-dma.org) The Direct Marketing Association (DMA) is the oldest and largest trade association for users and suppliers in the direct, database, and interactive marketing fields. The website provides extensive information on direct marketing advertising, including a library of white papers, research and statistics, demographics, and various free services that are available in exchange for online registration.

Radio Advertising Bureau (www.rab.com) The Radio Advertising Bureau (RAB) is a trade association that exists to promote radio as an advertising medium. The website has extensive information on radio-listening habits and the strength of the medium compared to other broadcast and print alternatives. The *Radio Marketing Guide and Fact Book for Advertisers*, which is available through the link to "Radio Facts," is especially valuable. Like the other media-specific websites, this one contrasts the strengths of radio to the weaknesses of other media. Some areas are limited to RAB members with no-cost registration.

National Association of Broadcasters (www.nab.org) The National Association of Broadcasters (NAB) is the principal trade association of the television industry. Its work focuses mostly on the business of broadcasting and governmental relations. The website contains reports on current events in the industry, regulatory issues, and technical advances. Although there is only limited information about advertising, the site provides useful background information at no cost for media planners.

Print-Planning Sites

MRI+ (www.mriplus.com) The website provides rates, circulation information, top-line MRI audience information, editorial calendars, and promotional media kits for more than 5,500 consumer magazines and business publications. This information is provided free on the Internet as a service to planners by MRI and the publications.

Audit Bureau of Circulations (www.accessabc.com) The Audit Bureau of Circulations (ABC) verifies the circulation statements made by major consumer magazines and newspapers. Although the audit data are password protected, the site contains information about how to use the various reports. A "Hot Links" button offers links to numerous media-related websites.

BPA Worldwide (www.bpaww.com) BPA provides a service that is similar to the ABC but deals primarily with controlled-circulation publications—magazines and newspapers that are subsidized entirely by advertising and offered at no cost to the reader. These tend to be trade or special-interest consumer publications whose readers request a subscription by filling out a questionnaire about their job titles, responsibilities, and product purchases. By using the BPA, advertisers can select the publications that most directly reach their particular marketing target. The website provides free access to all BPA reports and is a valuable resource for business-to-business advertisers.

Magazine Health Watch United States (http://www.ims.ca) A Canadian company, Inquiry Management Systems, makes available this free and exceptionally detailed overview of the U.S. magazine industry for the past three years up to the most recent month. For 95 business-to-business and 24 consumer market segments, it shows the number of magazines, issues, advertisers, insertions, and total revenue (calculated at rate card).

Magazine Publishers of America (www.magazine.org) The Magazine Publishers of America (MPA) exists to promote the value of magazines as an advertising medium. The MPA website provides a wealth of free information about the magazine industry and the way people read magazines. Because MPA is an industry group, however, the site has no data on individual titles that might be used to sell one versus another. The annual *Magazine Handbook* in the Research/Resources section provides especially useful information about the medium.

Newspaper Association of America (www.naa.org) The Newspaper Association of America (NAA) is a nonprofit organization that represents more than 1,800 newspapers in the United States and Canada. The website's Information Resource Center provides extensive free information about newspapers, readership, and advertising expenditures in the medium. However, most of the reports are limited to NAA members.

Verified Audit Circulation (www.verifiedaudit.com) Verified Audit Circulation (VAC) provides circulation audits for paid and free community newspapers; total market coverage flyers; shopping guides; alternative newsweeklies; ethnic, special interest, and niche publications; business, parenting, and senior periodicals; trade and consumer magazines; and Yellow Pages directories.

Outdoor-Planning Sites

Outdoor Advertising Association of America (www.oaaa.org) The Outdoor Advertising Association of America (OAAA) is the lead trade association representing the outdoor advertising industry. With nearly 1,100 member companies, the OAAA represents more than 90 percent of industry revenues. The association's website presents information about the medium and various creative units available. Links to outdoor companies can be used for gathering information about pricing and local market planning.

Lamar Advertising Company (www.lamar.com) An out-of-home media agency that covers all 50 U.S. states, Lamar Advertising also runs a useful website. The site offers resources and information for media buyers and planners. It also contains rates and poster details for the areas served by Lamar.

Eller Media Company (www.ellermedia.com) Eller Media is one of the largest outdoor advertising companies in the United States. The company's website provides links to outdoor companies, a glossary of outdoor terms, rates for various outdoor media in the major markets, and other information to help plan out-of-home media.

Internet-Planning Sites

Internet Advertising Bureau (www.iab.net) The Internet Advertising Bureau (IAB) presents itself as "the first global not-for-profit association devoted exclusively to maximizing the use and effectiveness of advertising on the Internet." The IAB website provides general information about digital advertising, industry standard ad sizes, and an exceptionally complete listing (including hot links) to the many tools of the trade.

Forrester Research, Inc. (www.forrester.com) A leading Internet marketing research company, Forrester provides strategic analysis and insight about the commerce on the Internet. It tracks industry trends and forecasts future business activity. The Forrester website offers summaries of the company's current presentations and top-line marketing information about the Internet in exchange for guest registration.

Glossary of Internet Terms (www.matisse.net/files/glossary.html) This extensive glossary of Internet terms is provided by Matisse Enzer, an Internet project manager who lives in San Francisco.

Advertising Publication Sites

Advertising Age (**www.adage.com**) *Advertising Age* is the oldest weekly trade publication of the advertising industry. Its website provides current information on all phases of advertising, media, creative, and Internet communication.

Adweek (**www.adweek.com**) *Adweek* is a weekly trade publication that covers the advertising industry. Its website, Adweek Online, provides daily headlines and excerpts from the magazine. See other Adweek websites: www.mediaweek.com and www.brandweek.com.

Advertising Industry Sites

American Association of Advertising Agencies (www.aaaa.org) The American Association of Advertising Agencies (AAAA or the 4As) is the national trade organization that represents the advertising industry. It offers its members information regarding the operation of ad agencies; management; media, print, and broadcast production; secondary research on advertising and marketing; and international advertising. The website lists current activities of the association and provides a catalog of available publications. It offers useful background for media planners but relatively little information for nonmembers.

American Marketing Association (www.marketingpower.com) The American Marketing Association (AMA) is the world's largest and most comprehensive professional society of marketers, consisting of more than 40,000 worldwide members in 82 countries and 400 chapters throughout North America. The AMA is the only organization that provides direct benefits to marketing professionals in both business and education and serves all levels of marketing practitioners, educators, and students. Its website contains information about the organization and its members, but has no media-planning resources.

American Advertising Federation (www.aaf.org) The American Advertising Federation (AAF) describes itself as "The Unifying Voice for Advertising." The AAF says, "We are the only professional advertising association that binds the mutual interests of corporate advertisers, agencies, media companies, suppliers and academia." The federation's website provides information about the organization and its publications, but there are no media-planning resources.

GLOSSARY

A Counties All counties belonging, as of June 30, 1999, to the largest metropolitan areas, which together account for 40 percent of U.S. households, according to the 2000 census.

ABC See *Audit Bureau of Circulations.*

Accumulation A method of counting audiences wherein each person exposed to a vehicle is counted once, either in a given time period such as four weeks for broadcast, or in one issue for print. (See also *Reach.*)

ADI (Area of Dominant Influence) Obsolete—a television market coverage area as defined by the Arbitron Company until 1992, when it stopped producing television ratings. Since then, Nielsen has been the only company producing local-market television ratings. Its comparable Nielsen area is the designated market area (DMA).

Adjacencies The specific time periods, usually two minutes long, that precede and follow regular television programming. These are commercial break positions available for local or spot advertisers. There is no such thing as a network adjacency; only spot adjacencies are available.

Adnorm A term used by Daniel Starch & Associates to indicate readership averages by publication, by space size and color, and by type of product for ads studied by Starch in a two-year period. It is used to provide a standard of comparison for individual ads against averages of similar types of ads.

Adstock The residual effect of advertising from the viewer's memory in the weeks following its appearance on television, in print, or in another medium. This effect decays over time as the viewer forgets the ad. The growth and decay of adstock is one of the factors accounted for in market mix modeling.

Advertising Allowance Money paid under contract by a manufacturer or its representative to a wholesaler or a retailer for spending to advertise a specified product, brand, or line of the manufacturer. Usually used for consumer advertising.

Advertising Appropriation A company's estimated dollar figure for an advertising effort of a short-term flight, seasonal campaign, and/or total marketing year. Usually refers to the combined budget for working media, production, promotion, and reserve and is based on projected business volume.

Advertising Checking Bureau (ACB) A service organization that supplies advertisers and agencies with tear sheets of advertisements run in publications and with other information used by clients to assess the impact of their advertising and competitors' advertising.

Advertising Impression One person or home exposed to a single advertisement; on a gross basis, gross impressions report the sum of all impressions to the ads in a schedule. This includes duplication, for some of those who may have been exposed more than once. In some instances, advertising impression refers to persons or homes exposed to a media vehicle (magazine, television show, etc.), the result of multiplying the audience of each vehicle (on a household or person basis) by the number of advertisements or commercials carried by each vehicle and obtaining the total. In other cases, it refers to the number of persons or homes exposed to an advertisement or commercial within the carrier. In these cases, data on advertising or commercial exposure are applied to the carrier audiences.

Advertising Weight A general term for the amount of advertising planned for or used by a brand. Although it is not limited to a particular measurement, it is most frequently stated in terms of the number of GRPs or gross impressions delivered or the number of broadcasts or insertions placed over a period of time.

Affidavit of Performance A notarized statement from a television or radio station that verifies that a media schedule ran as ordered.

Afternoon Drive Radio daypart between 3:00 P.M. and 7:00 P.M.

Agency Commission A commission that an advertising agency receives for media it has placed. Traditionally, this is in the form of a 15 percent discount on the cost of ad space or time that is offered by the media to recognized advertising agencies. The media grant this discount to compensate agencies for the effort of working with the advertiser to produce the ad, delivering it in the proper format, and ensuring the credit-worthiness of the advertiser. This form of agency compensation has been largely replaced by a negotiated fee that pays the agency for its work, regardless of fluctuations in the media budget. In recent years, agencies have experimented with payment based on performance that ties the agency's compensation to an advertiser's sales. Media costs that include this commission are called "gross" costs; those without are called "net" costs.

Agency of Record An agency that purchases media time or space for another agency or a group of agencies serving the same client.

Aided Recall A measurement technique in which an interviewer provides clues to help respondents remember portions or all of ads. (See *Unaided Recall*.)

Alternate Week Sponsor An advertiser who purchases full or participating sponsorship every other week of a network program for a full 52-week broadcast year. Each sponsor purchasing at least two minutes in a given program episode will receive billboard commercial time on its week of sponsorship. With the decline of program sponsorships, this form has largely disappeared.

Analytics The numerical data and the interpretation of that data in support of a point-of-view, recommendation, or other business application.

Announcement A commercial message between or within programs. Announcements may be live, recorded, or a combination of both. Common lengths in television are 60, 30, 20, 15, and 10 seconds.

Annual Discount A discount given to an advertiser by a media carrier based on the number of advertising insertions or units run during an established contract year.

Arbitron A radio rating service that measures the listening audience to local radio stations and national networks. (See also *RADAR.*)

As It Falls Concept In test marketing, a translation method that executes a national media plan exactly as it would appear in the local test market. This method accurately reflects the market-to-market differences that would occur in an actual buy, but may complicate interpretation of the results if network delivery in a given test market is abnormally above or below average.

Associated Business Publications A trade association of business (industrial, trade, and technical) publications.

Audience The number of people or households exposed to a medium. Exposure measurements indicate nothing about whether audiences saw, heard, or read either the advertisements or editorial contents of the medium.

Audience Composition The percent of a media vehicle's audience that falls into various demographic groups such as age, sex, income, geographic region, and so on.

Audience Duplication In broadcast, a measurement of the number of listeners or viewers reached by one program or station that are also reached by another program or station. In print, the measurement of the overlap of potential exposure between different issues of the same magazine or among issues of different magazines. (See also *Duplication.*)

Audience Deficiency Units (ADU) Additional telecasts of a commercial in order to deliver the guaranteed gross rating points in the event that delivered GRPs were below the original projection. Sometimes called "makegood units."

Audience Flow A measure of changes in audience between broadcast programs. May be reported on a minute-by-minute basis, by five-minute intervals, or from show to show.

Audience Holding Index A measurement of the retentive power or audience loyalty of a given program. Nielsen Media Research, for 30-minute programs, uses an index based on the percentage of homes tuned to the same program 25 minutes after the first measurement. It is a simple measure of the ratio of average audience rating to total audience rating of a given program. Also called *audience turnover.*

Audience, Potential In broadcasting, the number of sets in use in the time period to be studied, or the number of set owners. In print, the total audience of an issue.

Audience, Primary In print, all readers who live in households where someone subscribes to or purchases the magazine. May be called *primary readership.*

Audience Profile The characteristics of the people who make up the audience of a magazine, TV show, newspaper, radio show, and so on in terms of age, family size, location, education, income, and other factors.

Audience, Secondary Pass-along readers who read a publication they did not purchase. This would include visitors who read a magazine in someone else's home, readership in a barber shop or doctor's office, readership of a friend's copy of a magazine, and so on.

Audience Turnover See *Audience Holding Index*.

Audilog An old term for the diary that members of Nielsen's local rating panels fill out to show what they are viewing on television. It is the basis for demographic information about local television viewing in all 210 DMAs. The current name is "TV Viewing Diary."

Audimeter The old name for today's Recordimeter, an electronic device, developed by The Nielsen Company, that records set usage and tuning on a minute-by-minute basis. This passive TV set information is integrated with demographic information from the TV Viewing Diary to provide local market ratings in the meter/diary integration markets. Nielsen plans to replace this meter/diary integration process with the Local People Meter by 2012.

Audit Bureau of Circulations (ABC) A tripartite, nonprofit, self-regulatory organization of advertisers, agencies, and magazine and newspaper publishers that verifies the circulation figures of publishers and members and reports these data to advertiser and agency members.

Availability A specific period of broadcast commercial time offered for sale by a station or network for sponsorship.

Average Audience (AA) In broadcasting, the number of homes/persons tuned in to a TV program for an average minute (a Nielsen network TV measurement). In print, the number of persons who read or looked into an average issue of a publication.

Average Frequency The number of times the average home (or person) reached by a media schedule is exposed to the advertising. This is measured over a specific period of time, for example, four weeks in broadcast media.

Average Net Paid Average circulation per issue. To calculate, divide the total paid circulation for all the issues of the audit period by the total number of issues.

B Counties All counties in the next largest set of metropolitan areas after the top 40 percent (A Counties), which together account for 30 percent of U.S. households.

Back of Book The section of a magazine following the main editorial section.

Back-to-Back Scheduling Two or more commercials run one immediately following the other.

Banner A form of online advertising, typically 468 pixels wide by 60 pixels high but available in many other sizes. Web publishers include a blank space on the page that is filled with advertising delivered by third-party ad servers.

BAR (Broadcast Advertiser's Reports) An organization that monitored network and spot TV competitive activity through the 1980s. It has been replaced as one of the many media-tracking products of Kantar Media.

Barter Acquisition by an advertiser of sizable quantities of spot time or free mentions at rates lower than card rates from broadcast stations in exchange for operating capital or merchandise. Although direct negotiation between the advertiser and station is possible, it is more common for barter to be arranged through a middleman, a barter agency, or a film producer or distributor, who may have procured the time through an exchange of film or taped shows.

Base A demographic group, such as total women or men ages 35–49.

Base Rate See *Open Rate*.

Behavior Scan A test market service of SymphonyIRI, for measuring product and brand purchased through use of Universal Product Code (UPC) at checkout counters.

Billboard (a) An identifying announcement of sponsorship at the beginning, end, or breaks of radio and television sponsored programs. Billboards are not sold, but usually are a bonus, based on the advertiser's volume or commitment with the program or the broadcaster. Usually 5 to 10 seconds in length. (b) An outdoor poster.

Billing (a) A charge made to an advertiser by an advertising agency, based on the listed or gross charges of the media from which space or time has been purchased, along with any other charges and fees incurred by the agency that are passed on to the advertiser. (b) Loosely, the money spent by an advertiser through an agency. (c) The actual charge made by a medium of communication to an advertising agency; the gross charge less the agency discount.

Blanket Coverage Total coverage by television and radio of a given geographic area.

Bleed An advertisement in which part or all of the illustration or copy runs past the usual margins out to the edge of a page. Bleed insertions are generally sold at a premium price, usually 15 percent over the basic rate. Today, most full-page advertising is bleed.

Bonus Circulation Circulation delivered by a publication beyond the circulation on which an advertiser's rate is based.

BPA Worldwide (www.bpaww.com) A company that verifies the circulation of free-circulation magazines and newspapers—primarily industrial trade publications—that are delivered at no cost to readers. The company was formerly known as Business Press Audit.

Brand Development Index (BDI) The ratio of a brand's U.S. sales in a market divided by the market's percent of U.S. population $\times$ 100.

Branded Entertainment See *Product Placement*.

Broadcast Calendar A calendar that is used for accounting purposes in the radio and TV industry and that contains months of four or five whole weeks, ending on the last Sunday of each month. Each quarter in the broadcast calendar contains 13 weeks.

Bulk Circulation Sales in quantity lots of an issue of a magazine or newspaper. The purchases are made by individuals or concerns, and the copies are usually directed to lists of names supplied by the purchasers. In the Audit Bureau of Circulations report, bulk circulation is listed separately from single-copy sales.

Bulk Sales Sales of copies of a publication in quantity to one purchaser for the purchaser to give to others free. Many advertisers do not consider bulk sales to be a valuable part of a publication's circulation.

Business Building Test A test run by a specific brand and designed to determine whether a change in a marketing or advertising plan will produce enough additional business for the brand to pay the required costs of the change.

Business Paper A publication directed to a particular industry, trade, profession, or vocation. A horizontal business paper is designed to reach all groups in a broad trade or industry, regardless of location or occupational title. A vertical publication is for a specific profession, trade, or occupational level within or across various industries.

Buyout A one-time payment to television or radio talent for all rights to performance.

C3 See *Commercial Audience*.

C Counties All counties after the top 70 percent (A Counties: 40 percent, B Counties: 30 percent) and including both metropolitan areas and nonmetropolitan counties, which account for 15 percent of U.S. households.

Cable TV A system of broadcasting television whereby programs are first tuned in by a community antenna and then distributed to individual homes by cables. Cable operators typically receive programs transmitted by satellites and then transmit by cable to their subscribers.

Cancellation Date The last date on which it is possible to cancel advertising. Such dates occur for print, outdoor, and broadcasting.

Card Rate The cost of time and space quoted on a rate card.

Case Allowance An allowance or discount a manufacturer or wholesaler gives to a retailer on each case of product purchased, in return for which the retailer is to use the money to advertise the product.

Cash Discount A deduction allowed by print media (usually 2 percent of the net) for prompt payment (e.g., within 15 to 30 days), generally passed along by the agency to the advertiser to encourage collections.

Cash Refund Offer A type of mail-in offer, used by a brand or group of brands that offers cash to the consumer upon providing proof of purchase.

Category Development Index (CDI) The ratio of a market's percent of U.S. sales of a product category divided by the market's percent of U.S. population × 100. The category equivalent of the Brand Development Index (BDI).

Center Spread An advertisement appearing on the two facing pages in the center of a saddle-stitched publication.

Chain Break (a) The time between network programs during which a station identifies itself. (b) A commercial appearing in a chain break.

Checking Copy A copy of a publication sent to an advertiser and agency as proof that the advertisement appeared as ordered.

Circulation (a) In print, the number of copies of a vehicle distributed, based on an average of a number of issues. (b) In broadcast, the number of television or radio households that tune in to a station a minimum number of times within a specified time period (such as once a week or once a day). (c) In outdoor, the total number of people who have an opportunity to see a given showing of billboards within a specified time, such as a 24-hour period.

City Zone A geographic area that includes the corporate limits of the central city of the market plus any contiguous areas that have substantially the same built-up characteristics of the central city. This provides a method of reporting newspaper circulation according to the Audit Bureau of Circulations' standards.

Class A, B, C Rates Rates for television time, categorized by desirability of the time period. Class A rates are charged for the most desirable and costly television time, usually between 6 P.M. and 11 P.M. The next most costly level of rates is Class B; Class C is still less costly (and desirable). Each station sets its own time classifications. This system is seldom used today.

Class Magazine A publication that reaches select high-income readers, in contrast to magazines with larger circulations, generally referred to as *mass magazines.*

Clearance Obtaining a time period for a program or commercial on a station or obtaining approval to use advertising from clients, legal or medical counsel, or network continuity departments.

Clear Time Process used by an advertiser to reserve a time period with a local station and by a network to check with its affiliates on the availability of a time period.

Click-Through (Click-Through Rate) The percent of exposures to an Internet ad that result in the viewer clicking the mouse and being transferred to the advertiser's website. Click-through is used by many advertisers as the basis for payment to the site, because it can be a more useful measure of an exposure's value than ad impression.

Clipping Bureau An organization that examines newspapers and magazines and clips articles from them. It sends clients articles with references and allusions of interest to them.

Closing Date The final date to commit contractually for the purchase of advertising space, also called the *space closing date.* Generally, cancellations are not accepted after the closing date, although some publications have a separate cancellation date, which may fall earlier than this date. The *materials closing date* is the last date advertisers can supply production material to the publication.

Clutter Excessive amounts of advertising or nonprogram editorial material carried by media vehicles, both print and broadcast. The amount may be excessive both in terms of the total amount of advertising time and space and in terms of its scheduling—long strings of consecutive commercials for broadcasting and solid banks of advertisements in print.

Column Inch A measurement of newspaper space that is one column wide and one inch deep. The standard unit of measurement for newspaper pricing.

Combination Rate A discounted rate offered to encourage use of two or more stations, newspapers, magazines, and so on having common ownership. Occasionally, an advertiser has no choice but to buy the combination, as space or time may not be sold separately.

Commercial Audience The number of viewers or percent of population tuned to the average commercial minute of the program, viewed at normal speed. This can be reported as the live commercial audience or live plus DVR playback, typically over three days (the C3 audience). The commercial audience is distinguished from the "program" audience, which is the number of viewers to the average of all the minutes including entertainment.

Commercial Break In broadcasting, an interruption of programming during which commercials are broadcast.

Commercial Delivery The part of the audience that is actually exposed to a particular commercial.

Commercial Pool The selection of television or radio commercials that an advertiser has available for airing at any one time. Typically, different executions of the same creative theme.

Commercial Protection The amount of time that a network or station provides between the scheduling of competitive commercials.

Commission Compensation to a salesperson, agency, or others as a percent of the person's or agency's sales.

Competitive Parity Method A method of establishing a marketing or media budget based on matching anticipated competitive expenditures.

Composition The percent of a media vehicle's audience that is within an advertiser's target. For example, if Magazine A is read by 5 million women who are ages 18–34, and if the magazine has 10 million total adult readers, then the women 18–34 composition is 50 percent. This contrasts with *coverage*, which is the percent of the target exposed to the vehicle. In this example, since there are 34 million women ages 18–34 living in the United States, Magazine A's coverage of this target is 14.7 percent (5/34.0).

Concentration Campaign An advertising campaign that uses a small number of media vehicles to carry a relatively heavy amount of advertising.

Confirmation A broadcast media statement that a requested time slot is available to a prospective client.

Consecutive Weeks Discount A discount granted to an advertiser who uses a minimum number of weeks of advertising on a station or network without interruption.

Consumer Magazine A magazine whose editorial content appeals to the general public, or a specific segment or layer of the public. The term is used to differentiate these magazines from trade or business magazines.

Continuity A method of scheduling advertising at regular intervals over the year. Many patterns are possible, from advertising once each day of the year to once a month. Typically, a continuity advertiser is on air every week.

Controlled-Circulation Publications Publications that are offered at no charge to individuals who qualify by virtue of their job title or other characteristic. Most trade publications are controlled circulation. Some controlled circulation is solicited, although most is nonsolicited.

Cooperative Advertising Advertising run by a local advertiser in conjunction with a national advertiser. The national advertiser usually provides the copy and/or printing material and also shares the cost with the local retailer. In return, the national advertiser receives local promotion for its product. The name of the local advertiser and its address appear in the ad.

Cosponsorship The participation of two or more sponsors in a single broadcast program where each advertiser pays a proportionate share of the cost.

Cost-Efficiency The effectiveness of media as measured by a comparison of audience, either potential or actual, with cost and expressed as a CPM.

Cost per Rating Point (CPP) In broadcast, the cost of one household or demographic rating point (1 percent) in a given market. Used in media planning and evaluation, it is calculated by dividing the cost per spot by the rating. In the case of a number of spots, the CPP is their total cost divided by the total ratings or GRPs.

Cost per Thousand (CPM) The cost to deliver 1,000 people or homes. Used in comparing or evaluating the cost-efficiency of media vehicles, it is calculated by dividing the cost by the audience delivery, then multiplying the quotient by 1,000.

Counterprogramming A technique used by networks to regulate audience flow by offering a program of a different type from that broadcast by a strong competitor in the same time period.

Coverage A definition of a medium's geographical potential. In newspapers, coverage is the number of copies of a paper divided by the number of households in a given area. In magazines, it is the percentage of a given demographic market reached by a magazine. In radio and television, it is the percentage of television households that can tune in to a station (or stations) because they are in the signal area. In outdoor, coverage is the percentage of adults who pass a given showing and are exposed in a 30-day period. In previous years, coverage meant the same as reach. Today, the meaning depends on which medium is being discussed.

Cover Positions Premium-priced cover space for magazine or business publication advertisements. Cover positions are numbered: first cover is the outside front cover; second cover is the inside front cover; third cover is the inside back cover; fourth cover is the outside back cover. The first cover of consumer publications is seldom used for advertising.

CPG Abbreviation for consumer package goods—the broad range of products typically sold at grocery stores, drug stores, and mass merchandisers.

Cume A broadcast term that is Nielsen's shorthand for net cumulative audience of a program or of a spot schedule (radio or TV) in four weeks' time. The figure is based on total number of unduplicated TV homes or people reached.

Cumulative Audience The net unduplicated audience of a campaign, either in one medium or in a combination of media. Sometimes called *reach* or *cume.*

Cut-In Different broadcast copy or format that is used to replace an originating commercial in a network program in a specific market or region. Frequently used in test markets.

Cyberspace A term coined by author William Gibson in his novel *Neuromancer*. It represents the conceptual "place" where all Internet websites, networks, and online content resides. It has become a slang term for the Internet and the information in it.

Cycle (a) An interval within a contract year at the end of which, upon proper notice, an advertiser may cancel network stations, facilities, or both. Weekly and multiweekly program cycles usually last 13 weeks, while cosponsored program cycles usually encompass 13 major broadcasts. (b) A 13-week period used as a base for paying talent and use fees.

D Counties All remaining counties in the 15 percent of the United States that are not classified A, B, or C.

Daily Rate The rate a newspaper charges for space in its weekday editions, as opposed to the rate for the Sunday or weekend editions.

Data Fusion The process of combining the results of two surveys into a single database using common demographic "hooks." Fusion is necessary because no single survey can effectively capture all consumer behavior. The MRI survey is designed to measure the usage of thousands of products and services. The Nielsen Online survey captures all online activity across tens of thousands of websites. Each record in the fused database contains all the product usage information from a respondent in the MRI sample and all the online activity from a *demographically similar* respondent in Nielsen's online panel. The fusion concept assumes that demographics, such as age, sex, education, race, and so on, can accurately reflect both product usage and online browsing behavior. The quality of a data fusion depends on the validity, respondent matching process, and accuracy of the demographic hooks.

Day-After Recall Probably the most common method used to test television commercials. Test commercials are shown on the air in the normal fashion. Approximately 24 hours later, interviewers telephone people and ask about their previous day's viewing. Only those who viewed the program carrying the test commercial are questioned further. The test score consists of the proportion of the commercial audience who are able to provide specific correct audio or video details from the test commercial.

Daypart A part of the broadcast day, so designated for analytical purposes. In TV, the dayparts are usually early morning, daytime, early fringe, prime time, and late fringe. In radio, they are morning drive, daytime, afternoon drive, and evening.

Demographic Characteristics Physical characteristics, such as sex, age, education, and occupation, used to describe a population. Standard definitions, established by the 4As (American Association of Advertising Agencies), are used by many research companies.

Demographic Edition An edition of a national publication circulated only to individuals with known demographic characteristics. Usually these editions have the same editorial content as the national edition and differ only in their advertisements.

Designated Market Area (DMA) Nonoverlapping TV market coverage of the United States as defined by The Nielsen Company. Generally speaking, a DMA consists of all the counties that spend the largest share of viewing hours tuned to the TV stations in a given market. County assignments are reevaluated each September, with most changes occurring in the fringe counties. Each county is assigned to a single DMA, except where geographic features such as a mountain range splits viewing. In California, Contra Costa East spends the bulk of its time viewing Sacramento stations, while Contra Costa West mostly views San Francisco. Because DMA's are defined by television viewing, the counties are not necessarily adjacent. So Campbell County, Wyoming, is part of the Denver DMA even though it is widely separated from the cluster of counties that make up the bulk of the Denver DMA.

Diary Method A research technique in which a sample of respondents record in diaries specific behavior within a given period of time. This method is commonly used to measure the consumption of both media and products.

Differential (Newspaper) The difference in newspaper rates charged to local and national advertisers. Most newspapers charge higher rates to national advertisers than to retailers with a local street address.

Digital Video Recorder (DVR) An electronic attachment to a television set that records programs, either on command or at a set time or channel, to allow playback at a more convenient time. DVRs have the ability to fast-forward through the advertising, resulting in reduced exposure. The programs most likely to be recorded are the most popular scripted programs. News and sports programs are least likely to be recorded.

Discount A reduction from regular rates when an advertiser contracts to use quantities of advertising. Discounts in print may consider amount of space bought and frequency of insertion. Discounts in network broadcasting may be based upon number of dayparts used, frequency or weight, and length of contract. In local broadcasting, discounts will consider number of spots per week, length of contract, or purchase of plans or packages. Broadcast discounts are included in the negotiated price and are seldom formally spelled out.

Drive Time The radio dayparts when most people drive to or from work (about 6 to 10 A.M. and 3 to 7 P.M.). Drive time is the radio equivalent of television's prime time.

Duplication (a) The number or percentage of people in one vehicle's audience who are also exposed to another vehicle, best calculated as the percent of people exposed to either vehicle who are exposed to both. For example, if 80 people read either magazine A or magazine B, and if 40 people read only A, 30 people read only B, and 10 people read both magazines A and B, then the duplication would be 12.5% (10/80). (b) Audiences who are counted more than once in measurements, such as those who view the same TV program more than once a month (also called *audience duplication*).

Earned Rate The rate that an advertiser has earned, based on volume or frequency of space or time used to obtain a discount.

Effective Frequency The amount of frequency (or repetition) the planner judges to be necessary for advertisements to be effective in communicating the creative message.

Effective Reach The percent of the target audience exposed at the frequency level that is effective in the planner's judgment.

Eight-Sheet Poster See *Junior Panel*.

E-Mail Marketing A form of direct marketing that uses e-mail to deliver advertising and other marketing communication to the target consumers.

Exclusivity Freedom from competing advertising that one advertiser enjoys within a given communications medium; requires major purchases of space or time.

Expansion Plan An outline of the media to be used and timing thereof for a brand that plans to apply a theoretical national plan to portions of the country after testing and before actual national application. The expansion areas are the geographical units in which the product is to be sold.

Exposure Open eyes facing a medium. Practically, measurements are based on respondents who say with assurance that they have either read or looked into a given magazine during the most recent publication period (day, week, month, etc.). In broadcast, the measurement counts those who classify themselves as "watching" a television program or "listening" to a radio station, either by pushing a button on a people meter or by reporting exposure in a diary.

Exposure, Depth of The judgmentally determined additional value of an advertising exposure beyond the way it is defined in the standard methodology.

Exposure, Opportunity of The degree to which an audience may reasonably be expected to see or hear an advertising message.

Facebook One of the most popular social media websites as of summer 2010. Users create a profile of themselves with photographs, interests, and other personal information. They link up others ("friends") with similar interests to exchange informal messages about their daily life.

Federal Communications Commission (FCC) An independent United States government agency that was established by the Communications Act of 1934 and is charged with regulating interstate and international communications by radio, television, wire, satellite, and cable. The FCC's jurisdiction covers the 50 states, the District of Columbia, and U.S. possessions.

Fifteen and Two The financial terms on which advertising media are ordered by advertising agencies for their clients. Shorthand for saying a 15 percent commission is allowed by the media on the gross cost, with a 2 percent discount on the net amount for prompt payment.

Fifty-Fifty Plan In cooperative advertising, the equal sharing by a manufacturer and a dealer of the cost of a manufacturer's advertisement appearing over a dealer's name.

Fixed Position A specific period of station broadcasting time reserved for an advertiser and sold at a premium rate. Seldom used today.

Fixed Rate Station's price for a time slot that guarantees the advertiser's announcement will run in that position without preemption. Seldom used today—advertisers assume their announcements will run as ordered for the price they agreed to pay.

Flat Rate An advertisement rate that does not include any discounts.

Flighting A method of scheduling advertising for a period of time, followed by a hiatus period of no advertising, followed by a resumption of advertising.

Flowchart A system-analysis tool, either computerized or manual, that provides a graphical presentation of a procedure. In media plans, a flowchart is typically a one-year calendar, delineated by weeks and months, which shows all planned media activity. This includes publication dates, ad sizes, TV dayparts, weekly GRP levels, reach/frequency, budget, and any other information that might be needed by an advertiser.

Food & Drug Index A service of The Nielsen Company that uses store audits to collect data on retail sales movement.

Forced Combination Morning and evening newspapers owned by the same publisher and sold to national advertisers only in combination. Some forced combinations are morning and evening editions of the same newspapers. With the decline of newspapers, relatively few markets today have morning and evening editions.

Four-Color Process A halftone printing process that uses the colors magenta (red), cyan (blue), yellow, and black. This is the standard process used for color magazine ads.

Fourth Cover The outside back cover of a magazine.

Fractional Showing In outdoor, a showing of less than 25, offered in certain areas.

Franchise Position A specified position in a publication (e.g., back cover, inside front cover) that an advertiser has the right of first refusal to continue using as long as needed. If the advertiser does not use a given position one year, the right usually must be renegotiated for the advertiser to regain it.

Free Publication A publication sent without cost to a selected list of readers. Its circulation may or may not be audited by BPA and the publication cannot qualify for an Audit Bureau of Circulations audit unless at least 70 percent of circulation is paid.

Freestanding Insert (FSI) Printed material, typically a cents-off coupon, that is printed by the advertiser or a company such as Valassis Communications, Inc. (www.valassis.com) and inserted into a newspaper. The FSI is an important tool of package goods advertisers to stimulate trial and repeat purchase.

Frequency The average number of exposures to people who were reached by an ad campaign. Some people saw the ad only once; others saw it many times. Frequency (also *average frequency*) is the number of times the average person saw it. Calculated as GRPs divided by reach.

Frequency Discount A discount given for running a certain number of insertions, irrespective of size of advertisement, within a contract year. In broadcasting, similar discounts may be of two types: frequency per week and total number of announcements in a contract year.

Frequency Distribution An array of reach according to the number of times people in each group saw the ad. In other words, the number of people or percent of the target exposed once, twice, three times, and so on. Also the number of people exposed *at least* once, twice, three times, and so on.

Frequency-of-Reading Technique The most commonly used method for determining the number of people who read a magazine. Respondents are asked to record the number of copies of each magazine they have read out of the last four issues—one out of four, two out of four, and so on. Average issue audience is calculated as 25 percent of the one out of fours, 50 percent of the people who read two out of four issues, 75 percent of the three out of fours, and all of the four out of fours.

Fringe Time Time periods preceding and following peak set-usage periods and adjacent network programming blocks. For television, usually classified as *early fringe* (4:00 to 7:30 P.M.) and *late fringe* (after 11 P.M. EST).

Full Position Preferred position for a newspaper advertisement, generally following and next to reading matter, or top of column next to reading matter. When specifically ordered, it costs more than an ROP position.

Full-Program Sponsorship A regular program sponsored by only one advertiser.

Full Showing In car card advertising, usually denotes one card in each car of a line in which space is bought. In New York subways, a full showing consists of two cards in each car; a half showing is two cards in every other car. In outdoor poster advertising, a full or 100 showing indicates use of a specified number of panels whose total daily traffic on the average day (number of people passing the boards) is equal to the market population.

Fusion See *data fusion*.

Gatefold A special space unit in magazines, usually consisting of one full page plus an additional page or part of page that is an extension of the outer edge of the original page and folds outward from the center of the magazine as a gate.

General Editorial Magazine A consumer magazine not classified as to specific audience.

Geographic Market Weighting The practice of giving extra consideration to one or more markets that have more varying sales potential than other markets, because of location, demographics, or other reasons.

Geographic Split Run A way of buying a magazine ad where one creative execution is placed in the copies delivered to one geographic area and another ad is placed in other geographic areas or the balance of the country. Used by a national advertiser who sells different products in different geographic areas of the country.

Google An Internet website located at www.google.com that serves as a search engine that can locate desired content from anywhere in the world on the Internet. Google's search capability has been expanded to include search engine marketing, detailed satellite and terrestrial maps, and text translation. Offers news, video, images, shopping services, free e-mail, and other services.

Grade A and B Contours Areas in a television station's coverage pattern in which the transmission signal should have specific levels of strength according to requirements. Grade A service is defined as providing a picture expected to be satisfactory to the median (average) observer at least 90 percent of the time in at least 70 percent of the receiving locations within the contour, in the absence of interfering cochannel and adjacent-channel signals. Grade B service is satisfactory at least 90 percent of the time in at least 50 percent of the receiving locations. With 90 percent of American homes subscribing to cable or satellite, the contour is more important to station licensing than it is to advertisers.

Grid Card   A rate card in which a broadcast station's spots are priced individually, with charges related to the audience delivered. This is seldom used today.

Gross Audience   The total number of impressions to a medium or a combination of media. For example, if Medium A and Medium B have audiences of 7 million and 6 million, respectively, their gross audience is 13 million. To go from gross audience to net audience, one must subtract all duplicated audiences. The same as *gross impressions*.

Gross Impressions   The duplicated sum of audiences of all vehicles used in a media plan. This number represents the message weight of a media plan. The number is sometimes called the *tonnage* of the plan, because it is so large. (See *Gross Audience*.) Expressed as a percent, gross impressions X 100 divided by the population universe is GRPs.

Gross Rate   The published rate for space or time quoted by an advertising medium, including agency commission, cash discount, and any other discounts.

Gross Rating Point (GRP)   GRPs are the simple addition of the ratings from all of the media in a campaign. Also calculated as gross impressions divided by the population base times 100. GRPs are duplicated ratings. Also, reach X frequency = GRPs.

Guaranteed Circulation   The circulation level of a print vehicle; the basis for the advertising space rate. Similar to rate base circulation, except that an advertiser is assured of an adjustment if the circulation level is not achieved.

Half-Page Spread   An advertisement composed of two half-pages facing each other in a publication.

Half Run   (a) In transportation advertising, a car card placed in every other car of the transit system used; also called a *half service*. (b) For certain publications, advertising in half of the publication's circulation.

Half Showing   One half of a full showing of cards; a 50-intensity showing of outdoor posters or panels.

Hall's Magazine Reports (www.hallsreports.com)   A study of the number of editorial pages a magazine devotes to various categories of product interest over a period of time (e.g., the number of pages a magazine devotes to articles on food, home furnishings, fiction, news). This information is frequently used in analyzing the editorial content of a magazine before advertising is placed in it.

Hiatus   A period of time during which there is no advertising activity.

Holding Power The degree to which a program retains its audience throughout a broadcast. This percentage equals the average audience divided by the total audience. (See *Audience Holding Index*; *Audience Turnover*.)

Holdover Audience The audience a program acquires from listeners or viewers who tuned to the preceding program on the station and remained with the station.

Home Service Magazine A publication with editorial content keyed to the home and home living. Examples are *Better Homes & Gardens* and *House Beautiful*.

Horizontal Cume The cumulative audience rating for two programs in the same time period on different days.

Horizontal Half Page A half-page advertisement running horizontally across the page. (See *Vertical Half Page*.)

Horizontal Trade Publications A business publication editorially designed to be of interest to a variety of businesses or business functions.

Households Using TV (HUT) Also called *Homes Using Television*. A term used by The Nielsen Company that refers to the total number of TV households using their television sets during a given time period. Can be used for the total United States or a local market. The comparable term for persons is PUT, Persons Using Television.

Hyping Intense activity on the part of a broadcaster to increase rating during a rating survey.

ID Any short-length "identification" commercial on radio or TV (e.g., a 10-second ID).

Impressions See *Gross Impressions*.

Imprint In cooperative poster advertising programs, the local dealer's name placed on the bottom portion of the poster design (about 20 percent of the total copy area) to identify that store as the place to buy the product advertised. Sometimes the local dealer pays a portion of the cost of the poster space, and the parent company pays the remaining portion.

Index The ratio of two percentages times 100. The numerator represents the marketing information the planner is interested in; that is, a market's percent of U.S. sales. The denominator is usually the population base. If the market's percent of U.S. sales equals its percent of U.S. population, the index is 100 and the market is said to be an average market. If the numerator is greater, the index is over 100, and the market would be viewed as above average. The converse is true for markets with an index below 100. In calculating an index, the selection of the denominator base is important. The index for women's products should be calculated against a base of all women, not total adults.

Industrial Advertising Advertising of capital goods, supplies, and services directed mainly to industrial or professional firms that require them in the course of manufacturing.

Inherited Audience On a radio or television station, the carryover of a portion of one program's audience to the next program. (See *Holdover Audience*.)

In-Home Audience The portion of media exposure (reading, listening, or viewing) that occurs in the home.

Insertion Order Authorization from an advertiser or agency to a publisher to print an advertisement of specified size on a given date or dates at a definite rate. Copy instructions and printing materials may accompany the order or be sent later.

In-Store Media (In-Store Marketing) Print or broadcast ads that appear in stores. Print options include shopping carts, billboards, shelf talkers, and aisle posters. TV options include end-of-aisle monitors and shopping cart and checkout monitors.

Integrated Commercial A commercial that features more than one product or service in the form of a single commercial message.

Integration (or Origination or Networking) Charge A moderate extra charge to an advertiser for each commercial occurrence by a TV network for the integration of a commercial into a program. This anachronistic charge began in the early days of television when the commercials and entertainment were "integrated" by hand into a single reel of videotape. Technology and electronic switching have eliminated this process, but the charge continues as a bone of contention between media buyers and the networks.

Intensity In outdoor advertising, the strength of combinations of poster locations throughout a city in terms of coverage or repetition opportunities. A 100 showing has a 100 intensity. The number of posters that comprise a 100 showing (therefore, a 100 intensity) varies from city to city.

Interim Statement Sworn circulation statement of a publisher made quarterly to the Audit Bureau of Circulations at the publisher's option and issued unaudited but subject to audit. A situation that might call for an interim statement would occur when a community served by more than one newspaper loses one of them through consolidation or discontinuance and its circulation is absorbed by the other newspaper. (See *Publisher's Statement.*)

Intermedia Comparison In the planning process, a comparison among different media—such as among TV, radio, and magazines.

Internet A network of computer networks derived from the U.S. Department of Defense system for scientific communication and considered by many to be the freest and most flexible form of communication that exists today. A complete glossary of Internet terms can be found at www.matisse.net/files/glossary.html. This site is operated by Matisse Enzer, an Internet consultant in San Francisco.

Intramedia Comparison In the planning process, comparisons among media vehicles in the same class, such as among three magazines.

Island Position A newspaper or magazine advertisement entirely surrounded by editorial matter or margin.

Isolated 30 A 30-second commercial surrounded only by programming—virtually unheard of in today's broadcast environment.

Issue Life The time during which a publication accrues its total readership. For a weekly, this is generally five weeks; for a monthly, three months.

Junior Page In print, a page size that permits an advertiser to use the same printing materials for small- and large-page publications. The advertisement is prepared as a full-page unit in the smaller publication, and in the larger publication as a junior page with editorial around it.

Junior Panel A small-scale version of the 30-sheet poster. Also called an *eight-sheet poster*.

Junior Spread A print advertisement that appears on two facing pages and occupies only part of each page.

Keying an Advertisement Identification within an advertisement or coupon that permits inquiries or requests to be traced to a specific advertisement.

Keyline An assembly of all elements of a print ad pasted on a board. This camera-ready art is photographed to make the negative that in turn is used to make the printing plate. Also called a *mechanical*. This physical process has been largely replaced by computerized digital composition.

Lead-In (a) Words spoken by an announcer or narrator at the beginning of some shows to perform a scene-setting or recapitulation function. (b) A broadcast program positioned before another program.

Lead-Out In relation to audience flow, the program following an advertiser's program on the same station.

Lifestyle Targeting A target-audience classification system that categorizes people based on their activities, interests, and opinions.

Linage (a) A newspaper term denoting the number of (agate) lines in an ad or an ad schedule. (b) The amount of total space run by a publication in certain categories (e.g., retail grocery linage). Newspaper line rates have been replaced by column inch rates.

List Broker In direct-mail advertising, an agent who rents prospect lists from the advertiser that compiled the data, and sells those lists to another advertiser. The agent receives a commission for these services.

Listener Diary Method of TV or radio research whereby the audience keeps a continuing record of viewing or listening in a diary.

Listening Area The geographic area covered by a station's signal, usually divided into primary and secondary areas.

Little U.S.A. Concept In test marketing, a media plan translation method that executes a national media plan in a small market that has the same demographics and product usage habits as the entire country. Contrast with *As It Falls Concept*.

Live Time The time that the actual performance of a program is transmitted by interconnected facilities directly to the receiving stations at the moment of performance.

Live-Time Delay A delay that coincides with the local live time. Usually occurs when the station is noninterconnected and thus unable to take a live feed.

Local Advertising Advertising by local retailers (as opposed to national companies advertising in local markets), usually at a lower rate than that charged national advertisers.

Local-Channel Station A radio station that is allowed just enough power to be heard near its point of transmission and is assigned a radio channel set aside for low-power local-channel stations (usually 250 watts).

Locally Edited Supplement Sunday magazine supplement similar in character to syndicated magazine supplements but owned and edited by the newspaper distributing it. In the past, such supplements were available in most of the largest cities throughout the United States. These have been largely eliminated in recent years due to the financial challenges facing newspapers. A few major newspapers, such as the *New York Times*, have continued their locally edited supplement.

Local Media Media whose coverage and circulation are confined to or concentrated in their market of origin. Usually, they offer different sets of rates to the national advertiser and the local advertiser.

Local Rate Rate charged by a medium to the local retail trade.

Local Time Availabilities or times of broadcasting quoted in terms of local time rather than eastern standard time.

Loyalty Index Frequency of listenership to a particular station.

Magazine Supplement A magazine section of a Sunday or daily newspaper distributed either locally or nationally.

Mail-In Premium A premium offered at the point of sale in a retail store to be obtained by the consumer by mailing a box top, coin, or label to the manufacturer.

Mail Survey Map A broadcast coverage map prepared by tabulating cumulative, unsolicited mail received during a certain period or by tabulating listener response to a special order or contest run during a certain period. A throwback to the early days of radio, before the advent of syndicated research.

Makegood An announcement or advertisement run as a replacement for one that was scheduled but did not run, or that ran incorrectly. Also, no-charge units given to honor audience delivery guarantees (called *audience deficiency units* or *ADUs*).

Market The geographic area that can receive the program; can range from the entire United States down to a local market.

Market-by-Market Allocation (MBM) A system of media/marketing planning that allocates a brand's total available advertising dollars against current or potential business on the basis of each individual TV market. MBM spends all advertising dollars (national and local) available in each market in proportion to current or anticipated business in the market. The result of MBM planning is spending more accurately against anticipated sales and thereby generating greater business for a brand.

Market Development Index See *Category Development Index; Market Index.*

Market Index The factor chosen to measure relative sales opportunities in different geographic or territorial units. Any quantitative information that makes estimation of such opportunities possible might be used as a market index. A general market index is a factor that influences the purchase of a specific product or groups of related products. Sometimes called a *market development index* or *category development index.*

Marketing Mix A group of elements used to sell a product or service: product, place (or distribution), price, and promotion.

Market Outline The measurement of the share of market based on total purchases of a particular brand or groups of similar brands with a product category during a specific time period.

Market Pattern The pattern of a product's sales in terms of the relation between the volume and concentration either by total market or by individual market. A thick market pattern is one in which a high portion of all people are prospects for a product. A thin market pattern is one in which a low portion of all people are prospects for a product.

Market Potential The portion of a market that a company can hope to capture for its own product.

Market Profile A demographic description of the people or the households in a product's market. The description may also include economic and retailing information about a territory.

Market Segmentation A strategy of implementing different kinds of marketing programs to various segments of the total consumer market based on demographic or lifestyle characteristics.

Market Share A product's share of an industry's sales volume.

"Marriage" Split Ad placement that occurs when more than one advertiser buys the total circulation of a magazine and each of the advertisers runs its ad in only a portion of that circulation. For example, an advertiser with distribution in the western United States and one with distribution in the eastern United States may split an ad in a magazine that permits this. In this case, the advertiser with distribution in the West would use only the part of the magazine's circulation that reaches the West, and the other advertiser would use the remainder.

Masked-Recognition Test A method of assessing an ad's effectiveness by finding the percentage of respondents who can identify the advertiser or brand when all identifying marks are concealed.

Mass Magazine A magazine of a general nature that appeals to all types of people in all localities.

Mechanical See *Keyline.*

Mechanical Requirements The physical specifications of a publication that advertising material must meet to be reproduced in the publication. Such requirements are brought about by the physical requirements of the vehicle and the characteristics of its printing process. Broadcast media have similar requirements governing the physical characteristics of material acceptable for broadcast.

Media Consortia A group of advertisers or advertising agencies that pool their media budgets to obtain maximum buying discounts through their greater combined negotiating leverage.

Media Objectives The goals a media plan is expected to accomplish.

Media Plan The blueprint for how the advertising message will be delivered to the target audience. The plan also serves as a persuasive document that communicates the rationale behind a recommendation to spend significant amounts of money. Generally includes the media objectives, competitive analysis, target audience analysis and media habits, media strategy, time line, flowchart, and budget.

Media Records A detailed report of advertising volume by selected brands in selected daily and Sunday newspapers in selected cities. Today this has been replaced by Kantar Media's newspaper expenditure reports.

Media Strategy Statement A document prepared by an agency and outlining the specific media that the agency believes will best accomplish the brand's marketing objectives (as outlined in the market strategy statement) with the funds available.

Media Translation (a) The process of reducing a national advertising media plan to local level to test a product or campaign inexpensively. (b) The expansion of a local advertising campaign to a national level.

Media Value The judgment that a given medium has been found, through experience, to be more effective for a brand and its creative message, thus justifying more frequency in that medium.

Media Weight The total size of an advertising campaign in terms of number of commercials, impressions, GRPs, insertions, reach and frequency, advertising dollars, and so on.

Medium Any media class used to convey an advertising message to the public; includes newspapers, magazines, direct mail, radio, television, the Internet, and billboards.

Message Dispersion A measure indicating how widely a message is received in a target universe. Reach is a measure of message dispersion.

Message Weight The gross number of advertising messages or impressions delivered by a vehicle or a group of vehicles in a schedule.

Metro Area A county or group of counties comprising the central core of a geographical market (usually based on governmental lines).

Metropolitan and Micropolitan Statistical Areas Geographic entities defined by the U.S. Office of Management and Budget for use in publishing federal statistics. According to the U.S. Census Bureau, "A metro area contains a core urban area of 50,000 or more population, and a micro area contains an urban core of at least 10,000 (but less than 50,000) population. Each metro or micro area consists of one or more counties and includes the counties containing the core urban area, as well as any adjacent counties that have a high degree of social and economic integration (as measured by commuting to work) with the urban core." The metro area is the geographic base for radio ratings.

Middle Break Station identification at about the halfway point of a show.

Milline Rate A means of comparing rates of newspapers; the cost of one agate line per million circulation. The milline rate is computed by multiplying the line rate by 1 million, then dividing by the circulation. The factor of 1 million is used merely to provide an answer in convenient terms of dollars and cents, rather than in fractions of a cent. Today the line rate has been replaced by the inch rate in standard advertising units (SAU).

Minimum Depth At most newspapers, a requirement for the minimum size of advertisements— generally that an ad must be at least one inch high for every column it is wide. For example, if an advertiser wants to run an ad that is eight columns wide, the ad must be at least eight inches high.

Minute-by-Minute Profile Nielsen data reporting the minute-by-minute program audience. Used to study audience gains and losses during specific minutes of the program and to aid in placing commercials at times when they receive maximum audiences.

Mobile The access and delivery of Internet content on cellular telephones that have been equipped with a keyboard, a browser, and the ability contact the Internet. See *Smart Phone*.

Morning Drive Radio daypart from 6:00 to 10:00 A.M.

Multistation Lineup Purchase of commercial time on more than one station in a market.

NAB Codes Radio and television codes promulgated by the National Association of Broadcasters (NAB) to help its members meet their obligation to serve the American public. The codes include both program and advertising standards. Included in the advertising standards are sections dealing with presentation techniques, contests, premiums and offers, and time standards. These codes are extended by other documents providing interpretations and guidelines (e.g., *Children's Television Advertising Guidelines* and *Alcoholic Beverage Advertising Guidelines*). Discontinued in 1982.

Narrowcasting Service by a cable system to a small community; the delivery of programming that addresses a specific need or audience.

National Advertising Rates Rates for newspaper space charged to a national advertiser, as distinguished from local rates applying to local retailers. National advertising rates are generally higher than local rates.

National Media Media that are national in scope.

National Plan A media plan that is national in scope, as opposed to a local plan covering less than the entire United States.

National Rating A rating of all households or individuals tuned in to a program on a national base. Sometimes the base is all television or radio households in the country. Other times, the base is only those households that can tune in to the program because they are served by a cable system carrying the program.

Net Controlled Circulation The number of purchased and unpurchased copies of a controlled-circulation publication that are actually distributed to its intended readership.

Net Plus The net cost of a print ad, commercial, or program with an earned discount added on.

Net Unduplicated Audience The combined cumulative audience for a single issue of a group of magazines or broadcasts.

Net Weekly Audience In broadcast research, the number of families tuned in at least once to a program aired more than once a week.

Network Two or more stations contractually united to deliver broadcast programs (e.g., network programs).

Network Affiliate A broadcast station that is part of a network and therefore offers network programs.

Network Franchise A brand's right to retain the sponsorship of a program at the sponsoring brand's discretion. Advertisers acquire this right by agreeing to sponsor a program on a continuing basis.

Network Identification Acknowledgment of a network affiliation at the end of a network broadcast.

Network Option Time Time on network affiliates for which the network has selling priority.

Newspaper-Distributed Magazine A supplement inserted into a Sunday newspaper.

Newspaper Syndicate A business concern that sells special material (columns, photographs, comic strips) for simultaneous publication in a number of newspapers.

Newsstand Circulation Copies of publications purchased at outlets selling copies. These outlets may include hotels, vending machines, street vendors, drugstores, and supermarkets, in addition to the traditional newsstand or kiosk.

Nielsen Shorthand for The Nielsen Company, an international research giant with services covering virtually every aspect of consumer product marketing. Although formerly divided into separate units that had little contact with each other, in recent years the company has made it a corporate mission to integrate and cross-pollinate its many divisions.

Nielsen Rating See *Rating*.

Nielsen Station Index (NSI) The local television rating service of The Nielsen Company.

Ninety-Day Cancellation For all poster advertising, a policy that the advertising may be cancelled on 90 days' notice to the plant. This means that the advertiser or agency must notify the poster plant owner of cancellation 90 days before the contract posting date.

Noted The basic measure in the Starch method for testing print ads. This score represents the percentage of respondents (claimed readers of the issue) who say they saw the ad when they first read or looked into the magazine issue. In other words, they claimed recognition of the ad.

Obtained Score A Gallup & Robinson term for the actual percentage of respondents who prove recall of a print ad before the score is adjusted for color and size or converted to an index score. It is the basis for the final score.

Off Card Using a special rate not covered by a rate card.

Offensive Spending Advertising activity intended to secure new business.

On-Air Test A test of a commercial that uses a real broadcast response before the advertiser uses that commercial on a larger scale. An on-air test measures audience response to the creative executions, such as recall, attitude, or purchase interest for that product.

One-Time Rate The highest rate charged by a medium not subject to discounts. Sometimes called *open rate*.

Open End A broadcast that leaves the commercial spots blank to be filled in locally.

Open-End Transcription A recorded program usually sold on a syndicated basis in various cities and produced so that local commercial announcements may be inserted at various points throughout the show.

Open Rate In print, the highest rate charged to an advertiser, on which all discounts are based. Also called *base rate* or *one-time rate*.

Opportunities Marketing facts that exist and, without much money or effort, sell the product naturally.

Option Time (a) Time reserved by the networks in contract with their affiliates and for which the network has prior call under certain conditions for sponsored network programs; called *network option time*. (b) Time reserved by the local stations for local and national spot shows; called *station option time*.

Orbit A scheduling method in which stations rotate an advertiser's commercial among different programs, time periods, or both—typically in prime time. Seldom used today.

Organic Search See *Search*.

OTO One time only, describing a spot that runs only once. An OTO spot may be bought outright or provided as a makegood.

Outdoor Advertising Display advertising (billboards, posters, signs, etc.) placed out-of-doors, along highways and railroads, or on walls and roofs of buildings.

Out-of-Home Audience (a) Listeners to auto and battery-operated radios outside their homes. (b) The audience of a publication derived from exposure that occurred outside the reader's own home. (See *In-Home Audience*.)

Overlapping Circulation Duplication of circulation when advertising is placed in two or more media reaching the same prospects. Overlapping circulation is sometimes desirable to give additional impact to advertising.

Overnights Nielsen household ratings and shares provided to clients the morning following the day or evening of telecast.

Package (a) A combination of programs or commercials offered by a network for sponsorship at one price. Spot TV is sometimes sold as a package. (b) A program property in which all elements from script to finished production are owned and controlled by an individual or organization, commonly known as a *packager*.

Packaged Goods Mostly food, soap, and household products that are marketed in the manufacturer's package, wrapper, or container. Also known as Consumer Packaged Goods (CPG).

Package Insert Separate advertising material included in packaged goods.

Package Plan A plan by which an advertiser purchases a certain number of TV or radio announcements per week, in return for which the station gives the advertiser a lower rate per announcement. The advertiser agrees to run the specific number of announcements each week and cannot split them up over a period of time.

Package Plan Discount In spot television, a price discount based upon frequency within a week, for example, "5-plan," "10-plan."

Packager An individual or company producing a broadcast program or series of programs that are sold as complete units.

Painted Bulletin A billboard that is approximately 48 feet long by 14 feet high, with the copy message painted on the face of this structure, as contrasted to the poster panel that is composed of preprinted sheets that are pasted up like wallpaper.

Painted Display See *Painted Bulletin.*

Painted Wall An outdoor advertising unit, purchased individually, usually situated on a high-traffic artery or in a neighborhood shopping area.

Panel (a) A fixed sample of respondents or stores selected to participate in a research project in which they report periodically on their knowledge, attitudes, and activities. This sampling technique is in contrast to the technique of using fresh samples each time. (b) A master TV or radio control board, usually in a master control room.

Panels Regular and illuminated units of outdoor advertising. A regular panel is a billboard that is not lighted at night. An illuminated panel is a billboard that is lighted from dusk until midnight.

Pantry Audit A consumer survey to tabulate brands, items, and varieties of grocery store products in the home.

Parallel Location An outdoor advertising location in which the poster panel is parallel to the road.

Participation An announcement inside the context of a program, as opposed to sponsorship or to chain or station breaks placed between programs. A station or network may program a segment of time to carry participation announcements, which it sells to various advertisers for commercial use. The announcements are usually 10, 30, or 60 seconds long, but may be longer.

Participation Program (a) A commercial program cosponsored by a number of advertisers. (b) A program in which the audience participates (e.g., a quiz show).

Pass-Along Reader A person who reads a publication not purchased by the person or a member of his or her family. These readers are included in determining the total numbers of readers of a particular issue or a particular publication. (See *Audience, Secondary.*)

Pay Cable Any of a number of program services for which cable subscribers pay a monthly charge in addition to the basic cable subscription fee.

Penalty Costs In a test market and expansion operation, the premium paid for local replacement media, compared with the national media that the brand uses for its national plan.

Penetration The percentage of total homes or people in a specified area who are physically able to be exposed to a medium or who purchase a given product or service.

People Meter An electronic device that measures viewership of TV programs. Present meters require members of a sample household to push their designated button when they consider themselves to be "watching" television. This information is sent via telephone lines to the computers of The Nielsen Company, which tally the number of viewers watching each program.

Percent Composition See *Composition*.

Percent Coverage See *Coverage*.

Per Inquiry Advertising (PI Advertising) An agreement between a media owner and an advertiser in which the owner agrees to accept payment for advertising on the basis of the number of inquiries or completed sales resulting from advertising, soliciting inquiries, or direct sales. It is the least desirable way for a station to sell inventory.

Persons Using Radio (PUR) The percentage of an area's population (older than age 12) listening to a radio at any given time.

P4C Abbreviation for "page/four-color," meaning a full-page ad printed in the four-color process. Other abbreviations include *P2C* (page/two-color), *PB&W* (page/black and white), *3/5P4C* (3/5 page/four-color), *2C* (second cover), and *BC* (back cover).

Piggyback The back-to-back scheduling of two or more brand commercials of one advertiser in network or spot positions.

Plan Rate The rate paid by an advertiser who purchased a TV or radio package plan. The rates are lower than if the spots were purchased individually, since the advertiser agreed to run a specific number of spots each week.

Pod A bank of consecutive commercials within a television program.

Position An advertisement's place on a page and the location of the page in the publication. A preferred position is an especially desirable position obtained by paying an extra charge or granted to an advertiser that has placed a heavy schedule in a publication. Publications occasionally rotate preferred positions among advertisers that have contracted for space above a specified minimum.

Poster A product sign intended to be displayed on a store window or on an inside wall, large enough to be legible at a reasonable distance.

Poster Panel A standard surface on which outdoor advertisements are mounted. The poster panel is the most widely used form of outdoor advertising. The standard panel measures 12 feet by 25 feet and is usually made of steel with a wood, fiberglass, or metal molding around the outer edges. The 24-sheet poster is posted on this structure.

Poster Showing Poster advertising is sold in packages called *showings*. It is possible to buy #25, #50, #75, #100, and #200 showings. A showing equals the percent of the market's population passing one or more of the boards each day and is sometimes referred to as *daily GRPs*. This is based on the Traffic Audit Bureau's count of cars passing each site multiplied by an estimated number of persons per car. So a #50 showing equals 50 GRPs per day or 1,500 GRPs per month. The #100 showing is designed to provide more intense coverage of practically all major streets in the market. The #200 showing is one designed for maximum impact. Each poster plant owner decides how many panels will constitute a #50 showing or a #100 showing in his or her city. The outdoor industry has plans to replace the showing metric with measured GRPs.

Post Test Study of the response to finished advertising after it has been published and telecast in media. Post tests rely on normal patterns of behavior to expose respondents to advertising.

Potential Audience See *Audience, Potential.*

Preemptible Spot A spot announcement sold at a reduced rate because the station has the option to sell that same spot to another advertiser willing to pay full rate. No longer used.

Preemption Recapture by the station network of an advertiser's time to substitute a special program of universal value. For example, when the president speaks, the show regularly scheduled at that time is preempted.

Preferred Position A position in a magazine or newspaper that is regarded as excellent in terms of its ability to generate a large readership. Preferred position is usually located next to editorial material that has a high interest among the publication's readers.

Preprint A reproduction of an advertisement before it appears in a publication.

Pretest Study of advertisements or commercials prior to distribution via regular media channels. Advertising may be studied in rough or finished form. Pretesting relies on some special means of exposing respondents to the advertisement other than the regular media planned—portfolios, dummy magazines, and so on.

Primary Audience See *Audience, Primary.*

Primary Households Households into which a publication has been introduced by purchase, either at the newsstand or by subscription, rather than by pass-along.

Primary Readers The readers of a publication who reside in primary households.

Primary Research Original research conducted for one client or to meet a specific agency need. Contrasts with syndicated research.

Primary Service Area In AM or standard broadcasting, the area in which a station signal is strongest and steadiest. Defined by FCC rules as the area in which the ground wave (the primary wave for broadcast transmission) is not subject to objectionable interference or objectionable fading. No similar term is officially used in TV broadcasting, although television engineering standards recognize three zones of signal service existing in concentric rings from the transmitting tower: City Grade Service, A Contour, B Contour. An irrelevant metric for media planners.

Prime Time The period of peak television set usage—between 8:00 and 11 P.M. in the eastern and Pacific time zones and between 7:00 and 10 P.M. in the central and mountain time zones. On Sundays, prime time begins an hour earlier.

Prime Time Access Rule (PTAR) An FCC rule that allows television stations to put on a specified amount of their own local programming during prime time. Under this rule, regular network programming starts at 8 P.M. eastern standard time Monday through Saturday and 7 P.M. on Sunday. The period from 7:30 to 8:00 P.M. is generally referred to as *prime access time*.

Product Placement A form of advertising where the physical product or service is incorporated into the script or is used as a prop in a movie, television entertainment, or news program. Sometimes called *branded entertainment*.

Product Protection Protection that an advertiser wants and sometimes gets against being positioned adjacent to a competitive product. A concept honored more in the breech than in the practice.

Program Coverage The number (or percentage) of television households that can receive a program over one or more stations because they are in the signal area of some station carrying the program.

Program Lineup A listing of stations carrying a program on either a live or delayed basis. The information on the list may be supplied by the network or received directly from their affiliates.

Program Station Rating A rating that is based on the television homes located in the area in which a program was telecast. This type of rating permits an unbiased comparison of different programs regardless of variation in the number of homes capable of receiving the programs.

Promotion Allowance Money received by a wholesaler or a retailer from a manufacturer or its representative for sales promotion other than advertising. (See *Advertising Allowance*.)

Psychographic A term that describes consumers or audience members on the basis of some psychological trait, characteristic of behavior, or lifestyle.

Public Access FCC rule that requires any cable system with 3,500 or more subscribers to have at least one noncommercial channel available to the public on a first-come nondiscriminatory basis.

Public Service Announcement (PSA) Promotional material for a nonprofit cause, usually prepared at no cost to the service advertised and carried by vehicles at no cost.

Publishers Information Bureau (PIB) PIB is a membership organization that tracks the amount and type of advertising carried by consumer magazines. It accounts for about 85 percent of consumer magazine ad volume. Data is reported quarterly and is designed to give convenient summaries of national magazine expenditures by advertiser and by publication.

Publisher's Statement A notarized statement made by a publisher regarding total circulation, geographic distribution, methods of securing subscriptions, and so on. These statements are issued twice a year by the Audit Bureau of Circulations, for the six months ending June 30 and December 31. They contain detailed information about a magazine's circulation, copy distribution, price, and other information used by media planners.

Pulsing A media scheduling technique in which periods of heavy activity alternate with lower-activity periods.

Pure Program Ratings A measurement of audience size in which estimates exclude program pre-emptions that occurred during the survey period.

Qualified Issue Reader A respondent who qualifies to be interviewed about advertisements in a magazine on the basis of having read the study issue of a magazine. Requirements for such qualification vary. For Daniel Starch & Associates interviews, readers merely have to claim they looked into the issue when shown the cover. For Gallup & Robinson studies, respondents must prove reading by correctly describing some article when shown the issue's cover and table of contents.

Qualified Viewer A respondent who has demonstrated viewing of a TV program (on the basis of recall of at least one part of the episode), thus becoming eligible or qualified for interview about commercials aired on that show.

Quantity Discount (a) A graduated discount on quantity purchases scaled to the number of cases in a single order. (b) A periodic refund based upon the value of purchases over a period of time.

Quintile The division of any sample of respondents into five equal-sized groups ranging from the heaviest to the lightest amount of exposure to the medium. Samples may also be divided into tertiles (thirds), quartiles (fourths), deciles (tenths), and so on.

Quota A predetermined media goal in a market. Goals can be established in terms of dollars spent, number of spots to be purchased, or GRPs to be achieved. The agency's time buyer uses quotas in implementing a media plan. In research a quota sample establishes the target number of respondents in each age or gender group to match the U.S. Census. Although the final sample may match the census, panelists in difficult-to-recruit populations, such as young men, may not be representative of all the members of that group.

RADAR (Radio's All Dimension Audience Research) The network radio rating service provided by the National Radio Services division of Arbitron Company. It is set up to service national customers such as radio networks, syndicators, representative firms, public radio, and satellite radio companies.

Rate Base The circulation level of a print vehicle, used in setting rates for advertising space.

Rate Card A medium's listing of advertising costs, mechanical requirements, issue dates, closing dates, cancellation dates, and circulation data. Rate cards are issued magazines and newspapers. Broadcast stations no longer issue rate cards for their negotiated time.

Rate Differential Among newspapers, the difference between the national and the local rates.

Rate Holder (a) A minimum-sized advertisement placed in a publication during a contract period to hold a time or quantity discount rate. (b) An ID spot bought by the advertiser for the same reason.

Rate Protection A guarantee that an advertiser's rate under the old rate card will be protected for a period, usually from three to six months, should a new rate be introduced.

Rating In television or radio, the percent of the target audience in a market that is tuned in to a program or a daypart. In national television, ratings refer to the average minute. In local TV and radio, ratings refer to the average quarter hour.

Reach The number of different persons or homes exposed to a specific media vehicle or schedule at least once. Usually measured over a specific period of time (e.g., four weeks). Also known as *cume*, *cumulative*, *unduplicated*, or *net audience*.

Reader Interest (a) Expression of interest by readers in advertisements they have read. Sometimes evaluated by unsolicited mail. Sometimes evaluated by the numbers of people who can remember having read material with interest. (b) An evaluation of the relative level of general interest in different types of products.

Readers People who are exposed to a print vehicle.

Readers per Copy The average number of readers of a magazine per copy of circulation. When multiplied by a magazine's circulation, the result equals its audience.

Readership or Magazine Audience The average number of persons who are exposed to a publication as distinguished from the circulation or number of copies distributed.

Reader Traffic The movement from page to page by readers of a publication.

Read Most As defined by Daniel Starch & Associates for measurement of ad readership, magazine or newspaper readers who read 50 percent or more of the copy of a specific advertisement.

Rebate A refund that reduces the contract price for merchandise. The term is frequently used for advertising allowances. Also given to advertisers by a certain media vehicle as a result of an advertiser's exceeding the contract minimum and earning a greater discount.

Recent-Reading Technique In measurement of magazine readership, a technique in which survey respondents read a list of magazines and check the names of magazines they are sure they have read in the most recent publication period (week, month, quarter, etc.).

Recognition A technique used to determine whether a person saw or heard a given print advertisement or broadcast commercial; the researcher shows (or plays) the ad or commercial and inquires whether the person saw or heard it at a previous date in a specific medium. This technique was pioneered and is still being used by Daniel Starch & Associates.

Regional Edition A geographical section of a national magazine's circulation that an advertiser can purchase without having to purchase the rest of the magazine's circulation (as is required in a split run). The magazine usually charges a higher premium for regional editions and demographic editions.

Regional Network A network of stations serving a limited geographic area.

Regular Panel See *Panels*.

Remnant Space Magazine space sold at reduced price to help fill out regional editions.

Renewals (a) In print, magazine or newspaper subscriptions that people extend past their expiration dates. (b) In outdoor advertising, extra posters over and above the quantity actually needed to post the exact number of panels in a showing. They are shipped to the plant operator, and if one of the posters on display is damaged, the plant operator has a complete poster design on hand to replace the damaged poster immediately.

Repetition A measure indicating to what extent audience members were exposed to the same vehicle or group of vehicles. Frequency is a measure of repetition.

Replacement Media Local media that are being used to offset deficiencies in national media delivery in a test market or expansion area (e.g., local rotogravure supplements, comic sections, black-and-white daily newspapers). In television, additional spot TV weight to compensate for network underdelivery.

Representative (or Rep) A general term used to describe sales representatives for media vehicles. A representative firm usually handles several vehicles, serving as their sales agent and taking commissions on the sales they make; salespersons may also be directly employed by stations or publications.

Response Function A table that quantifies differences in a target's response to advertising after varying numbers of exposures.

Retail Trading Zone The area beyond the city zone whose residents regularly trade to an important degree with retail merchants in the city zone. These are defined by the Audit Bureau of Circulations.

Returns per Thousand Circulation A gauge of the effectiveness of media used in support of promotions; computed by dividing the total number of returns by the circulation of the publication to which the returns are attributable. (See *Keying an Advertisement*.)

Rollout A marketing strategy technique in which a brand is introduced in a limited geographical area. If the brand succeeds in that area, it is then introduced in adjacent areas and, if successful, in other adjacent areas until the entire country is covered.

Roster Recall Method of research in which a list of radio or TV programs is submitted to respondents for recall.

Rotating Painted Bulletins Moving the advertiser's copy from one painted bulletin location to another, usually every 60 days. This service, available in most major cities, offers advertisers an opportunity to cover a large area or a given market (over a long period of time) with a limited number of painted bulletins.

Rotation (a) The process of continuing a series of advertisements over and over again in a regular order. (b) The practice in store management of moving the older stock forward when restocking shelves or cases. (c) The practice, in retail advertising, of scheduling a branded product or group of products to be featured at intervals throughout the year to maintain a desired stock balance.

Run of Press (ROP) (a) A newspaper advertisement for which a definite position is not specified, but which usually appears in the general news sections. Also called *run of book*. (b) In connection with color newspaper advertising, color advertising in the main portion of the paper, as distinguished from that placed in the magazine section (Sunday supplement).

Run of Schedule (ROS) A broadcast commercial for which a definite time is not specified. For example, a nighttime commercial during prime time may be run at any time during this period. The time at which an announcement runs may also vary from week to week, depending upon other requirements.

Runs In television film syndication, the number of times a film has been telecast in a given area. The number of times a film may be run according to an advertiser's lease. A rerun among television film syndicators is an available program previously telecast in an area.

Russell Hall See *Hall's Magazine Reports*.

Sales Promotion Sales activities that supplement personal selling and advertising, coordinate the two, and help make them effective; for example, sales incentives.

Saturation A level of advertising weight several times above normal reach and frequency levels standard for the market or product involved. Saturation implies simultaneous achievement of high reach and frequency designed to achieve maximum impact.

Saturation Showing In outdoor advertising, a showing of maximum intensity, designed to surpass complete coverage (the 100 showing) with repeat impressions. Often a 200 showing.

Scatter Market The purchase of network or cable TV time on a quarterly basis, after the "upfront" selling season.

Scatter Plan The placing of announcements in a number of different network TV programs.

Schedule (a) A list of media to be used during an advertising campaign. (b) A list of a product's advertising to be included in a media vehicle during a specific time. (c) A chronological list of programs broadcast by a station. Also called a *flowchart*.

Search The use of a search engine such as Google to locate information on the Internet. After the user enters a keyword that describes what he or she is looking for, the software retrieves related content as *organic search* based on complex rules that reflect the popularity of the site and many other factors. Also on the screen are paid listings from advertisers who want to send a message and link to people with a demonstrated interest in the product. This is called *paid* or *sponsored search*.

Search Engine The websites and underlying statistical processes that organize content from all over the Internet, locate content that has been requested by the user, and deliver it to the user's screen. Examples are Google, Bing, Yahoo, and others.

Search Engine Marketing (SEM) Also called *paid search*, the process of buying keywords and phrases at auction that trigger a short message and a link to the advertiser's website. These appear on the screen next to related content that has been requested from a search engine such as Google. The goal of SEM is to have the advertiser's link near the top of the paid search listing. This contrasts with SEO, which attempts to have the advertiser's link near the top of the free (natural, organic) listing.

Search Engine Optimization (SEO) The process of organizing and writing a website to maximize the likelihood that Google's organic or natural search will present the site near the top of the list, resulting in more traffic to the advertiser's website. This contrasts with SEM, the effort to influence the ranking of the advertiser's link in *paid search*.

Secondary Audience See *Audience, Secondary.*

Secondary Research Research information gathered from a published study conducted by another person or group. (See *Syndicated Research.*)

Secondary Service Area The distant area in which a broadcast station's signal is subject to interference or fading but can still be received. This applies mostly to radio. With the conversion to all-digital television, there is no fringe area—the station is either received or not.

Sectional Magazine A magazine that is distributed only sectionally and not nationally (such as *Sunset,* which is confined to the western states). Also called a *regional magazine.*

Selective Magazine A magazine that because of its nature and editorial content appeals only to a certain type of audience.

Sets in Use The total number of sets tuned in to some program at a given time of day and day of week. At one time, "sets in use" was equivalent to HUT, but today its meaning is limited to sets, not households. (See *Households Using TV.*)

Share, or Share of Audience The audience for a program as a percentage of all households or persons using television (HUT/PUT) at the time of the program's broadcast.

Share of Market The percentage of the total sales of a specified class of products that is held by or attributed to a particular brand at a given time.

Share of Mind The percentage of relevant population (or sample of that population) who indicate awareness of or preference for the various brands within a product group. The specific meaning varies considerably with the method of measurement. It may be a test of salience or a test of total recall, aided or unaided. The term usually refers to consumer awareness of brands relative to like measures of awareness for competing brands. For food products, it is "share of stomach."

Share of Voice A brand's share of the total advertising dollars or impressions for a product or commodity classification.

Shelter Magazines Magazines dealing editorially with the home, covering topics such as decorating, maintenance, and gardening. Additionally, these magazines carry a considerable amount of food editorial. An example is *Better Homes & Gardens.*

Shopper A newspaper that is published in a local community and contains mainly local news, shopping hints and suggestions, and advertisements. Sometimes called a *shopping newspaper.*

Shopper Marketing The use of marketing and merchandising materials such as freestanding inserts, co-op advertising, digital coupon centers, product reviews, shelf talkers, end aisle displays, and other promotional material designed to enhance the shopping experience and boost sales.

Short Rate The additional charge incurred when an advertiser fails to use enough media time or space to earn the contract discount envisaged at the time of the original order.

Showing (a) In outdoor advertising, the number of posters offered as a unit in terms of 100 GRPs per day and variations thereof. (b) In transit advertising, the number of cards included in a unit of sale. (See *Poster Showing.*) The outdoor industry plans to replace showing with an "eyes on" metric that is expressed in GRPs.

Significantly Viewed As defined by the FCC, describing a station in a given county if (a) it is a network affiliate and achieves among noncable households a share of total viewing hours of at least 3 percent and a net weekly circulation of at least 25 percent; or (b) it is an independent station and achieves among noncable households a share of total viewing hours of at least 2 percent and a net weekly circulation of at least 5 percent. A station that is significantly viewed becomes "local" for regulatory purposes. It therefore can demand carriage on cable systems, and the systems need not delete the duplicate programming of a significantly viewed station at the request of a higher-priority (local) station.

Simmons Data Data on print and broadcast media audience exposure and product usage reported by Experian Simmons.

Simmons (Experian Simmons or its earlier name, Simmons Market Research Bureau [SMRB]) A media and marketing research firm that uses a single sample to measure product usage, media audience, and consumer behavior. Separate studies cover adults, teens, children, Hispanics, consumer online users, and computer professionals.

Single-Source Data Data on product usage and media behavior gathered from a single sample. This technique makes the results more reliable and avoids the need to match samples that have different characteristics.

Situation Analysis Research prepared in document format to provide background for a media planner. The analysis includes history of the market, distribution channels, consumer analysis, product analysis, and advertising and media analysis.

Sliding Rate A space or time rate in a medium that is reduced as the volume purchased increases over a period of time.

Smart Phone A portable, cellular telephone that has been augmented with a physical or graphic keyboard, allowing it to access the Internet, play games, download music or custom ring tones, serve as a global positioning device, or provide other online services.

Social Media (also called *social networks*) Internet websites that allow people to form semipublic groups of family members, friends, business associates, and others who share a common interest for the purpose of frequent informal communication.

Space Position Value In outdoor advertising, an estimate of the effectiveness of a particular poster location. The factors considered are the length of approach, the speed of travel, the angle of the panel to its circulation, and the relation of the panel to adjacent panels.

Space Schedule A schedule that the agency sends to the advertiser, showing the media to be used, dates on which advertising is to appear, size of advertisements, and cost of space.

Special A one-time TV show generally employing known talent and usually running an hour or longer. Also called a *spectacular.*

Spill-In (or Spill-Out) The degree to which programming is viewed in adjacent television markets. Depending on the perspective, this is either spill-in or spill-out. Milwaukee television programming spills out of the Milwaukee DMA and spills into the Madison, Wisconsin, area, and vice versa. The primary source of this information is Nielsen's DMA Audience Allocation report that shows the number of GRPs delivered in a neighboring market for every 100 GRPs in the home market.

Spinoff A line extension of a magazine on a short-term basis. Also called a *"one-shot" annual edition.*

Split Run The running of two or more versions of an advertisement in every other copy of the same magazine or newspaper. In a variation of split runs, one version of the ad appears in newsstand copies and another in mail subscription copies. Splits may also occur geographically.

Split-Run Test Research designed to test the effectiveness of various copy elements, prices, or types of offers by placing them in alternative copies of an issue. The researchers evaluate various forms of the advertisements by means of coupon or inquiry returns, or by orders placed for trial offers.

Sponsored Search See *Search.*

Sponsor Identification (SI) The extent to which a program's sponsor is identified or its product or service remembered. The percentage of listeners or viewers who correctly associate a program with the sponsor or his product is the Sponsor Identification Index (SII). Single-sponsor programs are rare these days.

Sponsor Relief The process whereby an advertiser who has contracted for broadcast time that is no longer needed is granted relief by having another advertiser purchase the unneeded time.

Sponsorship The purchase of more than one announcement in a program (usually a majority of commercials) by one advertiser. Partial sponsorships are common and give the advertisers sponsorship billboards.

Spot (a) A time period filled entirely by a commercial or public service message and sold separately from the adjacent time periods. Such announcements may be placed between network programs or within local programs. (b) To buy time (for programs or announcements) on a market-by-market basis from stations through their representatives.

Spot Announcement A commercial placed on individual radio and TV stations.

Spot Programming The process by which an advertiser secures the rights to a television program and places the program on stations in selected markets without regard to network affiliation. The advertiser may own the television program outright, have rights to the program for a specific length of time, or have rights to the program in only a certain part of the country.

Spot Radio The use of stations in selected markets without regard to network affiliation. May involve spot announcements or complete programs.

Spot Schedule A local spot announcement buy or a standard form that agencies submit showing specific times, adjacencies, and so on of a brand's current spot announcements in a market.

Spot Television The use of stations in selected markets without regard to network affiliation. May involve spot announcements or complete local programs.

Spread An advertisement appearing on any two facing pages of a publication.

SRDS (formerly Standard Rate & Data Service) A service that publishes the rates and discount structures of all major media. It also publishes marketing research studies, often on media or market areas. See www.srds.com.

Staggered Schedule Several advertisements scheduled in two or more publications, arranged so as to alternate or rotate the dates of insertion.

Standard Advertising Unit (SAU) The 56 advertising units in broadsheet and 33 units in tabloid newspapers that are fixed sizes in depth and width and are measured in standard column inches.

Standby Space An order accepted by some magazines to run an advertisement whenever and wherever they wish, at an extra discount. The advertiser forwards print production materials with the order. This practice helps magazines fill odd pages or spaces.

Starch Method The recognition method used by Daniel Starch & Associates in the company's studies of advertising readership. For each measured ad, Starch reports the percent of a publication's readers who "noted" the ad, "associated" the ad with the advertiser, and "read most" of the body copy. This system has been in use in the same format for more than 50 years, giving the company a valuable database of average (normative) scores by ad size, publication, and other characteristics.

Station Break A time period between two programs when a station announces its call letters and channel number, and also broadcasts commercials.

Station Log The official, chronological listing of a radio or television station's programming and commercial announcements throughout the day.

Station Rep A sales organization or person representing individual stations to national advertisers. Short for *station representative*.

Store-Distributed Magazine Any one of several magazines (e.g., *Family Circle, Woman's Day*) whose primary channel of distribution was retail grocery stores. In recent years these "store books" have shifted to more than 60 percent of subscription sales.

Store Panel A selected sample of stores used repeatedly for marketing research to collect data on retail sales movement (e.g., The Nielsen Company's food store panel). (See *Panel.*)

Strip Programming (a) Running of a television or radio series at the same hour on each weekday. (b) Similar but different programs telecast at the same time throughout the week. (c) The same program, but different episodes, broadcast several times weekly at the same time.

Sunday Newspaper Supplement Any printed matter that is inserted in a Sunday edition of a newspaper on a continuing basis and is not part of the newspaper itself. Two main publications fitting into this category are magazine supplements and comic sections. A supplement may be either syndicated nationally or edited locally. (See *Syndicated Sunday Magazine Supplement*.)

Sweeps Periods during which Nielsen surveys all 210 local television markets. Sweeps are conducted four times yearly (November, February, May, and July), so these months are called *sweep months*.

Syndicated Program A method of selling a TV or radio program on a market-by-market (station-by-station) basis, as opposed to a network of affiliated stations.

Syndicated Research Research that is available for general purchase, as contrasted with custom research for a single advertiser or user. Examples include MRI, The Nielsen Company, Arbitron, Experian Simmons, Kantar Media, and so on.

Syndicated Sunday Magazine Supplement A magazine supplement that is distributed through a group of newspapers and is owned by a single publisher. The distributing newspapers pay the publisher for the privilege of distributing the supplement, which in turn helps build circulation for the distributing newspapers. There are general-interest nationally syndicated supplements: *Parade* and *USA Weekend*. *American Profile* is a Sunday supplement distributed to mid-size and smaller markets.

Tabloid A smaller than standard-sized newspaper, with five columns and about 1,000 lines per page.

Tagline A final line of a dramatic scene or act that is treated to give point or impact to the preceding dialogue.

Target Audience The desired or intended audience for advertising, as described or determined by the advertiser. Usually defined in terms of specific demographic (age, sex, income, etc.), purchase, or ownership characteristics.

Targetcasting Another term for narrowcasting, where cable programming is created to meet the interests of a special demographic audience.

Tear Sheets Actual pages of advertising as they appear in an issue of any publication, used to serve as proofs of insertion.

Telecast A broadcast, program, or show on television.

Telemarketing The sale of goods and services through the use of a telephone. There are two classes of telemarketing: inbound telemarketing—consumers initiate the call to ask questions or order a product; and outbound telemarketing—calls are initiated by a telemarketing firm to consumers' homes.

Telephone Coincidental Survey In research, the interview method in which telephone calls are made while a particular activity, usually a broadcast program, is in progress.

Test Market A given marketing area, usually a metropolitan census region, in which a market test is conducted. Sometimes used as a verb to refer to introducing a new product.

Test-Market Translation The use of local media that are available in a specific market to represent the national media included in a brand's national plan. The theoretical national plan must be reproduced as carefully and as accurately as possible in the test market, since company management will use sales results to determine whether the product should be expanded to national distribution. (See *Little U.S.A. Concept* and *As It Falls Concept*.)

Thirty-Sheet Poster An outdoor poster that is about 12 feet by 25 feet. In the early days of advertising, the poster consisted of 24 individual panels pasted together to form an ad. Today about 10 to 12 panels are used, depending on the type of artwork and copy.

Through-the-Book A technique of determining a print medium's audience size by having respondents go through a stripped-down issue with an interviewer to learn which articles are most interesting. After this preliminary examination, respondents are asked whether they are sure they looked into the magazine. Only those who answer positively are counted as readers. No longer used because of the limited number of magazines that can be carried by interviewers.

Tie-In A retail outlet's newspaper advertisement referring to or associating with another ad in the same newspaper. Tie-ins are paid for by the retail outlets that run them.

Time Shifting The practice of recording a program off the air and playing it back at a different time using a DVR.

Total Audience The total number of unduplicated readers of a magazine.

Total Audience Rating The percent of households tuning to all or to any portion of a program for at least five minutes.

Total Net Paid The total of all classes of a publication's circulation for which the ultimate purchasers have paid in accordance with the standards set by the Audit Bureau of Circulations' rules. Includes single-copy sales, mail subscriptions, and specials.

TPT (Total Prime Time) A television research project of Gallup & Robinson (G & R) evaluating all paid commercials aired during the evening period when national network programming is shown, that is, both program commercials and station breaks. Offers data on percentage of commercial audience able to recall the commercial, plus an estimate of actual audience in station coverage. TPT has been replaced by other G & R services. See www.gallup-robinson.com.

Traceable Expenditures Published reports on advertising expenditures by media for different advertisers. Currently, traceable expenditures are available for 18 media including national consumer magazines, local magazines, national Sunday supplements, local Sunday supplements, local newspapers, national newspapers, spot TV, network TV, cable TV, syndication TV, outdoor, network radio, and spot radio, Hispanic network TV, Hispanic cable TV, Internet, business-to-business trade publications, and freestanding insert coupons.

Trade Advertising Advertisements of consumer items directed to wholesalers and retailers in the distribution channel.

Trade Magazine See *Business Paper*.

Trade Paper Publication covering the commercial activities of wholesale and retail outlets, but many reach the sales departments of manufacturers. Trade papers include all publications that offer a manufacturer the opportunity to reach those who will sell the product for the company, at either the retail or wholesale level.

Trading Area The area surrounding a city, as defined by the Audit Bureau of Circulations, whose residents would normally be expected to use the city as their trading center.

Traffic Audit Bureau (TAB) An organization sponsored by outdoor advertising plants, advertising companies, and national advertisers for the purpose of authenticating circulation as related to outdoor advertising. See www.tabonline.com.

Traffic Count The evaluation of outdoor poster circulation by an actual count of traffic passing the poster.

Traffic Flow Map (Outdoor) An outline map of a market's streets scaled to indicate the relative densities of traffic.

Traffic Pattern Comparisons of customer count to establish averages; behavior of customers in terms of shopping time, hour of day, day of week, frequency.

Transit Advertising Advertising that uses poster-type ads on transportation vehicles such as buses, subways, and streetcars.

Turnover The ratio of a single telecast rating to a four-week reach. This ratio serves as an indication of the relative degree to which a program's audience changes. The greater the turnover in the audience, the higher the ratio. Also the ratio of total viewers of a telecast divided by the average minute rating.

Twitter A free social networking site that enables its users to send and receive text messages, known as "tweets," that are up to 140 characters. These are displayed on the author's profile page and are delivered to the author's subscribers, known as "followers," who can be select friends or can be open to anyone who wishes.

Two-Sheet Posters Outdoor posters placed at transit or train stops, which measure 60 inches by 46 inches.

Unaided Recall The process of determining whether a person saw or heard a given ad or commercial sometime after exposure with only minimal cueing such as mention of product class (not brand).

Universe The estimated number of actual households or people from which the sample will be taken and to which data from the sample will be projected; also called *Universe Estimate*.

Up-Front The purchase of national television time (network, cable, or syndication) in the spring or summer for the coming broadcast year that begins in September. Up-front buying usually includes a guaranteed audience delivery and a full commitment without options after the first quarter. Advertisers expect lower prices and a better selection of programs in the up-front than in the scatter market later in the year.

Upscale A general description of a medium's audience indicating membership in an upper socio-economic class.

URL (Uniform Resource Locator) The address of a page on the Internet. The first part consists of a string of letters that identify the protocol. For typical websites, this is http:// or hypertext transfer protocol, the computer language in which websites are written. The second part is the file and domain name that serve as the website's location or domain. An example of a complete URL, http://www.draftfcb.com.

Vehicle A particular component of a media class, such as a particular magazine or broadcast program.

Vertical Cume In broadcast research, a cumulative rating for two or more programs broadcast on the same day.

Vertical Half Page A half-page ad where the long dimension of the ad is vertical. (See *Horizontal Half Page*.)

Vertical Publication A business publication that serves a specific trade, industry, business, or profession.

Viewers per Set (VPS) The average number of persons watching or listening to a program in each home.

Viewers per Viewing Household (VPVH) "Estimated number of viewers, usually classified by age and sex, comprising the audience within those households viewing a given station or program or using television during a particular time period." Also called *Viewers per Tuning Household (VPTH)*. (Source: The Nielsen Company.)

Volume Discount A discount that a publisher gives an advertiser in exchange for running ads in a certain volume of space in the publication. An advertiser might use many small insertions to make up the required number of pages.

Waste Circulation (a) The audience members of a magazine or newspaper who are not prospects for a particular advertised product. (b) Circulation in an area where an advertiser does not have distribution of its product.

Website An interconnected set of text, graphics, and other content that constitutes an organization, person, or other entity's place on the Internet. Websites are displayed on a computer or mobile device using browser software such as Microsoft's Internet Explorer. A website's location is identified by its URL, which is put into the browser to obtain access.

WOM (Word of Mouth) Person-to-person communication of news, gossip, or other content in the course of daily human interaction.

Women's Service Magazine Magazine appealing to women (homemakers specifically), and whose editorial contents are designed to further their knowledge as homemakers.

Working Media Budget The portion of the budget set aside for the purchase of advertising space and time, as distinguished from other advertising-related expenses such as commercial production, talent payments, tapes, shipping, and so on.

WWW (World Wide Web) The organized storehouse of billions of pages of alphanumeric and multi-media content that is made available to worldwide users who have access to the Internet.

Yahoo! An Internet portal at www.yahoo.com that includes news, search capability, shopping, e-mail, video, graphics, and other capabilities.

Yesterday-Reading Technique Research technique that asks respondents in a selected sample which newspapers they read yesterday; similar to recent-reading magazine technique.

Zapping Using a remote-control device to change television channels from across the room, especially to avoid viewing commercials.

Zipping Using a remote-control device to skip ahead of any portion of a television or VCR program, especially to skip over commercials.

INDEX

Jack Z. Sissors spent more than 40 years teaching and working in media at Northwestern University before retiring with the rank of professor emeritus. He created and edited *The Journal of Media Planning* and directed various media symposia for media planners. He worked on the Advertising Research Foundation's committees on single-source data, effective frequency, and media model building. Before working in academia, he held positions with Leo Burnett and other advertising agencies.

Roger B. Baron is senior vice president, director of media research at DRAFTFCB. He received a BA in communications and public policy from the University of California, Berkeley, and an MA in telecommunications from the University of Southern California. Following graduate school he spent three years on active duty as a Supply Officer in the U.S. Navy, retiring with the rank of captain in the U.S. Naval Reserve.

His professional experience includes five years at Leo Burnett in media research and as a media planner and supervisor on the Kellogg cereal account. He then spent 12 years at D'Arcy Masius Benton & Bowles in San Francisco—the last four as VP/media director. In 1987, he returned to Chicago and assumed the post of media research director at Foote, Cone & Belding, now DRAFTFCB.

Mr. Baron is active in the Advertising Research Foundation, the American Association of Advertising Agencies, the Media Rating Council, and the Market Research Council. He is also a past president of the Media Research Club of Chicago. Baron is an accomplished computer programmer and has developed several computer models for media planning. He is married and has two adult sons. Outside the office he spends time reading, working around the house, and driving his midlife-crisis Audi convertible.